Learning MySQL and MariaDB

Russell J.T. Dyer

Beijing · Cambridge · Farnham · Köln · Sebastopol · Tokyo

Learning MySQL and MariaDB

by Russell J.T. Dyer

Editor: Andy Oram	**Indexer:** Lucie Haskins
Production Editor: Matt Hacker	**Cover Designer:** Ellie Volckhausen
Copyeditor: Jasmine Kwityn	**Interior Designer:** David Futato
Proofreader: Troy Mott	**Illustrator:** Rebecca Demarest

April 2015:   First Edition

Revision History for the First Edition:

2015-03-23:   First release

See *http://oreilly.com/catalog/errata.csp?isbn=9781449362904* for release details.

To Fortunata Serio, my mother, who gave me life, taught me to be kind and loving, and to speak—which is a precursor to being a writer.

And to Andrew Gambos, who had the thankless job of being my stepfather, but taught me how to assert myself in life and in my career.

Table of Contents

Part II. Database Structures

Part III. Basics of Handling Data

Part IV.   Built-In Functions

Part V. Administration and Beyond

Foreword

Before you begin to read the main chapters of this book to learn about MySQL and MariaDB, it might be useful to understand what we were trying to accomplish when we first created MySQL about 20 years ago and MariaDB about 5 years ago, as well as the current state of these database systems and my expectations of them going forward. And I'd like to encourage you in your decision to learn these database systems and to assure you that they will be in use for a long time and that you will benefit from the time and energy you put into reading this book and learning what it has to teach you.

Origins of MySQL

When my business partner David Axmark and I started MySQL, there weren't any good, free, open source database systems. There was *mSQL*, which wasn't open source, but it inspired us to create a new database system for our clients, which would later become MySQL. We had no plans to do anything more with this embryo of MySQL other than satisfy the needs of our clients. We were learning, discovering, and creating out of practical concerns and needs, much as you might and perhaps should be doing as a reader of this book and a newcomer to MySQL and MariaDB.

Although we had accomplished our task in creating a straightforward database to meet our requirements, it wasn't long before we noticed that there were many other organizations that were looking for a solution similar to what we had already developed. So we decided to make the software available to the public and we named it *MySQL*.

Part of our motivation for doing this was that we felt that it was a way in which we could give something back to the open source community that would be very useful. Most open source projects at that time weren't as useful. We wanted to make the world a little better—we had no idea at that time how much of an impact MySQL would have on the world. At the same time, we were hoping that by going public with the software, it might finance further development of MySQL for as long as we might want. We had expectations of getting rich from MySQL. We hoped only to be able to work full-time on this project because we believed in it. The result, though, was that we contributed much to the world—much more than we thought possible.

Given the fact that over 80% of the websites in the world are now running on MySQL, one could easily argue that we accelerated the growth of the internet and almost everything that has grown out of it. The impact it's had is immeasurable. Many of the sites and businesses that have been successful, including the ones that are now huge, probably would never have started if it were not for MySQL being free and dependable. At that time, those founders and startup companies just didn't have the financial resources to start their sites. The cost of commercial database software was a barrier to some of the most creative web-based organizations being launched, including organizations like Google, Wikipedia, and Facebook. Plus, the commercial database systems posed other problems for startups of that time. First, they were too slow—they weren't optimized for the Web and that was critical for organizations like these. The commecial alternatives were also too difficult to use and manage, requiring higher paid developers.

Because of these factors, we were able to give fledgling organizations what they needed to become the significant components of the Internet and a major part of the lives of most people in the world today. We were a critical component of the development of the Internet and we still are. There's nothing to indicate that we won't continue to be so. The growth of MySQL and especially of MariaDB is increasing. It's not decreasing as some people expected with the introduction of new databases systems and methods such as NoSQL.

MySQL became a dominant database system long ago. Once something becomes dominant, it's difficult to replace it. Even if something better comes along, people prefer what's already familiar to them and what they already know and are using. For something to replace MySQL as the dominant open source database, it would have to be not only critically better, but also offer a way for people to migrate without much effort, and without wasting all of the knowledge they accumulated from their current system. This is why MariaDB can replace MySQL: it's basically the same thing, but with more features and more potential for the future.

State of MySQL and MariaDB

MySQL and MariaDB aren't perfect—no database is that, nor will ever be that—but MySQL and MariaDB are good enough for most people and they're excellent in many ways. The balance we strive for is to develop a database system that works easily on the Web and has one of the fastest connectors. Thanks to the fact that we're using threads, we can handle much higher loads than other database systems. We used some of the most advanced technologies available when we started MySQL and we have always striven to adapt to new hardware and to optimize the software for all commonly used systems and methods of deployment. Because we're continuously improving the software, we can have a new release each month for the community edition and we can have a new version every year. That's an indication that things are happening and improving regularly.

As someone learning and intending to use MySQL and MariaDB, you can take comfort in that we are always improving and adjusting for a changing environment. You can count on us for the future. I think that's the main thing: people like that they can depend on us. Although it may be fun and exciting to learn something new, after a while it can become tiresome to have to learn a totally new system every couple of years. You won't have to do that with MySQL and MariaDB.

I mentioned before about how difficult it is to supplant a dominant software. In the case of MariaDB, it's not much of a change in practice for those who have been using MySQL. As a result, most people can migrate to MariaDB without the usual obstacles, but they can take advantage of the new features included in MariaDB and the ones that are planned when they're added. MariaDB is relevant because we continue to make improvements and we care about giving developers what they need to get the most out of their databases.

Beyond the Server

In addition to web usage, MySQL and MariaDB can be used for stand-alone applications, embedded with other software. Embedded MySQL and MariaDB are growing more than ever. Many applications are moving to cloud environments, but database systems that many businesses used in the past are typically too expensive to use in a cloud environment. As a result, they need an inexpensive database system that is easily deployed in a cloud environment. For this situation, MySQL and MariaDB are the obvious choices.

The use of mobile devices and websites and applications through mobile devices has increased dramatically; for some sites, it now exceeds access and usage through desktop computers. For sites and applications that run on mobile devices and use a database located in the cloud or in house, we're the best choice among all the open source and commercial database systems. We have the best scale-out technologies for when your site or application experiences major spikes in traffic or rapid growth in business. With the encryption that we're adding in version 10.1 of MariaDB, you can be assured that your databases will be very secure by default. Most other database systems don't have encryption by default.

MariaDB: The Differences and Expectations

Regarding my hopes and expectations for the MariaDB database system, I'm working at the foundation to ensure that we get more companies actively involved in the development of MariaDB. That's something we lacked during the history of MySQL. We want to develop something that will satisfy everyone—not only now, but for the future. To do that, we need more organizations involved. We're happy to see Google involved in the MariaDB Foundation. I'd like to see 10 or 15 companies as significant as Google involved. That's something they've managed to do at FOSS, the Free and Open Source Software Foundation. They have several companies that assist in development. That's their strength. Their weakness is that they don't have one company coordinating the development of software. My hope is that the MariaDB Foundation will act as a coordinator for the effort, but with many companies helping. That would benefit everyone. It is this collaborative effort that I don't expect from Oracle regarding MySQL. That's the difference and advantage of MariaDB. With Oracle, there's no certainty in the future of the open source code of MySQL. With MariaDB, by design it will always be open source and everything they do will be open source. The foundation is motivated and truly want to be more closely aligned with open source standards.

The MariaDB Foundation was created to be a sanctuary. If something goes wrong in the MariaDB Corporation, the Foundation can guarantee that the MariaDB software will remain open—always. That's its main role. The other role is to ensure that companies that want to participate in developing MariaDB software can do so on equal terms as anyone else because the foundation is there. So if someone creates and presents a patch for MariaDB software, they can submit it to be included in the next release of MariaDB. With many other open source projects, it's difficult to get a patch included in the software. You have to struggle and learn how to conform to their coding style. And it's even harder to get the patch accepted. In the case of MySQL with Oracle, it could be blocked by Oracle. The situation is inherently different with MariaDB.

For example, if Percona, a competitor of MariaDB Corporation, wants to add a patch to MariaDB software that will help their background program XtraBackup to run better, but the management of MariaDB Corporation doesn't like that it would be helping their competitor, it doesn't matter. MariaDB Corporation has no say in which patches are adopted. If the Foundation accepts the patch, it's added to the software. The Foundation review patches on their technical merits only, not based on any commercial agenda.

The open source projects that survived are those that were created for practical reasons. MySQL wasn't in the beginning the best database solution. People complained that it didn't have many features at that time. However, it was always practical. It solved problems and met the needs of developers and others. And it did so better than other solutions that were supposedly better choices. We did that by actively listening to people and with a willingness to make changes to solve problems. Our goal with MariaDB is to get back to those roots and be more interactive with customers and users. By this method, we can create something that might not be perfect for everyone, but pretty good.

The Future of MySQL and MariaDB

As for the future, if you want MariaDB to be part of your professional life, I can assure you that we will do everything possible to support and develop the software. We have many brilliant people who will help to ensure MariaDB has a long future.

In the near term, I think that MariaDB version 10.1 will play a large role in securing the future of MariaDB. It offers full integration with Galera cluster—an add-on for MariaDB for running multiple database servers for better performance—because of the new encryption features. That's important. In recent months, all other technologies have been overshadowed with security concerns because the systems of some governments and major companies have been hacked. Having good encryption could have stopped most of those attacks from achieving anything. These improvements will change the perception that open source databases are not secure enough. Many commercial database makers have said that MySQL and MariaDB are not secure, and they have been able to convince some businesses to choose a commercial solution instead as a result. With MariaDB 10.1, though, we can prove easily that their argument is not true. So that's good. If you've chosen to use MariaDB, you can make this point when you're asked about the difference between MySQL and MariaDB, and you can feel good about your choice over the long term for this same reason.

Looking at the future, many companies are leery about using commercial database software because they don't know for sure if the compiled code contains backdoors for accessing the data or if there is some special way in which the software is using encryption that could allow hackers to get at their databases. On the other hand, countries like Russia and China question whether open source databases are secure. The only way we can assure them of that is to provide access to the source code, and that means they must use open source software. So I do hope and expect that in the future we will see MySQL and MariaDB growing rapidly in these countries and similar organizations, because we can address their concerns when commercial solutions cannot. Ironically, a more transparent software system is preferred by a less transparent government. It's better not only for less transparent organizations, but also for those that want to keep their databases more secure. This applies to an organization that wants to keep their data private and doesn't want someone else such as a hacker, or a competitor, a government to have access to their data.

Your Future in Learning MySQL and MariaDB

Both MySQL and MariaDB follow the SQL convention for database languages, which was created about 30 years ago. The nice thing about SQL is that it hasn't changed much in the last 30 years. Mostly, one can do more with it. So if you learn one SQL system well, you can easily make a transition to another. The basic concepts that you'll acquire in learning an SQL system like MySQL or MariaDB, will be useful for your entire career as a database developer or administrator. There's nothing to indicate that MySQL or MariaDB will go away for the next 50 years. All of the concepts for the past 20 years of MySQL are the same as they are today and will probably be the same for the next several decades. There are just some new features and tools to be able to do extra tasks. But the skills you always need are basic ones and they're contained in this book. These skills are ones that will always be of benefit to you.

Advice on Learning MySQL and MariaDB

You shouldn't just read this book. You should install MySQL or MariaDB, try executing the examples given, and complete the exercises at the end of each chapter. You should also try to do something useful with the software and the SQL statements and functions described in each chapter. You should use the tools or utilities presented. If you don't get practical experience, any book like this one will be useless to you. If you're not sure what you can do to get practical experience, perhaps you could try to build a website using MySQL or MariaDB. Try to solve some data-related problem with one of these database systems. Begin to make it part of your life. Then what you're learning may help you immediately in some way. By this method, you will become more excited by what you're learning. You will better learn the basics by using the software from almost the beginning.

Another way to learn more, as well as make yourself known in the community and to develop a business network that could lead to more work and better jobs, is by participating in the forums and mailing lists and IRC channels for MySQL and MariaDB. By using what you're learning to help others, you'll not only become popular, but you'll learn more in the process of having to explain the concepts you'll learn in this book.

—Monty Widenius
Málaga, Spain, January 2015

Preface

MySQL is the most popular open source database system available. It's particularly useful for public websites that require a fast and stable database. Even if you're not familiar with MySQL, you've used it many times. You use it when you use Google, Amazon, Facebook, Wikipedia, and many other popular websites. It's the keeper of the data behind huge websites with thousands of pages of data, and small sites with only a few pages. It's also used in many non-web-based applications. It's fast, stable, and small when needed.

The software was started by Michael "Monty" Widenius and David Axmark in 1995 and is licensed under the GNU General Public License. In time, they founded the Swedish company MySQL Ab (the Ab stands for *aktiebolag*, or stock company), which years later became MySQL, Inc., incorporated in the United States. In January 2008, the company was acquired by Sun Microsystems, which seemed promising for the future of the software. But in April 2009 Oracle—a major competitor of MySQL that offers closed source database software—acquired Sun. Many worried at the time that this acquisition would eventually end MySQL software as a free, open source alternative on which much of the Web and many sites that have changed the world were built. Five years after the acquisition, this hasn't proved to be the case. Many new features have been added to MySQL and the number of MySQL developers within and outside of Oracle has increased.

Displeased that Oracle took control of MySQL software, Monty started a new company (Monty Program Ab) that has developed a fork of the software called MariaDB.[1] Because MySQL software is licensed with the GPL, it is possible to freely and legally use the MySQL software and add to it. At the same time, Ulf Sandberg, the former Senior Vice President of Services at MySQL, Inc., along with other former employees of MySQL, left Sun and Oracle and started SkySQL Ab, providing support, consulting, training, and other services related to MySQL and MariaDB software. As of October 2013, Monty

---

1. Incidentally, MySQL is named for Monty Widenius' first daughter, My Widenius. MariaDB is named for his second daughter, Maria Widenius.

Program has merged into SkySQL, which was renamed to MariaDB Ab in October 2014. The software license, though, is now held by the MariaDB Foundation so that it cannot be bought by Oracle or any other corporation.

As for the community related to the software, some have been migrating to MariaDB, preferring software not associated with a large proprietary software company. Many operating systems distributors, hardware makers, and software packagers are now shipping their products with MariaDB, either together with MySQL or without it. Many websites that used MySQL software have switched to MariaDB. It's easy to do, and for most sites it requires no changes to applications that use MySQL—not a single line of code needs to be changed to switch to MariaDB. If you want to take advantage of new, advanced features of MariaDB, it is necessary to add or change code in an application that previously used MySQL, bu the rest is the same.

Although ownership, company names, and even the name of the software has changed, the vision that began almost 30 years ago and the spirit that has grown strong and vibrant in the community is the same and continues in MariaDB.

If you want to learn about MySQL and MariaDB software, you can do it. It's not difficult to understand or to use. This book has been written to be a primer for newcomers to MySQL and MariaDB, to get you started and help you be productive quickly. It's also useful for beginners who have learned only parts of MySQL and feel that there may be key aspects used commonly that they don't know, that they somehow missed or skipped over when first learning it. At the beginner level, there is no difference between MySQL and MariaDB. So when you learn one, you learn the other. Because of this, the names MySQL and MariaDB are used interchangeably.

Reading Strategy

The chapters of this book are written and ordered based on the assumption that the reader will read them in order. This does not assume that some chapters won't be skipped; it's assumed that most will skip Part I. For instance, in addition to skipping Chapter 1, the introductory chapter, if MySQL is already installed on your computer, you would probably skip Chapter 2, which covers installing MySQL and MariaDB. If you've never used MySQL, you probably should read Chapter 3, *The Basics and the mysql Client*. After that, all readers should read sequentially the chapters contained in the Parts II, III, and IV. The remaining chapters, contained in Part V, relate to administration and not all of those may be of use to you early on.

Most of the chapters conclude with a set of exercises. The exercises are designed to help you think through what you've read in the chapter. Working through the exercises will help reinforce what you should have learned from the examples in the chapter. Incidentally, it's useful to try entering the examples throughout the chapters for more practice. The exercises at the end of the chapters depend on a building of knowledge, if not from one chapter to the next, at least from previous chapters.

Text-Based Interface and Operating Systems

Many people feel that graphical user interfaces (GUIs) are faster when using a complex software program or system. This accounts for the popularity of Windows programs. However, while it is said that a picture is worth a thousand words, when you want to say only one word, you don't need to draw a picture. You don't need to use an elaborate GUI to make a minute change to a database.

In particular, I don't like GUIs for controlling a server or MySQL. Interfaces tend to change between versions of the interface. Command-line utilities are very stable and their basic commands don't usually change. If you know how to configure a server at the command line, it matters little what kind of server you're entering commands on. Any examples in this book that are executed within MySQL are universal. Examples shown at the command line are for Unix-like operating systems (e.g., Linux). I leave it to readers to make the necessary adjustments for their particular operating systems (i.e., how to get to the command prompt).

Conventions Used in This Book

The following typographical conventions are used in this book:

Italic

Indicates new terms, URLs, email addresses, filenames, and file extensions.

`Constant width`

Used for program listings, as well as within paragraphs to refer to program elements such as variable or function names, databases, data types, environment variables, statements, and keywords.

`Constant width bold`

Shows commands or other text that should be typed literally by the user.

`Constant width italic`

Shows text that should be replaced with user-supplied values or by values determined by context.

> This icon signifies a tip, suggestion, or general note.

This icon indicates a warning or caution.

Using Code Examples

All of the scripts and programs shown in the book are available for you to easily copy and modify for your own use. They can be found on the Web at *http://mysqlresources.com/files*.

This book is here to help you learn MySQL and MariaDB and to get your job done in relation to this software. In general, if this book includes code examples, you may use the code in your programs and documentation. You do not need to contact us for permission unless you're reproducing a significant portion of the code. For example, writing a program that uses several chunks of code from this book does not require permission. Selling or distributing a CD-ROM of examples from O'Reilly books does require permission. Answering a question by citing this book and quoting example code does not require permission. Incorporating a significant amount of example code from this book into your product's documentation does require permission.

We appreciate, but do not require, attribution. An attribution usually includes the title, author, publisher, and ISBN. For example: "*Learning MySQL and MariaDB* by Russell J.T. Dyer (O'Reilly). Copyright 2015 Russell J.T. Dyer, 978-1-449-36290-4."

If you feel your use of code examples falls outside fair use or the permission given above, you may contact us at *permissions@oreilly.com* to request special permission.

Safari® Books Online

 *Safari Books Online* is an on-demand digital library that delivers expert content in both book and video form from the world's leading authors in technology and business.

Technology professionals, software developers, web designers, and business and creative professionals use Safari Books Online as their primary resource for research, problem solving, learning, and certification training.

Safari Books Online offers a range of plans and pricing for enterprise, government, education, and individuals.

Members have access to thousands of books, training videos, and prepublication manuscripts in one fully searchable database from publishers like O'Reilly Media, Prentice Hall Professional, Addison-Wesley Professional, Microsoft Press, Sams, Que, Peachpit Press, Focal Press, Cisco Press, John Wiley & Sons, Syngress, Morgan Kaufmann, IBM

Redbooks, Packt, Adobe Press, FT Press, Apress, Manning, New Riders, McGraw-Hill, Jones & Bartlett, Course Technology, and hundreds more. For more information about Safari Books Online, please visit us online.

How to Contact Us

Please address comments and questions concerning this book to the publisher:

O'Reilly Media, Inc.
1005 Gravenstein Highway North
Sebastopol, CA 95472
800-998-9938 (in the United States or Canada)
707-829-0515 (international or local)
707-829-0104 (fax)

We have a web page for this book, where we list errata, examples, and any additional information. You can access this page at *http://bit.ly/lrng_mysql_and_mariadb*.

To comment or ask technical questions about this book, send email to *bookquestions@oreilly.com*.

For more information about our books, courses, conferences, and news, see our website at *http://www.oreilly.com*.

Find us on Facebook: *http://facebook.com/oreilly*

Follow us on Twitter: *http://twitter.com/oreillymedia*

Watch us on YouTube: *http://www.youtube.com/oreillymedia*

Acknowledgments

Thanks to my colleagues Colin Charles, Kenneth Dyer, Chad Hudson, Caryn-Amy Rose, and Sveta Smirnova for reviewing this book for technical accuracy and for advice and other information critical to its creation. Thanks to my editor, Andy Oram, for his help and his confidence in me over the many years I've known him. Thanks to my two bosses from the MySQL and MariaDB world: Ulf Sandberg and Max Mether, both of whom worked at MySQL AB and SkySQL/MariaDB Ab. Both of them have been very encouraging and excellent managers. Thanks also to my friend and coworker, Rusty Osborne Johnson for her friendship and patience while working on this book.

## PART I

The Software

At the heart of what is collectively known as MySQL and MariaDB is the server. The term *server* in this context refers to software, not a primary computer on which it may be running. The server maintains, controls, and protects your data, storing it in files on the computer where the server is running in various formats. The server listens for requests from other software that is running (called clients in this context). The term *client* refers to software, not a computer. A client and server software may be running on the same computer, which can be a personal laptop computer.

We'll start by using a command-line client where you type in requests manually. Then we'll graduate to issuing the requests from programs that can back up web servers and other uses for the data. It's not necessary for you to know all of the files and programs that make up MySQL. There are, though, a few key ones of which you should be aware.

One key program is the server itself, `mysqld` (the *d* stands for *daemon* and is a common term for a server). The name is the same in both MySQL and MariaDB. This daemon must be running in order for users to be able to access data and make changes. As an administrator, you have the ability to configure and set `mysqld` to suit your database system needs. The daemon is mentioned where relevant in various chapters throughout this book.

Another key program, used extensively through this book, is the basic MySQL client, called simply, `mysql`. With it, you can interact with the `mysqld` daemon, and thereby the databases. It's a textual user interface. There's nothing fancy about it—a mouse is not needed to use it. You simply type in the SQL statements that you will learn about in this book. The results of queries are displayed in ASCII text. It's very clean looking, but no graphics are involved. It's also very fast, as there's nothing but text (i.e., there are no binaries or image files). We'll cover this in Chapter 3. There are GUI clients available, but because most MySQL developers and administrators prefer the `mysql` client, and what you type in `mysql` is the same as what is passed to the server by a GUI client, I cover it exclusively.

## CHAPTER 1

Introduction

MySQL is an open source, multithreaded, relational database management system created by Michael "Monty" Widenius in 1995. In 2000, MySQL was released under a dual-license model that permitted the public to use it for free under the GNU General Public License (GPL). All of this, in addition to its many features and stability, caused its popularity to soar.

It has been estimated that there are more than six million installations of MySQL worldwide, and reports of over 50,000 downloads a day of MySQL installation software. The success of MySQL as a leading database is due not only to its price—after all, other cost-free and open source databases are available—but also its reliability, performance, and features. MariaDB is rapidly becoming the replacement to MySQL, and is seen by many as the heir apparent to the spirit of the MySQL community.

If you're embarking on a career in computer programming, web development, or computer technology more generally, learning MySQL and MariaDB will prove useful. Many businesses develop and maintain custom software with MySQL. Additionally, many of the most popular websites and software use MySQL for their database—or they use another SQL database system that you can learn once you understand MySQL. It's highly likely that you will be required to know or will benefit from knowing MySQL during the course of working as a database or website developer. Therefore, learning MySQL and MariaDB is a good foundation for your career in computer technology.

The Value of MySQL and MariaDB

Many features contribute to MySQL's standing as a superb database system. Its speed is one of its most prominent features (refer to its benchmarks page (*http://www.mysql.com/it-resources/benchmarks*) for its performance over time). MySQL and MariaDB are remarkably scalable, and are able to handle tens of thousands of tables and billions of rows of data. They can also manage small amounts of data quickly and smoothly, making them convenient for small businesses or amateur projects.

The critical software in any database management system is its storage engine, which manages queries and interfaces between a user's SQL statements and the database's back-end storage. MySQL and MariaDB offer several storage engines with different advantages. Some are transaction-safe storage engines that allow for rollback of data (i.e., the often needed *undo* feature so familiar in desktop software). Additionally, MySQL has a tremendous number of built-in functions, which are detailed in several chapters of this book. MariaDB offers the same functions and a few more. MySQL and MariaDB are also very well known for rapid and stable improvements. Each new release comes with speed and stability improvements, as well as new features.

Mailing Lists and Forums

When learning MySQL and MariaDB, and especially when first using MySQL for your work, it's valuable to know where to find help when you have problems with the software and your databases. For problems that you may have with your databases, you can receive assistance from the MySQL community at no charge through several Oracle-hosted forums (*http://forums.mysql.com/*). You should start by registering on the forums so that you may ask questions, as well as help others. You can learn much when helping others, as it forces you to refine what you know about MySQL. You can find similar resources related to MariaDB on MariaDB Ab's website (*https://mariadb.com/resources/community-tools*).

When you have a problem with MySQL, you can search the forums for messages from others who may have described the same problem that you are trying to resolve. It's a good idea to search the forums and the documentation before starting a new topic in the forums. If you can't find a solution after searching, post a question. Be sure to post your question in the forum related to your particular topic.

Other Books and Other Publications

MariaDB provides online documentation (*https://mariadb.com/kb/en/mariadb/documentation/*) of their software that generally applies to MySQL software. Oracle provides extensive online documentation (*http://dev.mysql.com/doc*) for the MySQL server and all of the other software it distributes. The documentation is organized by version of MySQL. You can read the material online or download it in a few different formats (e.g., HTML, PDF, EPUB). In PDF and EPUB, you can download a copy to an ereader. I maintain a website (*http://mysqlresources.com*) that contains some documentation and examples derived from my book, *MySQL in a Nutshell* (2008). Other people have also contributed examples and other materials to the site.

In addition to the book that you're now reading, O'Reilly publishes a few other MySQL books worth adding to your library. O'Reilly's mainline reference book on MySQL is written by me, *MySQL in a Nutshell*. For solving common practical problems, there's *MySQL Cookbook* (2006) by Paul DuBois. For advice on optimizing MySQL and performing administrative tasks, such as backing up databases, O'Reilly has published *High Performance MySQL* (2012) by Baron Schwartz, Peter Zaitsev, and Vadim Tkachenko. At MySQL, Inc., I worked with the writers of both *MySQL Cookbook* and *High Performance MySQL*, and they are authorities on the topic and well respected in the MySQL community.

O'Reilly also publishes several books about the MySQL application programming interfaces (APIs). For PHP development with MySQL, there's *Learning PHP, MySQL, JavaScript, CSS, and HTML5* (2014) by Robin Nixon. For interfacing with Perl to MySQL and other database systems, there's *Programming the Perl DBI* (published in 2000 and still very useful) by Alligator Descartes and Tim Bunce. To interface to MySQL with Java, you can use the JDBC and JConnector drivers; George Reese's book, *Database Programming with JDBC & Java* (2000) is a useful resource on this topic.

In addition to published books on MySQL, a few websites offer brief tutorials on using MySQL. Incidentally, I've contributed a few articles to O'Reilly blogs and several other publications on MySQL and related topics. MySQL's site also provides some in-depth articles on MySQL (*http://dev.mysql.com/tech-resources/articles*). Many of these articles deal with new products and features, making them ideal if you want to learn about using the latest releases available even while they're still in the testing stages. All of these online publications are available for no cost, except the time invested in reading them. If you are a MySQL support customer, though, you can get information about MySQL from their private Knowledge Base, of which I was the editor for many years.

Once you've mastered the material in this book, if you require more advanced training on MySQL, MariaDB, or related topics, MariaDB Ab offers training courses. Some are for one or two days, others are week-long courses offered in locations around the world. You can find a list of courses and when they're offered on MariaDB Ab's training page (*http://www.skysql.com/products/mysql-training*). I'm currently the Curriculum Manager for MariaDB Ab.

## CHAPTER 2

Installing MySQL and MariaDB

The MySQL and MariaDB database server and client software works on several different operating systems, notably several distributions of Linux, Mac OS X, FreeBSD, Sun Solaris, and Windows.

This chapter briefly explains briefly the process of installing MySQL or MariaDB on Linux, Mac OS X, and Windows operating systems. For some operating systems, this chapter has additional sections for different distribution formats. For any one platform, you can install MySQL by reading just three sections of this chapter: the next section on choosing a distribution; the section that applies to the distribution that you choose; and "Post-Installation" on page 24 at the end of the chapter. There's no need to read how to install every version of MySQL.

The Installation Packages

The MySQL and MariaDB packages come with several programs. Foremost is the server, represented by the mysqld daemon.[1] It has the same name in both MySQL and MariaDB. This daemon is the software that actually stores and maintains control over all of the data in the databases. The mysqld daemon listens for requests on a particular port (3306, by default) by which clients submit queries. The standard MySQL client program is called simply mysql. With this text-based interface, a user can log in and execute SQL queries. This client can also accept queries from text files containing queries, and thereby execute them on behalf of the user or other software. However, most MySQL interaction is done by programs using a variety of languages. The interfaces for Perl, PHP, and others are discussed in Chapter 16.

---

1. A *daemon* is a background process that runs continuously; a Unix term for what most people call a "server."

A few wrapper scripts for `mysqld` come with the server installation. The `mysqld_safe` script is the most common way to start `mysqld`, because this script can restart the daemon if it crashes. This helps ensure minimal downtime for database services. You don't need to know the details of how all of this works if you're just starting to learn MySQL and MariaDB, but it gives you a sense of how powerful and versatile this database system can be.

MySQL, and thereby MariaDB, also comes with a variety of utilities for managing the server. The `mysqlaccess` tool creates user accounts and sets their privileges. The `mysqladmin` utility can be used to manage the database server itself from the command line. This kind of interaction with the server includes checking a server's status and usage, and shutting down a server. The `mysqlshow` tool may be used to examine a server's status, as well as information about databases and tables. Some of these utilities require Perl, or ActivePerl for Windows, to be installed on the server. See the Perl site (*http://www.perl.org*) to download and install a copy of Perl on non-Windows systems, and the ActivePerl site (*http://www.activestate.com/activeperl*) to download and install a copy of ActivePerl on Windows systems.

MySQL and MariaDB also come with a few utilities for importing and exporting data from and to databases. The `mysqldump` utility is the most popular one for exporting data and table structures to a plain-text file, known as a *dump* file. This can be used for backing up data or for copying databases between servers. The `mysql` client can be used to import the data back to MySQL from a dump file. These topics and utilities are explained in detail in Part I, The Software.

You can opt not to install the helper utilities. However, there's no cost for them and they're not large files. So you may as well install and use them.

Licensing

Although MySQL can be used for free and is open source, the company that develops MySQL—currently Oracle—holds the copyright to the source code. The company offers a dual-licensing program for its software: one allows cost-free use through the GPL under certain common circumstances, and the other is a commercial license requiring the payment of a fee. They're both the same software, but each has a different license and different privileges. The website for the Free Software Foundation, which created the GPL (*http://www.fsf.org/licenses/license-list.html*), has details on the license.

Oracle allows you to use the software under the GPL if you use it without redistributing it, or if you redistribute it only with software that is licensed under the GPL. You can even use the GPL if you redistribute MySQL with software that you developed, as long as you distribute your software under the GPL as well. This is how MariaDB was created and why it is a legal fork of MySQL.

However, if you have developed an application that requires MySQL for its functionality and you want to sell your software with MySQL under a non-free license, you must purchase a commercial license from Oracle. There are other scenarios in which a commercial license may be required. For details on when you must purchase a license, see the MySQL legal site (*http://www.mysql.com/about/legal*).

Besides holding the software copyright, Oracle also holds the MySQL trademark. As a result, you cannot distribute software that includes MySQL in its name. None of this is important to learning how to use MySQL, but it's good for you to be aware of these things for when you become an advanced MySQL developer.

Finding the Software

You can obtain a copy of MySQL from MySQL's site (*http://dev.mysql.com/downloads/mysql/*), which requires an Oracle login but is still free, or from one of its mirror sites (*http://dev.mysql.com/downloads/mirrors.html*). You can instead download MariaDB, which contains the latest release of MySQL and some additional features. You can get a copy of MariaDB from the MariaDB Foundation site (*https://downloads.mariadb.org/mariadb/*), which is also free and requires registration.

When downloading the software on both sites, you'll have to provide some information about yourself, your organization, and how you intend to use the software. They're collecting information to understand how the software is used and to give to their sales department. But if you indicate that you don't want to be contacted, you can just download the software and not have to interact further with them.

If your server or local computer has MySQL or MariaDB installed on it, you can skip this chapter. If you're not sure whether MySQL or MariaDB is running on the computer you're using, you could enter something like this from the command line of a Linux or Mac machine:

```
ps aux | grep mysql
```

If MySQL is running, the preceding command should produce results like the following:

```
2763 ?        00:00:00 mysqld_safe
2900 ?        5-23:48:51 mysqld
```

On a Windows computer, you can use the `tasklist` tool to see whether MySQL is running. Enter something like the following from the command line:

```
tasklist /fi "IMAGENAME eq mysqld"
```

If it's running, you will get results like this:

```
Image Name           PID  Session Name      Session#   Mem Usage
================ ======= ================ ========= ==========
mysqld.exe          1356  Services                 0      212 K
```

If it's not running, you may get results like this from tasklist:

```
INFO:  No tasks are running which match the specified criteria.
```

This isn't conclusive proof that you don't have MySQL installed. It just shows that the daemon isn't running. You might try searching your computer for `mysqld`, using a file manager or some other such program. You might also try running `mysqladmin`, assuming it's installed on your server, and use the first line shown here to test MySQL (an example of the results you should see follow):

```
mysqladmin -p version status

mysqladmin  Ver 9.0 Distrib 5.5.33a-MariaDB, for Linux on i686
Copyright (c) 2000, 2013, Oracle, Monty Program Ab and others.

Server version          5.5.33a-MariaDB
Protocol version        10
Connection              Localhost via UNIX socket
UNIX socket             /var/lib/mysql/mysql.sock
Uptime:                 30 days 23 hours 37 min 12 sec

Threads: 4  Questions: 24085079  Slow queries: 0  Opens: 10832  Flush tables: 3
Open tables: 400  Queries per second avg: 8.996 Uptime: 2677032  Threads: 4
Questions: 24085079  Slow queries: 0  Opens: 10832  Flush tables: 3
Open tables: 400  Queries per second avg: 8.996
```

If one of these tests shows that MySQL is running on your computer, you may move onto Chapter 3. If MySQL is not running, it may be just that you need to start it. That's covered in this chapter, at the end of each section for each version of MySQL. Look for the section related to your distribution of MySQL or MariaDB (e.g., Mac OS X) and skip to the end of that section to see how to start the daemon. Try then to start it. If it starts, skip to the end of this chapter and read "Post-Installation" on page 24. There are a few important points made in that section, in particular some security steps you should follow. If you're unable to start the daemon, though, read the whole section for the distribution you choose.

Choosing a Distribution

Before beginning to download an installation package, you must decide which version of MySQL or MariaDB to install. For MySQL, the best choice is usually the latest stable version recommended by Oracle on its site, the version called the generally available (GA) release. This is the best way to go if you're new to MySQL. There's no need as a beginner to use a beta version, or a development release. Unless you have a support contract with Oracle, which would provide you access to the Enterprise version of MySQL, you will have to use the MySQL Community Server version. For a beginner, it's essentially the same as the Enterprise version.

For MariaDB, the latest GA release will be the current stable version. You can download it from the MariaDB Foundation's download page (*https://downloads.mariadb.org/mariadb/*).

When installing one of these database systems, you also have the option of using either a source distribution or a binary distribution. The binary distribution is easier to install and is recommended. Use a source distribution only if you have special configuration requirements that must be set during the installation or at compile time. You may also have to use a source distribution if a binary distribution isn't available for your operating system. Otherwise, install the binary; there's no need to make installation difficult when your goal at this point should be to learn the basics of MySQL.

The _AMP Alternatives

The following sections describe different methods for downloading and installing MySQL or MariaDB for different operating systems, in different formats. An easy method, though, is to use one of the *_AMP* packages. These letters stand for Apache, MySQL/MariaDB, and PHP/Perl/Python. Apache is the most popular web server. PHP is the most popular programming language used with MySQL. An *AMP* package or stack is based on an operating system: the Linux stack is called LAMP, the Macintosh stack is called MAMP, and the Windows stack is called WAMP. If you download and install one of these stacks, it will install Apache, MySQL, PHP, and any software upon which they depend on your local computer or server. It's a simple, turnkey method. If you install MySQL using a stack installation, you still need to make some post-installation adjustments. They're explained in the last section of this chapter. So after installing, skip ahead to it.

Sites for these packages include:

- The Apache XAMPP site (*http://www.apachefriends.org/en/xampp-linux.html*) for the latest Linux version (the extra P in LAMPP stands for Perl). Even though the site calls the package XAMPP instead of LAMPP, it's the same thing.

- The SourceForge MAMP site (*http://sourceforge.net/projects/mamp/*) for the latest Mac version.

- The EasyPHP WAMP site (*http://www.easyphp.org/download.php*) for the latest Windows vision.

All of these packages have easy-to-follow installation programs. The default installation options are usually fine.

Linux Binary Distributions

If your server is running on a version of Linux that installs software through the RPM package format (where RPM originally stood for RedHat Package Manager) or the DEB package format (where DEB stands for Debian Linux), it is recommended that you use a binary package instead of a source distribution. Linux binaries are provided based on a few different Linux distributions: various versions of Red Hat, Debian, SuSE Linux. For all other distributions of Linux, there are generic Linux packages for installing MySQL. There are also different versions of a distribution related to the type of processor used by the server (e.g., 32-bit or 64-bit).

Before proceeding, though, if you have the original installation disks for Linux, you may be able to use its installation program to easily install MySQL from the disks. In this case, you can skip the remainder of this section and proceed to "Post-Installation" on page 24. If your installation disks are old, though, they may not have the latest version of MySQL. So you may want to install MySQL using the method described in the following paragraphs.

For each version of MySQL, there are a few binary installation packages that you can download: the *MySQL Server*, the *Shared Components*, the *Compatibility Libraries*, *Client Utilities*, *Embedded*, and the *Test Suite*. The most important ones are the *Server*, the *Client Utilities*, and the *Shared Components*. In addition to these main packages, you may also want to install the one named *Shared Libraries*. It provides the files necessary for interacting with MySQL from programming languages such as PHP, Perl, and C. The other packages are for advanced or special needs that won't be discussed in this book and that you may not need to learn until you're a more advanced MySQL developer.

The naming scheme for these packages is generally *MySQL-server-version.rpm*, *MySQL-client-version.rpm* and *MySQL-shared-version.rpm*, where *version* is the actual version number. The corresponding package names for Debian-based distributions end in *.deb* instead of *.rpm*.

To install .rpm files after downloading them to your server, you can use the rpm utility or something more comprehensive like yum. yum is better about making sure you're not installing software that conflicts with other things on your server. It also upgrades and installs anything that might be missing on your server. In addition, it can be used to upgrade MySQL for newer editions as they become available. On Debian-based systems, apt-get is similar to yum. For MySQL, Oracle provides a yum repository (*http:// dev.mysql.com/downloads/repo/yum/*) and an apt repository (*http://dev.mysql.com/ downloads/repo/apt/*). For MariaDB, there is a repository configuration tool (*https:// downloads.mariadb.org/mariadb/repositories/*) for each operating system.

To install the binary installation files for MySQL using yum, you would enter something like the following from the command line on the server:

```
yum install MySQL-server-version.rpm \
MySQL-client-version.rpm MySQL-shared-version.rpm
```

You would, of course, modify the names of the RPM or DEB files to the precise name of the packages you want to install. The yum utility will take you through the installation steps, asking you to confirm the installation, any removals of conflicting software, and any upgrades needed. Unless the server is a critical one for use in business, you can probably agree to let it do what it wants.

To install the binary installation files for MariaDB using yum, you would enter something like the following from the command line on the server:

```
yum install MariaDB-server MariaDB-client
```

To install MySQL or MariaDB using the rpm utility, enter something like the following from the command line in the directory where the RPM files are located:

```
rpm -ivh MySQL-server-version.rpm \
MySQL-client-version.rpm MySQL-shared-version.rpm
```

If an earlier version of MySQL is already installed on the server, you will receive an error message stating this problem, and the installation will be canceled. If you want to upgrade an existing installation, you can replace the -i option in the example with an upper case -U like so:

```
rpm -Uvh MySQL-server-version.rpm
MySQL-client-version.rpm MySQL-shared-version.rpm
```

When the RPM files are installed, the mysqld daemon will be started or restarted automatically. Once MySQL is installed and running, you need to make some post-installation adjustments, as explained in "Post-Installation" on page 24. So skip ahead to it.

Mac OS X Distributions

Recent versions of Mac OS X no longer come with MySQL installed, but previous ones did—they stopped shipping it after Oracle took over MySQL. If your computer started with an older version, it may already be installed, but not running. To see if you have MySQL installed on your system, open the Terminal application (located in *Applications/Utilities*). Once you have a command prompt, enter the first line shown here (the results you should see are on lines 2–4):

```
whereis mysql mysqld mysqld_safe

/usr/bin/mysql
/usr/bin/mysqld
/usr/bin/mysqld_safe
```

If you get the results just shown, MySQL is installed on your computer. Check now whether the MySQL daemon (`mysqld`) is running. Enter the following from the command line:

```
ps aux | grep mysql
```

If it shows that `mysqld` is running, you don't need to install it, but skip instead to "Post-Installation" on page 24.

If the daemon is present on your system but not running, enter the following from the command line as *root* to start it:

```
/usr/bin/mysqld_safe &
```

If MySQL is not installed on your Mac system or you want to upgrade your copy of MySQL by installing the latest release, directions are included in the remainder of this section. If MySQL isn't already installed on your system, you may need to create a system user named *mysql* before installing MySQL. Oracle's MySQL package automatically creates a user called *_mysql*.

Binary file packages (DMG files) are available for installing MySQL. For Mac servers that do not have a GUI or a desktop manager, or for when you want to install it remotely, there are TAR files for installing MySQL.[2] Whether you will be downloading a DMG file or a TAR file, be sure to download the package related to the type of processor on your server (e.g., 32-bit or 64-bit), and for the minimum version of the server's operating system (e.g., Mac OS X, version 10.6 or higher).

If an older version of MySQL is already installed on your server, you will need to shut down the MySQL service before installing and running the newer version or replacing it with MariaDB. You can do this with the MySQL Manager Application, which is a GUI application that was probably installed when the operating system was first installed along with MySQL. It's typically installed on recent versions of Mac OS X by default. If your server doesn't have the MySQL Manager Application, you can enter the following from the command line to shut down the MySQL service:

```
/usr/sbin/mysqladmin -u root -p shutdown
```

If you've never used MySQL and didn't set the password, it's probably blank. When you're prompted for it after entering the preceding command, just press the Enter key.

To install the MySQL package file, from the Finder desktop manager, double-click on the disk image file (the DMG file) that you downloaded. This will reveal the disk image file's contents. Look for the PKG files; there will be two. Double-click on the one named *mysql-version.pkg* (e.g., *mysql-5.5.29-osx10.6-x86.pkg*). This will begin the installation

---

2. `tar` is an archive tool developed on Unix, but its format is understood by many archiving tools on many operating systems.

program. The installer will take you through the installation steps from there. The default settings are recommended for most users and developers.

To have MySQL started at boot time, add a *startup item*. Within the disk image file that you downloaded, you should see an icon labeled *MySQLStartupItem.pkg*. Just double-click it, and it will create a *startup item* for MySQL. You should also install the MySQL preferences pane so that you can start and stop MySQL easily from Systems Preferences in the Mac system, as well as set it to start automatically at start up time. To do this, click on the icon labeled *MySQL.prefPane*. If you have problems using the installer, read the *ReadMe.txt* file included in the DMG image file.

There is not yet an official installer for MariaDB on a Mac machine. However, you can use *homebrew (http://brew.sh/)* to download and install the needed packages, including required libraries. The homebrew utility works much like yum does on Linux systems, but is made for Mac OS X. After you install homebrew, you can run the following from the command line to install MariaDB:

```
brew install mariadb
```

To install MySQL with the TAR package instead of the DMG package, download the TAR file from Oracle's site and move it to the */usr/local* directory, then change to that directory. Next, untar and unzip the installation program like so:

```
cd /usr/local
tar xvfz mysql-version.tar.gz
```

Change the name of the installation package in the example to the actual name. From here, create a symbolic link for the installation directory, and then run the configuration program. Here is an example of how you might do this:

```
ln -s /usr/local/mysql-version /usr/local/mysql
cd /usr/local/mysql

./configure --prefix=/usr/local/mysql \
  --with-unix-socket-path=/usr/local/mysql/mysql_socket \
  --with-mysqld-user=mysql
```

The first line creates the symbolic link to give MySQL a universal location regardless of future versions; change *version* to the actual version number. By making a symbolic link to a generic directory of */usr/local/mysql*, you'll always know where to find MySQL when you need it. You could also just rename the directory with the version name to just *mysql*. But then you can't test new versions and keep old versions when upgrading.

With the second line, you enter the directory where the installation files are now located. The third line runs the configuration program to install MySQL. I've included a few options that I think will be useful for solving some problems in advance. Depending on your needs, you might provide more options than these few. However, for most beginners, these should be enough.

Next, you should set who owns the files and directories created, and which group has rights to them. Set both the user and group to mysql, which should have been created by the installation program. For some systems, you may have to enable permissions for the hard drive or volume first. To do that, use the vsdbutil utility. If you want to check whether permissions are enabled on the volume first, use the -c option; to just enable it, use -a option for vsdbutil. You should also make a symbolic link from the */usr/bin* directory to the mysql and mysqladmin clients:

```
vsdbutil -a /Volumes/Macintosh\ HD/

sudo chown -R _mysql /usr/local/mysql/.

alias mysql=/usr/local/mysql/bin/mysql
alias mysqladmin=/usr/local/mysql/bin/mysqladmin
```

The first line of this example enables the main drive of the Mac machine. The name of the drive on which you locate MySQL may be different on your server. The second line changes the owner to the user *mysql*. The last two lines create aliases for the two key MySQL clients mentioned earlier so that you can run them from anywhere on your system.

At this point, you should be able to start the daemon and log into MySQL or MariaDB. If you installed the preference pane for MySQL with the installer, you can go to the Systems Preference of the operating system and start it there instead:

```
sudo /usr/bin/mysqld_safe &
mysql -u root -p
```

Depending on the release of MySQL, the file path for a *dmg* installation may be different from what is shown in the first line here. An ampersand (&) sends the process to the background. The second line will start the mysql client and let you log in as *root*, the MySQL user who is in control of the whole server—MySQL users are different from operating system users, so the *root* user is also different even though the name is the same. The command will prompt you for a password, which will probably be blank. So you can just press Enter for the password and you'll be in.

Success here simply shows that you can connect to the MySQL or MariaDB server and that you have correctly added the symbolic links for the mysql client. There's more to do before you start trying MySQL. So type exit and press Enter to exit the mysql client.

Now that MySQL or MariaDB is installed and running, you need to make some post-installation adjustments, as explained in "Post-Installation" on page 24. Skip ahead to that section.

Windows Distributions

Installing MySQL or MariaDB on a server using Microsoft Windows is fairly easy. MySQL's website now provides one installation package for everything, offering different methods and versions to meet your needs and preference. The MariaDB Foundation's website provides installation packages for installing MariaDB on servers using Windows. The easiest and best choice for installing MySQL is to download and use the MySQL Installer for Windows. It's a single file that does everything for you. There are also older versions still available that may be downloaded in a TAR file, but the new installer is easier and will give you the latest version. For both the installer packages and the TAR packages, there are 32-bit and 64-bit versions, which you would choose based on which kind of processor is in your server.

Both the installer and TAR packages contain the essential files for running MySQL or MariaDB, including all of the command-line utilities covered in this book (e.g., `mysql`, `mysqladmin`, `mysqlbackup`), some useful scripts for handling special needs, and the libraries for APIs. They also contain the */usr/local/mysql/docs* directory for the version that you download.

If you decide to use the TAR package for Windows, because it does not include an installer to handle everything for you, you will have to do a few things manually at the beginning. First, you will need to unzip the TAR file to get at the installation files. To do this, you need WinZip (*http://www.winzip.com*) or another utility that you might have installed on your server to uncompress the files. These files need to be copied into the *c:\mysql* directory. You'll have to create that directory if it does not already exist on your server. Then, using a plain-text editor (e.g., Notepad) you must create a configuration file that is generally called *my.ini* in the *c:\windows* directory. Several examples of this configuration file are provided with the distribution package. Once you have the files in the appropriate place, you can run the setup program. It does provide some assistance, but not as much as the installer.

Before running the installer or the setup program, if MySQL is already installed and running on your server, and you want to install a newer version, you will first need to shut down the one that's currently running on your server. For server versions of Windows, it's generally installed as a service. You can enter something like the following within a command window to shut down the service and remove it:

```
mysqld -remove
```

If MySQL is running on your server, but not as a service, you can enter the following within a command window to shut it down:

```
msyqladmin -u root -p shutdown
```

If that returns an error message, you may have to figure out the absolute path for `mysqladmin`. Try entering something like the following, adjusting the file path to wherever `mysqladmin` is located:

```
"C:\Program Data\MySQL\MySQL Server 5.1\bin\mysqladmin" -u root -p shutdown
```

After you download the MySQL Installer for Windows from the Windows desktop, double-click on the file's icon and the Windows Installer program will start. If you're installing from a ZIP package, look for the file named *setup.exe* wherever you put the MySQL installation files. Double-click on it to start the installation. From this point, the installation process is pretty much the same for both types of packages.

After you've started the installation, once you get past the licensing question and so forth, you will be given a few choices of which type of installation. The *Developer* choice is the recommended one. However, it will not install the files need for an API, or some other utilities. It will install the MySQL server, libraries, and several MySQL clients on your computer. This is probably the best choice. However, if you're installing the software on a server and you will be connecting to it from a different computer such as your deskop, you could select "Server only" to install the MySQL server on your server. If you do so, run the installer on your desktop machine and select "Client only" to install only the MySQL clients locally. The MySQL files aren't very large, though. You could also install the "Server only" on your server and the Developer package on your desktop. This would allow you to use your desktop as a development environment to learn and test a database before uploading it to your server and making it active. Choose the packages and combinations that work best for you. Just be sure to have both the MySQL server and the MySQL clients installed somewhere that you can access them.

On the same screen where you choose the setup type, there will be two boxes for file paths: one where you install the utilities and the other where MySQL stores your data. You can accept the default paths for these or change them, if you want to use a different hard drive or location. The default settings are usually fine. Just make a copy of the paths somewhere, because you may want to know this information later. You can find it later in the configuration file for MySQL, but while it's handy now, copy it down: it might save you some time later.

Next, the installer will check whether your computer has the required additional files, besides the MySQL package. Allow it to install whatever files it says you need. For the TAR package, you will have to decide which directory to use and put the files where you want them. A typical choice is *C:\Program Data\MySQL* for the installation path, and *C:\Program Data\MySQL\MySQL Server version\data* for the data path, where the word *version* is replaced with the version number.

The last section before the installer finishes is the Configuration screen, where you can set some configuration options. If you want to set options, you can check the box labeled Advanced Configuration, but because you're still learning about MySQL, you should leave this unchecked and accept the basic default settings for now. You can change the server settings later.

If you're installing the MySQL server on this machine and not just the clients, you will see a "Start the MySQL Server at System Startup" checkbox. It is a good idea to check that box. In the Configuration section, you can also enter the password for the MySQL *root* user. Enter a secure password and don't forget it. You can also add another user. We'll cover that in "Post-Installation" on page 24. But if you want to make that process easier, you can add a user here for yourself—but I recommend waiting and using MySQL to add users, so you learn that important skill. As for the rest of the choices that the installer gives you, you can probably accept the default settings.

In this book, you will be working and learning from the command line, so you will need to have easy access to the MySQL clients that work from the command line. To invoke the command-line utilities without having to enter the file path to the directory containing them, enter the following from the command line, from any directory:

```
PATH=%PATH%;C:\Program Data\MySQL\MySQL Server version\bin
export PATH
```

Replace the word *version* with the version number and make sure to enter the actual path where MySQL is installed. If you changed the location when you installed MySQL, you need to use the path that you named. The line just shown will let you start the client by entering simply `mysql` and not something like, *C:\Program Data\MySQL\MySQL Server version\bin\mysql* each time. For some Windows systems, you may need to change the start of the path to *C:\Program Files*. You'll have to search your system to see where the binary files for MySQL were installed—look for the *bin* subdirectory. Any command windows you may already have open won't get the new path. So be sure to close them and open a new command window.

Once you've finished installing MySQL and you've set up the configuration file, the installer will start the MySQL server automatically. If you've installed MySQL manually without an installer, enter something like the following from a command window:

```
mysqld --install
net start mysql
```

Now that MySQL is installed and running, you need to make some post-installation adjustments, as explained in "Post-Installation" on page 24. So jump ahead to the last couple of pages of this chapter.

FreeBSD and Sun Solaris Distributions

Installing MySQL or MariaDB with a binary distribution is easier than using a source distribution. If a binary distribution is available for your platform, it's the recommended choice. For Sun Solaris distributions, there are PKG files for MySQL on Oracle's site and PKG files for MariaDB on the MariaDB Foundation's site. For MySQL, you will have to decide between 32-bit, 64-bit, and SPARC versions, depending on the type of processor used on your server. For MariaDB, there is only a 64-bit version.

There are also TAR files, combining the MySQL files. The FreeBSD files are available only in TAR packages and only for MySQL. For MariaDB, you will have to compile the source files. If you download the TAR files, you will need a copy of GNU's `tar` and

GNU's gunzip to unpack the installation files. These tools are usually included on Sun Solaris and FreeBSD systems. If your system doesn't have them, though, you can download them from the GNU Foundation site (*http://www.gnu.org*).

Once you've chosen and downloaded an installation package, enter something like the following from the command line as *root* to begin the installation process:

```
groupadd mysql
useradd -g mysql mysql
cd /usr/local
tar xvfz /tmp/mysql-version.tar.gz
```

These commands are the same for both MySQL and MariaDB. The first command creates the user group, *mysql*. The second creates the user, *mysql*, and adds it to the *mysql* group at the same time. The next command changes to the directory where the MySQL files are about to be extracted. The last line uses the tar utility (along with gunzip via the z option) to unzip and extract the distribution files. The word *version* in the name of the installation file should be replaced with the version number—that is to say, use the actual file path and name of the installation file that you downloaded as the second argument of the tar command. For Sun Solaris systems, you should use gtar instead of tar.

After running the previous commands, you need to create a symbolic link to the directory created by tar in */usr/local*:

```
ln -s /usr/local/mysql-version /usr/local/mysql
```

This creates */usr/local/mysql* as a link to */usr/local/mysql-version*, where *mysql-version* is the actual name of the subdirectory that tar created in */usr/local*. The link is necessary, because MySQL is expecting the software to be located in */usr/local/mysql* and the data to be in */usr/local/mysql/data* by default.

At this point, MySQL or MariaDB is basically installed. Now you must generate the initial user privileges or grant tables, and change the file ownership of the related programs and data files. To do these tasks, enter the following from the command line:

```
cd /usr/local/mysql
./scripts/mysql_install_db

chown -R mysql /usr/local/mysql
chgrp -R mysql /usr/local/mysql
```

The first command changes to the directory containing MySQL's files. The second line uses a script provided with the distribution to generate the initial privileges or *grant tables*, which consist of the mysql database with MySQL's superuser, *root*. This is the same for MariaDB. The third line changes the ownership of the MySQL directories and programs to the filesystem user, *mysql*. The last line changes the group owner of the same directory and files to the user, *mysql*.

With the programs installed and their ownerships set properly, you can start MySQL. This can be done in several ways. To make sure that the daemon is restarted in the event that it crashes, enter the following from the command line:

```
/usr/local/mysql/bin/mysqld_safe &
```

The mysqld_safe daemon, started by this command, will in turn start the MySQL server daemon, mysqld. If the mysqld daemon crashes, mysqld_safe will restart it. The ampersand at the end of the line instructs the shell to run the command in the background. This way you can exit the server and it will continue to run without you staying connected.

To have MySQL or MariaDB start at boot time, copy the *mysql.server* file located in the *support-files* subdirectory of */usr/local/mysql* to the */etc/init.d* directory. To do this, enter the following from the command line:

```
cp support-files/mysql.server /etc/init.d/mysql
chmod +x /etc/init.d/mysql
chkconfig --add mysql
```

The first line follows a convention of placing the start up file for the server in the server's initial daemons directory with the name, mysql. The second line makes the file executable. The third sets the run level of the service for *startup* and *shutdown*.

Now that MySQL or MariaDB is installed and running, you need to make some post-installation adjustments, as explained in "Post-Installation" on page 24.

Source Distributions

Although a binary distribution of MySQL and MariaDB is recommended, sometimes you may want to use a source distribution, either because binaries are not available for your server's operating system, or because you have some special requirements that require customizing the installation. The steps for installing the source files of MySQL or MariaDB on all Unix types of operating systems are basically the same. This includes Linux, FreeBSD, and Sun Solaris. These steps are explained in this section.

To install a source distribution, you will need copies of GNU gunzip, GNU tar, GNU gcc (at least Version 2.95.2), and GNU make. These tools are usually included in Linux systems and most Unix systems. If your system doesn't have them, you can download them from the GNU Foundation site (*http://www.gnu.org*).

Once you've chosen and downloaded the source distribution files for MySQL or MariaDB, enter the following commands as *root* from the directory where you want the source files stored:

```
groupadd mysql
useradd -g mysql mysql
tar xvfz /tmp/mysql-version.tar.gz
cd mysql-version
```

These commands are the same for installing MariaDB, except that the name of the installation package file will be something like *mariadb-5.5.35.tar.gz* and the name of the directory created when expanding the TAR file will be different. The first line creates the filesystem user group, *mysql*. The second creates the system user, *mysql*, and adds it to the *mysql* group at the same time. The next command uses the `tar` utility (along with `gunzip` via the `z` option) to unzip and extract the source distribution file you downloaded. Replace the word *version* with the version number. Use the actual file path and name of the installation file that you downloaded for the second argument of the `tar` command. The last command changes the directory to the one created by `tar` in the previous line. That directory contains the files needed to configure MySQL.

This brings you to the next step, which is to configure the source files to prepare them for building the binary programs. This is where you can add any special build requirements you may have. For instance, if you want to change the default directory from where MySQL or MariaDB is installed, use the `--prefix` option with a value set to equal the desired directory. To set the Unix socket file's path, use `--with-unix-socket-path`. If you would like to use a different character set from the default of `latin1`, use `--with-charset` and name the character set you want as the default. Here is an example of how you might configure MySQL with these particular options before building the binary files:

```
./configure --prefix=/usr/local/mysql \
            --with-unix-socket-path=/tmp \
            --with-charset=latin2
```

You can enter this command on one line without the backslashes. Several other configuration options are available. To get a complete and current listing of options permitted with the installation package you downloaded, enter the following from the command line:

```
./configure --help
```

You may also want to look at the latest online documentation for compiling MySQL (*http://bit.ly/compiling_mysql*).

Once you've decided on any options that you want, run the `configure` script with those options. It will take quite a while to run, and it will display a great amount of information, which you can ignore usually if it ends successfully. After the `configure` script finishes, the binaries will need to be built and MySQL needs to be initialized. To do this, enter the following:

```
make
make install
cd /usr/local/mysql
./scripts/mysql_install_db
```

The first line here builds the binary programs. There may be plenty of text displayed after that line and the next one, but I omitted that output to save space. If the command is successful, you need to enter the second line to install the binary programs and related files in the appropriate directories. The third line changes to the directory where MySQL was installed. If you configured MySQL to be installed in a different directory, you'll have to use that directory path instead. The last command uses a script provided with the distribution to generate the initial user privileges or grant tables.

All that remains is to change the ownership of the MySQL programs and directories. You can do this by entering the following:

```
chown -R mysql /usr/local/mysql
chgrp -R mysql /usr/local/mysql
```

The first line here changes ownership of the MySQL directories and programs to the filesystem user, *mysql*. The second line changes the group owner of the same directories and files to the group *mysql*. These file paths may be different depending on the version of MySQL you installed and whether you configured MySQL for different paths.

With the programs installed and their file ownerships set properly, you can start the daemon. You can do this in several ways. To make sure that the daemon is restarted in the event that it crashes, enter the following from the command line:

```
/usr/local/mysql/bin/mysqld_safe &
```

This method is the same for both MySQL and MariaDB, and it starts the mysqld_safe daemon, which will in turn start the server daemon, mysqld. If the mysqld daemon crashes, mysqld_safe will restart it. The ampersand at the end of the line instructs the shell to run the daemon in the background. This way you can exit the server and it will continue to run without you staying connected.

To have MySQL or MariaDB started at boot time, copy the *mysql.server* file, located in the *support-files* subdirectory of */usr/local/mysql*, to the */etc/init.d* directory. To do this, enter the following from the command line:

```
cp support-files/mysql.server /etc/init.d/mysql
chmod +x /etc/init.d/mysql
chkconfig --add mysql
```

The first line follows a convention of placing the startup file for the server in the server's initial daemons directory with the name, *mysql*. The second command makes the file executable. The third sets the run level of the service for *startup* and *shutdown*. All of this is the same for MariaDB.

At this point, MySQL or MariaDB is installed and running. All that remains now are some post-installation adjustments, as explained in the next section.

Post-Installation

After you've finished installing MySQL or MariaDB on your server, you should perform a few tasks before allowing others to begin using the service. You may want to change the server's default behavior by making changes to the configuration file. At a minimum, you should change the password for the database administrator, *root*, and add some nonadministrative users. Some versions of MySQL have some anonymous users initially, and you should delete them. This section will explain these tasks.

Although the creators of MySQL and MariaDB have set the server daemon to the recommended configuration, you may want to change one or more settings. For instance, you may want to turn on error logging.

Special Configuration

To enable error logging and other such settings, you will need to edit the main configuration file for MySQL. On Unix-like systems, this file is */etc/my.cnf*. On Windows systems, the main configuration file is usually either *c:\windows\my.ini* or *c:\my.cnf*. The configuration file is a text file that you can edit with a plain-text editor—don't use a word processor, as it will introduce hidden binary characters that will cause problems.

The configuration file is organized into sections or groups under a heading name contained within square brackets. For instance, settings for the server daemon, mysqld, are listed under the group heading, [mysqld]. Under this heading you could add something like log = /var/log/mysql to enable logging and to set the directory for the log files. You can list many options in the file for a particular group. Here is an example of how a server configuration file might look:

```
[mysqld]
datadir=/data/mysql
user=mysql
default-character-set=utf8
log-bin=/data/mysql/logs/binary_log
max_allowed_packet=512M

[mysqld_safe]
ulimit -d 256000
ledir=/usr/sbin
mysqld=mysqld
log-error=/var/log/mysqld.log
pid-file=/data/mysql/mysqld.pid

[mysql.client]
default-character-set=utf8
```

As a beginner, you probably won't need to make any changes to the server's configuration file. For now, just know that the configuration file exists, where it's located on your server, and how to change settings. What is necessary is to set the password for the MySQL user, *root*. It's initially blank.

Setting Initial Password for root

You can change the password for the *root* user in MySQL in a few ways. One way is to use the administration utility, `mysqladmin`. Enter the following from the command line:

```
mysqladmin -u root -p flush-privileges password "new_pwd"
```

Replace the word *new_pwd* in quotes with a strong password that you want to use for *root*. If you get a message saying something like, *mysqladmin command is not found*, it may be because you didn't make a symbolic link to the MySQL directory where `mysqladmin` is located or you haven't added it to your command path. See the instructions for the distribution you installed on how to do one or the other. For now, you can just add the file path to the preceding line and re-enter it. On Linux and other Unix like systems, try running the command as `/usr/local/mysql/bin/mysqladmin`. On a Windows system, try `c:\mysql\bin\mysqladmin`.

If you're working on a networked server, though, it's better not to enter a password in this way. Someone might be looking over your shoulder or may find it in the server logs later. As of version 5.5.3 of MySQL, you can and should enter it like this:

```
mysqladmin -u root -p flush-privileges password
```

After entering this line, you will be prompted for the old password, which will be initially blank, so press the Enter key. Then you will be prompted to enter the new password twice. By this method, the password you enter won't be displayed on the screen as you type it. If everything was installed properly and if the `mysqld` daemon is running, you should not get any message in response.

The MySQL user *root* is completely different from the operating system's *root* user, even though it has the same name. It is meaningful only within MySQL or MariaDB. Throughout this book, I will be referring to this MySQL user by default when I use the term *root*. On the rare occasion where I have to refer to the operating system *root* user, I will explain that.

More on Passwords and Removing Anonymous Users

Privileges in MySQL are set based on a combination of the user's name and the user's host. For instance, the user *root* is allowed to do everything from the localhost, but very little or nothing from a remote location. This is for security. Therefore, there may be more than one username/host combination for *root*. Using `mysqladmin`, you changed the password for *root* on the localhost, as you would have executed it while logged into the server where MySQL is located locally. Now you should set the password for all of the username/host combinations for *root*. To get a list of username and host combinations on the server, execute the following from the command line:

```
mysql -u root -p -e "SELECT User,Host FROM mysql.user;"
```

```
+------+---------------------+
| User | Host                |
+------+---------------------+
| root | 127.0.0.1           |
| root | localhost           |
| root | %                   |
|      | localhost           |
+------+---------------------+
```

If this didn't work for you, it may be that you don't have the `mysql` client in your command path. You may have to preface `mysql` with `/bin/` or `/usr/bin/`, or the path for wherever the binary files for MySQL are installed. The command will be the same for MariaDB. The results here are contrived. It's unlikely you will see exactly these results. But there are versions of MySQL whose host for *root* is %, which is a wildcard meaning any host. This is not good for security, because it allows anybody to claim to be *root* and to gain access from any location. And there have been versions of MySQL in which the username is left blank, meaning that any username from the `localhost` is accepted. This is an anonymous user. All of the users you will see in the results, though, will initially have no password. You should delete any unnecessary users and set passwords for those that you want to keep. Although 127.0.0.1 and `localhost` translate to the same host, the password should be changed for both. To change the *root* user's password for the first two entries shown in the previous example and to delete the second two user/host combinations shown, you would enter the following at the command prompt:

```
mysql -u root -p -e "SET PASSWORD FOR 'root'@'127.0.0.1' PASSWORD('new_pwd');"
mysql -u root -p -e "SET PASSWORD FOR 'root'@'localhost' PASSWORD('new_pwd');"
mysql -u root -p -e "DROP USER 'root'@'%';"
mysql -u root -p -e "DROP USER ''@'localhost';"
```

When you've finished making changes to the initial batch of users, you should flush the user privileges so that the new passwords will take effect. Enter the following from the command line:

```
mysqladmin -u root -p flush-privileges
```

From this point on, you'll have to use the new password for the user, *root*.

Creating a User

The next step regarding users is to create at least one user for general use. It's best not to use the *root* user for general database management. To create another user, enter commands like:

```
mysql -u root -p -e "GRANT USAGE ON *.*
TO 'russell'@'localhost'
IDENTIFIED BY 'Rover#My_1st_Dog&Not_Yours!';"
```

These lines create the user *russell* and allow him to access MySQL from the localhost. The *.* means all databases and all tables. We'll cover this in more depth later in the book. The statement also sets his password as *Rover#My_1st_Dog&Not_Yours!*.

This user has no privileges, actually: he can't even view the databases, much less enter data. When you set up a new user, you should consider which privileges to allow the user. If you want her to be able only to view data, enter something like the following from the command line:

```
mysql -u root -p -e "GRANT SELECT ON *.* TO 'russell'@'localhost';"
```

In this line, the user *russell* may use only the SELECT statement, a command for viewing data. If you would like to see the privileges granted to a user, you could enter something like this from the command line:

```
mysql -u root -p -e "SHOW GRANTS FOR 'russell@'localhost' \G"

*************************** 1. row ***************************
Grants for russell@localhost:
GRANT SELECT ON *.* TO 'russell'@'localhost'
IDENTIFIED BY PASSWORD '*B1A8D5415ACE5AB4BBAC120EC1D17766B8EFF1A1'
```

These results show that the user is granted only privileges to use the SELECT statement for viewing data. We'll cover this in more depth later in the book. Notice that the password is returned encrypted. There's no way to retrieve someone's password unencrypted from MySQL.

The user in the previous example, *russell* on localhost, cannot add, change, or delete data. If you want to give a user more than viewing privileges, you should add additional privileges to the SELECT command, separated by commas. That is covered in Chapter 13. For now, to give a user all privileges, replace SELECT with ALL. Here's another example using the ALL setting:

```
mysql -u root -p -e "GRANT ALL ON *.* TO 'russell'@'localhost';"
```

The user in this example, *russell* on localhost, has all basic privileges. So that you can experiment while reading this book, you should create a user with full privileges, but use a name other than mine, something that better suits you.

With the MySQL or MariaDB installation software downloaded and installed, all of the binary files and minimal data in place and properly set, and a full privileged user created, the database system is now ready to use and you can begin learning how to use it.

## CHAPTER 3

The Basics and the mysql Client

There are various methods of interacting with a MySQL or MariaDB server to develop or work with a database. A program that interfaces with the server is known as a *MySQL client*. There are many such clients, but this book focuses on one that best serves the need of interactive users, a text-based client known simply as mysql. It's the most commonly used interface, recommended for beginners and preferred by advanced users.

There are alternative clients with GUIs, but in the long run they're not as useful. First, you don't learn as much while using them. Because they give you visual hints about what to do, you may be able to carry out some basic queries quickly, but you won't be as well prepared for advanced work. The text-based mysql client causes you to think and remember more—and it's not that difficult to use or confusing. More importantly, GUIs tend to change often. When they do, you will need to learn where to find what you want in the new version. If you change jobs or go to a customer's site, or for whatever reason use someone else's system, they may not use the same GUI with which you are familiar. However, they will always have the mysql client, because it's installed with the MySQL server. So all examples in this book assume that this is the client you will use. I recommend that when examples are shown, that you try entering them on your computer with the mysql client so that you can reinforce what you're learning.

The mysql Client

With the mysql client, you may interact with the MySQL or MariaDB server from either the command line or within an interface environment called the *monitor*. The command-line method of using mysql allows you to interact with the server without much overhead. It also allows you to enter MySQL commands in scripts and other programs. For instance, you can put lines in cron to perform maintenance tasks and make backups automatically of databases. The monitor is an ASCII display of mysql that makes the text a little more organized and provides more information about commands you execute. Almost all of the examples in this book are taken from the monitor display. If they're not, I will note that they are from the command line.

If MySQL or MariaDB was installed properly on your server, mysql should be available for you to use. If not, see "Post-Installation" on page 24 to make sure everything is configured correctly on your system and make sure you created the necessary symbolic links or aliases. The mysql client should be in the */bin/* or */usr/bin/* directory. Windows, Macs, and other operating systems with GUIs have file location utilities for finding a program. Look for the directory containing the mysql client and the other binary files for MySQL.

Assuming that everything is working, you will need a MySQL username and password to be able to connect to MySQL, even with the mysql client. If you're not the administrator, you must obtain these credentials from the appointed person. If MySQL or MariaDB was just installed and the *root* password is not set yet, its password is blank—that is to say, just press the Enter key when prompted for the password. To learn how to set the *root* password and to create new users and grant them privileges, see "Post-Installation" on page 24 for starting pointers and Chapter 13 for more advanced details.

Connecting to the Server

Once you know your MySQL username and password, you can connect to the MySQL server with the mysql client. For instance, I gave myself the username *russell* so I can connect as follows from a command line:

```
mysql -u russell -p
```

It's useful to understand each element of the previous line. The -u option is followed by your username. Notice that the option and name are separated by a space. You would replace *russell* here with whatever username you've created for yourself. This is the MySQL user, not the user for the operating system. Incidentally, it's not a good security practice to use the *root* user, unless you have a specific administrative task to perform for which only *root* has the needed privileges. So if you haven't created another user for yourself, go back and do that now. To log into MariaDB, you would enter the same command and options as for MySQL.

The -p option instructs the mysql client to prompt you for the password. You could add the password to the end of the -p option (e.g., -pRover#My_1st_Dog&Not_Yours!, where the text after -p is the password). If you do this, leave no space between -p and the password. However, entering the password on the command line is not a good security practice either, because it displays the password on the screen (which others standing behind you may see), and it transmits the password as clear text through the network, as well as making it visible whenever someone gets a list of processes that are running on the server. It's better to give the -p option without the password and then enter the password when asked by the server. Then the password won't be displayed on the screen or saved anywhere.

If you're logged into the server filesystem with the same username as you created for MySQL, you won't need the -u option; the -p is all you'll need. You could then just enter this:

```
mysql -p
```

Once you've entered the proper mysql command to connect to the server, along with the password when prompted, you will be logged into MySQL or MariaDB through the client. You will see something that looks like this:

```
Welcome to the MySQL monitor.  Commands end with ; or \g.
Your MySQL connection id is 1419341
Server version: 5.5.29 MySQL Community Server (GPL)

Type 'help;' or '\h' for help. Type '\c' to clear the current input statement.

mysql>
```

If MariaDB is installed on your server, you will see something like the following:

```
Welcome to the MariaDB monitor.  Commands end with ; or \g.
Your MariaDB connection id is 360511
Server version: 5.5.33a-MariaDB MariaDB Server, wsrep_23.7.6.rXXXX

Copyright (c) 2000, 2013, Oracle, Monty Program Ab and others.

Type 'help;' or '\h' for help. Type '\c' to clear the current input statement.

MariaDB [(none)]>>
```

The first line, after "Welcome to the MySQL/MariaDB monitor," says that commands end with a semicolon (;) or a slash-g (\g). When you enter a command, or rather an SQL statement, you can press Enter at any point to go to the next line and continue entering more text. Until you enter either ; or \g, the mysql client will not transmit what you've entered to the MySQL server. If you use \G, with an uppercase G, you'll get a different format. We'll cover that format later. For now, just use the semicolon.

The second line in the output shown tells you the identification number for your connection to the server. One day you may get in trouble and need to know that. For now you can ignore it.

The third line tells you which version of MySQL or MariaDB is installed on the server. That can be useful when you have problems and discover in reading the online documentation that the problem is in a particular version, or when you want to upgrade the server but need to know which version you have now before upgrading.

The next line talks about getting online help. It provides help for all of the SQL statements and functions. Try entering these commands to see what the client returns:

help

> This command provides help on using the `mysql` client.

help contents

> This command shows you a list of categories for help on major aspects of MySQL or MariaDB. In that list, you will see one of the categories is called Data Manipulation. These are SQL statements related to inserting, updating, and deleting data.

hep Data Manipulation

> This command will display all of those statements for which help is available from the client. One of those SQL statements is SHOW DATABASES.

help SHOW DATABASES

> This command shows how to retrieve the help information related to that SQL statement. As you can see, there is plenty of useful information accessible within the client. If you can't quite remember the syntax of an SQL statement, it's a quick way to retrieve the information.

The first `help` command provides help on using the `mysql` client. The second `help` command shows you a list of categories for help on major aspects of MySQL or MariaDB. In that list, you will see one of the categories is called, *Data Manipulation.* These are SQL statements related to inserting, updating, and deleting data. The third `help` command will display all of those statements for which help is available from the client. One of those SQL statements is SHOW DATABASES. The last `help` command shows how to retrieve the help information related to that SQL statement. As you can see, there is plenty of useful information accessible within the client. If you can't quite remember the syntax of an SQL statement, it's a quick way to retrieve the information.

A minor but sometimes useful tip is included in the third line of the opening results: to cancel an SQL statement once you've started typing it, enter \c and press Enter without a closing semicolon. It will clear whatever you have been entering, even on previous lines, from the buffer of the `mysql` client, and return you to the `mysql>` prompt.

The very last line, the `mysql>`, is known as the *prompt*. It's prompting you to enter a command, and is where you'll operate during most of this book. If you press Enter without finishing a command, the prompt will change to -> to indicate that the client hasn't yet sent the SQL statement to the server. On MariaDB, the default prompt is different. It shows `MariaDB [(none)]>>` to start. When you later set the default database to be used, the *none* will be changed to the name of the current default database.

Incidentally, it is possible to change the prompt to something else. To do so, enter the client command `prompt` followed by the text you want to display for the prompt. There are a few special settings (e.g., \d for default database). Here's how you might change the prompt:

```
prompt SQL Command \d>\_
```

And here's how the prompt will look after you run the preceding command to change it:

```
SQL Command (none)>
```

Right now you have no default database. So now that you have the `mysql` client started, let's start exploring databases.

Starting to Explore Databases

The next few chapters cover how to create databases, add data to them, and run queries to find interesting relationships. In this chapter, while you're logged into MySQL or MariaDB with the `mysql` client, let's get familiar with the core aspects of the database system. We'll consider a few basic concepts of databases so that you may enter a few commands within the `mysql` monitor. This will help you get comfortable with the `mysql` client. Because you may be in a very early stage of learning, we'll keep it simple for now.

In SQL terminology, data is always stored in a *table*, a term that reflects the way a user generally views the data. In a table about movies, for example, you might see a horizontal row about each movie, with the title as one column, and other columns to indicate more information on each movie:

```
+----------+--------------------+--------+
| movie_id | title              | rating |
+----------+--------------------+--------+
|        1 | Casablanca         | PG     |
|        2 | The Impostors      | R      |
|        3 | The Bourne Identity | PG-13  |
+----------+--------------------+--------+
```

That's just a simple example. Don't try to create that table. Let's first take a look at what you already have on your server, to see these elements. From the `mysql>` prompt, enter the following and press the Enter key:

```
SHOW DATABASES;
```

The following output (or something similar) should be displayed in response:

```
+--------------------+
| Database           |
+--------------------+
| information_schema |
| mysql              |
| test               |
+--------------------+
```

First, let me mention a book convention. MySQL is not case sensitive when you enter keywords such as `SHOW`. You could just as well enter `show` or even `sHoW`. However, the names of databases, tables, and columns may be case sensitive, especially on an operating system that is case sensitive, such as Mac OS X or Linux. Most books and documentation use all upper case letters to indicate keywords while respecting the case of the things that you can change. We use all lower case letters for database, table, and column names because it's easier on the eyes and easier to type, and mostly because it's easier for the reader to distinguish between what is set by the SQL convention and what is flexible.

The list just displayed shows that you have three databases at the start of using MySQL, created automatically during installation. The information_schema database contains information about the server. The next database in the list is mysql, which stores usernames, passwords, and user privileges. When you created a user for yourself at the end of Chapter 2, this is where that information was stored. You may have noticed that some commands shown in Chapter 2 referenced this database. Don't try to change the mysql database directly. Later, I'll show you commands for manipulating this database. At least for now, access the mysql database only through administrative functions and utilities. The last database listed is called test. That's there for you to test things and to use when learning. Let's use that for a bit in this chapter.

First SQL Commands

The test database is initially empty; it contains no tables. So let's create one. Don't worry about understanding what you're doing in detail. I'll introduce concepts gradually as we go along.

So enter the following in the mysql client (remember the terminating semicolon):

```
CREATE TABLE test.books (book_id INT, title TEXT, status INT);
```

This is your first SQL statement. It creates a table in the test database and names it books. We specified the name of the database and table with test.books (i.e., the format is *database.table*). We also defined, within the parentheses, three columns for the table. We'll talk about that in more depth later.

If you correctly type that SQL statement, you'll receive a reply like this:

```
Query OK, 0 rows affected (0.19 sec)
```

This is a message from the server reporting how things went with the SQL statement you sent. What you need to take from the message is that everything is OK. With that, let's see the results of what we did. To see a list of tables within the test database, enter:

```
SHOW TABLES FROM test;
```

The output should be:

```
+----------------+
| Tables_in_test |
+----------------+
| books          |
+----------------+
1 row in set (0.01 sec)
```

You now have one table, books. Notice that the results are enclosed with ASCII text to look like a table of data, as you might draw it on a piece of paper. Notice also the message after the table. It says that one row is in the set, meaning that books is the only table in the database. The time in parentheses that you will see after running every SQL statement indicates how long it took for the server to process the request. In this case, it took my server 0.01 seconds. I ran that statement from my home computer in Milan, Italy, but using my server in Tampa, Florida in the U.S. That's a pretty quick response. Sometimes it's even faster and shows 0.00 seconds, because the lapse in time was not enough to register.

From this point forward, I will leave out these lines of status to save space and to keep the clutter down, unless there's something relevant to discuss. For the same reason, I'm not including the mysql> prompts. You'll have to learn when something is entered from the mysql client versus the operating system shell—although I will usually indicate when to enter something from the operating system shell. So from now on, I'll combine input and output like this:

```
SHOW TABLES FROM test;

+-----------------+
| Tables_in_test  |
+-----------------+
| books           |
+-----------------+
```

You can tell what you're supposed to enter because it's bold, whereas the output is not.

For each of these SQL statements, we have to specify the database name. If you will be working mainly in one database (you usually will be), you can set the default database so that you don't have to specify the database each time. To do this, enter a USE command:

```
USE test
```

 Incidentally, if your server doesn't have the test database, you can create it by just entering CREATE DATABASE test; on the server first.

Because this is an instruction for the mysql client and not the server, the usual ending semicolon is not needed. The client will change the default database on the server for the client to the one given, making it unnecessary to specify table names without a preceding database name—unless you want to execute an SQL statement for a table in another database. After entering the USE command, you can re-enter the earlier SQL statement to list the tables in the database without specifying that you want test. It's taken for granted:

```
SHOW TABLES;

+----------------+
| Tables_in_test |
+----------------+
| books          |
+----------------+
```

Now that we've peeked at a database, which is not much more than a grouping of tables (in this example, only one table), and created a table, let's look inside the table that we created. To do that, we'll use the SQL statement DESCRIBE, like so:

```
DESCRIBE books;

+---------+---------+------+-----+---------+-------+
| Field   | Type    | Null | Key | Default | Extra |
+---------+---------+------+-----+---------+-------+
| book_id | int(11) | YES  |     | NULL    |       |
| title   | text    | YES  |     | NULL    |       |
| status  | int(11) | YES  |     | NULL    |       |
+---------+---------+------+-----+---------+-------+
```

In these results you can see that we created three fields for entering data, named book_id, title, and status. That's pretty limited, but we're keeping things simple in this chapter. The first and third fields, book_id and status, are integer types, meaning they can contain only numbers. We stipulated that when we created the table by adding the INT keyword when specifying those columns. The other field, title, can contain text, which includes anything you can type at the keyboard. We set that earlier with the TEXT keyword. Don't worry about remembering any of this now. We're just looking around to get a feel for the system and the mysql client.

Inserting and Manipulating Data

Let's put some data in this table. Enter the following three SQL statements within the mysql client:

```
INSERT INTO books VALUES(100, 'Heart of Darkness', 0);
INSERT INTO books VALUES(101, 'The Catcher of the Rye', 1);
INSERT INTO books VALUES(102, 'My Antonia', 0);
```

All three lines use the SQL statement INSERT to insert, or add data, to the books table. Each line will be followed by a status message (or an error message if you mistype something), but I didn't bother to include those messages here. Notice that numbers don't need to be within quotes, but text does. The syntax of SQL statements like this one is pretty structured—hence the name *Structured Query Language*. You can be casual about spacing between elements of the statements, but you must enter everything in the right order and use the parentheses, commas, and semicolons as shown. Keeping SQL statements structured makes queries predictable and the database faster.

The previous examples insert the values given in parentheses into the table. The values are given in the same order and format as we told MySQL to expect when we created the table: three fields, of which the first and third will be numbers, and the second will be any kind of text. Let's ask MySQL to display the data we just gave it to see how it looks:

```
SELECT * FROM books;
```

```
+---------+-------------------------+--------+
| book_id | title                   | status |
+---------+-------------------------+--------+
|     100 | Heart of Darkness       | 0      |
|     101 | The Catcher of the Rye  | 1      |
|     102 | My Antonia              | 0      |
+---------+-------------------------+--------+
```

In this table, you can see more easily why they call records *rows* and fields *columns*. We used the SELECT statement to select all columns—the asterisk (*) means "everything"—from the table named. In this example, book_id functions as a record identification number, while title and status contain the text and numbers we want to store. I purposely gave status values of *0* or *1* to indicate status: *0* means inactive and *1* means active. These are arbitrary designations and mean nothing to MySQL or MariaDB. Incidentally, the title of the second book is not correct, but we'll use it later as an example of how to change data.

Let's play with these values and the SELECT statement to see how it works. Let's add a WHERE clause to the SQL statement:

```
SELECT * FROM books WHERE status = 1;
```

```
+---------+-------------------------+--------+
| book_id | title                   | status |
+---------+-------------------------+--------+
|   101   | The Catcher of the Rye  |     1  |
+---------+-------------------------+--------+
```

In these results, we've selected only rows in which status equals *1* (i.e., only records that are active). We did this using the WHERE clause. It's part of the SELECT statement and not an SQL statement on its own. Let's try another SQL statement like this one, but ask for the *inactive* records:

```
SELECT * FROM books WHERE status = 0 \G
```

```
*************************** 1. row ***************************
book_id: 100
  title: Heart of Darkness
 status: 0
*************************** 2. row ***************************
book_id: 102
```

```
    title: My Antonia
   status: 0
```

Notice that this time we changed the ending of the SQL statement from a semicolon to \G. This was mentioned earlier in this chapter as an option. It shows the results not in a table format, but as a batch of lines for each record. Sometimes this is easier to read, usually when the fields are so long that a tabular format would be too wide for your screen and would wrap around. It's a matter of preference for each situation.

We've added data to this minimal table. Now let's change the data a little. Let's change the status of one of the rows. To do this, we will use the UPDATE statement. It produces two lines of status output:

```
UPDATE books SET status = 1 WHERE book_id = 102;

Query OK, 1 row affected (0.18 sec)
Rows matched: 1  Changed: 1  Warnings: 0
```

You can learn how to read and remember SQL statement syntax better if you read and interpret them in the way and order they're written. Let's do that with this SQL statement, the first line in the preceding code block. It says to *update* books by *setting* the value of status to *1* for all rows *where* book_id equals *102*. In this case, there is only one record with that value, so the message that follows says that one row was affected, and only one was changed or updated—however you want to say that. To see the results, run the SELECT statement shown earlier, the one where we check for active status:

```
SELECT * FROM books WHERE status = 1;
```

```
+---------+------------------------+--------+
| book_id | title                  | status |
+---------+------------------------+--------+
|     101 | The Catcher of the Rye | 1      |
|     102 | My Antonia             | 1      |
+---------+------------------------+--------+
```

Thanks to our update, we get two rows back this time, where the rows have a status of active. If we execute the UPDATE statement again, but for a different book_id, we can change the book, *The Catcher in the Rye* to inactive:

```
UPDATE books SET status = 0 WHERE book_id = 101;

SELECT * FROM books WHERE status = 0;
```

```
+---------+------------------------+--------+
| book_id | title                  | status |
+---------+------------------------+--------+
|     100 | Heart of Darkness      | 0      |
|     101 | The Catcher of the Rye | 0      |
+---------+------------------------+--------+
```

Let's enter one more UPDATE statement so you can see how to do more with just one statement. As I mentioned earlier, the title of this book is not correct. It's not The Catcher of the Rye. The correct title is The Catcher in the Rye. Let's change that text in the title column, while simultaneously setting the value of status back to *1*. We could do this with two SQL statements, but let's do it in one like so:

```
UPDATE books
SET title = 'The Catcher in the Rye', status = 1
WHERE book_id = 101;
```

Notice that we've given the same syntax as before with the UPDATE statement, but we've given two pairs of columns and values to set. That's easier than entering the UPDATE statement twice. It also saves some network traffic when communicating with a server on another continent.

A Little Complexity

Let's increase the pace a little. Let's create another table and insert a couple of rows of data in it. Enter these two SQL statements from within the mysql client:

```
CREATE TABLE status_names (status_id INT, status_name CHAR(8));

INSERT INTO status_names VALUES(0, 'Inactive'), (1,'Active');
```

Now we've created the table status_names, but with only two columns. The CREATE TABLE statement is similar to the one we used to create the first table. There's one difference I'd like you to notice: instead of using the column type of TEXT, we're using the column type of CHAR, which stands for "character." We can add text to this column, but its size is limited: each row can have only a maximum of eight characters in this column. That makes a smaller field and therefore a smaller and faster table. It doesn't matter in our examples here, as we're not entering much data, but little specifications like this will make a huge performance difference in large databases. It's good for you to start thinking this way from the beginning.

The second SQL statement added two sets of values. Doing multiple sets of values in one INSERT is allowed, and is easier than entering a separate line for each. Here's how the data looks in that table:

```
SELECT * FROM status_names;

+-----------+-------------+
| status_id | status_name |
+-----------+-------------+
|         0 | Inactive    |
|         1 | Active      |
+-----------+-------------+
```

That's probably a seemingly useless table of data. But let's combine this table with the first table, books, to see a glimpse of the potential of database system like MariaDB. We'll use the SELECT statement to join both tables together to get nicer results, and we'll be selective about which data is displayed. Try this on your computer:

```
SELECT book_id, title, status_name
FROM books JOIN status_names
WHERE status = status_id;
```

```
+---------+------------------------+-------------+
| book_id | title                  | status_name |
+---------+------------------------+-------------+
|     100 | Heart of Darkness      | Inactive    |
|     101 | The Catcher in the Rye | Active      |
|     102 | My Antonia             | Active      |
+---------+------------------------+-------------+
```

First, notice that I broke this SQL statement over three lines. That's allowed. Nothing is processed until you type a semicolon and then press the Enter key. Breaking apart a statement like this makes it easier to read, but has no effect on MySQL. In this SQL statement, the first line selects book_id and title, which are both in books, and status_name, which is in the status_names table. Notice that we didn't use an asterisk to select all of the columns, but named the specific ones we want. We also chose columns from two tables.

On the second line, we say to select these columns listed from books and from status_names. The JOIN clause is where we named the second table.

In the WHERE clause, on the third line, we tell MySQL to match the values of the status column from books to the values of the status_id column from the status_names table. This is the point in which the rows from each will be joined. If the idea of joining tables seems difficult, don't worry about it at this point. I've included it just to show you what can be done with MySQL and MariaDB. I'll explain joins more fully later.

When we created books, we could have made status a text or character field and entered the words *Active* or *Inactive* for each row. But if you have a table with thousands or maybe millions of rows of data, entering 0 or 1 is much easier and you're less likely to make typos (e.g., you might enter *Actve* sometimes). Databases are tedious, but creating tables with better structures and using better written SQL statements makes them less tedious and helps you to leverage your time and resources.

Summary

There's plenty more you can do to explore the simple tables we've created, but in this chapter I wanted just to give you an overview of MySQL and MariaDB, and to show you around. The chapters in Part II will delve into details, starting with Chapter 4, which will cover creating tables in detail.

Before jumping ahead, you might want to reinforce what you just learned from this chapter. A few exercises follow for you to play some more on your own with the test database and the mysql client. When you're finished, to exit mysql, type quit or exit, and press the Enter key.

Exercises

In addition to logging into MySQL or MariaDB with the mysql client and entering the SQL statements shown already in this chapter, here are a few exercises to get some more practice playing with the mysql client and to help you better understand the basics. Rather than use generic names like books and book_id, you're asked to use more realistic names. In that same spirit, use fairly realistic data (e.g., "John Smith" for a person's name) when entering data in these exercises.

1. Log into MySQL or MariaDB using the mysql client and switch the default database to the database, test. Create two tables called contacts and relation_types. For both tables, use column type INT for number columns and CHAR for character columns. Specify the maximum number of characters you want with CHAR—otherwise MySQL wills set a maximum of one character, which is not very useful. Make sure that you allow for enough characters to fit the data you will enter later. If you want to allow characters between numbers (e.g., hyphens for a telephone number), use CHAR. For the contacts, you will need six columns: name, phone_work, phone_mobile, email, relation_id. For the relation_types table, there should be only two columns: relation_id and relationship.

   When you're finished creating both tables, use the DESCRIBE statement to see how they look.

2. Enter data in the two tables created in the previous exercise. Enter data in the second table, relation_types first. Enter three rows of data in it. Use single-digit, sequential numbers for the first column, but the following text for the second column: Family, Friend, Colleague. Now enter data in the table named contacts. Enter at least five fictitious names, telephone numbers, and email addresses. For the last column, relation_id, enter single digits to correspond with the relation_id numbers in the table, relation_types. Make sure you have at least one row for each of the three potential values for relation_id.

3. Execute two SELECT statements to retrieve all of the columns of data from both tables that you created and filled with data from the previous two exercises. Then run a SELECT statement that retrieves only the person's name and email address from the table named contacts.

4. Change some of the data entered in the previous exercises, using the UPDATE statement. If you don't remember how to do that, refer back to the examples in this chapter on how to change data in a table. First, change someone's name or telephone

number. Next, change someone's email address and his or her relationship to you (i.e., relation_id). Do this in one UPDATE statement.

5. Run a SELECT statement that joins both tables created in the first exercise. Use the JOIN clause to do this (the JOIN clause was covered in this chapter, so look back at the example if you don't remember how to use it). Join the tables on the common column named relation_id—this will go in the WHERE clause. To help you with this, here's how the clauses for the tables should look:

```
...
FROM contacts JOIN relation_types
WHERE contacts.relation_id = relation_types.relation_id
...
```

Select the columns name and phone_mobile, but only for contacts who are marked as a Friend—you'll have to add this to the WHERE with AND. Try doing this based on the value of relation_id and then again based on the value of the relationship column.

## PART II

Database Structures

The primary organizational structure in MySQL and MariaDB is the database. Separate databases are usually created for each separate business or organization, or for individual departments or projects. The basis by which you might want to create separate databases is mostly based on your personal preference. It does allow a convenient method of providing different permissions and privileges to different users or groups of users. However, for a beginner, one database for one organization is enough on which to learn.

As explained in "Starting to Explore Databases" on page 33, databases contain *tables* that contain one *row* or *record* for each item of data, and information about that item in *columns* or *fields*. Compared to databases, there are well-established, practical considerations for determining what separate tables to create. Although some beginners may create one large table within a database, a table with many columns, it is almost always an inefficient method of handling data. There is almost never a situation in which it makes sense to have only one table. So expect to create many small tables and not a few wide tables (a wide table is one with many columns).

When creating a table, you specify the fields or columns to be created, called the table's *schema*. When specifying the columns of a table being created, you may specify various properties of each column. At a minimum, you must specify the type of column to create: whether it contains characters or just integers; whether it is to contain date and time information; or possibly binary data. When first creating a column, you may also specify how the data to be contained in the column is indexed, if it is to be collated based on particular alphabets (e.g., Latin letters or Chinese characters), and other factors.

The first chapter of this part, Chapter 4, covers how to create a database—a very simple task—and how to create a table. I also touch on how to put data into a table and retrieve it, topics to be greatly expanded in later chapters. Presenting only how to create a table without showing you how to use it would be a very dry approach. It's better to show you quickly the point of why you would create a table before moving on to other details related to tables.

When you first create tables, especially as a beginner, it's difficult to know exactly what to put in each table's schema. Invariably, you will want to change a table's structure after the table is created. Thus, in Chapter 5 we'll look at how to alter tables after they have been created. I could have placed the chapter on altering tables after the chapters on manipulating data, but you would inevitably need to jump ahead to it at some point when you realize that you created a table incorrectly while experimenting with MySQL.

## CHAPTER 4

Creating Databases and Tables

In order to be able to add and manipulate data, you first have to create a database. There's not much to this. You're creating just a container in which you will add tables. Creating a table is more involved and offers many choices. There are several types of tables from which to choose, some with unique features. When creating tables, you must also decide on the structure of each table: the number of columns, the type of data each column may hold, how the tables will be indexed, and several other factors. However, while you're still learning, you can accept the default setting for most of the options when creating tables.

There are a few basic things to decide when creating a structure for your data:

- The number of tables to include in your database, as well as the table names
- For each table, the number of columns it should contain, as well as the column names
- For each column, what kind of data is to be stored

For the last part, in the beginning, we'll use just four types of columns: columns that contain only numbers; columns that contain alphanumeric characters, but not too many (i.e., a maximum of 255 characters); columns that contain plenty of text and maybe binary files; and columns for recording date and time information. This is a good starting point for creating a database and tables. As we get further along, we can expand that list of column data types to improve the performance of your databases.

This chapter contains examples of how to create a database and tables. The text is written on the assumption that you will enter the SQL statements shown on your server, using the mysql client. The exercises at the end of this chapter will require that you make some changes and additions to the database and its tables on your computer. So, when instructed, be sure to try all of the examples on your computer.

The database and the tables that we create in this chapter will be used in several chapters in this book, especially in Part III, Basics of Handling Data. In those later chapters, you will be asked to add, retrieve, and change data from the tables you create in this chapter. Exercises in subsequent chapters assume that you have created the tables you are asked to create in this chapter. Thus, in order to get the most value possible from this book, it's important that you complete the exercises included for each chapter. It will help reinforce what you read, and you will learn more.

Creating a Database

Creating a database is simple, mostly because there's nothing much to it. Use the SQL statement CREATE DATABASE. You will have to provide a name for the database with this SQL statement. You could call it something bland like db1. However, let's do something more realistic and interesting. I'm a fan of birds, so I've used a database of a fictitious bird-watching website for the examples in this book. Some birds live in groups, or a colony called a *rookery*. To start, let's create a database that will contain information about birds and call it rookery. To do this, enter the following from within the mysql client:

```
CREATE DATABASE rookery;
```

As previously mentioned, this very minimal, first SQL statement will create a subdirectory called rookery on the filesystem in the data directory for MySQL. It won't create any data. It will just set up a place to add tables, which will in turn hold data. Incidentally, if you don't like the keyword DATABASE, you can use SCHEMA instead: CREATE SCHEMA *database_name*. The results are the same.

You can, though, do a bit more than the SQL statement shown here for creating a database. You can add a couple of options in which you can set the default types of characters that will be used in the database and how data will be sorted or collated. So, let's drop the rookery database and create it again like so:

```
DROP DATABASE rookery;

CREATE DATABASE rookery
CHARACTER SET latin1
COLLATE latin1_bin;
```

The first line in this SQL statement is the same as the earlier one—remember, all of this is one SQL statement spread over two lines, ending with the semicolon. The second line, which is new, tells MySQL that the default characters that will be used in tables in the database are Latin letters and other characters. The third line tells MySQL that the default method of sorting data in tables is based on binary Latin characters. We'll discuss binary characters and binary sorting in a later chapter, but it's not necessary to understand that at this point. In fact, for most purposes, the minimal method of creating a database without options, as shown earlier, is fine. You can always change these two options later if necessary. I'm only mentioning the options here so that you know they exist if you need to set them one day.

Now that we've created a database, let's confirm that it's there, on the MySQL server. To get a list of databases, enter the following SQL statement:

```
SHOW DATABASES;
```

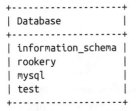

```
+--------------------+
| Database           |
+--------------------+
| information_schema |
| rookery            |
| mysql              |
| test               |
+--------------------+
```

The results here show the rookery database, and three other databases that were created when MySQL was installed on the server. We saw the other three in "Starting to Explore Databases" on page 33, and we'll cover them in later chapters of this book as needed.

Before beginning to add tables to the rookery database, enter the following command into the mysql client:

```
USE rookery
```

This little command will set the new database that was just created as the default database for the mysql client. It will remain the default database until you change it to a different one or until you exit the client. This makes it easier when entering SQL statements to create tables or other SQL statements related to tables. Otherwise, when you enter each table-related SQL statement, you would have to specify each time the database where the table is located.

Creating Tables

The next step for structuring a database is to create tables. Although this can be complicated, we'll keep it simple to start. We'll initially create one main table and two smaller tables for reference information. The main table will have a bunch of columns, but the reference tables will have only a few columns.

For our fictitious bird-watchers site, the key interest is birds. So we want to create a table that will hold basic data on birds. For learning purposes, we won't make this an elaborate table. Enter the following SQL statement into mysql on your computer:

```
CREATE TABLE birds (
bird_id INT AUTO_INCREMENT PRIMARY KEY,
scientific_name VARCHAR(255) UNIQUE,
common_name VARCHAR(50),
```

```
family_id INT,
description TEXT);
```

This SQL statement creates the table `birds` with five fields, or columns, with commas separating the information about each column. Note that all the columns together are contained in a pair of parentheses. For each colum, we specify the name, the type, and optional settings. For instance, the information we give about the first column is:

- The name, `bird_id`
- The type, `INT` (meaning it has to contain integers)
- The settings, `AUTO_INCREMENT` and `PRIMARY KEY`

The names of the columns can be anything other than words that are reserved for SQL statements, clauses, and functions. Actually, you can use a reserve word, but it must always be given within quotes to distinguish it. You can find a list of data types from which to choose on the websites of MySQL and MariaDB, or in my book, *MySQL in a Nutshell*.

We created this table with only five columns. You can have plenty of columns (up to 255), but you shouldn't have too many. If a table has too many columns, it can be cumbersome to use and the table will be sluggish when it's accessed. It's better to break data into multiple tables.

The first column in the `birds` table is a simple identification number, `bird_id`. It will be the primary key column on which data will be indexed—hence the keywords, `PRIMARY KEY`. We'll discuss the importance of the primary key later.

The `AUTO_INCREMENT` option tells MySQL to automatically increment the value of this field. It will start with the number 1, unless we specify a different number.

The next column will contain the scientific name of each bird (e.g., *Charadrius vociferus*, instead of *Killdeer*). You might think that the `scientific_name` column would be the ideal identifier to use as the primary key on which to index the `birds` table, and that we wouldn't need the `bird_id` column. But the scientific name can be very long and usually in Latin or Greek (or sometimes a mix of both languages), and not everyone is comfortable using words from these languages. In addition, would be awkward to enter the scientific name of a bird when referencing a row in the table. We've set the `scientific_name` column to have a variable-width character data type (`VARCHAR`). The 255 that we specify in the parentheses after it sets the maximum size (255 should be sufficient for the long names we'll need to accommodate).

If the scientific name of a bird has fewer than 255 characters, the storage engine will reduce the size of the column for the row. This is different from the `CHAR` column data type. If the data in a `CHAR` column is less than its maximum, space is still allocated for the full width that you set. There are trade-offs with these two basic character data types.

If the storage engine knows exactly what to expect from a column, tables run faster and can be indexed more easily with a CHAR column. However, a VARCHAR column can use less space on the server's hard drive and is less prone to fragmentation. That can improve performance. When you know for sure that a column will have a set number of characters, use CHAR. When the width may vary, use VARCHAR.

Next, we set the column data type for the common_name of each bird to a variable-width character column of only 50 characters at most.

The fourth column (family_id) will be used as identification numbers for the family of birds to which each bird belongs. They are integer data types (i.e., INT). We'll create another table for more information on the families. Then, when manipulating data, we can join the two tables, use a number to identify each family, and link each bird to its family.

The last column is for the description of each bird. It's a TEXT data type, which means that it's a variable-width column, and it can hold up 65,535 bytes of data for each row. This will allow us to enter plenty of text about each bird. We could write multiple pages describing a bird and put it in this column.

There are additional factors to consider when searching for a bird in a database, so there are many columns we could add to this table: information about migratory patterns, notable features for spotting them in the wild, and so on. In addition, there are many other data types that may be used for columns. We can have columns that allow for larger and smaller numbers, or for binary files to be included in each row. For instance, you might want a column with a binary data type to store a photograph of each bird. However, this basic table gives you a good sampling of the possibilities when creating tables.

To see how the table looks, use the DESCRIBE statement. It displays information about the columns of a table, or the table schema—not the data itself. To use this SQL statement to get information on the table we just created, you would enter the following SQL statement:

```
DESCRIBE birds;
```

```
+-----------------+--------------+------+-----+---------+----------------+
| Field           | Type         | Null | Key | Default | Extra          |
+-----------------+--------------+------+-----+---------+----------------+
| bird_id         | int(11)      | NO   | PRI | NULL    | auto_increment |
| scientific_name | varchar(255) | YES  | UNI | NULL    |                |
| common_name     | varchar(50)  | YES  |     | NULL    |                |
| family_id       | int(11)      | YES  |     | NULL    |                |
| description     | text         | YES  |     | NULL    |                |
+-----------------+--------------+------+-----+---------+----------------+
```

Notice that these results are displayed in a table format made with ASCII characters. It's not very slick looking, but it's clean, quick, and provides the information requested. Let's study this layout, not the content, per se.

The first row of this results set contains column headings describing the rows of information that follow it. In the first column of this results set, *Field* contains the fields or columns of the table created.

The second column, *Type*, lists the data type for each field. Notice that for the table's columns in which we specified the data type VARCHAR with the specific widths within parentheses, those settings are shown here (e.g., varchar(255)). Where we didn't specify the size for the INT columns, the defaults were assumed and are shown here. We'll cover later what INT(11) means and discuss the other possibilities for integer data types.

The third column in the preceding results, *Null*, indicates whether each field may contain NULL values. NULL is nothing; it's nonexistent data. This is different from blank or empty content in a field. That may seem strange: just accept that there's a difference at this point. You'll see that in action later in this book.

The fourth column, *Key*, indicates whether a field is a key field—an indexed column. It's not an indexed column if the result is blank, as it is with common_name. If a column is indexed, the display will say which kind of index. Because of the limited space permitted in the display, it truncates the words. In the example shown, the bird_id column is a primary key, shortened to PRI in this display. We set scientific_name to another type of key or index, one called UNIQUE, which is abbreviated UNI here.

The next-to-last column in the display, *Default*, would contain any default value set for each field. We didn't set any when creating the birds table, but we could have done so. We can do that later.

The last column, *Extra*, provides any extra information the table maintains on each column. In the example shown, we can see that the values for bird_id will be incremented automatically. There's usually nothing else listed in this column.

If we don't like something within the structure of the table we created, we can use the ALTER TABLE statement to change it (this SQL statement is covered in Chapter 5). If you made some mistakes and just want to start over, you can delete the table and try again to create it. To delete a table completely (including its data), you can use the DROP TABLE statement, followed by the table name. Be careful with this SQL statement, as it's not reversible and it deletes any data in the table.

Incidentally, when using the mysql client, you can press the up arrow on your keyboard to get to the previous lines you entered. So if you create a table, then run the DESCRIBE statement and catch a mistake, you can just drop the table, and use the up arrow to go back to your previous entry in which you created the table. Use the left arrow to move the cursor over to the text you want to change and fix it. When you've finished modifying the CREATE TABLE statement, press Enter. The modified CREATE TABLE statement will then be sent to the server.

Inserting Data

Those were a lot of details to absorb in the last section. Let's take a break from creating tables and enter data in the birds table. We'll use an INSERT statement, which was covered briefly in Chapter 3, and will be covered in more detail in the next section. For now, don't worry too much about understanding all of the possibilities with the IN SERT statement. Just enter the following on your server using the mysql client:

```
INSERT INTO birds (scientific_name, common_name)
VALUES ('Charadrius vociferus', 'Killdeer'),
('Gavia immer', 'Great Northern Loon'),
('Aix sponsa', 'Wood Duck'),
('Chordeiles minor', 'Common Nighthawk'),
('Sitta carolinensis', ' White-breasted Nuthatch'),
('Apteryx mantelli', 'North Island Brown Kiwi');
```

This will create six rows of data for six birds. Enter the following from the mysql client to see the contents of the table:

```
SELECT * FROM birds;
```

```
+---------+----------------------+---------------------+-----------+-------------+
| bird_id | scientific_name      | common_name         | family_id | description |
+---------+----------------------+---------------------+-----------+-------------+
|       1 | Charadrius vociferus | Killdeer            |      NULL | NULL        |
|       2 | Gavia immer          | Great Northern...   |      NULL | NULL        |
|       3 | Aix sponsa           | Wood Duck           |      NULL | NULL        |
|       4 | Chordeiles minor     | Common Nighthawk    |      NULL | NULL        |
|       5 | Sitta carolinensis   | White-breasted...   |      NULL | NULL        |
|       6 | Apteryx mantelli     | North Island...     |      NULL | NULL        |
+---------+----------------------+---------------------+-----------+-------------+
```

As you can see from the results, MySQL put values in the two columns we gave it, and set the other columns to their default values (i.e., NULL). We can change those values later.

Let's create another table for a different database. We have information on birds in the rookery database. Let's create another database that contains information about people who are interested in bird-watching. We'll call it `birdwatchers` and we'll create one table for it that we'll call `humans`, to correlate with the name of `birds` table:

```
CREATE DATABASE birdwatchers;

CREATE TABLE birdwatchers.humans
(human_id INT AUTO_INCREMENT PRIMARY KEY,
formal_title VARCHAR(25),
name_first VARCHAR(25),
name_last VARCHAR(25),
email_address VARCHAR(255));
```

This isn't much of a table; we're not collecting much information on members, but it will do well for now. Let's enter some data into this table. The following adds four people to our table of members of the site:

```
INSERT INTO birdwatchers.humans
(name_first, name_last, email_address)
VALUES
('Mr.', 'Russell', 'Dyer', 'russell@mysqlresources.com'),
('Mr.', 'Richard', 'Stringer', 'richard@mysqlresources.com'),
('Ms.', 'Rusty', 'Osborne', 'rusty@mysqlresources.com'),
('Ms.', 'Lexi', 'Hollar', 'alexandra@mysqlresources.com');
```

This enters information for four humans. Notice that we left the first column NULL so that MySQL can assign an identification number automatically and incrementally.

We've created some simple tables. We could do more, but this is enough for now to better understand tables and their structure.

More Perspectives on Tables

Besides the DESCRIBE statement, there's another way to look at how a table is structured. You can use the SHOW CREATE TABLE statement. This basically shows how you might enter the CREATE TABLE to create an existing table, perhaps in a different database. What's particularly interesting and useful about the SHOW CREATE TABLE statement is that it shows the default settings assumed by the server, ones that you might not have specified when you ran the CREATE TABLE statement. Here's how you would enter this statement, with the results shown after it:

```
SHOW CREATE TABLE birds \G

*************************** 1. row ***************************
       Table: birds
Create Table: CREATE TABLE `birds` (
  `bird_id` int(11) NOT NULL AUTO_INCREMENT,
  `scientific_name` varchar(255) COLLATE latin1_bin DEFAULT NULL,
  `common_name` varchar(50) COLLATE latin1_bin DEFAULT NULL,
  `family_id` int(11) DEFAULT NULL,
```

```
  `description` text COLLATE latin1_bin,
  PRIMARY KEY (`bird_id`),
  UNIQUE KEY `scientific_name` (`scientific_name`)
) ENGINE=MyISAM DEFAULT CHARSET=latin1 COLLATE=latin1_bin
```

As mentioned earlier, there are more options that you can set for each column; if you don't specify them, the server will use the default choices. Here you can see those default settings. Notice that we did not set a default value for any of the fields (except the first one when we said to use an automatically incremented number), so it set each column to a default of NULL. For the third column, the common_name column, the server set the set of characters (i.e., the alphabet, numbers, and other characters) by which it will collate the data in that column to *latin1_bin* (i.e., Latin binary characters). The server did the same for three other columns. That's because of how we set the database at the beginning of this chapter, in the second CREATE DATABASE statement. This is where that comes into play. We could set a column to a different one from the one we set for the database default, but it's usually not necessary.

You may have noticed in looking at the results that the options for the bird_id column don't indicate that it's a primary key, although we specified that in CREATE TABLE. Instead, the list of columns is followed by a list of keys or indexes used in the table. Here it lists the primary key and specifies that that index is based on bird_id. It then shows a unique key. For that kind of key, it gives a name of the index, scientific_name, which is the same as the column it indexes, and it then shows in parentheses a lists of columns from which the index is drawn. That could be more than one column, but it's just one here. We'll cover indexes in Chapter 5 (see "Indexes" on page 80).

There's one more aspect you should note in the results of SHOW CREATE TABLE. Notice that the last line shows a few other settings after the closing parentheses for the set of columns. First is the type of table used, or rather the type of storage engine used for this table. In this case, it's *MyISAM*, which is the default for many servers. The default for your server may be different. Data is stored and handled in different ways by different storage engines. There are advantages and disadvantages to each.

The other two settings are the default character set (latin1) and the default collation (latin1_bin) in the table. These come from the default values when the database was created, or rather they came indirectly from there. You can set a different character and collation, and you can even set a different character set and collation for an individual column.

Let me give you an example where setting explicit values for the character set and collation might be useful. Suppose you have a typical database for a bird-watcher group located in England with most of its common names written in English. Suppose further that the site attracts bird-watchers from other countries in Europe, so you might want to include common bird names in other languages. Let's say that you want to set up a table for the Turkish bird-watchers. For that table, you would use a different character set and collation, because the Turkish alphabet contains both Latin and other letters.

For the character set, you would use latin5, which has both Latin and other letters. For collation, you would use latin5_turkish_ci, which orders text based on the order of the letters in the Turkish alphabet. To make sure you don't forget to use this character set and collation when adding columns to this table later, you could set the CHARSET and COLLATE for the table to these values.

Before moving on, let me make one more point about the SHOW CREATE TABLE statement: if you want to create a table with plenty of special settings different from the default, you can use the results of the SHOW CREATE TABLE statement as a starting point for constructing a more elaborate CREATE TABLE statement. Mostly you would use it to see the assumptions that the server made when it created a table, based on the default settings during installation.

The next table we'll create for the examples in this book is bird_families. This will hold information about bird families, which are groupings of birds. This will tie into the family_id column in the birds table. The new table will save us from having to enter the name and other information related to each family of birds for each bird in the birds table:

```
CREATE TABLE bird_families (
family_id INT AUTO_INCREMENT PRIMARY KEY,
scientific_name VARCHAR(255) UNIQUE,
brief_description VARCHAR(255) );
```

We're creating three columns in the table. The first is the most interesting for our purposes here. It's the column that will be indexed and will be referenced by the birds table. That sounds like there is a physical connection or something similar within the birds table, but that's not what will happen. Instead, the connection will be made only when we execute an SQL statement, a query referencing both tables. With such SQL statements, we'll join the bird_families table to the birds table based on the family_id columns in both. For instance, we would do this when we want a list of birds along with their corresponding family names, or maybe when we want to get a list of birds for a particular family.

Now we can put all the information we want about a family of birds in one row. When we enter data in the birds table, we'll include the family_id identification number that will reference a row of the bird_families table. This also helps to ensure consistency of data: there's less chance of spelling deviations when you only enter a number and not a Latin name. It also saves space because you can store information in one row of bird_families and refer to it from hundreds of rows in birds. We'll see soon how this works.

The scientific_name column will hold the scientific name of the family of birds (e.g., *Charadriidae*). The third column is basically for the common names of families (e.g., *Plovers*). But people often associate several common names to a family of birds, as well as vague names for the types of birds contained in the family. So we'll just call the column `brief_description`.

Let's next create a table for information about the orders of the birds. This is a grouping of families of birds. We'll name it `bird_orders`. For this table, let's try out some of the extra options mentioned earlier. Enter the following SQL statement:

```
CREATE TABLE bird_orders (
   order_id INT AUTO_INCREMENT PRIMARY KEY,
   scientific_name VARCHAR(255) UNIQUE,
   brief_description VARCHAR(255),
   order_image BLOB
) DEFAULT CHARSET=utf8 COLLATE=utf8_general_ci;
```

This SQL statement creates a table named `bird_orders` with four columns to start. The first one, `order_id`, is the key in which rows will be referenced from the `bird_fami lies` table. This is followed by `scientific_name` for the scientific name of the order of birds, with a data type of `VARCHAR`. We're allowing the maximum number of characters for it. It's more than we'll need, but there won't be many entries in this table and it's difficult to guess what what the longest description will be. So we'll set it to the maximum allowed for that data type. We're naming this column `brief_description`, as we did in the earlier `bird_families` table.

Because all three tables that we've created so far have similar names for some of the columns (e.g., `scientific_name`), that may cause us a little trouble later if we try to join all of these tables together. It might seem simpler to use distinct names for these columns in each of these tables (e.g., `order_scientific_name`). However, we can resolve that ambiguity easily when necessary.

In the previous SQL statement, notice that we have a column for an image to represent the order of birds. We might put a photo of the most popular bird of the order or a drawing of several birds from the order. Notice that for this image file, the data type we're using is a `BLOB`. While the name is cute and evocative, it also stands for *binary large object*. We can store an image file, such as a JPEG file, in the column. That's not always a good idea. It can make the table large, which can be a problem when backing up the database. It might be better to store the image files on the server and then store a file path or URL address in the database, pointing to where the image file is located. I've included a BLOB here, though, to show it as a possibility.

After the list of columns, we've included the default character set and collation to be used when creating the columns. We're using UTF-8 (i.e., UCS Transformation Format, 8-bit), because some of the names may include characters that are not part of the default `latin1` character set. For instance, if our fictitious bird-watcher site included German words, the column `brief_description` would be able to accept the letters with umlauts over them (i.e., *ä*). The character set `utf8` allows for such letters.

For a real bird-watching database, both the `bird_families` and `bird_orders` tables would have more columns. There would also be several more tables than the few we're creating. But for our purposes, these few tables as they are here will be fine for now.

Summary

You have many more possibilities when creating tables. There are options for setting different types of storage engines. We touched on that in this chapter, but there's much more to that. You can also create some tables with certain storage engines that will allow you to partition the data across different locations on the server's hard drives. The storage engine can have an impact on the table's performance. Some options and settings are rarely used, but they're there for a reason. For now, we've covered enough options and possibilities when creating tables.

What we have covered in this chapter may actually be a bit overwhelming, especially the notion of reference tables like `bird_families` and `bird_orders`. Their purpose should become clearer in time. Chapter 5 provides some clarification on tables, and will show you how to alter them. There are additional examples of inserting and selecting data interspersed throughout that chapter. Before moving on, make sure to complete the exercises in the following section. They should help you to better understand how tables work and are used.

Exercises

Besides the SQL statements you entered on your MySQL server while reading this chapter, here are a few exercises to further reinforce what you've learned about creating databases and tables. In some of these exercises, you will be asked to create tables that will be used in later chapters, so it's important that you complete the exercises that follow.

1. Use the `DROP TABLE` statement to delete the table `bird_orders` that we created earlier in this chapter. Look for the `CREATE TABLE` statement that we used to create that table. Copy or type it into a text editor and make changes to that SQL statement: change the `brief_description` column to `TEXT` column type. Watch out for extra commas when you remove columns from the list. When you're finished, copy that modified SQL statement into the `mysql` monitor on your computer and press Enter to execute it.

   If you get an error, look at the error message (which will probably be confusing) and then look at the SQL statement in your text editor. Look where you made changes and see if you have any mistakes. Make sure you have keywords and values in the correct places and there are no typos. Fix any mistakes you find and try running the statement again. Keep trying until you succeed.

2. I mentioned in this chapter that we might want to store data related to identifying birds. Instead of putting that data in the birds table, create a table for that data, which will be a reference table. Try creating that table with the CREATE TABLE statement. Name it birds_wing_shapes. Give it three columns: the first column should be named wing_id with a data type of CHAR with the maximum character width set to 2. Make that column the index, as a UNIQUE key, but not an AUTO_IN CREMENT. We'll enter two-letter codes manually to identify each row of data—a feasible task because there will be probably only six rows of data in this table. Name the second column wing_shape and set its data type to CHAR with the maximum character width set to 25. This will be used to describe the type of wings a bird may have (e.g., tapered wings). The third column should be called wing_example and make it a BLOB column for storing example images of the shapes of wings.

3. After creating the birds_wing_shapes table in the previous exercise, run the SHOW CREATE TABLE statement for that table in mysql. Run it twice: once with the semicolon at the end of the SQL statement and another time with \G to see how the different displays can be useful given the results.

Copy the results of the second statement, the CREATE TABLE statement it returns. Paste that into a text editor. Then use the DROP TABLE statement to delete the table birds_wing_shapes in mysql.

In your text editor, change a few things in the CREATE TABLE statement you copied. First, change the storage engine—the value of ENGINE for the table—to a MyISAM table, if it's not already. Next, change the character set and collation for the table. Set the character set to utf8 and the collation to utf8_general_ci.

Now copy the CREATE TABLE statement you modified in your text editor and paste it into the mysql monitor and press [Enter] to run it. If you get an error, look at the confusing error message and then look at the SQL statement in your text editor. Look where you made changes and see if you have any mistakes. Make sure you have keywords and values in the correct places and there are no typos. Fix any mistakes you find and try running the statement again. Keep trying to fix it until you're successful. Once you're successful, run the DESCRIBE statement for the table to see how it looks.

4. Create two more tables, similar to birds_wing_shapes. One table will store information on the common shapes of bird bodies, and the other will store information on the shapes of their bills. They will also be used for helping bird-watchers to identify birds. Call these two tables birds_body_shapes and birds_bill_shapes.

For the birds_body_shapes table, name the first column body_id, set the data type to CHAR(3), and make it a UNIQUE key column. Name the second column body_shape with CHAR(25), and the third column body_example, making it a BLOB column for storing images of the bird shapes.

For the `birds_bill_shapes` table, create three similar columns: `bill_id` with CHAR(2) and UNIQUE; `bill_shape` with CHAR(25); and `bill_example`, making it a BLOB column for storing images of the bird shapes. Create both tables with the ENGINE set to a MyISAM, the DEFAULT CHARSET, utf8, and the COLLATE as utf8_general_ci. Run the SHOW CREATE TABLE statement for each table when you're finished to check your work.

## CHAPTER 5

Altering Tables

Despite the best planning, you will need occasionally to change the structure or other aspects of your tables. We cannot imagine everything that we might want to do with a table, or how the data might look when it's entered. Altering a table, though, is not very difficult. Because of these factors, you shouldn't worry too much about getting the table structure exactly right when creating a table. You should see tables as more fluid. Perhaps the term *table structure* makes that difficult to accept: the words *table* and *structure* have such rigid senses to them. To offset these images, perhaps a modified version of a cliché would be useful to give you a truer sense of the reality of table structures: they're not made of stone or wood, but of digital confines that are easily altered. I suspect that sentence won't be quoted much, but it's a useful perspective.

In this chapter, we will explore the ways to alter tables: how to add and delete columns, how to change their data types, how to add indexes, and how to change table and column options. This chapter will also include some precautions about potential data problems you can cause when altering a table containing data.

Prudence When Altering Tables

Before doing any structural changes to a table, especially if it contains data, you should make a backup of the table to be changed. You should do this even if you're making simple changes. You might lose part of the data if you inadvertently change the column to a different size, and may lose all of the data contained in a column if you change the column type to one that's incompatible (e.g., from a string to a numeric data type).

If you're altering only one table, you can make a copy of the table within the same database to use as a backup in case you make a mistake and want to restore the table to how it was before you started. A better choice would be to make a copy of the table and then alter the copy. You may even want to put the copy in the test database and alter the table there. When you're finished altering it, you can use it to replace the original table. We'll cover this method in more detail later in this chapter.

The best precaution to take, in addition to working with copies of tables, would be to use the `mysqldump` utility to make a backup of the tables you're altering or the whole database. This utility is covered in Chapter 14. However, to make it easier for you, here is an example of what you should enter from the command line—not from the `mysql` client—to make a backup of the `birds` table with `mysqldump` (you'll need to have read and write permission for the directory where you're executing it; it's set to the */tmp* directory here, but you should change that to a different directory, perhaps one to which only you have access and the filesystem `mysql` user has read and write permission):

```
mysqldump --user='russell' -p \
rookery birds > /tmp/birds.sql
```

As you can see, the username is given on the first line (you would enter your username instead of mine) within single or double quotes, with the `-p` option to tell `mysqldump` to prompt you for the password. There are many other `mysqldump` options, but for our purposes, these are all that are necessary. Incidentally, this statement can be entered in one line from the command line, or it can be entered on multiple lines as shown here by using the back-slash (\) to let the shell know that more is to follow. On the second line in the preceding code block, the database name is given, followed by the table name. The redirect (>) tells the shell to send the results of the dump to a text file called *birds.sql* in the */tmp* directory.

The previous example makes a backup of just the `birds` table. It may be best to make a backup of the whole `rookery` database. To do this with `mysqldump`, enter the following from the command line:

```
mysqldump --user='russell' -p \
rookery > rookery.sql
```

You should definitely do this, because having a backup of the `rookery` database will be helpful in case you accidentally delete one of the tables or its data and then get confused later when you're working on the exercises in later chapters. In fact, it's a good idea to make a backup of the `rookery` database at the end of each chapter. Each dump file should be named according to its chapter name (e.g., *rookery-ch1-end.sql*, *rookery-ch2-end.sql*, etc.) so that you can rewind to a specific point in the book.

Later on, if you have a problem and need to restore the database back to where you were at the end of a chapter, you would enter something like the following from the command line:

```
mysql --user='russell' -p \
rookery < rookery-ch2-end.sql
```

Notice that this line does not use the `mysqldump` utility. We have to use the `mysql` client at the command line to restore a dump file. When the dump file (*rookery-ch2-end.sql*) is read into the database, it will delete the `rookery` database with its tables and data before restoring the back up copy with its tables and data. Any data that users entered in the interim into the `rookery` database will be lost. Notice that to restore from the dump file, we're using a different redirect, the less-than sign (<) to tell `mysql` to take input from the contents of the text file, *rookery-ch2-end.sql*. It's possible to restore only a table or to set other limits on what is restored from a back up file. You can read about how to do that in Chapter 14. Let's move on to learning the essentials of altering tables in MySQL and MariaDB.

Essential Changes

After you have created a table, entered data into it, and begun to use it, you will invariably need to make changes to the table. You may need to add another column, change the data type of the column (e.g., to allow for more characters), or perhaps rename a column for clarity of purpose or to align the columns better with columns in other tables. To improve the speed at which data is located in the column (i.e., make queries faster), you might want to add or change an index. You may want to change one of the default values or set one of the options. All of these changes can be made through the `ALTER TABLE` statement.

The basic syntax for the `ALTER TABLE` is simple:

```
ALTER TABLE table_name changes;
```

Replace *table_name* with the name of the table you want to change. Enter the changes you want to make on the rest of the line. We'll cover the various changes possible with the `ALTER TABLE` statement one at a time in this chapter.

This SQL statement starts simply. It's the specifics of the changes that can make it confusing. Actually, that isn't always the reason for the confusion. The reason many developers have trouble with the `ALTER TABLE` statement is because they most likely don't use it often. When you need to make a change to a table, you will probably look in a book or in the documentation to see how to make a change, enter it on your server, and then forget what you did. In contrast, because you will frequently use the SQL statements for entering and retrieving data (i.e., `INSERT` and `SELECT`), their syntax will be easier to remember. So it's natural that database developers don't always remember how to make some of the changes possible with the `ALTER TABLE` statement.

One of the most common alterations you will need to make to a table is adding a column. To do this, include the `ADD COLUMN` clause as the *changes* at the end of the syntax shown earlier. As an example of this clause, let's add a column to the `bird_families` table to be able to join it to the `bird_orders` table. You should have created these two tables in Chapter 4. We'll name the column `order_id`, the same as in the `bird_orders` table. It's acceptable and perhaps beneficial for it to have the same name as the related column in the `bird_orders` table. To do this, enter the following from the `mysql` client:

```
ALTER TABLE bird_families
ADD COLUMN order_id INT;
```

This is pretty simple. It adds a column to the table with the name order_id. It will contain integers, but it will not increment automatically like its counterpart in the bird_orders table. You don't want automatic increments for the column being added to bird_families, because you're just referring to existing orders, not adding new ones.

As another example of this clause, let's add a couple of columns to the birds table to be able to join it to the two tables you should have created in the exercises at the end of Chapter 4 (i.e., birds_wing_shapes and birds_body_shapes). Before we do that, let's make a copy of the table and alter the copy instead of the original. When we're finished, we'll use the table we altered to replace the original table.

To make a copy of the birds table, we'll use the CREATE TABLE statement with the LIKE clause. This was covered in Chapter 4) In fact, let's create the new table in the test database just to work separately on it (this isn't necessary, but it's a good practice to have a development database separate from the live one. To do this, enter the following in mysql on your server:

```
CREATE TABLE test.birds_new LIKE birds;
```

Next, enter the following two lines in mysql to switch the default database of the client and to see how the new table looks:

```
USE test

DESCRIBE birds_new;
```

This DESCRIBE statement will show you the structure of the new table. Because we copied only the structure of the birds table when we created the new table, there is no data in this table. To do that, we could use an INSERT statement coupled with a SELECT like so:

```
INSERT INTO birds_new
SELECT * FROM rookery.birds;
```

This will work fine. However, there's another method that creates a table based on another table and copies over the data in the process:

```
CREATE TABLE birds_new_alternative
SELECT * FROM rookery.birds;
```

This will create the table birds_new_alternative with the data stored in it. However, if you execute a DESCRIBE statement for the table, you will see that it did not set the bird_id column to a PRIMARY KEY and did not set it to AUTO_INCREMENT. So in our situation, the first method we used to create the table is preferred, followed by an INSERT INTO...SELECT statement. Enter the following to delete the alternative table:

```
DROP TABLE birds_new_alternative;
```

Be careful with the DROP TABLE statement. Once you delete a table, there is usually no way (or at least no easy way) to get it back, unless you have a backup copy of the database. That's why I suggested that you make a backup at the beginning of this chapter.

Let's now alter the new table and add a column named wing_id to be able to join the table to the birds_wing_shapes table. To add the column, enter the following SQL statement in mysql:

```
ALTER TABLE birds_new
ADD COLUMN wing_id CHAR(2);
```

This will add a column named wing_id to the table with a fixed character data type and a maximum width of two characters. I have made sure to give the column the exact same data type and size as the corresponding column in birds_wing_shapes, because that enables us to refer to the column in each table to join the tables.

Let's look at the structure of the birds_new table to see how it looks now. Enter the following in your mysql client:

DESCRIBE birds_new;

```
+-----------------+--------------+------+-----+---------+----------------+
| Field           | Type         | Null | Key | Default | Extra          |
+-----------------+--------------+------+-----+---------+----------------+
| bird_id         | int(11)      | NO   | PRI | NULL    | auto_increment |
| scientific_name | varchar(100) | YES  | UNI | NULL    |                |
| common_name     | varchar(50)  | YES  |     | NULL    |                |
| family_id       | int(11)      | YES  |     | NULL    |                |
| description     | text         | YES  |     | NULL    |                |
| wing_id         | char(2)      | YES  |     | NULL    |                |
+-----------------+--------------+------+-----+---------+----------------+
```

Looking over the results set for the table, you should recognize the first six columns. They're based on the birds table that we created in Chapter 4. The only change is the addition we just made. Notice that the new column, wing_id, was added to the end of the table. Where a column is located matters little to MySQL or MariaDB. However, it may matter to you as a developer, especially when working with wider tables or with tables that have many columns. Let's try adding this column again, but this time tell MySQL to put it after the family_id. First, we'll delete the column we just added. Because it's a new column, we can do this without losing data.

```
ALTER TABLE birds_new
DROP COLUMN wing_id;
```

This was even simpler than adding the column. Notice that we don't mention the column data type or other options. The command doesn't need to know that in order to drop a column. The DROP COLUMN clause removes the column and all of the data contained in the column from the table. There's no UNDO statement in MySQL or in MariaDB, so be careful when working with a live table.

Let's add the `wing_id` column again:

```
ALTER TABLE birds_new
ADD COLUMN wing_id CHAR(2) AFTER family_id;
```

This will put the `wing_id` column after the `family_id` in the table. Run the DESCRIBE statement again to see for yourself. By the way, to add a column to the first position, you would use the keyword FIRST instead of AFTER. FIRST takes no column name.

With the ADD COLUMN clause of the ALTER TABLE statement, we can add more than one column at a time and specify where each should go. Let's add three more columns to the `birds_new` table. We'll add columns to join the table to the `birds_body_shapes` and `birds_bill_shapes` tables we created in the exercises at the end of Chapter 4. We'll also add a field to note whether a bird is an endangered species. While we're making changes, let's change the width of the `common_name` column. It's only 50 characters wide now. That may not be enough for some birds that have lengthy common names. For that change, we'll use the CHANGE COLUMN clause. Enter the following in `mysql`:

```
ALTER TABLE birds_new
ADD COLUMN body_id CHAR(2) AFTER wing_id,
ADD COLUMN bill_id CHAR(2) AFTER body_id,
ADD COLUMN endangered BIT DEFAULT b'1' AFTER bill_id,
CHANGE COLUMN common_name common_name VARCHAR(255);
```

This is similar to the previous ALTER TABLE examples using the ADD COLUMN clause. There are a few differences to note. First, we entered the ADD COLUMN clause three times, separated by commas. You might think you should be able to specify the ADD COLUMN keywords once, and then have each column addition listed after it, separated by commas. This is a common mistake that even experienced developers make. You can include multiple clauses in ALTER TABLE, but each clause must specify just one column. This restriction may seem unnecessary, but altering a table can cause problems if you enter something incorrectly. Being emphatic like this is a good precaution.

In one of the columns added here, the `endangered` column, we're using a data type we haven't used yet in this book: BIT. This stores one bit, which takes a values of either set or unset—basically, 1 or 0. We'll use this to indicate whether a species is endangered or not. Notice that we specified a default value for this column with the DEFAULT keyword followed by the default value. Notice also that to set the bit, we put the letter b in front of the value in quotes. There is one quirk—a bug with this data type. It stores the bit fine, but it does not display the value. If the value is unset (0), it shows a blank space in the results of a SELECT statement. If the value is set, it does not show anything, causing the ASCII format of the results set to be indented by one space to the left. It's a bug in MySQL that they'll resolve eventually—it may even be fixed by the time you read this. We can still use the data type just fine with this bug. We'll see this in action after we finish loading the data into the table.

As for the CHANGE COLUMN clause, notice that we listed the name of the common_name column twice. The first time is to name the column that is to be changed. The second time is to provide the new name, if we wanted to change it. Even though we're not changing the name, we still must list it again. Otherwise, it will return an error message and reject the SQL statement. After the column names, you must give the data type. Even if you were using the CHANGE COLUMN statement to change only the name of the column, you must give the data type again. Basically, when you type CHANGE COLUMN, the server expects you to fully specify the new column, even if some parts of the specification remain the same.

There is one more thing to note about the previous ALTER TABLE example. Notice that we told the server where to locate each of columns that it's adding using the AFTER clause. We did this previously. However, what's different is that for the second column, where we're adding bill_id, we said to locate it after body_id. You might imagine that would cause an error because we're adding the body_id column in the same statement. However, MySQL executes the clauses of an ALTER TABLE statement in the order that they are given. Depending on the version and operation, it creates a temporary copy of the table and alters that copy based on the ALTER TABLE statement's instructions, one clause at a time, from left to right (or top to bottom in our layout). When it's finished, if there are no errors, it then replaces the original table with the altered temporary table—much like we're doing here, but rapidly and behind the scenes.

If there are errors in processing any clause of the ALTER TABLE statement, it just deletes the temporary table and leaves the original table unchanged, and then returns an error message to the client. So in the previous example, in the temporary table that MySQL creates, it first added the column body_id. Once that was done, it then added the bill_id column and put it after the body_id column in that temporary table. Your tendency might have been to have entered AFTER wing_id at the end of each of the ADD COLUMN clauses. That would have worked, but the columns would have been in reverse order (i.e., wing_id, endangered, bill_id, body_id). So if we want body_id to be located after wing_id, and bill_id to be located after body_id, and so on, we have to say so in the SQL statement as shown.

Let's change now the value of the endangered column. The table only has five rows in it at the moment and none of the birds they represent are endangered. Still, let's set the value of the endangered column to 0 for four of them. To do this, we use the UPDATE statement (you'll learn more about it in Chapter 8, so don't worry if this is unfamiliar):

```
UPDATE birds_new SET endangered = 0
WHERE bird_id IN(1,2,4,5);
```

This will set the value of the endangered column to 0, or rather unset it, for the rows in which the bird_id column has one of the values listed within the parentheses. Basically, we'll change four rows of data, but leave the one unchanged where bird_id equals 3. Remember that when we created the endangered column, we gave a default of b'1', meaning the bit is set by default. The preceding statement is unsetting that column for the four rows identified in the WHERE clause.

Now we'll retrieve data using the SELECT statement (covered in Chapters 3 and 7), based on whether the endangered column is set. Because the birds_new table is now wider, we'll enter the following SQL statement using the \G for an easier-to-read display:

```
SELECT bird_id, scientific_name, common_name
FROM birds_new
WHERE endangered \G

*************************** 1. row ***************************
        bird_id: 3
scientific_name: Aix sponsa
    common_name: Wood Duck

*************************** 2. row ***************************
        bird_id: 6
scientific_name: Apteryx mantelli
    common_name: North Island Brown Kiwi
```

Notice that in the WHERE clause of the SELECT statement we are selecting rows where the endangered column has a value. For the column data type of BIT, this is all that's needed, and it has the same effect as if we specified WHERE endangered = 1. To filter on the reverse—to select rows in which the bit for the endangered column is not set—use the NOT operator like so:

```
SELECT * FROM birds_new
WHERE NOT endangered \G
```

After looking over the display for the Wood Duck and that Kiwi bird, maybe we should allow for other values for the endangered column. There are several degrees of endangerment for birds. We could and should create a separate reference table for the possibilities, but let's just enumerate the choices in the column attributes so you can see how that's done. While we're at it, we'll also relocate the column to just after the family_id column. For this, we'll use a new clause, MODIFY COLUMN:

```
ALTER TABLE birds_new
MODIFY COLUMN endangered
ENUM('Extinct',
    'Extinct in Wild',
    'Threatened - Critically Endangered',
    'Threatened - Endangered',
    'Threatened - Vulnerable',
    'Lower Risk - Conservation Dependent',
    'Lower Risk - Near Threatened',
    'Lower Risk - Least Concern')
AFTER family_id;
```

Notice that the syntax for the `MODIFY COLUMN` clause lists the name of the column once. That's because the clause does not allow you to change the column name. For that, you must use the `CHANGE COLUMN` clause. Notice also that we used a new column data type that lets us enumerate a list of acceptable values: the `ENUM` data type. The values are enclosed in quotes, separated by commas, and the set is contained within a pair of parentheses.

Let's run the `SHOW COLUMNS` statement with the `LIKE` clause to see just the column settings for the endangered column:

```
SHOW COLUMNS FROM birds_new LIKE 'endangered' \G

*************************** 1. row ***************************
  Field: endangered
   Type: enum('Extinct','Extinct in Wild',
              'Threatened - Critically Endangered',
              'Threatened - Endangered',
              'Threatened - Vulnerable',
              'Lower Risk - Conservation Dependent',
              'Lower Risk - Near Threatened',
              'Lower Risk - Least Concern')
   Null: YES
    Key:
Default: NULL
  Extra:
```

In addition to the values enumerated, notice that a NULL value is allowed and is the default. We could have disallowed NULL values by including a `NOT NULL` clause.

If we want to add another value to the enumerated list, we would use the `ALTER TABLE` statement again with the `MODIFY COLUMN` clause, without the `AFTER` clause extension—unless we want to relocate the column again. We would have to list all of the enumerated values again, with the addition of the new one.

To set the values in a column that has an enumerated list, you can either give a value shown in the list, or refer to the value numerically, if you know the order of the values. The first enumerated value would be 1. For instance, you could do an UPDATE statement like this to set all birds in the table to *Lower Risk - Least Concern*, the seventh value:

```
UPDATE birds_new
SET endangered = 7;
```

I said earlier that using the `ENUM` data type can be an alternative to a reference table when there are a few values. However, the `endangered` column as shown in this example is cumbersome and not professional. We could still do a reference table in addition to this enumerated list within the table. The reference table would have a row for each of these choices, but with extra columns that would provide more information for them, for when we wanted to display more information. Based on that, we could change the values in the enumerated list in the `birds` table to something easier to type (e.g., *LR-LC* for

Lower Risk - Least Concern) and then put the lengthier description in the reference table that we'd create.

It will be simpler, however, to treat the endangered column like the other reference tables that we've created (e.g., `birds_wing_shapes`) and use numbers for the values in the `birds` table. We should change the column and create another reference table for it. We'll do that later, though.

Dynamic Columns

We just covered `ENUM`, so let's digress from `ALTER TABLE` for a moment to cover dynamic columns. This is something that is available only in MariaDB, as of version 5.3. It's similar to an `ENUM` column, but with key/value pairs instead of a plain list of options. That will initially sound confusing, but it make more sense when we look at some examples. So let's create a few tables with dynamic columns.

To make the bird-watchers site more interesting, suppose we've decided to do some surveys of the preferences of bird-watchers. We'll ask the members to rate birds they like the most. That will be a simple start. In time, we might ask them to rate the best places to see birds in an area, or maybe binocular makers and models they like the best. For this scenario, let's create a set of tables.

If you're not using MariaDB and don't want to replace MySQL with it, just read along. If you do have MariaDB installed on your server, enter the following:

```
USE birdwatchers;

CREATE TABLE surveys
(survey_id INT AUTO_INCREMENT KEY,
survey_name VARCHAR(255));

CREATE TABLE survey_questions
(question_id INT AUTO_INCREMENT KEY,
survey_id INT,
question VARCHAR(255),
choices BLOB);

CREATE TABLE survey_answers
(answer_id INT AUTO_INCREMENT KEY,
human_id INT,
question_id INT,
date_answered DATETIME,
answer VARCHAR(255));
```

The first table we created here will contain a list of surveys. The second table is where we'll put the questions. Because we intend to do only polls, the `choices` column will contain the survey choices. We defined it with a very generic type, `BLOB`, but we'll use it to store a dynamic column. The data type used has to be able to hold the data that will be given to it when we create the dynamic column. BLOB can be a good choice for that.

The third table is where we will store the answers to the survey questions. This time we define a VARCHAR column to hold the dynamic column. We will link survey_answers to survey_questions based on the question_id, and survey_questions to surveys based on the survey_id.

Now let's put some data in these tables. If you're using MariaDB, enter the following SQL statements to add SQL statements:

```
INSERT INTO surveys (survey_name)
VALUES("Favorite Birding Location");

INSERT INTO survey_questions
(survey_id, question, choices)
VALUES(LAST_INSERT_ID(),
"What's your favorite setting for bird-watching?",
COLUMN_CREATE('1', 'forest', '2', 'shore', '3', 'backyard') );

INSERT INTO surveys (survey_name)
VALUES("Preferred Birds");

INSERT INTO survey_questions
(survey_id, question, choices)
VALUES(LAST_INSERT_ID(),
"Which type of birds do you like best?",
COLUMN_CREATE('1', 'perching', '2', 'shore', '3', 'fowl', '4', 'rapture') );
```

That created two surveys: one with a set of choices about where the birders like to watch birds; the second with a simple, not comprehensive set of bird types they prefer. We used COLUMN_CREATE( ) to create the enumerated lists of choices: each choice has a key and a value. Thus, in survey_questions, choice 1 is "forest," choice 2 is "shore," and choice 3 is "backyard." Starting with MariaDB version 10.0.1, you can give strings for the keys instead of numbers.

Let's see now how data may be retrieved from a dynamic column:

```
SELECT COLUMN_GET(choices, 3 AS CHAR)
AS 'Location'
FROM survey_questions
WHERE survey_id = 1;

+----------+
| Location |
+----------+
| backyard |
+----------+
```

This returns the third choice. We used the COLUMN_GET( ) function to get the dynamic column within the column given as the first argument. The second argument specifies the key to use to get the data. We also included AS to indicate the type of data type it should use (i.e., CHAR) to cast the value it returns.

Now let's enter a bunch of answers for our members. If you're using an electronic version of this book, just copy and paste the following into your MariaDB server:

```
INSERT INTO survey_answers
(human_id, question_id, date_answered, answer)
VALUES
(29, 1, NOW(), 2),
(29, 2, NOW(), 2),
(35, 1, NOW(), 1),
(35, 2, NOW(), 1),
(26, 1, NOW(), 2),
(26, 2, NOW(), 1),
(27, 1, NOW(), 2),
(27, 2, NOW(), 4),
(16, 1, NOW(), 3),
(3, 1, NOW(), 1),
(3, 2, NOW(), 1);
```

This isn't many rows, but it's enough for now. Let's count the votes for the first survey question by executing the following:

```
SELECT IFNULL(COLUMN_GET(choices, answer AS CHAR), 'total')
AS 'Birding Site', COUNT(*) AS 'Votes'
FROM survey_answers
JOIN survey_questions USING(question_id)
WHERE survey_id = 1
AND question_id = 1
GROUP BY answer WITH ROLLUP;
```

```
+---------------+-------+
| Birding Site  | Votes |
+---------------+-------+
| forest        |     2 |
| shore         |     3 |
| backyard      |     1 |
| total         |     6 |
+---------------+-------+
```

In the WHERE clause, survey_id chose the survey we want from survey_questions while question_id chose the question we want from survey_answers. We retrieve all the answers, group them, and count the rows for each answer to see how many bird-watchers voted for each one.

That's not much data, though. I'll add more answers to give us a larger table with which to work. You can download the table from my site (*http://mysqlresources.com/files*).

We'll use it in examples later in this book. Dynamic columns are still new and very much under development, so this brief a review will suffice for now. Let's now get back to more standard table-related topics.

Optional Changes

In addition to the most common uses for the ALTER TABLE statement (i.e., adding and renaming columns), you can use it to set some of the options of an existing table and its columns. You can also use the ALTER TABLE statement to set the value of table variables, as well as the default value of columns. This section covers how to change those settings and values, as well as how to rename a table. Additionally, you can change indexes in a table. That is covered in the section on "Indexes" on page 80.

Setting a Column's Default Value

You may have noticed that the results of the DESCRIBE statements shown in earlier examples have a heading called *Default*. You may have also noticed that almost all of the fields have a default value of NULL. This means that when the user does not enter a value for the column, the value of NULL will be used. If you would like to specify a default value for a column, though, you could have done so when creating the table. For an existing table, you can use the ALTER TABLE statement to specify a default value other than NULL. This won't change the values of existing rows—not even ones that previously used a default value. You would use either the CHANGE clause or the ALTER clause. Let's look at an example of using the CHANGE clause first.

Suppose that most of the birds that we will list in our database would have a value of *Lower Risk - Least Concern* in the endangered column. Rather than enter *Lower Risk - Least Concern* or its numeric equivalent in each INSERT statement (which inserts data into a table), we could change the default value of the endangered column. Let's do that and change the column from an ENUM to an INT data type to prepare for the creation of a reference table for the conservation status of birds. Let's also make this a little more interesting by creating the reference table and inserting all of the data we had enumerated in the settings for the endangered. We'll start by entering the following in mysql to create the reference table:

```
CREATE TABLE rookery.conservation_status
(status_id INT AUTO_INCREMENT PRIMARY KEY,
conservation_category CHAR(10),
conservation_state CHAR(25) );
```

We named the reference table conservation_status, which is a better description than endangered. Notice that we split each status into two columns. A value like *Lower Risk - Least Concern* was meant to indicate the state of *Least Concern* in the category *Lower Risk*. So we created two columns for those values. We'll put *Lower Risk* in the conservation_category column and *Least Concern* in another column called, conservation_category.

Now let's insert all of the data into this new reference table. We'll use the INSERT statement (covered briefly in Chapter 3):

```
INSERT INTO rookery.conservation_status
(conservation_category, conservation_state)
VALUES('Extinct','Extinct'),
('Extinct','Extinct in Wild'),
('Threatened','Critically Endangered'),
('Threatened','Endangered'),
('Threatened','Vulnerable'),
('Lower Risk','Conservation Dependent'),
('Lower Risk','Near Threatened'),
('Lower Risk','Least Concern');
```

If you find this SQL statement confusing, just enter it and rest assured we'll cover such statements in detail in Chapter 6. For now, though, I wanted to show you a reference table with data in it. Let's use the SELECT statement to select all of the rows of data in the table. Enter just the SQL statement (shown in bold), not the results that follow it:

SELECT * FROM rookery.conservation_status;

```
+-----------+-----------------------+------------------------+
| status_id | conservation_category | conservation_state     |
+-----------+-----------------------+------------------------+
|         1 | Extinct               | Extinct                |
|         2 | Extinct               | Extinct in Wild        |
|         3 | Threatened            | Critically Endangered  |
|         4 | Threatened            | Endangered             |
|         5 | Threatened            | Vulnerable             |
|         6 | Lower Risk            | Conservation Dependent |
|         7 | Lower Risk            | Near Threatened        |
|         8 | Lower Risk            | Least Concern          |
+-----------+-----------------------+------------------------+
```

The first column gets default values, incrementing automatically as we asked when we created the table, while the other two columns get the values we specified during our insert.

Notice that we have been prefixing the table name with the database name (i.e., rookery.conservation_status). That's because we had set the default database to test with USE. Going back to the birds_new table, we're ready to change the endangered column. We decided earlier that we wanted to set the default value of this column to *Lower Risk - Least Concern*, or rather to the value of the status_id for that combination of columns in the conservation_status table. Looking at the results, you can see that the value for the status_id we want for the default is 8. We can change the endangered column's name and default value by entering the following on the server:

```
ALTER TABLE birds_new
CHANGE COLUMN endangered conservation_status_id INT DEFAULT 8;
```

The syntax of this is mostly the same as previous examples in this chapter that use the
CHANGE clause (i.e., list the name of the column twice and restate the data types, even if
you don't want to change them). The difference in this case is that we've added the
keyword DEFAULT followed by the default value—if the default value were a string, you
would put it within quotes. The example also changed the column name. But if we
wanted only to set the default value for a column, we could use the ALTER clause of the
ALTER TABLE statement. Let's change the default of conservation_status_id to 7:

```
ALTER TABLE birds_new
ALTER conservation_status_id SET DEFAULT 7;
```

This is much simpler. It only sets the default value for the column. Notice that the second
line starts with ALTER and not CHANGE. It's then followed by the column name, and the
SET subclause. Let's see how that column looks now, running the SHOW COLUMNS statement only for that column:

```
SHOW COLUMNS FROM birds_new LIKE 'conservation_status_id' \G

*************************** 1. row ***************************
   Field: conservation_status_id
    Type: int(11)
    Null: YES
     Key:
 Default: 7
   Extra:
```

As you can see, the default value is now 7. If we change our minds about having a default
value for conservation_status_id, we would enter the following to reset it back to
NULL, or whatever the initial default value would be based on the data type of the
column:

```
ALTER TABLE birds_new
ALTER conservation_status_id DROP DEFAULT;
```

This particular usage of the DROP keyword doesn't delete data in the columns. It just
alters the column settings so there is no default value. Run the SHOW COLUMNS statement
again on your computer to see that the default has been reset. Then put the default back
to 7.

Setting the Value of AUTO_INCREMENT

Many of the main tables in a database will have a primary key that uses the AUTO_IN
CREMENT option. That creates an AUTO_INCREMENT variable in the table called tables in
the information_schema database. You may recognize that database name. We saw the
information_schema database in the results of the SHOW DATABASE statement in "Starting to Explore Databases" on page 33. When you create a table, MySQL adds a row to

the table called `tables` in the `information_schema` database. One of the columns of that table is called `auto_increment`. That is where you can find the value of the next row to be created in a table. This is initially set to a value of 1, unless you set it to a different number when creating the table. Let's run a `SELECT` statement to get that value from the `information_schema` database, from the `tables` table:

```
SELECT auto_increment
FROM information_schema.tables
WHERE table_name = 'birds';
```

```
+----------------+
| auto_increment |
+----------------+
|              7 |
+----------------+
```

Because we entered data for only six birds in the `birds` table, and the value of `AUTO_IN CREMENT` was not set when the table was created, it started at 1 and now has a value of 7. That means the *next* row we add to the table will have 7 in the column.

If you would like to change the value of `AUTO_INCREMENT` for a particular table, you can do so with the `ALTER TABLE` statement. Let's set the value of `AUTO_INCREMENT` for the `birds` table to 10, just to see how to change it this way. While we're at it, let's switch the default database back to `rookery`. Enter the following in `mysql`:

```
USE rookery

ALTER TABLE birds
AUTO_INCREMENT = 10;
```

This will cause the `bird_id` to be set to 10 for the next row of data on a bird that we enter into the `birds` table. Changing the auto-increment value is not usually necessary, but it's good to know that you can do even this with `ALTER TABLE`.

Another Method to Alter and Create a Table

There may be times when you realize that you've created a table that is too wide, with too many columns. Perhaps some columns would be handled better in a separate table. Or perhaps you started adding new columns to an existing table and found it became unruly over time. In either case, you could create a smaller table and then move data from the larger table into the new, smaller one. To do this, you can create a new table with the same settings for the columns you want to move, then copy the data from the first table to the new table, and then delete the columns you no longer need from the first table. If you wanted to make this transition by the method just described, the individual column settings will need to be same in the new table to prevent problems or loss of data.

An easier method for creating a table based on another table is to use the CREATE TABLE with the LIKE clause. Let's try that to create a copy of the birds table. Enter the following in mysql on your server:

```
CREATE TABLE birds_new LIKE birds;
```

This creates an identical table like the birds table, but with the name birds_new. If you enter the SHOW TABLES statement in mysql, you will see that you now have a birds table and a new table, birds_new.

 You can use an underscore (i.e., _) in a table name, but you may want to avoid using hyphens. MySQL interprets a hyphen as a minus sign and tries to do a calculation between the two words given, which causes an error. If you want to use a hyphen, you must always reference the table name within quotes.

Execute the following three SQL statements to see what you now have:

```
DESCRIBE birds;

DESCRIBE birds_new;

SELECT * FROM birds_new;
Empty set (0.00 sec)
```

The first two SQL statements will show you the structure of both tables. They will confirm that they are identical except for their names. To save space, I didn't include the results of those two SQL statements here.

The third SQL statement should show you all of the rows of data in the birds_new table. Because we copied only the structure of the birds table when we created the new table, there is no data—as indicated by the message returned. We could copy the data over when we're finished altering the table if that's what we want to do.

This method can also be used when making major modifications to a table. In such a situation, it's good to work from a copy of the table. You would then use the ALTER TABLE statement to change the new table (e.g., birds_new). When you're finished making the changes, you would then copy all of the data from the old table to the new table, delete the original table, and then rename the new table.

In such a situation, you may have one minor problem. I said earlier that the tables are identical except for the table names, but that's not exactly true. There may be one other difference. If the table has a column that uses AUTO_INCREMENT for the default value, the counter will be set to 0 for the new table. You must determine the current value of AUTO_INCREMENT for the birds table to be assured that the rows in the new table have the correct identification numbers. Enter the following SQL statement in mysql:

```
SHOW CREATE TABLE birds \G
```

In the results, which are not shown, the last line will reveal the current value of the AUTO_INCREMENT variable. For instance, the last line may look as follows:

```
...
) ENGINE=MyISAM AUTO_INCREMENT=6 DEFAULT CHARSET=latin1 COLLATE=latin1_bin
```

In this excerpt of the results, you can see that the variable, AUTO_INCREMENT is currently 6. Set AUTO_INCREMENT to the same value in the birds_new table by entering the following SQL statement in mysql:

```
ALTER TABLE birds_new
AUTO_INCREMENT = 6;
```

When you're ready to copy the data from one table to the other, you can use the IN SERT...SELECT syntax. This is covered in "Other Possibilities" on page 104.

Instead of copying the data after you're finished modifying the new table, you can copy the data while creating the new table. This might be useful when you want to move only certain columns with their data to a new table, without any alterations to the columns. To do this, you would still use the CREATE TABLE statement, but with a slightly different syntax.

Let's suppose that we have decided that we want to create a new table for details about each bird (e.g., migratory patterns, habitats, etc.). Looking at the birds table, though, we decide that the description column and its data belong in this new table. So we'll create a new table and copy that column's settings and data, as well as the bird_id into the new table. We can do that by entering the following from mysql to get the table started:

```
CREATE TABLE birds_details
SELECT bird_id, description
FROM birds;
```

This creates the birds_details table with two columns, based on the same columns in the birds table. It also copies the data from the two columns in the birds table into the birds_details table. There is one minor, but necessary, difference in one of the columns in the new table. The difference has to do with AUTO_INCREMENT again, but not in the same way as earlier examples. Enter the DESCRIBE statement to see the difference:

DESCRIBE birds_details;

```
+-------------+---------+------+-----+---------+-------+
| Field       | Type    | Null | Key | Default | Extra |
+-------------+---------+------+-----+---------+-------+
| bird_id     | int(11) | NO   |     | 0       |       |
| description | text    | YES  |     | NULL    |       |
+-------------+---------+------+-----+---------+-------+
```

The difference here is that the bird_id does not use AUTO_INCREMENT. This is good because we have to manually set the value of the bird_id for each row that we enter.

We won't have details for each bird, though, and we won't necessarily be entering them in the same order as we will in the birds table. We could change the bird_id column in this table to an AUTO_INCREMENT column, but that would cause problems—trying to keep it in line with the birds table would be maddening. We could, however, make an index for the bird_id column in the birds_details table by using the ALTER TABLE statement and setting the column to a UNIQUE key. That would allow only one entry per bird, which may be a good idea. This is covered in "Indexes" on page 80.

The CREATE TABLE...SELECT statement created the birds_details table with only two columns. We said, though, that we want more columns for keeping other information on birds. We'll add those additional columns later with the ALTER TABLE statement, in the exercises at the end of the chapter. For now, let's remove the column description from the birds table by entering this from mysql:

```
ALTER TABLE birds
DROP COLUMN description;
```

This will delete the column and the data in that column. So be careful using it. This clause will be covered in more depth in Chapter 6.

Renaming a Table

Earlier sections covered how to make changes to the columns in a table. This included renaming columns. Sometimes, though, you may want to rename a table. You may do this for style reasons or to change the name of a table to something more explanatory. You may do it as a method of replacing an existing table, by deleting the existing table first and then renaming the replacement table to the deleted table's name. This is the situation in some of the examples in the previous section.

We created a copy of the birds table that we called birds_new in the test database. Our plan was to modify the birds_new table, then to delete the birds table from the rookery database and replace it with birds_new table from the test database. To fully replace the birds table, in this case, we will rename birds_new to birds. This is not done through the ALTER TABLE statement. That's used only for altering the structure of columns in a table, not for renaming a table. Instead, we will use the RENAME TABLE statement. Let's wait before doing that. For now, a generic example follows of how you would rename a table. Do not enter this statement, though:

```
RENAME TABLE table1_altered
TO table1;
```

This SQL statement would rename the table1_altered table to table1. This assumes that a table named table1 doesn't already exist in the database. If it does, it won't overwrite that table. Instead, you'll get an error message and the table won't be renamed.

The RENAME TABLE statement can also be used to move a table to another database. This can be useful when you have a table that you've created in one database, as we did in the test database, and now want to relocate it to a different database. Because you can both rename and relocate a table in the same RENAME TABLE statement, let's do that with our example instead of using the previous syntax. (Incidentally, relocating a table without renaming it is also allowed. You would give the name of the new database, with the same table name.) In our examples, we will have to either delete or rename the unaltered table in the rookery database first. Renaming the table that's being replaced is a safer choice, so we'll go with that option.

Let's rename the birds table in the rookery database to birds_old and then rename and relocate the birds_new table from the test database to birds in the rookery database. To do all of this in one SQL statement, enter the following:

```
RENAME TABLE rookery.birds TO rookery.birds_old,
test.birds_new TO rookery.birds;
```

If there was a problem in doing any of these changes, an error message would be generated and none of the changes would be made. If all of it went well, though, we should have two tables in the rookery database that are designed to hold data on birds.

Let's run the SHOW TABLES statement to see the tables in the rookery database. We'll request only tables starting with the word *birds* by using the LIKE clause with the wildcard, %. Enter the following in mysql:

```
SHOW TABLES IN rookery LIKE 'birds%';
```

```
+----------------------------+
| Tables_in_rookery (birds%) |
+----------------------------+
| birds                      |
| birds_bill_shapes          |
| birds_body_shapes          |
| birds_details              |
| birds_new                  |
| birds_old                  |
| birds_wing_shapes          |
+----------------------------+
```

The birds table used to be the birds_new table that we altered in the test database. The original birds table has been renamed to birds_old. The other tables in the results set here are the ones we created earlier in this chapter. Because their names start with *birds*, they're in the results. After running a SELECT statement to ensure that you haven't lost any data, you might want to delete the birds_old table. You would delete the birds_old table with the DROP TABLE statement in mysql. It would look like the following, but don't enter this:

```
DROP TABLE birds_old;
```

Reordering a Table

The SELECT statement, which is used to retrieve data from a table, has an ORDER BY clause that may be used to sort or order the results of the statement. This is useful when displaying data, especially when viewing a table with many rows of data. Although it's not necessary, there may be times in which it would be desirable to resort the data within a table. You might do this with tables in which the data is rarely changed, such as a reference table. It can sometimes make a sequential search of the table faster, but a good index will work fine and is usually better.

As an example of how to reorder a table, if you go to my website, you will find a table listing country codes. We might use such a table in conjunction with members of the site or maybe to have a list of birds spotted in each country. The country_codes table contains two-character country codes, along with the names of the countries. Rather than type the name of the country for each record in a related table for members or bird spottings, we could enter a two-character code for the country (e.g., us for *United States of America*). The table is already in alphabetical order by name, but you might want to reorder that table to put rows in alphabetical order. Or perhaps you want to add a new country to the list, perhaps a disputed territory that you want to recognize. You might want to reorder the list after making the addition.

First, let's see how the data in the table looks now. Let's enter the following SELECT statement in mysql, limiting the results to the first five rows of data:

```
SELECT * FROM country_codes
LIMIT 5;
```

```
+--------------+----------------+
| country_code | country_name   |
+--------------+----------------+
| af           | Afghanistan    |
| ax           | Åland Islands  |
| al           | Albania        |
| dz           | Algeria        |
| as           | American Samoa |
+--------------+----------------+
```

As you can see, the data is already in alphabetical order based on the values in the country_name column. Let's use the ALTER TABLE statement with its ORDER BY clause to reorder the data in the table based on the country_code column. We would probably not want the table in this order, but let's do it just to experiment with this clause of the ALTER TABLE statement. We can change it back afterwards. Enter the following in mysql:

```
ALTER TABLE country_codes
ORDER BY country_code;
```

That should have been processed quickly. Let's run the SELECT statement again to see what the first five rows in the table now contain:

```
SELECT * FROM
country_codes LIMIT 5;
```

```
+--------------+----------------------+
| country_code | country_name         |
+--------------+----------------------+
| ac           | Ascension Island     |
| ad           | Andorra              |
| ae           | United Arab Emirates |
| af           | Afghanistan          |
| ag           | Antigua and Barbuda  |
+--------------+----------------------+
```

Notice that the results are different and that the rows are now sorted on the coun
try_code columns without having to specify that order in the SELECT statement. To put
the rows back in order by country_name, enter the ALTER TABLE statement, but with the
country_name column instead of the country_code column.

Again, reordering a table is rarely necessary. You can order the results of a SELECT
statement with the ORDER BY clause like so:

```
SELECT * FROM country_codes
ORDER BY country_name
LIMIT 5;
```

The results of this SQL statement are the same as the previous SELECT statement, and
the difference in speed is usually indiscernible.

Indexes

One of the most irritating tasks for beginners in using the ALTER TABLE statement is
having to use it to change an index. If you try to rename a column that is indexed by
using only an ALTER TABLE statement, you will get a frustrating and confusing error
message. For instance, suppose we decide to rename the primary key column in the
conservation_status table from status_id to conservation_status_id. To do so,
we might try an SQL statement like this:

```
ALTER TABLE conservation_status
CHANGE status_id conservation_status_id INT AUTO_INCREMENT PRIMARY KEY;

ERROR 1068: Multiple primary key defined
```

When you first try doing this, you will probably think that you're remembering the
syntax incorrectly. So you'll try different combinations, but nothing will work. To avoid
this and to get it right the first time, you will need to understand indexes better and
understand that an index is separate from the column upon which the index is based.

Indexes are used by MySQL to locate data quickly. They work very much like the index
in the back of a book. Let's use that metaphor to compare methods of searching this

book. For example, if you want to find the syntax for the ALTER TABLE statement, you could start at the beginning of this book and flip through the pages rapidly and se-quentially—assuming you have a print version of this book—until you spot those key-words. That would be searching for data without an index. Instead, you could flip to the beginning of the book and search the Table of Contents, which is a broader index, for a chapter title using the words *alter table* and then search within the chapters con-taining those words in their title. That's an example of a simple or poor index. A better choice would be to go to the index at the back of this book, look for the list of pages in which ALTER TABLE can be found, and go straight to those pages to find what you want.

An index in MySQL works similarly to the last example. Without an index, rows are searched sequentially. Because an index is smaller and is structured to be traversed quickly, it can be searched rapidly and then MySQL can jump directly to the row that matches the search pattern. So when you create a table, especially one that will hold many rows of data, create it with an index. The database will run faster.

With this metaphor of a book index in mind, you can better understand that an index is not the same as a column, although it is related to columns. To illustrate this in a MySQL table, let's look at the index for the humans table we created in Chapter 4, by using the SHOW INDEX statement. Enter the following from mysql:

```
SHOW INDEX FROM birdwatchers.humans \G
```

```
*************************** 1. row ***************************
        Table: humans
   Non_unique: 0
     Key_name: PRIMARY
 Seq_in_index: 1
  Column_name: human_id
    Collation: A
  Cardinality: 0
     Sub_part: NULL
       Packed: NULL
         Null:
   Index_type: BTREE
      Comment:
```

The output shows that behind the scenes there is an index associated with the hu man_id (look in the preceding output where it says, *Column_name*). The human_id column is not the index, but the data from which the index is drawn. The name of the column and name of the index are the same and the index is bound to the column, but they are not the same. Let's alter this table and add another index to make this clearer.

Suppose that users of the humans table sometimes search based on the last name of the member. Without an index, MySQL will search the last_name column sequentially. Let's confirm that by using the EXPLAIN statement, coupled with the SELECT statement. This will return information on how the SELECT statement searches the table and on what basis. It will explain what the server did when executing the SELECT statement—so it won't return any rows from the table, but information on how the index would be used had you executed only the SELECT statement. Enter the following in `mysql`:

```
EXPLAIN SELECT * FROM birdwatchers.humans
WHERE name_last = 'Hollar' \G

*************************** 1. row ***************************
           id: 1
  select_type: SIMPLE
        table: humans
         type: ALL
possible_keys: NULL
          key: NULL
      key_len: NULL
          ref: NULL
         rows: 4
        Extra: Using where
```

The EXPLAIN statement here analyzes the SELECT statement given, which is selecting all of the columns in the humans table where the value for the name_last column equals *Hollar*. What is of interest to us in the results is the possible_keys field and the key field—a key is the column on which a table is indexed. However, the words *key* and *index* are fairly interchangeable. The possible_keys field would show the keys that the SELECT statement could have used. In this case, there is no index related to the name_last column. The key would list the index that the statement actually used. Again, in this case there were none, so it shows a value of NULL. There are only four names in this table, so an index would not make a noticeable difference in performance. However, if this table might one day have thousands of names, an index will greatly improve the performance of look-ups on people's names.

In addition to sometimes searching the humans table based on the member's last name, suppose that users sometimes search based on the first name, and sometimes based on both the first and last names. To prepare for those possibilities and to improve performance for a time when the table will have many records, let's create an index that combines the two columns. To do this, we will use the ALTER TABLE statement with the ADD INDEX clause like so:

```
ALTER TABLE birdwatchers.humans
ADD INDEX human_names (name_last, name_first);
```

Now let's run the SHOW CREATE TABLE statement to see how the index looks from that perspective:

```
SHOW CREATE TABLE birdwatchers.humans \G

*************************** 1. row ***************************
       Table: humans
Create Table: CREATE TABLE `humans` (
  `human_id` int(11) NOT NULL AUTO_INCREMENT,
  `formal_title` varchar(25) COLLATE latin1_bin DEFAULT NULL,
```

```
    `name_first` varchar(25) COLLATE latin1_bin DEFAULT NULL,
    `name_last` varchar(25) COLLATE latin1_bin DEFAULT NULL,
    `email_address` varchar(255) COLLATE latin1_bin DEFAULT NULL,
    PRIMARY KEY (`human_id`),
    KEY `human_names` (`name_last`,`name_first`)
) ENGINE=MyISAM DEFAULT CHARSET=latin1 COLLATE=latin1_bin
```

The results show a new KEY after the list of columns. The key, or index, is called hu
man_names and is based on the values of the two columns listed in parentheses. Let's use
another SQL statement to see more information about this new index. We'll use the
SHOW INDEX statement like so:

```
SHOW INDEX FROM birdwatchers.humans
WHERE Key_name = 'human_names' \G

*************************** 1. row ***************************
        Table: humans
   Non_unique: 1
     Key_name: human_names
 Seq_in_index: 1
  Column_name: name_last
    Collation: A
  Cardinality: NULL
     Sub_part: NULL
       Packed: NULL
         Null: YES
   Index_type: BTREE
      Comment:
*************************** 2. row ***************************
        Table: humans
   Non_unique: 1
     Key_name: human_names
 Seq_in_index: 2
  Column_name: name_first
    Collation: A
  Cardinality: NULL
     Sub_part: NULL
       Packed: NULL
         Null: YES
   Index_type: BTREE
      Comment:
```

This SQL statement shows the components of the human_names index. The results show
two rows with information on the columns that were used to create the index. There's
plenty of information here about this index. It's not important that you understand what
it all means at this point in learning MySQL and MariaDB. What I want you to see here
is that the name of the index is different from the columns upon which it's based. When
there's only one column in the index and the index for it has the same name, it doesn't
mean that they are the same thing.

Let's try the EXPLAIN...SELECT again to see the difference from earlier when we didn't have the human_names index:

```
EXPLAIN SELECT * FROM birdwatchers.humans
WHERE name_last = 'Hollar' \G

*************************** 1. row ***************************
           id: 1
  select_type: SIMPLE
        table: humans
         type: ref
possible_keys: human_names
          key: human_names
      key_len: 28
          ref: const
         rows: 1
        Extra: Using where
```

As shown in the results, this time the possible_keys field indicates that the human_names key could be used. If there were more than one possible key that could be used, the line would list them here. In line with the index's presence in possible_keys, the key shows that the human_names index was actually used. Basically, when a SELECT is run in which the user wants to search the table based on the person's last name, MySQL will use the human_names index that we created, and not search the name_last column sequentially. That's what we want. That will make for a quicker search.

Now that you hopefully have a better understanding of indexes in general and their relation to columns, let's go back to the earlier task of renaming the column in the conservation_status table from status_id to conservation_status_id. Because the index is associated with the column, we need to remove that association in the index. Otherwise, the index will be associated with a column that does not exist from its perspective: it will be looking for the column by the old name. So, let's delete the index and rename the column, and then add a new index based on the new column name. To do that, enter the following SQL statement in mysql:

```
ALTER TABLE conservation_status
DROP PRIMARY KEY,
CHANGE status_id conservation_status_id INT PRIMARY KEY AUTO_INCREMENT;
```

The clauses must be in the order shown, because the index must be dropped before the column with which it's associated can be renamed. Don't worry about losing data: the data in the columns is not deleted, only the index, which will be re-created easily by MySQL. We don't have to give the name of the associated column when dropping a PRIMARY KEY. There is and can be only one primary key.

At this point, you should have a better sense of indexes and the procedure for changing them with the ALTER TABLE statement. The order in which you make changes to indexes and the columns on which they are based matters. Why it matters should be clear now. So that you can get more practice with these concepts and syntax, though, in one of the exercises at the end of the chapter you will be asked to change some columns and indexes. Be sure to complete all of the exercises.

Summary

Good planning is certainly key to developing an efficient database. However, as you can see from all of the examples of how to use the ALTER TABLE statement, MySQL is malleable enough that a database and its tables can be reshaped without much trouble. Just be sure to make a backup before restructuring a database, and work from a copy of a table before altering it. Check your work and the data when you're finished, before committing the changes made.

With all of this in mind, after having had some experience altering tables in this chapter, you should feel comfortable in creating tables, as you now know that they don't have to be perfect from the beginning. You should also have a good sense of the options available with columns and how to set them. And you should have a basic understanding of indexes, how they're used, and how they may be created and changed.

If you have found this chapter confusing, though, it may be that you need more experience using tables with data. In the next part of this book, you will get plenty of experience working with tables, inserting data into columns, and changing the data. When you see how the data comes together, you'll have a better understanding of how to structure a table and how to set columns in preparation for data. You'll have a better appreciation of how multiple tables may be joined together to get the results you want.

Exercises

Besides the SQL statements you entered on your MySQL or MariaDB server while reading this chapter, here are a few practice exercises to further strengthen what we've covered. They're related to creating and altering tables. We'll use these tables with the modifications you'll make in later chapters, so make sure to complete all of the exercises here.

1. Earlier in this chapter, we created a table called birds_details. We created the table with two columns: bird_id and description. We took these two columns from the birds table. Our intention in creating this table was to add columns to store a description of each bird, notes about migratory patterns, areas in which they can be found, and other information helpful in locating each bird in the wild. Let's add a couple of columns for capturing some of that information.

   Using the ALTER TABLE statement, alter the birds_details table. In one SQL statement, add two columns named migrate and bird_feeder, making them both integer (INT) columns. These will contain values of 1 or 0 (i.e., *Yes* or *No*). In the same SQL statement, using the CHANGE COLUMN clause, change the name of the column, description to bird_description.

When you're finished altering the table, run the SHOW CREATE TABLE statement for this table to see the results.

2. Using the CREATE TABLE statement, create a new reference table named, habi tat_codes. Create this table with two columns: name the first column habi tat_id and make it a primary key using AUTO_INCREMENT and the column type of INT. Name the second column habitat and use the data type VARCHAR(25). Enter the following SQL statement to add data to the table:

```
INSERT INTO habitat_codes (habitat)
VALUES('Coasts'), ('Deserts'), ('Forests'),
('Grasslands'), ('Lakes, Rivers, Ponds'),
('Marshes, Swamps'), ('Mountains'), ('Oceans'),
('Urban');
```

Execute a SELECT statement for the table to confirm that the data was entered correctly. It should look like this:

```
+------------+---------------------+
| habitat_id | habitat             |
+------------+---------------------+
|          1 | Coasts              |
|          2 | Deserts             |
|          3 | Forests             |
|          4 | Grasslands          |
|          5 | Lakes, Rivers, Ponds|
|          6 | Marshes, Swamps     |
|          7 | Mountains           |
|          8 | Oceans              |
|          9 | Urban               |
+------------+---------------------+
```

Create a second table named bird_habitats. Name the first column bird_id and the second column habitat_id. Set the column type for both of them to INT. Don't make either column an indexed column.

When you're finished creating both of these tables, execute the DESCRIBE and SHOW CREATE TABLE statements for each of the two tables. Notice what information is presented by each statement, and familiarize yourself with the structure of each table and the components of each column.

Use the RENAME TABLE statement to rename the bird_habitats to birds_habi tats (i.e., make *bird* plural). This SQL statement was covered in "Renaming a Table" on page 77.

3. Using the ALTER TABLE statement, add an index based on both bird_id and the habitat_id columns combined (this was covered in "Indexes" on page 80). Instead

of using the INDEX keyword, use UNIQUE so that duplicates are not allowed. Call the index birds_habitats.

Execute the SHOW CREATE TABLE statement for this table when you're finished altering it.

At this point, you should enter some data in the birds_habitats table. Execute these two SELECT statements, to see what data you have in the birds and habitat_codes tables:

```
SELECT bird_id, common_name
FROM birds;

SELECT * FROM habitat_codes;
```

The results of the first SELECT statement should show you a row for a loon and one for a duck, along with some other birds. Both the loon and the duck can be found in lakes, but ducks can also be found in marshes. So enter one row for the loon and two rows for the duck in the birds_habitats table. Give the value of the bird_id for the loon, and the value of habitat_id for *Lakes, Rivers, Ponds*. Then enter a row giving the bird_id for the duck, and the value again of the habitat_id for lakes. Then enter a third row giving again the bird_id for the duck and this time the habitat_id for *Marshes, Swamps*. If you created the index properly, you should not get an error about duplicate entries. When you're done, execute the SELECT statement to see all of the values of the table.

4. Using the ALTER TABLE statement, change the name of the index you created for birds_habitats in the previous exercise (this was covered near the end of this chapter). The index is now called birds_habitats. Rename it to bird_habitat.

5. Using the ALTER TABLE statement again, add three columns to the humans table in the birdwatchers database. Use a single ALTER TABLE statement to add all three of these columns. Add one column named country_id to contain two-character codes representing the country where each member is located. Add another column named membership_type with enumerated values of *basic* and *premium*. Add a third column named membership_expiration with a data type of DATE so that we can track when the membership of premium members will expire. These members will have special privileges on the site and discounts for items that we sell related to bird-watching.

## PART III

Basics of Handling Data

The main point of a database is data. In Part II, Database Structures, you learned how to create and alter tables. As interesting as that may have been, the data that will go in tables is essential. If you felt a little confused when creating and altering tables in the previous chapters, it may be because it's difficult to envision how tables and their columns will come into play with data, without having more experience adding data.

In this part, we will explore some of the fundamental ways in which data may be entered into a database and inserted into tables. This will be covered in Chapter 6, *Inserting Data*. It primarily involves the INSERT statement. The SQL statement for retrieving data from tables is the SELECT statement, which is covered extensively in Chapter 7, *Selecting Data*. You've seen both of these SQL statements in use several times in the previous chapters. However, in the next two chapters you will learn more about the various syntax and options for each of them, and you will be given plenty of practical examples of their use.

Data often needs to be changed and sometimes deleted, so in Chapter 8, *Updating and Deleting Data* we'll take a look at how to update and delete data. This chapter will help you to learn how to use the UPDATE and the DELETE statements to do these common tasks. These are important for managing data in a database.

The final chapter of this part, Chapter 9, *Joining and Subquerying Data*, is an advanced one. It's not too difficult to follow, but you should definitely not rush through it. In it, you will learn how to select data from one or more tables, and to use that data as a basis for inserting, selecting, updating, or deleting data in other tables. Thus, you should make sure that you've mastered the material in the previous chapters before skipping ahead to Chapter 9.

In each chapter of this part, there are practical examples that are used to explain the various SQL statements and related factors. You should enter those examples into your server. Even if you are reading this book from a digital version on your computer, I recommend highly that you manually type all of the SQL statements you are instructed to enter. It may seem like a little thing, but the process of typing them will aid your learning process and help you remember the syntax and the deviations of each SQL statement. When you make a mistake and type something incorrectly, you'll get an error message. Deciphering error messages is part of being a good MySQL and MariaDB developer. If you copy and paste everything as I present it to you, you will only confirm the accuracy of the book's examples, and you will learn only a little. It's easy to learn when you don't make any mistakes. It's more difficult, but you will learn more when you manually enter the SQL statements and get errors and then have to determine where you went wrong.

At the end of each chapter of this part, as with almost all of the chapters in this book, there are exercises. For the same reasons that you should enter the SQL statements in the examples throughout the chapters, you should also complete the exercises. This is not just a book to be read. It's meant to be a tool to help you to learn MySQL and MariaDB. To accomplish that, you must do more than just read the chapters: you need to participate, experiment, and research. If you make this kind of effort, you will benefit greatly from this book. This is probably the most essential part of the book, so you should fully engage with these concluding chapters.

## CHAPTER 6

Inserting Data

After you have created a database and tables, the next step is to insert data. I'm intentionally using the word *insert* because the most common and basic way to enter data into a table is with the SQL statement INSERT. It's easier to learn the language of MySQL and MariaDB, if you use the keywords to describe what you are doing. In this chapter, we will cover the INSERT statement, its different syntax, and many of its options. We'll use the tables that we created in Chapter 4 and altered in Chapter 5. We'll also look at some related statements on retrieving or selecting data, but they will be covered in greater detail in Chapter 7.

When going through this chapter, participate. When examples are given showing the INSERT statement and other SQL statements, try entering them on your server using the mysql client. At the end of the chapter are some exercises—do them. They require you to enter data in the tables that you created in Chapter 4. In doing the exercises, you may have to refer back to the examples in this chapter and in Chapter 4. This will help to reinforce what you've read. When you're done, you should feel comfortable entering data in MySQL and MariaDB.

The Syntax

The INSERT statement adds rows of data into a table. It can add a single row or multiple rows at a time. The basic syntax of this SQL statement is:

```
INSERT INTO table [(column, …)]
    VALUES (value, …), (…), …;
```

The keywords INSERT INTO are followed by the name of the table and an optional list of columns in parentheses. (Square brackets in a syntax indicate that the bracketed material is optional.) Then comes the keyword VALUES and a pair of parentheses containing a list of values for each column. There are several deviations of the syntax, but this is the basic one. Commas separate the column names within the first list, and the values within the second.

Let's go through some examples that will show a few of the simpler syntaxes for the INSERT statement. Don't try to enter these on your system. These are generic examples using INSERT to add data to nonexistent tables.

Here's a generic example of the INSERT statement with the minimum required syntax:

```
INSERT INTO books
VALUES('The Big Sleep', 'Raymond Chandler', '1934');
```

This example adds text to a table called books. This table happens to contain only three columns, so we don't bother to list the columns. But because there are three columns, we have to specify three values, which will go into the columns in the order that the columns were defined in CREATE TABLE. So in our example, *The Big Sleep* will be inserted into the first column of the table, *Raymond Chandler* will go into the second column, and *1934* will go into the third.

For columns that have a default value set, you can rely on the server to use that value and omit the column from your INSERT statement. One way to do this is by entering a value of DEFAULT or NULL, as shown in the following example:

```
INSERT INTO books
VALUES('The Thirty-Nine Steps', 'John Buchan', DEFAULT);
```

MySQL will use the default value for the third column. If the default value is NULL— the usual default value if none is specified—that's what the statement will put in the column for the row. For a column defined with AUTO_INCREMENT, the server will put the next number in the sequence for that column.

Another way to use defaults is to list just the columns into which you want to enter non-default data, like so:

```
INSERT INTO books
(author, title)
VALUES('Evelyn Waugh','Brideshead Revisited');
```

Note that this example lists just two columns within parentheses. It's also significant that the statement lists them in a different order. The list of values must match the order of the list of columns. For the third column (i.e., year) of this table, the default value will be inserted.

When you have many rows of data to insert into the same table, it can be more efficient to insert all of the rows in one SQL statement. To do this, you need to use a slightly different syntax for the INSERT statement. Just add more sets of values in parentheses, each set separated by a comma. Here's an example of this:

```
INSERT INTO books
(title, author, year)
```

```
VALUES('Visitation of Spirits','Randall Kenan','1989'),
       ('Heart of Darkness','Joseph Conrad','1902'),
       ('The Idiot','Fyodor Dostoevsky','1871');
```

This SQL statement enters three rows of data into the books table. Notice that the set of column names and the VALUES keyword appear only once. Almost all SQL statements allow only one instance of each clause (the VALUES clause in this case), although that clause may contain multiple items and lists as it does here.

Practical Examples

Let's get back to the rookery database that we created and altered in Chapters 4 and 5 for more involved examples of inserting data into tables. If you haven't created those tables yet, I recommend you go back and do that before proceeding with this chapter.

Your natural tendency when putting data into a database will be to start by adding data to the main or primary table of the database first and to worry about ancillary or reference tables later. That will work well enough, but you may be creating more work for yourself than needed. Starting with the main table is more interesting, and entering data in reference tables is more tedious. But that's the way of databases: they are tedious. It's inescapable.

Nevertheless, we don't have to create all of the tables we will need for a database before entering data; we don't need to enter data into all of the secondary tables before working on the primary tables. It will be difficult to plan ahead for all of the possible tables that will be needed. Instead, database development is generally always a work in progress. You will often add more tables, change the schema of existing tables, and shift large blocks of data from one table to another to improve performance and to make the management of the database easier. That takes some of the tediousness out of databases and makes database management interesting.

With that approach in mind, we'll enter data in some of the tables, using some simple logic to decide which table to work on first. Remember how we are categorizing birds: a bird species is a member of a bird family, and a bird family is part of a bird order. The birds table needs the family_id to join with the bird_families table, and the bird_families table needs an order_id from the bird_orders table to join with it. So, we'll add data to bird_orders first, then to bird_families, and then to birds.

Most people don't know the scientific names of birds, bird families, and bird orders. However, you can find this information on Wikipedia and sites dedicated specifically to bird-watching and ornithology. But there's no need for you to do research about birds to participate in this book. I'll provide you with the information to enter a few rows for each table, and you can download complete tables from my website (*http://mysqlresour ces.com/files*).

The Table for Bird Orders

Before entering data in the `bird_orders` table, let's remind ourselves of the structure of the table by executing the following SQL statement:

```
DESCRIBE bird_orders;
```

```
+-------------------+--------------+------+-----+---------+----------------+
| Field             | Type         | Null | Key | Default | Extra          |
+-------------------+--------------+------+-----+---------+----------------+
| order_id          | int(11)      | NO   | PRI | NULL    | auto_increment |
| scientific_name   | varchar(255) | YES  | UNI | NULL    |                |
| brief_description | varchar(255) | YES  |     | NULL    |                |
| order_image       | blob         | YES  |     | NULL    |                |
+-------------------+--------------+------+-----+---------+----------------+
```

As you can see, this table has only four columns: an identification number that will be used by the `bird_families` to join to this table, a column for the scientific name of the bird order, a column for the description of the order; and a column with an image representing each order of birds. The `order_id` column starts with 1 for the first bird order and is set automatically to the next number in sequence each time we add a bird order (unless we told MySQL otherwise).

Before entering the orders of birds, let's prime the `order_id` by initially setting the `AUTO_INCREMENT` variable to 100, so that all of the bird order identification numbers will be at least three digits in length. The numbering means nothing to MySQL; it's only a matter of personal style. To do this, we'll use the `ALTER TABLE` statement (covered in Chapter 5). Enter the following in the `mysql` client:

```
ALTER TABLE bird_orders
AUTO_INCREMENT = 100;
```

This SQL statement alters the table `bird_orders`, but only the value set on the server for the `AUTO_INCREMENT` variable for the specified table. This will set the `order_id` to 100 for the first order that we enter in our `bird_orders` table.

Let's now enter the orders of birds. We can quickly enter a bunch of orders using the multiple-row syntax for the `INSERT` statement. Because there are only 29 modern orders of birds, let's enter all of them. The following gigantic SQL statement is what I used to insert data into the `bird_orders` table; you can download the table from my site or enter the SQL statement in `mysql` (perhaps by cutting and pasting it from an ebook):

```
INSERT INTO bird_orders (scientific_name, brief_description)
VALUES('Anseriformes', "Waterfowl"),
      ('Galliformes', "Fowl"),
      ('Charadriiformes', "Gulls, Button Quails, Plovers"),
      ('Gaviiformes', "Loons"),
      ('Podicipediformes', "Grebes"),
      ('Procellariiformes', "Albatrosses, Petrels"),
      ('Sphenisciformes', "Penguins"),
```

```
('Pelecaniformes', "Pelicans"),
('Phaethontiformes', "Tropicbirds"),
('Ciconiiformes', "Storks"),
('Cathartiformes', "New-World Vultures"),
('Phoenicopteriformes', "Flamingos"),
('Falconiformes', "Falcons, Eagles, Hawks"),
('Gruiformes', "Cranes"),
('Pteroclidiformes', "Sandgrouse"),
('Columbiformes', "Doves and Pigeons"),
('Psittaciformes', "Parrots"),
('Cuculiformes', "Cuckoos and Turacos"),
('Opisthocomiformes', "Hoatzin"),
('Strigiformes', "Owls"),
('Struthioniformes', "Ostriches, Emus, Kiwis"),
('Tinamiformes', "Tinamous"),
('Caprimulgiformes', "Nightjars"),
('Apodiformes', "Swifts and Hummingbirds"),
('Coraciiformes', "Kingfishers"),
('Piciformes', "Woodpeckers"),
('Trogoniformes', "Trogons"),
('Coliiformes', "Mousebirds"),
('Passeriformes', "Passerines");
```

As large as that statement was, it inserted only two of the four columns into each row. I left out order_id, which I know will be assigned by the server with a value that starts at what I asked for, 100, and increments for each row. The default of NULL will be assigned to the order_image column, and we can insert images later if we want. However, we can't pretend the columns don't exist. If we enter an INSERT statement and don't provide data for one or more of the columns that we specify, MySQL will reject the SQL statement and return an error message like this one:

```
ERROR 1136 (21S01):
Column count doesn't match value count at row 1
```

This indicates that we didn't give the server the number of columns it was expecting.

By now, I hope you see why I created a special table dedicated to orders and made it so you have to enter each name only here, and not on every single bird in the main table. Given the bird_orders table, you can use numbers in the order_id column to represent a bird order in the bird_families table. This is one of the benefits of a reference table. Typing in numbers is easier than typing in a scientific name each time, and should reduce the frequency of typos.

The Table for Bird Families

Now that the bird_orders table is filled with data, let's next add some data to the bird_families table. First, execute the following statement:

```
DESCRIBE bird_families;
```

This SQL statement will show you the layout of the columns for the `bird_families` table. We also need to know the `order_id` for the order of the families we will enter. To start, we'll enter a row for the *Gaviidae* bird family. This happens to be the family to which the *Great Northern Loon* belongs—a bird we entered already in the `birds` table. The *Gaviidae* family is part of the *Gaviiformes* order of birds. So enter the following on your server to determine the `order_id` for that order:

```
SELECT order_id FROM bird_orders
WHERE scientific_name = 'Gaviiformes';
```

```
+----------+
| order_id |
+----------+
|      103 |
+----------+
```

Now let's enter the *Gaviidae* family in the `bird_families` table. We'll do that like so:

```
INSERT INTO bird_families
VALUES(100, 'Gaviidae',
"Loons or divers are aquatic birds found mainly in the Northern Hemisphere.",
103);
```

This adds the name and description of the bird family, *Gaviidae*, into the `bird_families` table. You may have noticed that although the `family_id` column is set to increment automatically, I put a value of 100 here. That's not necessary, but it's another way of instituting my style of starting with an identification number that has a few digits. A `family_id` of 1 for an elegant and ancient bird family like that of the loons sounds either presumptuous or lame to me. By giving it a specific value, I'll not only give an ID of 100 to *Gaviidae*, but ensure that the server will give 101 to the next family I insert.

If we try to enter the `INSERT` statement with the correct number of columns, but not in the order the server expects to receive the data based on the schema for the table, the server may accept the data. It will generate a warning message if the data given for the columns don't match the column types. For instance, suppose we had tried to add another row to the same table—this one for the bird family, *Anatidae*, the family for the Wood Duck, another bird we entered already in the `birds` table. Suppose further that we had tried to give the data in a different order from the way the columns are organized in the table. The server would accept the SQL statement and process the data as best it can, but it would not work the way we might want. The following example shows such a scenario:

```
INSERT INTO bird_families
VALUES('Anatidae', "This family includes ducks, geese and swans.", NULL, 103);
Query OK, 1 row affected, 1 warning (0.05 sec)
```

Notice that in this SQL statement we put the family's name first, then the description, then NULL for the `family_id`, and 103 for the `order_id`. MySQL is expecting the first column to be a number or `DEFAULT` or `NULL`. Instead, we gave it text. Notice that the status line returned by `mysql` after the INSERT statement says, *Query OK, 1 row affected, 1 warning*. That means that one row was added, but a warning message was generated, although it wasn't displayed. We'll use the SHOW WARNINGS statement like so to see the warning message:

```
SHOW WARNINGS \G

*************************** 1. row ***************************
  Level: Warning
   Code: 1366
Message: Incorrect integer value: 'Anatidae' for column 'family_id' at row 1
1 row in set (0.15 sec)
```

Here we can see the warning message: the server was expecting an integer value, but received text for the column, `family_id`. Let's run the SELECT statement to see what we have now in the `bird_families` table:

```
SELECT * FROM bird_families \G

*************************** 1. row ***************************
      family_id: 100
 scientific_name: Gaviidae
brief_description: Loons or divers are aquatic birds
                  found mainly in the Northern Hemisphere.
       order_id: 103
*************************** 2. row ***************************
      family_id: 101
 scientific_name: This family includes ducks, geese and swans.
brief_description: NULL
       order_id: 103
```

The first row is fine; we entered it correctly, before. But because MySQL didn't receive a good value for the `family_id` column for the row we just entered, it ignored what we gave it and automatically set the column to 101—the default value based on AUTO_IN CREMENT. It took the description text that was intended for `brief_description` column and put that in the `scientific_name` column. It put the NULL we meant for the `family_id` column and put it in the `brief_description` column. This row needs to be fixed or deleted. Let's delete it and try again. We'll use the DELETE statement like this:

```
DELETE FROM bird_families
WHERE family_id = 101;
```

This will delete only one row: the one where the `family_id` equals 101. Be careful with the DELETE statement. There's no UNDO statement, per se, when working with the data like this. If you don't include the WHERE clause, you will delete all of the data in the table. For this table, which has only two rows of data, it's not a problem to re-enter the data. But on a server with thousands of rows of data, you could lose plenty of data—permanently, if you don't have a backup copy. Even if you do have a backup of the data, you're not going to be able to restore the data quickly or easily. So be careful with the DELETE statement and always use a WHERE clause that limits greatly the data that's to be deleted.

Let's re-enter the data for the duck family, *Anatidae*, but this time we'll try a different syntax for the INSERT statement so that we don't have to give data for all of the columns and so that we can give data in a different order from how it's structured in the table:

```
INSERT INTO bird_families
(scientific_name, order_id, brief_description)
VALUES('Anatidae', 103, "This family includes ducks, geese and swans.");
```

To let us give only three columns in this SQL statement, and in a different order, we put the names of the columns in parentheses before the set of values. Listing the names of the columns is optional, provided data is in the correct format for all of the columns and in order. Because we are not doing that with this SQL statement, we had to list the columns for which we are giving data, matching the order that the data is given in the VALUES clause in the set of values and in parentheses. Basically, we're telling the server what each value represents; we're mapping the data to the correct columns in the table. Again, for the columns that we don't provide data or don't name in the SQL statement, the server will use the default values. Let's see what we have now for data in the bird_families table:

```
SELECT * FROM bird_families \G

*************************** 1. row ***************************
       family_id: 100
 scientific_name: Gaviidae
brief_description: Loons or divers are aquatic birds
                  found mainly in the Northern Hemisphere.
        order_id: 103
*************************** 2. row ***************************
       family_id: 102
 scientific_name: Anatidae
brief_description: This family includes ducks, geese and swans.
        order_id: 103
```

That's better. Notice that the server put the family name, *Anatidae*, in the scientif ic_name column, per the mapping instructions stipulated in the INSERT statement. It also assigned a number to the family_id column. Because the family_id for the previous row was set to 101, even though we deleted it, the server remembers elsewhere in MySQL that the count is now at 101. So it incremented that number by 1 to set this new row to 102. You could change the value of this row and reset the counter (i.e., the AUTO_INCREMENT variable for the column of the table), but it's generally not important.

Let's prepare now to enter some more bird families. We'll keep the data simple this time. We'll give only the scientific name and the order identification number. To do that, we need to know the order_id of each order. We'll execute this SQL statement to get the data we need:

```
SELECT order_id, scientific_name FROM bird_orders;
```

```
+----------+---------------------+
| order_id | scientific_name     |
+----------+---------------------+
|      100 | Anseriformes        |
|      101 | Galliformes         |
|      102 | Charadriiformes     |
|      103 | Gaviiformes         |
|      104 | Podicipediformes    |
|      105 | Procellariiformes   |
|      106 | Sphenisciformes     |
|      107 | Pelecaniformes      |
|      108 | Phaethontiformes    |
|      109 | Ciconiiformes       |
|      110 | Cathartiformes      |
|      111 | Phoenicopteriformes |
|      112 | Falconiformes       |
|      113 | Gruiformes          |
|      114 | Pteroclidiformes    |
|      115 | Columbiformes       |
|      116 | Psittaciformes      |
|      117 | Cuculiformes        |
|      118 | Opisthocomiformes   |
|      119 | Strigiformes        |
|      120 | Struthioniformes    |
|      121 | Tinamiformes        |
|      122 | Caprimulgiformes    |
|      123 | Apodiformes         |
|      124 | Coraciiformes       |
|      125 | Piciformes          |
|      126 | Trogoniformes       |
|      127 | Coliiformes         |
|      128 | Passeriformes       |
+----------+---------------------+
```

Now let's enter one hefty INSERT statement to insert a bunch of bird families into the bird_families table. We just list each set of data within its own parentheses, separated by commas. After consulting our bird-watching guides, we determine which families belong to which orders and then enter this in the mysql client:

```
INSERT INTO bird_families
(scientific_name, order_id)
VALUES('Charadriidae', 109),
      ('Laridae', 102),
      ('Sternidae', 102),
      ('Caprimulgidae', 122),
      ('Sittidae', 128),
      ('Picidae', 125),
      ('Accipitridae', 112),
      ('Tyrannidae', 128),
```

```
('Formicariidae', 128),
('Laniidae', 128);
```

This statement enters 10 rows of data in one batch. Notice that we didn't have to list the names of the columns for each row. Notice also that we didn't mention the family_id column in this SQL statement. The server will assign automatically the next number in the column's sequence for that field. And we didn't give the statement any text for the brief_description column. We can enter that later if we want.

If you want a heftier bird_family table with more rows and the brief descriptions, you can download it later from my site. This is enough data for now. Let's execute the SELECT statement to get the family_id numbers. We'll need them when we enter birds in the birds table:

```
SELECT family_id, scientific_name
FROM bird_families
ORDER BY scientific_name;
```

```
+-----------+-----------------+
| family_id | scientific_name |
+-----------+-----------------+
|       109 | Accipitridae    |
|       102 | Anatidae        |
|       106 | Caprimulgidae   |
|       103 | Charadriidae    |
|       111 | Formicariidae   |
|       100 | Gaviidae        |
|       112 | Laniidae        |
|       104 | Laridae         |
|       108 | Picidae         |
|       107 | Sittidae        |
|       105 | Sternidae       |
|       110 | Tyrannidae      |
+-----------+-----------------+
```

I added an extra tweak to the previous SELECT statement: an ORDER BY clause, ensuring that the results would be ordered alphabetically by the scientific name of the order. We'll cover the ORDER BY clause in more depth in Chapter 7.

We're now ready to enter data in the birds table. The table already has a Killdeer, a small shore bird that is part of the *Charadriidae* family. Let's prepare to enter a few more shore birds from the same family as the Killdeer. Looking at the preceding results, we can determine that the family_id is 103, because the Killdeer is in the *Charadriidae* family. Incidentally, the values for the family_id column might be different on your server.

Now that we have the family_id for shore birds, let's look at the columns in the birds table and decide which ones we'll set. To do that, let's use the SHOW COLUMNS statement like this:

```
SHOW COLUMNS FROM birds;
```

```
+------------------------+--------------+------+-----+-------+----------------+
| Field                  | Type         | Null | Key |Default| Extra          |
+------------------------+--------------+------+-----+-------+----------------+
| bird_id                | int(11)      | NO   | PRI | NULL  | auto_increment |
| scientific_name        | varchar(100) | YES  | UNI | NULL  |                |
| common_name            | varchar(255) | YES  |     | NULL  |                |
| family_id              | int(11)      | YES  |     | NULL  |                |
| conservation_status_id | int(11)      | YES  |     | NULL  |                |
| wing_id                | char(2)      | YES  |     | NULL  |                |
| body_id                | char(2)      | YES  |     | NULL  |                |
| bill_id                | char(2)      | YES  |     | NULL  |                |
| description            | text         | YES  |     | NULL  |                |
+------------------------+--------------+------+-----+-------+----------------+
```

The results are the same as for the DESCRIBE statement. However, with SHOW COLUMNS, you can retrieve a list of columns based on a pattern. For instance, suppose you just want a list of reference columns—columns that we labeled with the ending, _id. You could enter this:

```
SHOW COLUMNS FROM birds LIKE '%id';
```

```
+------------------------+---------+------+-----+---------+----------------+
| Field                  | Type    | Null | Key | Default | Extra          |
+------------------------+---------+------+-----+---------+----------------+
| bird_id                | int(11) | NO   | PRI | NULL    | auto_increment |
| family_id              | int(11) | YES  |     | NULL    |                |
| conservation_status_id | int(11) | YES  |     | NULL    |                |
| wing_id                | char(2) | YES  |     | NULL    |                |
| body_id                | char(2) | YES  |     | NULL    |                |
| bill_id                | char(2) | YES  |     | NULL    |                |
+------------------------+---------+------+-----+---------+----------------+
```

We used the percent sign (%) as a wildcard—the asterisks won't work here—to specify the pattern of any text that starts with any characters but ends with _id. For a large table, being able to refine the results like this might be useful. When naming your columns, keep in mind that you can search easily based on a naming pattern (e.g., %_id). Incidentally, if you add the FULL flag to this SQL statement (e.g., SHOW FULL COLUMNS FROM birds;), you can get more information on each column. Try that on your system to see the results.

The Table for Birds

That was interesting, but let's get back to data entry—the focus of this chapter. Now that we have been reminded of the columns in the birds table, let's enter data on some of shore birds. Enter the following in mysql:

```
INSERT INTO birds
(common_name, scientific_name, family_id)
VALUES('Mountain Plover', 'Charadrius montanus', 103);
```

This adds a record for the *Mountain Plover*. Notice that I mixed up the order of the columns, but it still works because the order of the values agrees with the order of the columns. We indicate that the bird is in the family of *Charadriidae* by giving a value of 103 for the `family_id`. There are more columns that need data, but we'll worry about that later. Let's now enter a few more shore birds, using the multiple-row syntax for the INSERT statement:

```
INSERT INTO birds
(common_name, scientific_name, family_id)
VALUES('Snowy Plover', 'Charadrius alexandrinus', 103),
('Black-bellied Plover', 'Pluvialis squatarola', 103),
('Pacific Golden Plover', 'Pluvialis fulva', 103);
```

In this example, we've added three shore birds in one statement, all of the same family of birds. This is the same method that we used earlier to enter several bird families in the `bird_families` table and several bird orders in the `bird_orders` table. Notice that the number for the `family_id` is not enclosed here within quotes. That's because the column holds integers, using the INT data type. Therefore, we can pass exposed numbers like this. If we put them in quotes, MySQL treats them first like characters, but then analyzes them and realizes that they are numbers and stores them as numbers. That's the long explanation. The short explanation is that it doesn't usually matter whether numbers are in quotes or not.

Now that we have entered data for a few more birds, let's connect a few of our tables together and retrieve data from them. We'll use a SELECT statement, but we'll give a list of the tables to merge the data in the results set. This is much more complicated than any of the previous SELECT statements, but I want you to see the point of creating different tables, especially the reference tables we have created. Try entering the following SQL statement on your server:

```
SELECT common_name AS 'Bird',
       birds.scientific_name AS 'Scientific Name',
       bird_families.scientific_name AS 'Family',
       bird_orders.scientific_name AS 'Order'
FROM birds,
     bird_families,
     bird_orders
WHERE birds.family_id = bird_families.family_id
AND bird_families.order_id = bird_orders.order_id;
```

```
+----------------------+------------------------+--------------+---------------+
| Bird                 | Scientific Name        | Family       | Orders        |
+----------------------+------------------------+--------------+---------------+
| Mountain Plover      | Charadrius montanus    | Charadriidae | Ciconiiformes |
| Snowy Plover         | Charadrius alex...     | Charadriidae | Ciconiiformes |
```

```
| Black-bellied Plover  | Pluvialis squatarola | Charadriidae | Ciconiiformes |
| Pacific Golden Plover | Pluvialis fulva      | Charadriidae | Ciconiiformes |
+----------------------+---------------------+--------------+---------------+
```

In this SELECT statement, we are connecting together three tables. Before looking at the columns selected, let's look at the FROM clause. Notice that all three tables are listed, separated by commas. To assist you in making sense of this statement, I've added some indenting. The table names don't need to be on separate lines, as I have laid them out.

MySQL strings these three tables together based on the WHERE clause. First, we're telling MySQL to join the birds table to the bird_families table where the family_id from both tables equal or match. Using AND, we then give another condition in the WHERE clause. We tell MySQL to join the bird_families table to the bird_orders table where the order_id from both tables are equal.

That may seem pretty complicated, but if you had a sheet of paper in front of you showing thousands of birds, and a sheet of paper containing a list of bird families, and another sheet with a list of orders of birds, and you wanted to type on your screen a list of bird with their names, along with the family and order to which each belonged, you would do the same thing with your fingers, pointing from keywords on one sheet to the keyword on the other. It's really intuitive when you think about it.

Let's look now at the columns we have selected. We are selecting the common_name and scientific_name columns from the birds table. Again, I've added indenting and put these columns on separate lines for clarity. Because all three tables have columns named scientific_name, we must include the table name for each column (e.g., birds.sci entific_name) to eliminate ambiguity. I've added also an AS clause to each column selected to give the results table nicer column headings. The AS clause has nothing to do with the tables on the server; it affects only what you see in your output. So you can choose the column headings in the results through the string you put after the AS keyword.

Let's take a moment to consider the results. Although we entered the scientific name of each family and order referenced here only once, MySQL can pull them together easily by way of the family_id and order_id columns in the tables. That's economical and very cool.

As I said before, the SQL statement I've just shown is much more complicated than anything we've looked at before. Don't worry about taking in too much of it, though. We'll cover this kind of SQL statement in Chapter 7. For now, just know that this is the point of what we're doing. The kind of inquiries we can make of data this way is so much better than one big table with columns for everything. For each shore bird, we had to enter only 103 for the family_id column and didn't have to type the scientific name for the family, or enter the scientific name of the order for each bird. We don't have to worry so much about typos. This leverages your time and data efficiently.

Other Possibilities

A few times in this chapter, I mentioned that the INSERT statement offers extra options. In this section, we'll cover some of them. You may not use these often in the beginning, but you should know about them.

Inserting Emphatically

Besides the basic syntax of the INSERT statement, there is a more emphatic syntax that involves mapping individual columns to data given. Here's an example in which information on another bird family is inserted into the bird_families table; enter it in mysql to see how you like the visceral feel of this syntax:

```
INSERT INTO bird_families
SET scientific_name = 'Rallidae',
order_id = 113;
```

This syntax is somewhat awkward. However, there's less likelihood of making a mistake with this syntax, or at least it's less likely that you will enter the column names or the data in the wrong order, or not give enough columns of data. Because of its rigidity, most people don't normally use this syntax. But the precision it offers makes it a preferred syntax for some people writing automated scripts. It's primarily popular because the syntax calls for naming the column and assigning a value immediately afterwards, in a key/value pair format found in many programming languages. This makes it easier to visually troubleshoot a programming script. Second, if the name of a column has been changed or deleted since the creation of a script using this syntax, the statement will be rejected by the server and data won't be entered into the wrong columns. But it doesn't add any functionality to the standard syntax that we've used throughout the chapter, as long as you list the columns explicitly in the standard syntax. Plus, you can insert only one row at a time with this syntax

Inserting Data from Another Table

INSERT can be combined with a SELECT statement (we covered this briefly in Chapter 5). Let's look at an example of how it might be used. Before you do, I'll warn you that the examples in this section get complicated. You're not expected to do the examples in this section; just read along.

Earlier in this chapter, we entered data for a few bird families—13 so far. You have the option of downloading the table filled with data from my site, but I had to get the data elsewhere (or endure manually entering 228 rows of data on bird families). So I went to Cornell University's website. The Cornell Lab of Ornithology teaches ornithology and is a leading authority on the subject. On their site, I found a table of data that's publicly available. I loaded the table into the rookery database on my server and named it `cornell_birds_families_orders`. Here's how the table is structured and how the data looks:

```
DESCRIBE cornell_birds_families_orders;

+--------------+--------------+------+-----+---------+----------------+
| Field        | Type         | Null | Key | Default | Extra          |
+--------------+--------------+------+-----+---------+----------------+
| fid          | int(11)      | NO   | PRI | NULL    | auto_increment |
| bird_family  | varchar(255) | YES  |     | NULL    |                |
| examples     | varchar(255) | YES  |     | NULL    |                |
| bird_order   | varchar(255) | YES  |     | NULL    |                |
+--------------+--------------+------+-----+---------+----------------+

SELECT * FROM cornell_birds_families_orders
LIMIT 1;

+-----+---------------+----------+------------------+
| fid | bird_family   | examples | bird_order       |
+-----+---------------+----------+------------------+
|   1 | Struthionidae | Ostrich  | Struthioniformes |
+-----+---------------+----------+------------------+
```

This is useful. I can take the family names, use the *examples* for the brief description, and use them both to finish the data in the `bird_families` table. I don't need their identification number (i.e., `fid`) for each bird family—I'll use my own. What I need is a way to match the value of the `bird_order` column in this table to the `scientific_name` in the `bird_orders` table so that I can put the correct `order_id` in the `bird_families` table.

There are a couple of ways I could do that. For now, I'll add another column to my `bird_families` table to take in the `bird_order` column from this table from Cornell. I'll use the `ALTER TABLE` statement, as described in Chapter 5, and enter the following on my server:

```
ALTER TABLE bird_families
ADD COLUMN cornell_bird_order VARCHAR(255);
```

With this change, I can now execute the following SQL statement to copy the data from the Cornell table to my table containing data on bird families:

```
INSERT IGNORE INTO bird_families
(scientific_name, brief_description, cornell_bird_order)
SELECT bird_family, examples, bird_order
FROM cornell_birds_families_orders;
```

Look closely at this syntax. It may be useful to you one day. It starts with the normal syntax of the `INSERT` statement, but where we would put the `VALUES` clause, we instead put a complete `SELECT` statement. The syntax of the `SELECT` portion is the same as we've used so far in other examples in this book. It's simple, but neat and very powerful.

Conceptually, you can think of the embedded SELECT statement creating multiple rows, each containing values in the order you specify in the SELECT. These values work just like a VALUES clause, feeding values into the parent INSERT statement and filling the columns I carefully specify in the right order.

One thing is different at the start of the previous INSERT statement. I've added the IGNORE option. I used this because the bird_families table already had data in it. Because the scientific_name column is set to UNIQUE, it does not permit duplicate values. If a multiple-row INSERT statement like this encounters any errors, it will fail and return an error message. The IGNORE flag instructs the server to ignore any errors it encounters while processing the SQL statement, and to insert the rows that may be inserted without problems. Instead of failing and showing an error message, warning messages are stored on the server for you to look at later. When the server is finished, if you want, you can run the SHOW WARNINGS statement to see which rows of data weren't inserted into the table. This is a graceful solution if you just want the server to process the rows that aren't duplicates and to ignore the duplicates.

Now that the data has been inserted, I'll run the following SQL statement from mysql to look at the last row in the table—the first rows contain the data I entered previously:

```
SELECT * FROM bird_families
ORDER BY family_id DESC LIMIT 1;
```

```
+-----------+----------------+-----------------+----------+-----------------+
| family_id | scientific_name |brief_description| order_id | cornell_bird_order|
+-----------+----------------+-----------------+----------+-----------------+
|       330 | Viduidae       | Indigobirds     |     NULL | Passeriformes   |
+-----------+----------------+-----------------+----------+-----------------+
```

In the SELECT statement here, I added an ORDER BY clause to order the results set by the value of the family_id. The DESC after it indicates that the rows should by ordered in descending order based on the value of family_id. The LIMIT clause tells MySQL to limit the results to only one row. Looking at this one row of data, we can see that the INSERT INTO...SELECT statement worked well.

A Digression: Setting the Right ID

Our INSERT from the previous section helped me fill my table with data I took from a free database, but it's still missing data: the bird order for each bird. I defined my own orders of birds in the bird_orders table, giving each order an arbitrary order_id. However, the Cornell data had nothing to do with the numbers assigned when I created my bird_orders table. So now I need to set the value of the order_id column to the right order_id from the bird_orders table—and to figure out that value, I have to find the order in the cornell_bird_order column.

This is a bit complicated, but I am showing my process here to illustrate the power of relational databases. Basically, I'll join my own bird_orders table to the data I got from

Cornell. I loaded the bird orders from Cornell into a `cornell_bird_order` field. I have the exact same orders in the `scientific_name` field of my `bird_orders` table. But I don't want to use the scientific name itself when I label each individual bird: instead, I want a number (an `order_id`) to assign to that bird.

I need to set the value of the `order_id` column to the right `order_id` from the `bird_orders` table. To figure out that value, I have to find the order in the `cornell_bird_order` column.

For that, I'll use the UPDATE statement. Before I change any data with UPDATE, though, I'll construct a SELECT statement for testing. I want to make sure my orders properly match up with Cornell's. So I'll enter this on my server:

```
SELECT DISTINCT bird_orders.order_id,
cornell_bird_order AS "Cornell's Order",
bird_orders.scientific_name AS 'My Order'
FROM bird_families, bird_orders
WHERE bird_families.order_id IS NULL
AND cornell_bird_order = bird_orders.scientific_name
LIMIT 5;
```

```
+----------+------------------+------------------+
| order_id | Cornell's Order  | My Order         |
+----------+------------------+------------------+
|      120 | Struthioniformes | Struthioniformes |
|      121 | Tinamiformes     | Tinamiformes     |
|      100 | Anseriformes     | Anseriformes     |
|      101 | Galliformes      | Galliformes      |
|      104 | Podicipediformes | Podicipediformes |
+----------+------------------+------------------+
```

We're testing a WHERE clause here that we'll use later when updating our `bird_families` table. It's worth looking at what a WHERE clause give us before we put all our trust in it and use it in an UPDATE statement.

This WHERE clause contains two conditions. First, it changes the `bird_families` table only where the `order_id` hasn't been set yet. That's kind of a sanity check. If I already set the `order_id` field, there is no reason to change it.

After the AND comes the second condition, which is more important. I want to find the row in my `bird_orders` table that has the right scientific name, the scientific name assigned by Cornell. So I check where `cornell_bird_order` equals the `scientific_name` in the `bird_orders` table.

This shows how, if you want to change data with INSERT…SELECT, REPLACE, or UPDATE, you can test your WHERE clause first with a SELECT statement. If this statement returns the rows you want and the data looks good, you can then use the same WHERE clause with one of the other SQL statements to change data.

The SELECT statement just shown is similar to the one we executed in the previous section of this chapter when we queried the birds, bird_families, and bird_orders tables in the same SQL statement. There is, however, an extra option added to this statement: the DISTINCT option. This selects only rows in which all of the columns are distinct. Otherwise, because more than five bird families are members of the *Struthioniformes* order, and I limited the results to five rows (i.e., LIMIT 5), we would see the first row repeated five times. Adding the DISTINCT flag returns five distinct permutations and is thereby more reassuring that the WHERE clause is correct.

Because the results look good, I'll use the UPDATE statement to update the data in the bird_families table. With this statement, you can change or update rows of data. The basic syntax is to name the table you want to update and use the SET clause to set the value of each column. This is like the syntax for the SELECT statement in "Inserting Emphatically" on page 104. Use the WHERE clause you tested to tell MySQL which rows to change:

```
UPDATE bird_families, bird_orders
SET bird_families.order_id = bird_orders.order_id
WHERE bird_families.order_id IS NULL
AND cornell_bird_order = bird_orders.scientific_name;
```

This is fairly complicated, so let's reiterate what's happening here: the UPDATE statement tells MySQL to set the order_id in the bird_families table to the value of the order_id of the corresponding row in the bird_orders table—but thanks to the AND clause, I do the update only where the cornell_bird_order equals the scientific_name in the bird_orders table.

That's plenty to take in, I know. We'll cover this statement in more detail in Chapter 8.

Let's see the results now. We'll execute the same SQL statement we did earlier, but limit it to four rows this time to see a bit more:

```
SELECT * FROM bird_families
ORDER BY family_id DESC LIMIT 4;
```

```
+-----------+----------------+----------------------+----------+
| family_id | scientific_name | brief_description    | order_id |
+-----------+----------------+----------------------+----------+
|       330 | Viduidae       | Indigobirds          |      128 |
|       329 | Estrildidae    | Waxbills and Allies  |      128 |
|       328 | Ploceidae      | Weavers and Allies   |      128 |
|       327 | Passeridae     | Old World Sparrows   |      128 |
+-----------+----------------+----------------------+----------+
```

That seems to have worked. The order_id column for the *Viduidae* bird family now has a value other than NULL. Let's check the bird_orders to see whether that's the correct value:

```
SELECT * FROM bird_orders
WHERE order_id = 128;
```

```
+----------+-----------------+-------------------+-------------+
| order_id | scientific_name | brief_description | order_image |
+----------+-----------------+-------------------+-------------+
|      128 | Passeriformes   | Passerines        | NULL        |
+----------+-----------------+-------------------+-------------+
```

That's correct. The order_id of 128 is for *Passeriformes*, which is what the Cornell table said is the order of the *Viduidae* family. Let's see whether any rows in bird_families are missing the order_id:

```
SELECT family_id, scientific_name, brief_description
FROM bird_families
WHERE order_id IS NULL;
```

```
+-----------+------------------+----------------------+
| family_id | scientific_name  | brief_description    |
+-----------+------------------+----------------------+
|       136 | Fregatidae       | Frigatebirds         |
|       137 | Sulidae          | Boobies and Gannets  |
|       138 | Phalacrocoracidae | Cormorants and Shags |
|       139 | Anhingidae       | Anhingas             |
|       145 | Cathartidae      | New World Vultures   |
|       146 | Sagittariidae    | Secretary-bird       |
|       147 | Pandionidae      | Osprey               |
|       148 | Otididae         | Bustards             |
|       149 | Mesitornithidae  | Mesites              |
|       150 | Rhynochetidae    | Kagu                 |
|       151 | Eurypygidae      | Sunbittern           |
|       172 | Pteroclidae      | Sandgrouse           |
|       199 | Bucconidae       | Puffbirds            |
|       200 | Galbulidae       | Jacamars             |
|       207 | Cariamidae       | Seriemas             |
+-----------+------------------+----------------------+
```

For some reason, the data didn't match the 15 rows in the bird_orders table. I had to determine why these didn't match. Let's look at how I resolved a couple of them.

I looked up the name of the order to which the Osprey belongs and found that there are two possible names: *Accipitriformes* and *Falconiformes*. Cornell used the *Accipitriformes*, whereas my bird_orders table has the *Falconiformes* (i.e., order_id 112). I'll use that one and update the bird_families table:

```
UPDATE bird_families
SET order_id = 112
WHERE cornell_bird_order = 'Accipitriformes';
```

I could have used the family_id in the WHERE clause, but by doing what I did here, I discovered two more bird families that are in the *Accipitriformes* order and updated all three in one SQL statement. Digging some more, I found that four of these bird families are part of a new order called *Suliformes*. So I added that order to the `bird_orders` table and then updated the rows for those families in the `bird_families` table. This method of clean-up is common when creating a database or when importing large amounts of data from another database.

Next, I'll do some clean-up by dropping the extra column I added (`cornell_bird_or der`) to the `bird_families` table and the `cornell_birds_families_orders` table:

```
ALTER TABLE bird_families
DROP COLUMN cornell_bird_order;

DROP TABLE cornell_birds_families_orders;
```

That set of examples was complicated, so don't be discouraged if you were confused by it. In time, you will be constructing more complex SQL statements on your own. In fact, you will come to look at what I did here and realize that I could have performed the same tasks in fewer steps. For now, I wanted to show you the power of MySQL and MariaDB, as well as their communities. I mention the communities because in the MySQL and MariaDB communities, you can sometimes find tables with data like this that you can download for free and then manipulate for your own use, thus saving you plenty of work and taking some of the ever pesky tediousness out of database management. There are other methods for bulk importing data, even when it's not in a MySQL table. They're covered in Chapter 15.

Replacing Data

When you're adding massive amounts of data to an existing table and you're using the multiple-row syntax, you could have a problem if one of the fields you're importing gets inserted into a key field in the table, as in the preceding example with the `bird_fami lies` table. In that example, the `scientific_name` column was a key field, set to UNIQUE so that there is only one entry in the `birds_families` table for each bird family. When MySQL finds a duplicate key value while running an INSERT statement, an error is generated and the entire SQL statement will be rejected. Nothing will be inserted into the table.

You would then have to edit the INSERT statement, which might be lengthy, to remove the duplicate entry and run the statement again. If there are many duplicates, you'd have to run the SQL statement many times, watch for error messages, and remove duplicates until it's successful. We avoided this problem in the previous example by using the IGNORE option with the INSERT statement. It tells MySQL to ignore the errors, not insert the rows that are duplicates, and insert the ones that aren't.

There may be times, though, when you don't want to ignore the duplicate rows, but replace duplicate rows in the table with the new data. For instance, in the UPDATE example in the previous section, we have newer and better information, so we prefer to overwrite duplicate rows. In situations such as this, instead of using INSERT, you could use the

REPLACE statement. With it, new rows of data will be inserted as they would with an INSERT statement. Any rows with the same key value (e.g., same `scientific_name` code) will replace the matching row already in the table. This can be very useful, and not difficult. Let's look at an example:

```
REPLACE INTO bird_families
(scientific_name, brief_description, order_id)
VALUES('Viduidae', 'Indigobirds & Whydahs', 128),
('Estrildidae', 'Waxbills, Weaver Finches, & Allies', 128),
('Ploceidae', 'Weavers, Malimbe, & Bishops', 128);

Query OK, 6 rows affected (0.39 sec)
Records: 3  Duplicates: 3  Warnings: 0
```

Notice that the syntax is the same as an INSERT statement. The options all have the same effect as well. Also, multiple rows may be inserted, but there's no need for the IGNORE option because duplicates are just overwritten.

Actually, when a row is replaced using the REPLACE statement, it's first deleted completely and the new row is then inserted. For any columns without values, the default values for the columns will be used. None of the previous values are kept. So be careful that you don't replace a row that contains some data that you want. When you update a row with REPLACE, you can't choose to replace some columns and leave the others unchanged. REPLACE replaces the whole row, unlike UPDATE. To change just specific columns, use the UPDATE statement.

There are a couple of things that you should notice about this REPLACE statement and the content we entered. You can see something unusual in the results message. It says that six rows were affected by this SQL statement: three new records and three duplicates. The value of six for the number of rows affected may seem strange. What happened is that because three rows had the same value for the `scientific_name`, they were deleted. And then three new rows were added with the new values, the replacements. That gives a total of six affected rows: three deleted and three added.

The results contain no warnings, so all went well as far as MySQL knows. Let's look at the data for one of the bird families we changed in the `bird_families` table, the *Viduidae* family:

```
SELECT * FROM bird_families
WHERE scientific_name = 'Viduidae' \G

*************************** 1. row ***************************
        family_id: 331
   scientific_name: Viduidae
brief_description: Indigobirds & Whydahs
         order_id: 128
```

It may not be apparent, but everything was replaced. This row has a new value in the `family_id` column. If you look earlier in this chapter at the row for this family, you'll see that the `family_id` was 330. Because it was the last row in the table, when a new row was created for its replacement, 331 was assigned to it. The `brief_description` has the new value; it said before only *Indigobirds*.

The `REPLACE` statement is useful for replacing all of the data for a duplicate row and inserting new rows of data for data that isn't already in a given table. It has the potential problem of replacing all of the columns when you might want to replace only some of them. Also, in the previous examples, if the `scientific_name` column was not `UNIQUE` or otherwise a key column, new rows would be created for the three families we tried to replace with the `REPLACE` statement.

Priorities When Inserting Data

On a busy MySQL or MariaDB server, there will be times when many people will access the server at the same time. There will be times when SQL statements are entered simultaneously from different sources, perhaps many at the same instant. The server must decide which statements to process first.

Statements that change data (`INSERT`, `UPDATE`, and `DELETE`) take priority over read statements (`SELECT` statements). Someone who is adding data to the server seems to be more important than someone reading data. One concern is that the one inserting data might lose the connection and lose its opportunity. The user retrieving data, in contrast, can generally wait. For example, on a website that uses MySQL to store purchases, a customer entering an order will take priority over another customer who is just browsing through the list of products.

When the server is executing an `INSERT` statement for a client, it locks the related tables for exclusive access and forces other clients to wait until it's finished. This isn't the case with InnoDB: it locks the rows, rather than the entire table. On a busy MySQL server that has many simultaneous requests for data, locking a table could cause users to experience delays, especially when someone is entering many rows of data by using the multiple-row syntax of the `INSERT` statement.

Rather than accept the default priorities in MySQL, you can instead set the priority for an `INSERT`. You can decide which SQL statements need to be entered as soon as possible and which can wait. To specify you preferences, the `INSERT` statement offers priority options. Enter them between the `INSERT` keyword and the `INTO` keyword. There are three of them: `LOW_PRIORITY`, `DELAYED`, and `HIGH_PRIORITY`. Let's look at each of them.

Lowering the priority of an insert

For an example of `LOW_PRIORITY`, suppose that we've just received a file from a large bird-watcher group with thousands of rows of data related to bird sightings. The table is a MySQL dump file, a simple text file containing the necessary SQL statements to insert the data into a table in MySQL. We open the dump file with a text editor and see that it contains one huge INSERT statement that will insert all of the bird sightings (i.e., bird_sightings) with one SQL statement into a table on our server. We haven't created a table like this yet, but you can imagine what it might contain.

When the INSERT statement in the dump file from the large bird-watcher group is run, it might tie up our server for quite a while. If there are users who are in the middle of retrieving data from the bird_sightings table, we might prefer that those processes finish before starting our huge INSERT statement. The LOW_PRIORITY option instructs MySQL to enter the rows when it's finished with whatever else it's doing. Here's an abbreviated version of how we would do that:

```
INSERT LOW_PRIORITY INTO bird_sightings
...
```

Of course, a real INSERT will have all the column and value listings you want where I left the ellipsis (three dots).

The LOW_PRIORITY flag puts the INSERT statement in a queue, waiting for all of the current and pending requests to be completed before it's performed. If new requests are made while a low priority statement is waiting, they are put ahead of it in the queue. MySQL does not begin to execute a low priority statement until there are no other requests waiting.

The table is locked and any other requests for data from the table that come in after the INSERT statement starts must wait until it's completed. MySQL locks the table once a low priority statement has begun so it will prevent simultaneous insertions from other clients. The server doesn't stop in the middle of an insert to allow for other changes just because of the LOW_PRIORITY setting. Incidentally, LOW_PRIORITY and HIGH_PRIORITY aren't supported by InnoDB tables. It's unnecessary because it doesn't lock the table, but locks the relevant rows.

One potential inconvenience with an INSERT LOW_PRIORITY statement is that your mysql client will be tied up waiting for the statement to be completed successfully by the server. So if you're inserting data into a busy server with a low priority setting using the mysql client, your client could be locked up for minutes, maybe even hours, depending on how busy the server is at the time. Using LOW_PRIORITY causes your client to wait until the server starts the insert, and then the client is locked, as well as the related tables on the server are locked.

Delaying an INSERT

As an alternative, you can use the DELAYED option instead of the LOW_PRIORITY option. This is deprecated in 5.6.6 of MySQL. However, if you're using an older version, this is how you would use it:

```
INSERT DELAYED INTO bird_sightings
...
```

This is very similar to LOW_PRIORITY; MySQL will take the request as a low-priority one and put it on its list of tasks to perform when it has a break. The difference and advantage is that it will release the mysql client immediately so that the client can go on to enter other SQL statements or even exit. Another advantage of this method is that multiple INSERT DELAYED requests are batched together for block insertion when there is a gap in server traffic, making the process potentially faster than INSERT LOW_PRIORITY.

The drawback to this choice is that the client is never informed whether the delayed insertion is actually made. The client gets back error messages when the statement is entered—the statement has to be valid before it will be queued—but it's not told of problems that occur after the SQL statement is accepted by the server.

This brings up another drawback: delayed insertions are stored in the server's memory. So if the MySQL daemon dies or is manually killed, the inserts are lost and the client is not notified of the failure. You'll have to manually check the database or the server's logs to determine whether the inserts failed. As a result, the DELAYED option is not always a good alternative.

Raising the priority of an INSERT

The third priority option for the INSERT statement is HIGH_PRIORITY. INSERT statements by default are usually given higher priority over read-only SQL statements so there would seem to be no need for this option. However, the default of giving write statements priority over read statements (e.g., INSERT over SELECT) can be removed. "Post-Installation" on page 24 touched on the configuration of MySQL and MariaDB. One of the server options that may be set is --low-priority-updates. This will make write statements by default a low priority statement, or at least equal to read-only SQL statements. If a server has been set to this default setting, you can add the HIGH_PRIORITY option to an INSERT statement to override the default setting of LOW_PRIORITY so that it has high priority over read statements.

Summary

At this point, you should have a good understanding of MySQL and MariaDB. You should understand the basic structure of a database and its tables. You should now see the value of having smaller multiple tables. You should no longer envision a database as one large table or like a spreadsheet. You should have a good sense of columns and how to enter data into them, especially if you have done all of the exercises at the end of the previous two chapters. You should not be overwhelmed at this point.

Chapter 7 delves more deeply into how to retrieve data from tables using the SELECT statement. We have already touched on this SQL statement several times. However, you saw only a sampling of how you might use SELECT in this chapter and in previous ones, to give you a sense of why we were creating and adding data the way we did to tables. The next chapter will cover the SELECT statement in much more detail.

The INSERT, SELECT, and the UPDATE statements are the most used SQL statements. If you want to learn MySQL and MariaDB well, you need to know these statements well. You need to know how to do the basics, as well as be familiar with the more specialized aspects of using SELECT. You'll accomplish that in the next chapter.

Before moving on to the next chapter, though, complete the following exercises. They will help you to retain what you've learned about the INSERT statement in this chapter. Don't skip them. This is useful and necessary to building a solid foundation in learning MySQL and MariaDB.

Exercises

Here are some exercises to get practice using the INSERT statement and a few others that we covered in this chapter. So that these exercises won't be strictly mundane data entry, a couple of them call for you to create some tables mentioned in this chapter. The practice of creating tables will help you to understand data entry better. The process of entering data will help you to become wiser when creating tables. Both inform each other.

1. In the exercises at the end of Chapter 4, you were asked to create a table called birds_body_shapes. This table will be used for identifying birds. It will be referenced from the birds table by way of the column called body_id. The table is to contain descriptions of body shapes of birds, which is a key factor in identifying birds: if it looks like a duck, walks like a duck, and quacks like a duck, it may be a goose—but it's definitely not a hummingbird. Here is an initial list of names for general shapes of birds:

   Hummingbird
   Long-Legged Wader
   Marsh Hen
   Owl
   Perching Bird
   Perching Water Bird
   Pigeon
   Raptor
   Seabird
   Shore Bird
   Swallow
   Tree Clinging
   Waterfowl
   Woodland Fowl

Construct an INSERT statement using the multiple-row syntax—not the emphatic method—for inserting data into the birds_body_shapes table. You'll have to set the body_id to a three-letter code. You decide on that, but you might base it somewhat on the names of the shapes themselves (e.g., *Marsh Hen* might be *MHN* and *Owl* might be simply *OWL*). Just make sure each ID is unique. For the body_shape column, use the text I have just shown, or reword it if you want. For now, skip the third column, body_example.

2. You were asked also in the exercises at the end of Chapter 4 to create another table for identifying birds, called birds_wing_shapes. This describes the shapes of bird wings. Here's an initial list of names for general wing shapes:

   Broad
   Rounded
   Pointed
   Tapered
   Long
   Very Long

   Construct an INSERT statement to insert these items into the birds_wing_shapes table using the emphatic syntax—the method that includes the SET clause. Set the wing_id to a two-letter code. You decide these values, as you did earlier for body_id. For the wing_shape column, use the text just shown. Don't enter a value for the wing_example column yet.

3. The last bird identification table in which to enter data is birds_bill_shapes. Use the INSERT statement to insert data into this table, but whichever multiple-row method you prefer. You determine the two-letter values for bill_id. Don't enter values for bill_example. Use the following list of bill shapes for the value of bill_shape:

   All Purpose
   Cone
   Curved
   Dagger
   Hooked
   Hooked Seabird
   Needle
   Spatulate
   Specialized

4. Execute a SELECT statement to view the row from the birds_body_shapes table where the value of the body_shape column is *Woodland Fowl*. Then replace that row with a new value for the body_shape column. Replace it with *Upland Ground*

Birds. To do this, use the REPLACE statement, covered in "Replacing Data" on page 110. In the VALUES clause of the REPLACE statement, provide the same value previously set for the body_id so that it is not lost.

After you enter the REPLACE statement, execute a SELECT statement to retrieve all the rows of data in the birds_body_shapes table. Look how the data changed for the row you replaced. Make sure it's correct. If not, try again either using REPLACE or UPDATE.

## CHAPTER 7

Selecting Data

Previous chapters discussed the important topics of organizing your tables well and getting data in to them. In this chapter, we will cover a key objective that makes the others pay off: retrieving the data stored in a database. This is commonly called a *database query*.

The simplest way to retrieve data from a MySQL or MariaDB database—*to select* data—is to use the SQL statement, SELECT. We used this SQL statement a few times in previous chapters. In this chapter, we will cover it in greater detail. It's not necessary to know or use all of the may options, but some techniques such as joining tables together are basic to using relational databases.

We'll begin this chapter by reviewing the basics of the SELECT statement, and then progress to more involved variants. When you finish this chapter, you will hopefully have a good understanding of how to use SELECT for most of your needs as you start out as a database developer, as well as be prepared for the many possibilities and special situations that may arise over the years of developing databases with MySQL and MariaDB.

In previous chapters, especially in the exercises, you were asked to enter data into the tables that we created and altered in the chapters of the previous part of this book. Entering data on your own was good for training purposes, but we now need much more data in our database to better appreciate the examples in this chapter. If you haven't done so already, go to this book's website (*http://mysqlresources.com/files*) and download the dump files that contain tables of data.

Download *rookery.sql* to get the whole rookery database, with plenty of data for use in our explorations. Once you have the dump file on your system (let's assume you put it in */tmp/rookery.sql*), enter the following from the command line:

```
mysql --user='your_name' -p \
rookery < /tmp/rookery.sql
```

The command prompts for your password, logs you in using the username assigned to you, and runs the statements in the *rookery.sql* file on the `rookery` database. If everything goes well, there should be no message in response, just the command-line prompt when it's finished.

Basic Selection

The basic elements of the syntax for the `SELECT` statement are the `SELECT` keyword, the column you want to select, and the table from which to retrieve the data:

```
SELECT column FROM table;
```

If you want to select more than one column, list them separated by commas. If you want to select all of the columns in a table, you can use the asterisk as a wildcard instead of listing all of the columns. Let's use the `rookery` database you just loaded with data to see a practical example of this basic syntax. Enter the following SQL statement in `mysql` to get a list of all of the columns and rows in the `birds` table:

```
USE rookery;

SELECT * FROM birds;
```

This is the most minimal `SELECT` statement that you can execute successfully. It tells MySQL to retrieve all of the data contained in the `birds` table. It displays the columns in the order you defined them in the table's `CREATE` or `ALTER` statements, and displays rows in the order they are found in the table, which is usually the order that the data was entered into the table.

To select only certain columns, do something like this:

```
SELECT bird_id, scientific_name, common_name
FROM birds;
```

This `SELECT` statement selects only three columns from each row found in the `birds` table. There are also many ways to choose particular rows, change the order in which they are displayed, and limit the number shown. These are covered in the following sections of this chapter.

Selecting by a Criteria

Suppose that we want to select only birds of a certain family, say the *Charadriidae* (i.e., Plovers). Looking in the `bird_families` table, we find that its `family_id` is 103. Using a `WHERE` clause with the `SELECT` statement, we can retrieve a list of birds from the `birds` table for this particular family of birds like so:

```
SELECT common_name, scientific_name
FROM birds WHERE family_id = 103
LIMIT 3;
```

```
+-----------------------+-------------------------+
| common_name           | scientific_name         |
+-----------------------+-------------------------+
| Mountain Plover       | Charadrius montanus     |
| Snowy Plover          | Charadrius alexandrinus |
| Black-bellied Plover  | Pluvialis squatarola    |
+-----------------------+-------------------------+
```

This SELECT statement requests two columns, in a different order from the way the data is listed in the table—in the table itself, scientific_name precedes common_name. I also added the LIMIT clause to keep the results down to the first three rows in the table. We'll talk more about the LIMIT clause in a little while.

 Because we separated families into a separate table, you had to look at the bird_families table to get the right ID before selecting birds from the birds table. That seems round-about. There is a stream-lined way to ask for a family name such as *Charadriidae* instead of a number. They're called joins. We'll cover them later.

This is all fairly straightforward and in line with what we've seen in several other examples in previous chapters. Let's move on and take a look at how to change the order of the results.

Ordering Results

The previous example selected specific columns from the birds table and limited the results with the LIMIT clause. However, the rows were listed in whatever order they were found in the table. We've decided to see only a tiny subset of the birds in the *Charadriidae* family, so ordering can make a difference. If we want to put the results in alphabetical order based on the values of the common_name column, we add an ORDER BY clause like this:

```
SELECT common_name, scientific_name
FROM birds WHERE family_id = 103
ORDER BY common_name
LIMIT 3;
```

```
+-----------------------+-----------------------+
| common_name           | scientific_name       |
+-----------------------+-----------------------+
| Black-bellied Plover  | Pluvialis squatarola  |
| Mountain Plover       | Charadrius montanus   |
| Pacific Golden Plover | Pluvialis fulva       |
+-----------------------+-----------------------+
```

Notice that the ORDER BY clause is located after the WHERE clause and before the LIMIT clause. Not only will this statement display the rows in order by common_name, but it will retrieve only the first three rows based on the ordering. That is to say, MySQL will first retrieve all of the rows based on the WHERE clause, store those results in a temporary table behind the scenes, order the data based on the ORDER BY clause, and then return to the mysql client the first three rows found in that temporary table based on the LIMIT clause. This activity is the reason for the positioning of each clause.

By default, the ORDER BY clause uses ascending order, which means from A to Z for an alphabetic column. If you want to display data in descending order, add the DESC option, as in ORDER BY DESC. There's also a contrasting ASC option, but you probably won't need to use it because ascending order is the default.

To order by more than one column, give all the columns in the ORDER BY clause in a comma-separated list. Each column can be sorted in ascending or descending order. The clause sorts all the data by the first column you specify, and then within that order by the second column, etc. To illustrate this, we'll select another column from the birds table, family_id, and we'll get birds from a few more families. We'll select some other types of shore birds: Oystercatchers (i.e., *Haematopodidae*), Stilts (e.g., *Recurvirostridae*), and Sandpipers (e.g., *Scolopacidae*). First, we need the family_id for each of these families. Execute the following on your server:

```
SELECT * FROM bird_families
WHERE scientific_name
IN('Charadriidae','Haematopodidae','Recurvirostridae','Scolopacidae');
```

family_id	scientific_name	brief_description	order_id
103	Charadriidae	Plovers, Dotterels, Lapwings	102
160	Haematopodidae	Oystercatchers	102
162	Recurvirostridae	Stilts and Avocets	102
164	Scolopacidae	Sandpipers and Allies	102

In this SELECT statement, we added another item to the WHERE clause, the IN operator. It lists, within parentheses, the various values we want in the scientific_name column. Let's use the IN operator again to get a list of birds and also test the LIMIT clause:

```
SELECT common_name, scientific_name, family_id
FROM birds
WHERE family_id IN(103, 160, 162, 164)
ORDER BY common_name
LIMIT 3;
```

```
+--------------+-------------------------------------+-----------+
| common_name  | scientific_name                     | family_id |
+--------------+-------------------------------------+-----------+
|              | Charadrius obscurus aquilonius      |       103 |
|              | Numenius phaeopus phaeopus          |       164 |
|              | Tringa totanus eurhinus            |       164 |
+--------------+-------------------------------------+-----------+
```

Notice that we didn't put the numeric values in quotes as we did with the family names in the previous SQL statement. Single or double quotes are necessary for strings, but they're optional for numeric values. However, it's a better practice to not use quotes around numeric values. They can affect performance and cause incorrect results if you mix them with strings.

There is one odd thing about the results here: there aren't any common names for the birds returned. That's not a mistake. About 10,000 birds in the birds table are true species of birds, and about 20,000 are subspecies. Many subspecies don't have a unique common name. With about 30,000 species and subspecies of birds, with all of the minor nuances between the subspecies bird families, there just aren't common names for all of them. Each bird has a scientific name assigned by ornithologists, but everyday people who use the common names for birds don't see the subtle distinctions that ornithologists see. This is why the scientific_name column is necessary and why the common_name column cannot be a key column in the table.

Let's execute that SQL statement again, but add another factor to the WHERE clause to show only birds with a value for the common_name column:

```
SELECT common_name, scientific_name, family_id
FROM birds
WHERE family_id IN(103, 160, 162, 164)
AND common_name != ''
ORDER BY common_name
LIMIT 3;
```

```
+---------------------+--------------------------+-----------+
| common_name         | scientific_name          | family_id |
+---------------------+--------------------------+-----------+
| African Oystercatcher | Haematopus moquini     |       160 |
| African Snipe       | Gallinago nigripennis    |       164 |
| Amami Woodcock      | Scolopax mira            |       164 |
+---------------------+--------------------------+-----------+
```

In the WHERE clause, we added the AND logical operator to specify a second filter. For a row to match the WHERE clause, the family_id must be one in the list given and the common_name must not be equal to a blank value.

Nonprogrammers will have to learn a few conventions to use large WHERE clauses. We've seen that an equals sign says, "The column must contain this value," but the != construct says, "The column must not contain this value." And in our statement, we used ' ' to refer to an empty string. So we'll get the rows where the common name exists.

In this case, we couldn't ask for non-NULL columns. We could have set up the table so that birds without common names had NULL in the common_name column, but we chose to instead use empty strings. That's totally different in meaning: NULL means there is no value, whereas the empty string is still a string even if there are no characters in it. We could have used NULL, but having chosen the empty string, we must use the right value in our WHERE clause.

Incidentally, != is the same as <> (i.e., less-than sign followed by greater-than sign).

Limiting Results

The birds table has nearly 30,000 rows, so selecting data without limits can return more rows than you might want to view at a time. We've already used the LIMIT clause to resolve this problem. We limited the results of the SELECT statement to three rows, the first three rows based on the WHERE and ORDER BY clauses. If we'd like to see the subsequent rows, maybe the next two based on the criteria we gave previously, we could change the LIMIT clause to show five rows. But an alternative, which is often a better choice, is to do something like this:

```
SELECT common_name, scientific_name, family_id
FROM birds
WHERE family_id IN(103, 160, 162, 164)
AND common_name != ''
ORDER BY common_name
LIMIT 3, 2;
```

```
+-----------------------+----------------------------+-----------+
| common_name           | scientific_name            | family_id |
+-----------------------+----------------------------+-----------+
| American Avocet       | Recurvirostra americana    |       162 |
| American Golden-Plover | Pluvialis dominica        |       103 |
+-----------------------+----------------------------+-----------+
```

This LIMIT clause has two values: the point where we want the results to begin, then the number of rows to display. The result is to show rows 3 and 4. Incidentally, LIMIT 3 used previously is the same as LIMIT 0, 3: the 0 tells MySQL not to skip any rows.

Combining Tables

So far in this chapter we've been working with just one table. Let's look at some ways to select data from more than one table. To do this, we will have to tell MySQL the tables from which we want data and how to join them together.

For an example, let's get a list of birds with their family names. To keep the query simple, we'll select birds from different families, but all in the same order of birds. In earlier examples where we got a list of shore birds, they all had the same order_id of 102. We'll use that value again. Enter this SELECT statement on your server:

```
SELECT common_name AS 'Bird',
bird_families.scientific_name AS 'Family'
FROM birds, bird_families
WHERE birds.family_id = bird_families.family_id
AND order_id = 102
AND common_name != ''
ORDER BY common_name LIMIT 10;
```

```
+-------------------------+-------------------+
| Bird                    | Family            |
+-------------------------+-------------------+
| African Jacana          | Jacanidae         |
| African Oystercatcher   | Haematopodidae    |
| African Skimmer         | Laridae           |
| African Snipe           | Scolopacidae      |
| Aleutian Tern           | Laridae           |
| Amami Woodcock          | Scolopacidae      |
| American Avocet         | Recurvirostridae  |
| American Golden-Plover  | Charadriidae      |
| American Oystercatcher  | Haematopodidae    |
| American Woodcock       | Scolopacidae      |
+-------------------------+-------------------+
```

This SELECT statement returns one column from the birds table and one from the bird_families table. This is a hefty SQL statement, but don't let it fluster you. It's like previous statements in this chapter, but with some minor changes and one significant one. First, let's focus on the one significant change: how we've drawn data from two tables.

The FROM clause lists the two tables, separated by a comma. In the WHERE clause, we indicated that we want rows in which the value of family_id in the two tables is equal. Otherwise, we would have duplicate rows in the results. Because those columns have the same name (family_id) in both tables, to prevent ambiguity, we put the table name before the colum name, separated by a dot (e.g., birds.family_id). We did the same thing for the scientific name in the column list (bird_families.scientific_name). If we don't do that, MySQL would be confused as to whether we want the scientific_name from the birds or the bird_families table. This would generate an error like this:

```
ERROR 1052 (23000): Column 'scientific_name' in field list is ambiguous
```

You may have noticed that another new item was added to the SELECT statement: the AS keyword. This specifies a substitute name, or *alias*, for the heading in the results set for the column. Without the AS keyword for the column containing the family names, the heading would say `bird_families.scientific_name`. That's not as attractive. This is another style factor, but it can have more practical aspects that we'll see later. The keyword AS can also be used to specify a table name like so:

```
SELECT common_name AS 'Bird',
families.scientific_name AS 'Family'
FROM birds, bird_families AS families
WHERE birds.family_id = families.family_id
AND order_id = 102
AND common_name != ''
ORDER BY common_name LIMIT 10;
```

In this example, we provided an alias for the `bird_families` table. We set it to the shorter name `families`. Note that aliases for table names must not be in quotes.

After setting the alias, we must use it wherever we want to refer to the table. So we have to change the column selected in the field list from `bird_families.scientific_name` to `families.scientific_name`. We also have to change the column name `bird_fami` `lies.family_id` in the WHERE clause to `families.family_id`. If we don't make this final change, we'll get the following error:

```
ERROR 1054 (42S22):
Unknown column 'bird_families.family_id' in 'where clause'
```

Let's add a third table to the previous SQL statement, to get the name of the order of birds to which the birds belong. You can do that by entering this SQL statement on your server:

```
SELECT common_name AS 'Bird',
families.scientific_name AS 'Family',
orders.scientific_name AS 'Order'
FROM birds, bird_families AS families, bird_orders AS orders
WHERE birds.family_id = families.family_id
AND families.order_id = orders.order_id
AND families.order_id = 102
AND common_name != ''
ORDER BY common_name LIMIT 10, 5;
```

```
+------------------+------------------+------------------+
| Bird             | Family           | Order            |
+------------------+------------------+------------------+
| Ancient Murrelet | Alcidae          | Charadriiformes  |
| Andean Avocet    | Recurvirostridae | Charadriiformes  |
| Andean Gull      | Laridae          | Charadriiformes  |
| Andean Lapwing   | Charadriidae     | Charadriiformes  |
| Andean Snipe     | Scolopacidae     | Charadriiformes  |
+------------------+------------------+------------------+
```

Let's look at the changes from the previous statement to this one. We added the third table to the FROM clause and gave it an alias of orders. To properly connect the third table, we had to add another evaluator to the WHERE clause: families.order_id = orders.order_id. This allows the SELECT to retrieve the right rows containing the scientific names of the orders that correspond to the rows we select from the families. We also added a column to the field list to display the name of the order. Because the families we've selected are all from the same order, that field seems a little pointless in these results but can be useful as we search more orders in the future. We gave a starting point for the LIMIT clause so that we could see the next five birds in the results.

It's not necessary to put the field alias name for a column in quotes if the alias is only one word. However, if you use a reserved word (e.g., *Order*), you will need to use quotes.

Expressions and the Like

Let's change the latest SELECT statement to include birds from multiple orders. To do this, we'll focus in on the operator in the WHERE clause for the common_name:

```
AND common_name != ''
```

We'll change the simple comparison here (i.e., the LIKE operator, which we saw in Chapter 6) to select multiple names that are similar. Among many families of birds, there are often bird species that are similar but have different sizes. The smallest is sometimes referred to as the *least* in the common name. So let's search the database for birds with *Least* in their name:

```
SELECT common_name AS 'Bird',
families.scientific_name AS 'Family',
orders.scientific_name AS 'Order'
FROM birds, bird_families AS families, bird_orders AS orders
WHERE birds.family_id = families.family_id
AND families.order_id = orders.order_id
AND common_name LIKE 'Least%'
ORDER BY orders.scientific_name, families.scientific_name, common_name
LIMIT 10;
```

```
+------------------+---------------+-------------------+
| Bird             | Family        | Order             |
+------------------+---------------+-------------------+
| Least Nighthawk  | Caprimulgidae | Caprimulgiformes  |
| Least Pauraque   | Caprimulgidae | Caprimulgiformes  |
| Least Auklet     | Alcidae       | Charadriiformes   |
| Least Tern       | Laridae       | Charadriiformes   |
| Least Sandpiper  | Scolopacidae  | Charadriiformes   |
| Least Seedsnipe  | Thinocoridae  | Charadriiformes   |
| Least Flycatcher | Tyrannidae    | Passeriformes     |
| Least Bittern    | Ardeidae      | Pelecaniformes    |
| Least Honeyguide | Indicatoridae | Piciformes        |
| Least Grebe      | Podicipedidae | Podicipediformes  |
+------------------+---------------+-------------------+
```

In the preceding example, using the LIKE operator, MySQL selected rows in which the common_name starts with *Least* and ends with anything (i.e., the wildcard, %). We also removed the families.order_id = 102 clause, so that we wouldn't limit the birds to a single order. The results now have birds from a few different orders.

We also changed the ORDER BY clause to have MySQL order the results in the temporary table first by the bird order's scientific name, then by the bird family's scientific name, and then by the bird's common name. If you look at the results, you can see that's what it did: it sorted the orders first. If you look at the rows for the *Charadriiformes*, you can see that the families for that order are in alphabetical order. The two birds in the *Caprimulgidae* family are in alphabetical order.

> You cannot use alias names for columns in the ORDER BY clause, but
> you can use alias table names. In fact, they're required if you've used
> the aliases in the FROM clause.

The previous example used the LIKE operator, which has limited pattern matching abilities. As an alternative, you can use REGEXP, which has many pattern matching characters and classes. Let's look at a simpler example, of the previous SELECT statement, but using REGEXP. In the previous example we searched for small birds, birds with a common name starting with the word *Least*. The largest bird in a family is typically called *Great*. To add these birds, enter the following SQL statement on your server:

```
SELECT common_name AS 'Birds Great and Small'
FROM birds
WHERE common_name REGEXP 'Great|Least'
ORDER BY family_id LIMIT 10;
```

```
+-----------------------------+
| Birds Great and Small       |
+-----------------------------+
| Great Northern Loon         |
| Greater Scaup               |
| Greater White-fronted Goose |
| Greater Sand-Plover         |
| Great Crested Tern          |
| Least Tern                  |
| Great Black-backed Gull     |
| Least Nighthawk             |
| Least Pauraque              |
| Great Slaty Woodpecker      |
+-----------------------------+
```

The expression we're giving with REGEXP, within the quote marks, contains two string values: *Great* and *Least*. By default, MySQL assumes the text given for REGEXP is meant to be for the start of the string. To be emphatic, you can insert a carat (i.e., ^) at the start of these string values, but it's unnecessary. The vertical bar (i.e., |) between the two expressions signifies that either value is acceptable—it means *or*.

In the results, you can see some common bird names starting with *Greater*, not just *Great*. If we don't want to include the *Greater* birds, we can exclude them with the NOT REGEXP operator. Enter the following on your server:

```
SELECT common_name AS 'Birds Great and Small'
FROM birds
WHERE common_name REGEXP 'Great|Least'
AND common_name NOT REGEXP 'Greater'
ORDER BY family_id LIMIT 10;
```

```
+---------------------------+
| Birds Great and Small     |
+---------------------------+
| Great Northern Loon       |
| Least Tern                |
| Great Black-backed Gull   |
| Great Crested Tern        |
| Least Nighthawk           |
| Least Pauraque            |
| Great Slaty Woodpecker    |
| Great Spotted Woodpecker  |
| Great Black-Hawk          |
| Least Flycatcher          |
+---------------------------+
```

Using NOT REGEXP eliminated all of the *Greater* birds. Notice that it was included with AND, and not as part of the REGEXP.

Incidentally, we're ordering here by `family_id` to keep similar birds together in the list and to have a good mix of *Great* and *Least* birds. The results may seem awkward, though, as the names of the birds are not ordered. We could add another column to the ORDER BY clause to alphabetize them within each family.

REGEXP and NOT REGEXP are case insensitive. If we want an expression to be case sensitive, we'll need to add the BINARY option. Let's get another list of birds to see this. This time we'll search for Hawks, with the first letter in uppercase. This is because we want only Hawks and not other birds that have the word, *hawk* in their name, but are not a Hawk. For instance, we don't want Nighthawks and we don't want Hawk-Owls. The way the data is in the birds table, each word of a common name starts with an uppercase letter—the names are in title case. So we'll eliminate birds such as Nighthawks by using the BINARY option to require that "Hawk" be spelled with an uppercase *H* and the other letters in lowercase. We'll use NOT REGEXP to not allow *Hawk-Owls*. Try the following on your server:

```
SELECT common_name AS 'Hawks'
FROM birds
WHERE common_name REGEXP BINARY 'Hawk'
AND common_name NOT REGEXP 'Hawk-Owl'
ORDER BY family_id LIMIT 10;
```

```
+--------------------+
| Hawks              |
+--------------------+
| Red-tailed Hawk    |
| Bicolored Hawk     |
| Common Black-Hawk  |
| Cuban Black-Hawk   |
| Rufous Crab Hawk   |
| Great Black-Hawk   |
| Black-faced Hawk   |
| White-browed Hawk  |
| Ridgway's Hawk     |
| Broad-winged Hawk  |
+--------------------+
```

I stated that REGEXP and NOT REGEXP are case insensitive, unless you add the BINARY option as we did to stipulate the collating method as binary (e.g., the letter *H* has a different binary value fromn the letter *h*). For the common_name column, though, we didn't need to add the BINARY option because the column has a binary collation setting. We did this unknowingly when we created the rookery database near the beginning of Chapter 4. See how we created the database by entering this from the mysql client:

```
SHOW CREATE DATABASE rookery \G

*************************** 1. row ***************************
       Database: rookery
Create Database: CREATE DATABASE `rookery` /*!40100 DEFAULT
                 CHARACTER SET latin1 COLLATE latin1_bin */
```

The COLLATE clause is set to latin1_bin, meaning Latin1 binary. Any columns that we create in tables in the rookery database, unless we specify otherwise, will be collated using latin1_bin. Execute the following statement to see how the common_name column in the birds table is set:

```
SHOW FULL COLUMNS
FROM birds LIKE 'common_name' \G

*************************** 1. row ***************************
     Field: common_name
      Type: varchar(255)
 Collation: latin1_bin
      Null: YES
       Key:
   Default: NULL
     Extra:
Privileges: select,insert,update,references
   Comment:
```

This shows information just on the common_name column. Notice that the *Collation* is latin1_bin. Because of that, regular expressions using REGEXP are case sensitive without having to add the BINARY option.

Looking through the birds table, we discover some common names for birds that contain the words, "Hawk Owls," without the hyphen in between. We didn't allow for that in the expression we gave. We discover also that there are birds in which the word "Hawk" is not in title case—so we can't count on looking for the uppercase letter, *H*. Our previous regular expression left those birds out of the results. So we'll have to change the expression and try a different method. Enter this on your server:

```
SELECT common_name AS 'Hawks'
FROM birds
WHERE common_name REGEXP '[[:space:]]Hawk|[[.hyphen.]]Hawk'
AND common_name NOT REGEXP 'Hawk-Owl|Hawk Owl'
ORDER BY family_id;
```

This first, rather long REGEXP expression uses a *character class* and a *character name*. The format of character classes and character names is to put the type of character between two sets of double brackets. A character class is given between a pair of colons (e.g., [[:alpha:]] for alphabetic characters). A character name is given between two dots (e.g., [[.hyphen.]] for a hyphen). Looking at the first expression, you can deduce that we want rows in which the common_name contains either "Hawk" or "-Hawk"—that is to say, *Hawk* preceded by a space or a hyphen. This won't allow for *Hawk* preceded by a letter (e.g., *Nighthawk*). The second expression excludes *Hawk-Owl* and *Hawk Owl*.

Pattern matching in regular expressions in MySQL tends to be more verbose than they are in other languages like Perl or PHP. But they do work for basic requirements. For elaborate regular expressions, you'll have to use an API like the Perl DBI to process the data outside of MySQL. Because that may be a performance hit, it's better to try to accomplish such tasks within MySQL using REGEXP.

Counting and Grouping Results

In many of our examples, we displayed only a few rows of data because the results could potentially contain thousands of rows. Suppose we'd like to know how many are contained in the table. We can do that by adding a *function* to the statement. In this case, we want the COUNT( ) function. Let's see how that would work:

```
SELECT COUNT(*) FROM birds;
```

```
+----------+
| COUNT(*) |
+----------+
|    28891 |
+----------+
```

We put an asterisk within the parentheses of the function to indicate that we want all of the rows. We could put a column name instead of an asterisk to count only rows that have data. Using a column prevents MySQL from counting rows that have a NULL value in that column. But it will count rows that have a blank or empty value (i.e., ' ').

It's nice to know how many rows are in the birds table, but suppose we'd like to break apart that count. Let's use COUNT( ) to count the number of rows for a particular family of birds, the *Pelecanidae*—those are Pelicans. Enter this SQL statement in the mysql client on your server:

```
SELECT families.scientific_name AS 'Family',
COUNT(*) AS 'Number of Birds'
FROM birds, bird_families AS families
WHERE birds.family_id = families.family_id
AND families.scientific_name = 'Pelecanidae'
```

```
+-------------+-----------------+
| Family      | Number of Birds |
+-------------+-----------------+
| Pelecanidae |              10 |
+-------------+-----------------+
```

As you can see, there are 10 bird species recorded for the *Pelecanidae* family in the birds table. In this example, we used the WHERE clause to limit the results to the *Pelecanidae* family. Suppose we want to know the number of birds for other bird families in the same order to which Pelicans belong, to the order called *Pelecaniformes*. To do this, we'll add the bird_orders table to the previous SELECT statement. Enter the following from the mysql client:

```
SELECT orders.scientific_name AS 'Order',
families.scientific_name AS 'Family',
COUNT(*) AS 'Number of Birds'
FROM birds, bird_families AS families, bird_orders AS orders
WHERE birds.family_id = families.family_id
AND families.order_id = orders.order_id
AND orders.scientific_name = 'Pelecaniformes';
```

```
+-----------------+--------------+-----------------+
| Order           | Family       | Number of Birds |
+-----------------+--------------+-----------------+
| Pelecaniformes  | Pelecanidae  |             224 |
+-----------------+--------------+-----------------++
```

This tells us that there are 224 birds in the birds table that belong to *Pelecaniformes*. There are five families in that order of birds, but it returned only the first family name found. If we want to know the name of each family and the number of birds in each family, we need to get MySQL to group the results. To do this, we have to tell it the column by which to group. This is where the GROUP BY clause comes in. This clause tells MySQL to group the results based on the columns given with the clause. Let's see how that might look. Enter the following on your server:

```
SELECT orders.scientific_name AS 'Order',
families.scientific_name AS 'Family',
COUNT(*) AS 'Number of Birds'
FROM birds, bird_families AS families, bird_orders AS orders
WHERE birds.family_id = families.family_id
AND families.order_id = orders.order_id
AND orders.scientific_name = 'Pelecaniformes'
GROUP BY Family;
```

```
+-----------------+--------------------+-----------------+
| Order           | Family             | Number of Birds |
+-----------------+--------------------+-----------------+
| Pelecaniformes  | Ardeidae           |             157 |
| Pelecaniformes  | Balaenicipitidae   |               1 |
| Pelecaniformes  | Pelecanidae        |              10 |
| Pelecaniformes  | Scopidae           |               3 |
| Pelecaniformes  | Threskiornithidae  |              53 |
+-----------------+--------------------+-----------------+
```

We gave the GROUP BY clause the Family alias, which is the scientific_name column from the bird_families table. MySQL returns one results set for all five families, for one SELECT statement.

The GROUP BY clause is very useful. You'll use it often, so learn it well. This clause and related functions are covered in greater detail in Chapter 12.

Summary

The SELECT statement offers quite a number of parameters and possibilities that I had to skip to keep this chapter from becoming too lengthy and too advanced for a learning book. For instance, there are several options for caching results and a clause for exporting a results set to a text file. You can learn about these from other sources if you need them.

At this point, make sure you're comfortable with the SELECT statement and its main components: choosing columns and using field aliases; choosing multiple tables in the FROM clause; how to construct a WHERE clause, including the basics of regular expressions; using the ORDER BY and the GROUP BY clauses; and limiting results with the LIMIT clause. It will take time and practice to become very comfortable with all of these components. Before moving on to Chapter 8, make sure to complete the exercises in the next section.

Exercises

The following exercises will help cement your understanding of the SELECT statement. The act of typing SQL statements, especially ones that you will use often like SELECT, helps you to learn, memorize, and know them well.

1. Construct a SELECT statement to select the common names of birds from the birds table. Use the LIKE operator to select only Pigeons from the table. Order the table by the common_name column, but give it a field alias of Bird'. Don't limit the results; let MySQL retrieve all of the rows that match. Execute the statement on your server and look over the results.

   Next, use the same SELECT statement, but add a LIMIT clause. Limit the results to the first ten rows and execute it. Compare the results to the previous SELECT statement to make sure the results show the 1st through 10th row. Then modify the SELECT statement again to display the next 10 rows. Compare these results to the results from the first SELECT statement to make sure you retrieved the 11th through 20th row. If you didn't, find your mistake and correct it until you get it right.

2. In this exercise, you'll begin with a simple SELECT statement and then make it more complicated. To start, construct a SELECT statement in which you select the scientific_name and the brief_description from the bird_orders table. Give the field for the scientific_name an alias of *Order*—and don't forget to put quotes around it because it's a reserved word. Use an alias of *Types of Birds in Order* for brief_description. Don't limit the results. When you think that you have the SELECT statement constructed properly, execute it. If you have errors, try to determine the problem and fix the statement until you get it right.

   Construct another SELECT statement in which you retrieve data from the birds table. Select the common_name and the scientific_name columns. Give them field aliases: *Common Name of Bird* and *Scientific Name of Bird*. Exclude rows in which the common_name column is blank. Order the data by the common_name column. Limit the results to 25 rows of data. Execute the statement until it works without an error.

Merge the first and second SELECT statements together to form one SELECT statement that retrieves the same four columns with the same alias from the same two tables (this was covered in "Combining Tables" on page 124). It involves giving more than one table in the FROM clause and providing value pairs in the WHERE clause for temporarily connecting the tables to each other. This one may seem tricky. So take your time and don't get frustrated. If necessary, refer back to "Combining Tables" on page 124.

Limit the results to 25 rows. If you do it right, you should get the same 25 birds from the second SELECT of this exercise, but with two more fields of data. Be sure to exclude rows in which the common_name column is blank.

3. Use the SELECT statement in conjunction with REGEXP in the WHERE clause to get a list of birds from the birds table in which the common_name contains the word "Pigeon" or "Dove" (this was covered in "Expressions and the Like" on page 127). Give the field for the common_name column the alias >*Type of Columbidae*—that's the name of the family to which Doves and Pigeons belong.

## CHAPTER 8

Updating and Deleting Data

Data in databases will change often. There's always something to change, some bit of information to add, some record to delete. For these situations in which you want to change or add pieces of data, you will mostly use the UPDATE statement. For situations in which you want to delete an entire row of data, you'll primarily use the DELETE statement. Both of these SQL statements are covered extensively in this chapter.

Updating Data

The UPDATE statement changes the data in particular columns of existing records. The basic syntax is the UPDATE keyword followed by the table name, then a SET clause. Generally you add a WHERE clause so as not to update all of the data in a given table. Here is a generic example of this SQL statement:

```
UPDATE table
SET column = value, ... ;
```

This syntax is similar to the emphatic version of the INSERT statement, which also uses the SET clause. There isn't a less emphatic syntax for UPDATE, as there is with INSERT. An important distinction is that there is no INTO clause. Instead, the name of the affected table is just given immediately after the UPDATE keyword.

Let's look at an example of the UPDATE statement. In Chapter 5, we created a database called birdwatchers and a table within it called humans that would contain data about people who watch birds and use the rookery site. We then entered information on some of those people. In one of the exercises at the end of Chapter 5, we added a column (country_id) which contains the country code where the member resides. Suppose that of the few members that we've entered already in the table, all of them live in the United States. We could set the default value for the country_id column to *us*, but we're expecting most of our members to be in a few countries of Europe. For now, we just want to update all of the rows in the humans table to set the country_id to *us*. Execute an UPDATE statement like this:

```
UPDATE birdwatchers.humans
SET country_id = 'us';
```

This statement will set the value for the country_id for all of the rows in the table. All of them had a NULL value before this, but if they had some other value—a different country code—those values would be changed to *us*. That's a very broad and comprehensive action. Once you do this, there's generally no way to undo it—unless you do so in an InnoDB table and do it as part of a transaction. So be careful when you use the UPDATE statement. Use a WHERE clause to pinpoint the rows you want to change, and test it first, as we will soon see.

Note that the previous UPDATE statement included the name of the database, because in previous chapters we set the mysql client to use rookery as the default database. Because all of the examples in this chapter will use the birdwatchers database, let's change the default database to it with USE:

```
USE birdwatchers;
```

For the remainder of the examples in this chapter, you should download the rookery and the birdwatchers databases from the MySQL Resources site (*http://mysqlresour ces.com/files*). They will provide you larger tables on which to work.

Updating Specific Rows

Most of the time, when you use the UPDATE statement you will need to include the WHERE clause to stipulate which rows are updated by the values in the SET clause. The conditions of a WHERE clause in an UPDATE statement are the same as that of a SELECT statement. In fact, because they're the same, you can use the SELECT statement to test the conditions of the WHERE clause before using it in the UPDATE statement. We'll see examples of that soon in this chapter. For now, let's look at a simple method of conditionally updating a single row.

The humans table contains a row for a young woman named *Rusty Osborne*. She was married recently and wants to change her last name to her husband's name, *Johnson*. We can do this with the UPDATE statement. First, let's retrieve the record for her. We'll select data based on her first and last name. There may be only one *Rusty Osborne* in the database, but there may be a few members with the family name of *Osborne*. So we would enter this in the mysql client:

```
SELECT human_id, name_first, name_last
FROM humans
WHERE name_first = 'Rusty'
AND name_last = 'Osborne';
```

```
+----------+------------+-----------+
| human_id | name_first | name_last |
+----------+------------+-----------+
|        3 | Rusty      | Osborne   |
+----------+------------+-----------+
```

Looking at the results, we can see that there is indeed only Rusty Osborne, and that the value of her human_id is 3. We'll use that value in the UPDATE statement to be sure that we update only this one row. Let's enter the following:

```
UPDATE humans
SET name_last = 'Johnson'
WHERE human_id = 3;

SELECT human_id, name_first, name_last
FROM humans
WHERE human_id = 3;
```

```
+----------+------------+-----------+
| human_id | name_first | name_last |
+----------+------------+-----------+
|        3 | Rusty      | Johnson   |
+----------+------------+-----------+
```

That worked just fine. It's easy to use the UPDATE statement, especially when you know the identification number of the key column for the one row you want to change. Let's suppose that two of our members who are married women have asked us to change their title from *Mrs.* to *Ms.* (this information is contained in an enumerated column called formal_title). After running a SELECT statement to find their records, we see that their human_id numbers are 24 and 32. We could then execute the following UP DATE statement in MySQL:

```
UPDATE humans
SET formal_title = 'Ms.'
WHERE human_id IN(24, 32);
```

Things get slightly more complicated when you want to change more than one row, but it's still easy if you know the key values. In this example, we used the IN operator to list the human_id numbers to match specific rows in the table.

Suppose that after updating the title for the two women just shown, we decide that we want to make this change for all married women in the database, to get with the modern times. We would use the UPDATE statement again, but we'll have to modify the WHERE clause. There may be too many women with the formal_title of *Mrs.* in the table to manually enter the human_id for all of them. Plus, there's an easier way to do it. First, let's see how the formal_title column looks now:

```
SHOW FULL COLUMNS
FROM humans
```

```
LIKE 'formal_title' \G
```

```
*************************** 1. row ***************************
     Field: formal_title
      Type: enum('Mr.','Miss','Mrs.','Ms.')
 Collation: latin1_bin
      Null: YES
       Key:
   Default: NULL
     Extra:
Privileges: select,insert,update,references
   Comment:
```

Looking at the enumerated values of this column, we decide that the choices seem somewhat sexist to us. We have one choice for boys and men, regardless of their age and marital status, and three choices for women. We also don't have other genderless choices like *Dr.*, but we decide to ignore those possibilities for now. In fact, we could eliminate the column so as not to be gender biased, but we decide to wait before making that decision. At this point, we want to change our schema so it limits the list of choices in the column to *Mr.* or *Ms.* however, we should not make that change to the schema until we fix all the existing values in the column. To do that, we'll enter this UPDATE statement:

```
UPDATE humans
SET formal_title = 'Ms.'
WHERE formal_title IN('Miss','Mrs.');
```

Now that all of the members have either a value of *Mr.* or *Ms.* in the `formal_title` column, we can change the settings of that column to eliminate the other choices. We'll use the ALTER TABLE statement covered in Chapter 4. Enter the following to change the table on your server:

```
ALTER TABLE humans
CHANGE COLUMN formal_title formal_title ENUM('Mr.','Ms.');
```

```
Query OK, 62 rows affected (0.13 sec)
Records: 62  Duplicates: 0  Warnings: 0
```

As you can see from the message in the results, the column change went well. However, if we had forgotten to change the data for one of the rows (e.g., didn't change *Miss* to *Ms.* for one person), the Warnings would show a value of 1. In that case, you would then have to execute the SHOW WARNINGS statement to see this warning:

```
SHOW WARNINGS \G
```

```
*************************** 1. row ***************************
  Level: Warning
   Code: 1265
Message: Data truncated for column 'formal_title' at row 44
```

This tells us that MySQL eliminated the value for the `formal_title` column of the 44th row. We'd then have to use the `UPDATE` statement to try to set the `formal_title` for the person whose title was clobbered and hope we set the title correctly. That's why it's usually better to update the data before altering the table.

Sometimes, when changing bulk data, you have to alter the table before you can do the update. For example, suppose that we decide that we prefer to have the enumerated values of the `formal_title` set to *Mr* or *Ms*, without any periods. To do this, we would need to add that pair of choices to the `ENUM` column before we eliminate the old values. Then we can easily change the data to the new values. In this situation, we can tweak the criteria of the `WHERE` clause of the `UPDATE` statement. The values have a pattern: the new values are the same as the first two characters of the old value. So we can use a function to extract that part of the string. We would do something like this:

```
ALTER TABLE humans
CHANGE COLUMN formal_title formal_title ENUM('Mr.','Ms.','Mr','Ms');

UPDATE humans
SET formal_title = SUBSTRING(formal_title, 1, 2);

ALTER TABLE humans
CHANGE COLUMN formal_title formal_title ENUM('Mr','Ms');
```

The first `ALTER TABLE` statement adds the two new choices of titles without a period to the column, without yet eliminating the previous two choices because existing table contents use them. The final `ALTER TABLE` statement removes the two old choices of titles with a period from the column. Those two SQL statements are fine and not very interesting. The second one is more interesting, the `UPDATE`.

In the `SET` clause, we set the value of the `formal_title` column to a substring of its current value. We're using the `SUBSTRING( )` function to extract the text. Within the parentheses, we give the column from which to get a string (`formal_title`). Then we give the start of the substring we want to extract: 1, meaning the first character of the original string. We specify the number of characters we want to extract: 2. So wherever `SUBSTRING( )` encounters "Mr." it will extract "Mr", and wherever it encounters "Ms." it will extract "Ms".

It's critical to note that fuctions don't *change* the data in the table. `SUBSTRING( )` simply gives you back the substring. In order to actually change the column, you need the `SET formal_title` = clause. That changes `formal_title` to the value you got back from `SUBSTRING( )`. Note that, if you wanted, you could just as easily have run `SUBSTRING( )` on one column and used it to set the value of a different one.

In this chapter, we'll work with a few string functions that are useful with the `UPDATE` statement. We'll cover many more string functions in Chapter 10.

Limiting Updates

As mentioned near the beginning of this chapter, UPDATE can be a powerful tool for quickly changing large amounts of data in a MySQL database. As a result, you should almost always use a WHERE clause with an UPDATE statement to limit updates to rows based on certain conditions. There are times when you might also want to limit updates to a specific number of rows. To do this, use the LIMIT clause with the UPDATE statement. This clause functions the same as in the SELECT statement, but its purpose is different with UPDATE. Let's look at an example of how and why you might use the LIMIT clause with the UPDATE statement.

Suppose that we decide to offer a small prize each month to two of the members of our site to encourage people to join. Maybe we'll offer them the choice of a booklet with a list of birds found in their area, a nice pen with the Rookery name on it, or a water bottle with a bird image on it. Suppose also that we want a person to win only once, and we want to make sure that everyone wins eventually. To keep track of the winners, let's create a table to record who won and when, as well as what prize they were sent and when. We'll use the CREATE TABLE statement like so:

```
CREATE TABLE prize_winners
(winner_id INT AUTO_INCREMENT PRIMARY KEY,
 human_id INT,
 winner_date DATE,
 prize_chosen VARCHAR(255),
 prize_sent DATE);
```

In this statement, we created a table called prize_winners and gave it five columns: the first (winner_id) is a standard identifier for each row; the second (human_id) is to associate the rows in this table to the humans table; the third column (winner_date) is to record the date that the winner was determined; the next (prize_chosen) is the prize the member chose ultimately; and the last column (prize_sent) is to record the date the prize was sent to the winner.

> The IDs in this table may be a bit confusing. winner_id will be used to select items from this table, such as the prize and the dates. hu man_id will be used to find data about the winner in the humans table. You might think that there is no need for two IDs, as they both refer to the same person. But think back to the ways we used IDs to link birds, bird families, and bird orders. Giving each table its own identifier is more robust.

We could have set the prize_chosen column to an enumerated list of the choices, but the choices may change over time. We may eventually create another table containing a list of the many prizes and replace this column with a column that contains a reference number to a table listing prizes. For now, we'll use a large variable character column.

Because we want to make sure every member wins eventually, we'll enter a row in the prize_winners table for each member. Otherwise, we would enter a row only when the member won. This is probably the better choice for maintaining the data, but we'll use the more straightforward method of inserting an entry for each member in the prize_winners table. We'll use an INSERT...SELECT statement to select the winners and insert them in the new table (this type of SQL statement was covered in "Inserting Data from Another Table" on page 104):

```
INSERT INTO prize_winners
(human_id)
SELECT human_id
FROM humans;
```

This inserted a row in the prize_winners table for each member in the humans table. It added only the value of the human_id column, because that's all we need at this point as no one has yet to win anything. The statement also automatically sets the winner_id column, thanks to its AUTO_INCREMENT modifier, giving it a unique value for each human. There is no reason this ID should be the same as the human_id column, because we'll use the human_id column whenever we need information from it. The other columns currently have NULL for their values. We'll update those values when someone wins a prize.

Now that we have a separate table for recording information about winners and their prizes each month, let's pick some winners. We'll do that in the next subsection.

Ordering to Make a Difference

In the previous subsection, we decided to award prizes to members so as to encourage new people to join the Rookery site, as well as to make current members feel good about continuing their membership. So that new and old members have an equal chance of winning, we'll let MySQL randomly choose the winners each month. To do this, we'll use the UPDATE statement with the ORDER BY clause and the RAND( ) function. This function picks an arbitrary floating-point number for each row found by the SQL statement in which it's used. By putting this function in the ORDER BY clause, we will order the results based on the random values chosen for each row. If we couple that with the LIMIT clause, we can limit the results to a different pair of rows each month we select winners:

```
UPDATE prize_winners
SET winner_date = CURDATE()
WHERE winner_date IS NULL
ORDER BY RAND()
LIMIT 2;
```

There are flaws in the RAND( ) function. It's not so random and can sometimes return the same results. So be careful about when you use it and for what purpose.

Let's start at the bottom of this UPDATE statement. The ORDER BY clause is a bit ironic here because the order it puts the columns in is random. The LIMIT clause limits the results to only two rows. So everyone has an equal chance of being one of our two winners.

We can't be sure that the top two rows are new winners, though; we might happen to choose the same person through a random process on different months. So we add a WHERE clause to update only rows in which winner_date has a value of NULL, which indicates that the member hasn't won previously. Finally, at the top of the statement, we set the winner_date column for the winner to the current date, using a function we'll learn about in Chapter 11.

However, there are some problems with this SQL statement that may not be obvious. First, the use of the RAND( ) function in an ORDER BY clause can be absurdly slow. You won't notice the difference when used on a small table, but it performs poorly on an extremely large table that is used by a very active server. So, be mindful of which tables and situations you use the RAND( ) function within the ORDER BY clause. Second, using the ORDER BY clause with a LIMIT clause can cause problems if you use MySQL replication, unless you use row-based replication. This is a feature that allows you to have a master server and slave servers that replicate or copy exactly the databases on the master. That's an advanced topic, but I want to mention this potential problem because when you use this combination of clauses with the UPDATE statement, you'll see a warning message like this:

```
SHOW WARNINGS \G

*************************** 1. row ***************************
  Level: Warning
   Code: 1592
Message: Statement is not safe to log in statement format.
```

If you're not using MySQL replication, you can ignore this warning. If you are using it, though, you'll have a situation in which one slave may update its data differently from the data on the master or the other slaves—especially if you use the RAND( ) function (i.e., the slave will have different random results). Again, at this stage of learning MySQL, you can probably ignore this warning, and can safely use these clauses and this function. What's important is that you're aware of these potential problems and that you get of a sense of how extensive MySQL is.

Updating Multiple Tables

Thus far in this chapter, we have updated only one table at a time with the UPDATE statement. We've also made updates based on the values of the table for which the changes were made. You can also update values in one table based on values in another table. And it's possible to update more than one table with one UPDATE statement. Let's look at some examples of how and why you might do this.

Suppose that we've been giving out prizes for a couple of years now and that we've decided we want to make a special bid to recruit and retain members from the United Kingdom. To do this, we've decided to give four prizes each month to members of the Rookery site: two prizes to members in the U.K, and two prizes to members in all other countries. We'll announce this change so that our skewing will be perceived fairly by members of the site. We'll even allow U.K. members who won previously to win again. For this last component, we'll need to reset the values of rows in the prize_winners table based on the value of the country_id in the humans table. Let's see how that would look:

```
UPDATE prize_winners, humans
SET winner_date = NULL,
    prize_chosen = NULL,
    prize_sent = NULL
WHERE country_id = 'uk'
AND prize_winners.human_id = humans.human_id;
```

This SQL statement checks rows in one table, associates those rows to the related rows in another table, and changes those rows in that second table. Notice that we listed the two tables involved in a comma-separated list. We then used the SET clause to set the values of the columns related to winning a prize to NULL. In the WHERE clause, we give the condition that the country_id from the humans table has a value of *uk* and that the human_id in both tables equal.

Now that we've reset the prize information for the U.K. members, we're ready to award prizes for the new month. Let's try the UPDATE statement that we used previously to randomly select winners, but this time we'll straddle both the humans and prize_win ners tables by entering the following:

```
UPDATE prize_winners, humans
SET winner_date = CURDATE()
WHERE winner_date IS NULL
AND country_id = 'uk'
AND prize_winners.human_id = humans.human_id
ORDER BY RAND()
LIMIT 2;
```

```
ERROR 1221 (HY000): Incorrect usage of UPDATE and ORDER BY
```

You would expect this to work well, but it doesn't work at all. Instead, it fails and returns the error message shown. When using the multiple-table syntax of UPDATE, it causes problems for MySQL if you include an ORDER BY or a LIMIT clause—those clauses apply to one table, not to multiple tables as in this UPDATE. Limitations like this can be frustrating, but there are ways around them. For our current task, because the ORDER BY RAND( ) and LIMIT clauses work with one table without problems, we can use a subquery (i.e., a query within a query) to randomly select the winners from the humans table and then update the prize_winners table. Let's see how we would do that in this situation:

```
UPDATE prize_winners
SET winner_date = CURDATE()
WHERE winner_date IS NULL
AND human_id IN
  (SELECT human_id
   FROM humans
   WHERE country_id = 'uk'
   ORDER BY RAND())
LIMIT 2;
```

That may seem pretty complicated, but if we pull it apart, it's not too difficult. First, let's look at the inner query, the SELECT statement contained within the parentheses. It's selecting the human_id for all members in the humans table, where the country_id has a value of *uk*, and randomly ordering the results. Notice that we're selecting all rows for U.K. members and we're not distinguishing whether the member was a previous winner. That's because the inner query cannot query the table that is the target of the UPDATE. So we have to separate the conditions like we're doing here: in the WHERE clause of the UPDATE, we're updating only rows in which the value of the winner_date is NULL. That will be all of the U.K. members.But we could change the statement to select non-U.K. members simply by changing the operator in the subquery to !=.

In the UPDATE statement, using the IN operator, we specify that only rows whose hu man_id is in the results of the subquery should be updated. The LIMIT clause says to update only two rows. The LIMIT clause here is part of the UPDATE, not the subquery (i.e., the SELECT).

Because MySQL executes the subquery first, and separately from the UPDATE, there's no problem with using the ORDER BY clause in it. Because the LIMIT clause is in an UPDATE that's not using the multiple-table syntax, there's no problem using it either.

The preceding example may seem cumbersome, but it solves the problem. When you can't do something the way you would think in MySQL, you can sometimes accomplish a task with methods like using a subquery. Subqueries are covered extensively in Chapter 9.

Handling Duplicates

In Chapter 6, we covered the INSERT statement in detail. We saw several variants on its syntax and interesting ways to use it. This included INSERT...SELECT, a combination of the INSERT and SELECT statements. There is another combination related to updating rows, INSERT...ON DUPLICATE KEY UPDATE.

When inserting multiple rows of data, you may attempt inadvertently to insert rows that would be duplicates: that is to say, rows with the same value that is supposed to be unique. With the INSERT statement, you can add the IGNORE flag to indicate that duplicate rows should be ignored and not inserted. With the REPLACE statement, MySQL will replace the existing rows with the new data, or rather it will delete the existing rows and insert the new rows. As an alternative, you might want to keep the existing rows, but make a notation to them in each row. Such a situation is when INSERT...ON DUPLICATE KEY UPDATE is useful. This will make more sense with an example.

Suppose there is another bird-watchers website similar to ours that's called *Better Birders*. Because that site has become inactive and the owner wants to close it, he contacts us and offers to redirect the site's traffic to our domain if we'll add its members to our membership. We accept this offer, so he gives us a plain-text file with a list of each member's name and email address. There are a few ways we might import those names; some are covered in Chapter 15. But because some of the members of the other site may already be members of our site, we don't want to import them and have duplicate entries. However, we do want to make note of those people as being members of the other site in case we want that information later. Let's try using INSERT...ON DUPLICATE KEY UPDATE to do that. First we'll add a column to indicate that a member came from the *Better Birders* site by using the ALTER TABLE statement like so:

```
ALTER TABLE humans
ADD COLUMN better_birders_site TINYINT DEFAULT 0;
```

This statement added a column named better_birders_site with a default value of 0. If someone is a member of the *Better Birders* site, we'll set the column to 1. We'll set the column to a value of 2 to indicate they are a member of both sites. Because two people can have the same name, we use the email address to determine whether a row is a duplicate. In the humans table, the email_address column is already set to UNIQUE. It will be the basis by which rows will be updated with the combined SQL statement we'll use. With these factors in mind, let's try to insert a few members:

```
INSERT INTO humans
(formal_title, name_first, name_last, email_address, better_birders_site)
VALUES('Mr','Barry','Pilson', 'barry@gomail.com', 1),
      ('Ms','Lexi','Hollar', 'alexandra@mysqlresources.com', 1),
      ('Mr','Ricky','Adams', 'ricky@gomail.com', 1)
ON DUPLICATE KEY
UPDATE better_birders_site = 2;
```

Because of the ON DUPLICATE KEY component, when there are rows with the same email address, the better_birders_site column will be set to 2. The rest will be inserted with their better_birders_site column set to 1. That's what we wanted.

We now need to insert rows for these new members in the prize_winners table. We'll use the INSERT...SELECT statement as we did earlier, but this time we'll just insert rows where the value of the better_birders_site column is 1:

```
INSERT INTO prize_winners
(human_id)
SELECT human_id
```

```
FROM humans
WHERE better_birders_site = 1;
```

Although these two SQL statements worked well, it's possible that there might be two entries for someone in the humans table if they used a different email address on the other site. That possibility may already exist with our existing members if they registered on the site more than once. Let's check for this possibility and add a column to note it. We'll enter the following SQL statements to prepare:

```
ALTER TABLE humans
ADD COLUMN possible_duplicate TINYINT DEFAULT 0;

CREATE TEMPORARY TABLE possible_duplicates
(name_1 varchar(25), name_2 varchar(25));
```

The first statement added a column to the humans table to note a row as a possible duplicate entry. The second creates a temporary table. A temporary table is accessible only to your MySQL client connection. When you exit from the client, the temporary table will be dropped automatically. Because we cannot update the same table for which we're checking for duplicates, we can note them in this temporary table. We'll use INSERT...SELECT to do this:

```
INSERT INTO possible_duplicates
SELECT name_first, name_last
FROM
  (SELECT name_first, name_last, COUNT(*) AS nbr_entries
   FROM humans
   GROUP BY name_first, name_last) AS derived_table
WHERE nbr_entries > 1;
```

This statement uses a subquery that selects the names and counts the number of entries based on the GROUP BY clause. We saw how to use GROUP BY and COUNT( ) together in "Counting and Grouping Results" on page 132, but their use here calls for a reiteration of how they work. The subquery selects name_first and name_last, and groups them so that any rows containing the same first and last names will be grouped together. They can then be counted. We give the result of COUNT(*) an alias of nbr_entries so that we can reference it elsewhere.

Back in the main SQL statement, the WHERE clause selects only rows from the subquery in which there are more than one entry (i.e., nbr_entries is greater than 1). These are duplicate entries. This SQL statement will insert a row into the temporary table for rows found in the humans table that have the same first and last name. It should enter only one row in the temporary table for each person.

Now that we have a list of possible duplicates in the temporary table, let's update the humans table to note them:

```
UPDATE humans, possible_duplicates
SET possible_duplicate = 1
```

```
WHERE name_first = name_1
AND name_last = name_2;
```

That will set the value of the `possible_duplicate` column to 1 where the names in the humans table match the names in `possible_duplicates`. When we're ready, we can send an email to these members telling them that we have two entries for their names and asking if the entries are duplicates. If they are, we might be able to merge the information together (such as by creating another column for a second email address) and delete the duplicate rows. As for the temporary table, it will be deleted when we close the MySQL client.

Deleting Data

With most databases, you will eventually need to delete rows from a table. To do this, you can use the `DELETE` statement. As mentioned a few times earlier in this book, there is no `UNDELETE` or `UNDO` statement for restoring rows that you delete. You can recover data from backups, if you're making backups as you should, but it's not quick and easy to restore data from them. If you use a storage engine like InnoDB, there is a method for wrapping SQL statements in a transaction that can be rolled back after you delete rows. However, once you commit such a transaction, you'll have to look to backups or other cumbersome methods to restore deleted data. Thus, you should alwaysbe careful when using the `DELETE` statement.

The `DELETE` statement works much like the `SELECT` statement in that you may delete rows based on conditions in the `WHERE` clause. You should always use the `WHERE` clause, unless you really want to leave an empty table with no rows. You may also include an `ORDER BY` clause to specify the order in which rows are deleted, and a `LIMIT` clause to limit the number of rows deleted in a table. The basic syntax of the `DELETE` statement is:

```
DELETE FROM table
[WHERE condition]
[ORDER BY column]
[LIMIT row_count];
```

As the formatting indicates with square brackets, the `WHERE`, `ORDER BY`, and `LIMIT` clauses are optional. There are additional options that may be given and deviations to the syntax for deleting rows in multiple tables and for deletions based on multiple tables. Let's look at an example using this simpler syntax for now.

Suppose after sending out a notice to members who we suspect of having duplicate entries in the humans table, one of them confirms that her membership has been duplicated. The member, *Elena Bokova* from Russia, asks us to delete the entry that uses her old *yahoo.com* email address. To do that, we could, but we won't, enter this SQL statement:

```
DELETE FROM humans
WHERE name_first = 'Elena'
AND name_last = 'Bokova'
AND email_address LIKE '%yahoo.com';
```

This SQL statement will delete any rows in which the criteria expressed in the WHERE clause are met. Notice that for checking the email address, we used the LIKE operator and the wildcard (i.e., %) to match any email ending with *yahoo.com*.

The statement just shown would work fine, but we also need to delete the related entry in the prize_winners table. So we should first get the human_id for this row before deleting it. That's why I said we won't enter this SQL statement. It's tedious, though, to execute one SQL statement to retrieve the human_id, then another to delete the row in the humans table, and then execute a third SQL statement to delete the related row in the prize_winners table. Instead, it would be better to change the DELETE statement to include both tables, deleting the desired rows from both in one SQL statement. We'll cover that in the next subsection.

Deleting in Multiple Tables

There are many situations where data in one table is dependent on data in another table. If you use DELETE to delete a row in one table on which a row in another table is dependent, you'll have orphaned data. You could execute another DELETE to remove that other row, but it's usually better to delete rows in both tables in the same DELETE statement, especially when there may be many rows of data to delete.

The syntax for the DELETE that deletes rows in multiple tables is:

```
DELETE FROM table[, table]
USING table[, . . . ]
[WHERE condition];
```

In the FROM clause, list the tables in a comma-separated list. The USING clause specifies how the tables are joined together (e.g., based on human_id). The WHERE clause is optional. Like the UPDATE statement, because this syntax includes multiple tables, the ORDER BY and LIMIT clauses are not permitted. This syntax can be tricky, but how much so may not be evident from looking at the syntax. Let's look at an example.

In the example at the end of the previous subsection, we needed to delete rows from two tables that are related. We want to delete the rows for *Elena Bokova* in which she has a *yahoo.com* email address in both the humans and the prize_winners tables. To do that efficiently, we'll enter this from the mysql client:

```
DELETE FROM humans, prize_winners
USING humans JOIN prize_winners
WHERE name_first = 'Elena'
AND name_last = 'Bokova'
```

```
AND email_address LIKE '%yahoo.com'
AND humans.human_id = prize_winners.human_id;
```

This DELETE statement is similar to other data manipulation statements (e.g., SELECT, UPDATE). However, there is a difference in the syntax that may be unexpected and confusing. The FROM clause lists the tables from which data is to be deleted. There is also a USING clause that lists the tables again and how they are joined. What is significant about this distinction is that we must list the tables in which rows are to be deleted in the FROM clause. If we did not include prize_winners in that list, no rows would be deleted from it—only rows from humans would be deleted.

There are several contortions and options in the syntax for DELETE. However, at this stage, the methods we reviewed in this chapter will serve well for almost all situations you will encounter as a MySQL and MariaDB developer or administrator.

Summary

The UPDATE and DELETE statements are very useful for changing data in tables; they are essential to managing a MySQL or MariaDB database. They have many possibilities for effecting changes to tables with ease. You can construct very complex SQL statements with them to change precisely the data you want to change or to delete exactly the rows you want to delete. However, it can be confusing and difficult at times. So be careful and learn these SQL statements well.

If you're nervous at times about using the UPDATE and DELETE statements, it's because you should be. You can change all of the rows in a table with one UPDATE statement, and you can delete all of the rows in a table with one DELETE statement. On a huge database, that could be thousands of rows of data changed or deleted in seconds. This is why good backups are always necessary. Whenever using these two SQL statements, take your time to be sure you're right before you execute them. While you're still learning especially, it can be a good idea to make a duplicate of a table with its data using the CREATE TABLE...SELECT statement before updating or deleting data. This SQL statement was covered in "Essential Changes" on page 61. This way if you make a major mistake, you can put the data back as it was before you started.

Because of the problems you can cause yourself and others who will use the databases on which you will work, practice using the UPDATE and DELETE statements. More than any other chapter in this book so far, you should make sure to complete the exercises in the next section.

Exercises

Exercises follow for you to practice using the UPDATE and DELETE statements. If you haven't already, download the rookery and the birdwatchers databases from the

MySQL Resources site (*http://mysqlresources.com/files*)). This will give you some good-sized tables on which to practice these SQL statements.

1. Use the CREATE TABLE...SELECT statement (see "Essential Changes" on page 61) to make a copies of the humans and the prize_winners tables. Name the new tables humans_copy and prize_winners_copy. Once you've created the copies, use the SELECT statement to view all of the rows in both of the new tables. You should see the same values as are contained in the original tables.

2. After you've done the previous exercise, use the SELECT statement to select all of the members from Austria in the humans table. You'll need to use a WHERE clause for that SQL statement. The country_id for Austria is *au*. If you have problems, fix the SQL statement until you get it right.

   Next, using the same WHERE clause from the SELECT statement, construct an UPDATE statement to change the value of the membership_type column for Austrian members to *premium*. In the same UPDATE statement, set the value of the membership_ex piration to one year from the date you execute the SQL statement. You will need to use the CURDATE( ) function inside the DATE_ADD( ) function. The DATE_ADD( ) function was shown in an example earlier in this chapter (see "Updating Specific Rows" on page 138). The CURDATE( ) has no arguments to it, nothing to go inside its parentheses. Both functions are covered in Chapter 11. If you can't figure out how to combine these function, you can enter the date manually (e.g., '*2014-11-03*' for November 3, 2014; include the quote marks). Use the SELECT statement to check the results when you're done.

3. Using the DELETE statement, delete the rows associated with the member named *Barry Pilson* from the humans and prize_winners tables. This was explained, along with an example showing how to do it, in "Deleting in Multiple Tables" on page 150. After you do this, use the SELECT statement to view all of the rows in both tables to make sure you deleted both rows.

4. Using the DELETE statement, delete all of the rows in the humans table. Then delete all of the rows of data in the prize_winners tables. Use the SELECT statement to confirm that both tables are empty.

   Now copy all of the data from the humans_copy and prize_winners_copy tables to the humans and prize_winners tables. Do this with the INSERT...SELECT statement (covered in "Inserting Data from Another Table" on page 104).

   After you've restored the data by this method, execute the SELECT statement again to confirm that both tables now have all of the data. If you were successful, use the DROP TABLE statement to eliminate the humans_copy and prize_winners_copy tables. This SQL statement was covered in Chapters 4 and 5. If you drop the wrong tables or if you delete data from the wrong tables, you can always download the whole database again from the MySQL Resources site.

## CHAPTER 9

Joining and Subquerying Data

Most of the examples used in this book thus far have intentionally involved one table per SQL statement in order to allow you to focus on the basic syntax of each SQL statement. When developing a MySQL or MariaDB database, though, you will often query multiple tables. There are a few methods by which you may do that—you've seen some simple examples of them in previous chapters. This chapter covers how to merge results from multiple SQL statements, how to join tables, and how to use subqueries to achieve similar results.

Unifying Results

Let's start this chapter by looking at a simple method of unifying results from multiple SQL statements. There may be times when you just want the unified results of two SELECT statements that don't interact with each other. In this situation, you can use the UNION operator, which merges two SELECT statements to form a unified results set. You can merge many SELECT statements together simply by placing the UNION between them in a chain. Let's look at an example.

In "Counting and Grouping Results" on page 132, we queried the birds table to get a count of the number of birds in the *Pelecanidae* family (i.e., Pelicans). Suppose we want to also know how many birds are in the *Ardeidae* family (i.e., Herons). That's easy to do: we'd use a copy of the same SELECT, but change the value in the WHERE clause. Suppose further that we want to merge the results of the SELECT statement counting Pelicans with the results of a SELECT counting Herons. We'll do this with a UNION operator, so we can enter two complete SELECT statements and unite them into one results set. Enter the following in the mysql client:

```
SELECT 'Pelecanidae' AS 'Family',
  COUNT(*) AS 'Species'
  FROM birds, bird_families AS families
  WHERE birds.family_id = families.family_id
```

```
      AND families.scientific_name = 'Pelecanidae'
UNION
  SELECT 'Ardeidae',
    COUNT(*)
    FROM birds, bird_families AS families
    WHERE birds.family_id = families.family_id
    AND families.scientific_name = 'Ardeidae';
```

```
+-------------+----------+
| Family      | Species  |
+-------------+----------+
| Pelecanidae |       10 |
| Ardeidae    |      157 |
+-------------+----------+
```

First notice that the column headings in the results is taken only from the first SELECT
statement. Next notice that for the first fields in both SELECT statements, we didn't reference a column. Instead, we gave plain text within quotes: 'Pelecanidae' and 'Ar
deidae'. That's an acceptable choice in MySQL and MariaDB. It works well when you
want to fill a field with text like this. Notice that we gave field aliases for the columns in
the first SELECT statement, but not in the second one. MySQL uses the first ones it's given
for the column headings of the results set when using the UNION operator. It ignores any
field aliases in subsequent SELECT statements, so they're not needed. If you don't give
aliases, it uses the column names of the first SQL statement of the UNION.

The reason a UNION was somewhat necessary in the preceding example is because we're
using an aggregate function, COUNT( ) with GROUP BY. We can group by multiple columns, but to get results like this which show separate counts for two specific values of
the same column, a UNION or some other method is necessary.

There are a few minor things to know about using a UNION. It's used only with SELECT
statements. The SELECT statements can select columns from different tables. Duplicate
rows are combined into a single column in the results set.

You can use the ORDER BY clause to order the unified results. If you want to order the
results of a SELECT statements, independently of the unified results, you have to put that
SELECT statement within parentheses and add an ORDER BY clause to it. When specifying
the columns in the ORDER BY clauses, you cannot preface column names with the table
names (e.g., families.scientific_name). If using the column names would be am-
biguous, you should instead use column aliases. Let's expand our previous example to
better illustrate how to use the ORDER BY clause with UNION. Let's get a count for each
bird family within two orders: *Pelecaniformes* and *Suliformes*. Enter the following:

```
SELECT families.scientific_name AS 'Family',
  COUNT(*) AS 'Species'
  FROM birds, bird_families AS families, bird_orders AS orders
  WHERE birds.family_id = families.family_id
  AND families.order_id = orders.order_id
  AND orders.scientific_name = 'Pelecaniformes'
```

```
      GROUP BY families.family_id
UNION
  SELECT families.scientific_name, COUNT(*)
    FROM birds, bird_families AS families, bird_orders AS orders
    WHERE birds.family_id = families.family_id
    AND families.order_id = orders.order_id
    AND orders.scientific_name = 'Suliformes'
    GROUP BY families.family_id;
```

```
+--------------------+---------+
| Family             | Species |
+--------------------+---------+
| Pelecanidae        |      10 |
| Balaenicipitidae   |       1 |
| Scopidae           |       3 |
| Ardeidae           |     157 |
| Threskiornithidae  |      53 |
| Fregatidae         |      13 |
| Sulidae            |      16 |
| Phalacrocoracidae  |      61 |
| Anhingidae         |       8 |
+--------------------+---------+
```

The first five rows are are *Pelecaniformes* and the remaining rows are *Suliformes*. The results are not in alphabetical order, but in the order of each SELECT statement and the order that server found the rows for each SELECT statement based on the family_id. If we want to order the results alphabetically by the family name, we have to use an ORDER BY clause, but after the unified results are generated. To do this, we'll wrap the results set in parentheses to tell MySQL to treat it as a table. Then we'll select all of the columns and rows of that results set and use the ORDER BY clause to order them based on the family name. To avoid confusion, we'll add the name of the order to the results. Enter the following:

```
SELECT * FROM
(
    SELECT families.scientific_name AS 'Family',
    COUNT(*) AS 'Species',
    orders.scientific_name AS 'Order'
    FROM birds, bird_families AS families, bird_orders AS orders
    WHERE birds.family_id = families.family_id
    AND families.order_id = orders.order_id
    AND orders.scientific_name = 'Pelecaniformes'
    GROUP BY families.family_id
UNION
  SELECT families.scientific_name, COUNT(*), orders.scientific_name
    FROM birds, bird_families AS families, bird_orders AS orders
    WHERE birds.family_id = families.family_id
    AND families.order_id = orders.order_id
    AND orders.scientific_name = 'Suliformes'
    GROUP BY families.family_id ) AS derived_1
ORDER BY Family;
```

```
+--------------------+---------+----------------+
| Family             | Species | Order          |
+--------------------+---------+----------------+
| Anhingidae         |       8 | Suliformes     |
| Ardeidae           |     157 | Pelecaniformes |
| Balaenicipitidae   |       1 | Pelecaniformes |
| Fregatidae         |      13 | Suliformes     |
| Pelecanidae        |      10 | Pelecaniformes |
| Phalacrocoracidae  |      61 | Suliformes     |
| Scopidae           |       3 | Pelecaniformes |
| Sulidae            |      16 | Suliformes     |
| Threskiornithidae  |      53 | Pelecaniformes |
+--------------------+---------+----------------+
```

In these examples, it may seem to be a lot of typing to achieve very little. But there are times—albeit rare times—when UNION is the best or simplest choice. It's more useful when you retrieve data from very distinct, separate sources or other situations that would require contortions to fit into a single SELECT statement and are executed more easily as separate ones, still giving you a unified results set.

You can get the same results as the previous examples, though, with less effort by using a subquery. Actually, when we put the UNION within parentheses, that became a subquery, just not much of one. We'll cover subqueries later in this chapter. For now, let's consider how to join multiple tables in one SQL statement.

Joining Tables

The JOIN clause links two tables together in a SELECT, UPDATE, or DELETE statement. JOIN links tables based on columns with common data for purposes of selecting, updating, or deleting data. In "A Little Complexity" on page 39, for instance, we joined two tables named books and status_names, taking advantage of the design that put identical values in the status column of books and the status_id column of status_names. That way, we could show data from each table about the same book:

```
SELECT book_id, title, status_name
FROM books JOIN status_names
WHERE status = status_id;
```

Let's review the way a join works, using this example. The status and status_id fields both contain numbers that refer to a status. In the books table, the numbers have no intrinsic meaning. But the status_names table associates the numbers with meaningful text. Thus, by joining the tables, you can associate a book with its status.

Sometimes there are alternatives to the JOIN clause. For instance, when constructing an SQL statement that includes multiple tables, a simple method is to list the tables in a comma-separated list in the appropriate position of the SQL statement—for a SELECT statement, you would list them in the FROM clause—and to provide pairing of columns in the WHERE clause on which the tables will be joined. This is the method we have used several times in the previous chapters. Although this method works fine and would seem fairly straightforward, a more agreeable method is to use a JOIN clause to join both tables and to specify the join point columns. When you have an error with an SQL statement, keeping these items together and not having part of them in the WHERE clause makes troubleshooting SQL statements easier.

With JOIN, tables are linked together based on columns with common data for purposes of selecting, updating, or deleting data. The JOIN clause is entered in the relevant statement where tables referenced are specified usually. This precludes the need to join the tables based on key columns in the WHERE clause. The ON operator is used to indicate the pair of columns by which the tables are to be joined (indicated with the equals-sign operator). If needed, you may specify multiple pairs of columns, separated by AND. If the column names by which the two tables are joined are the same in both tables, as an alternative method, the USING operator may be given along with a comma-separated list of columns that both tables have in common, contained within parentheses. The columns must be contained in each table that is joined. To improve performance, join to a column that is indexed.

Here is how the first of these two syntax looks using a JOIN:

```
SELECT book_id, title, status_name
FROM books
JOIN status_names ON(status = status_id);
```

This is the same example as before, but without the WHERE clause. It doesn't need it, because it uses ON instead to indicate the join point. If we were to alter the books table to modify the name of the status column to be status_id, so that the names of both columns on which we join these two tables are the same, we could do the join like this:

```
SELECT book_id, title, status_name
FROM books
JOIN status_names USING(status_id);
```

Here we use the keyword USING in the JOIN clause to indicate the identical column by which to join.

These syntaxes are only two of a few possible with the JOIN. They show how you might construct a SELECT statement using a JOIN. It's basically the same for the UPDATE and DELETE statements. In the next subsections, we'll consider the methods for using JOIN with each of these three SQL statements, and look at some examples for each.

Selecting a Basic Join

Suppose we want to get a list of species of Geese whose existence is Threatened—that's a category of conservation states. We will need to construct a SELECT statement that takes data from the birds table and the conservation_status table. The shared data in the birds and the conservation_status tables is the conservation_status_id column of each table. We didn't have to give the column the same name in each table, but doing so makes it easier to know where to join them.

Enter the following in the mysql client:

```
SELECT common_name, conservation_state
FROM birds
JOIN conservation_status
ON(birds.conservation_status_id = conservation_status.conservation_status_id)
WHERE conservation_category = 'Threatened'
AND common_name LIKE '%Goose%';
```

```
+-------------------------------+--------------------+
| common_name                   | conservation_state |
+-------------------------------+--------------------+
| Swan Goose                    | Vulnerable         |
| Lesser White-fronted Goose    | Vulnerable         |
| Hawaiian Goose                | Vulnerable         |
| Red-breasted Goose            | Endangered         |
| Blue-winged Goose             | Vulnerable         |
+-------------------------------+--------------------+
```

The ON operator specifies the conservation_status_id columns from each table as the common item on which to join the tables. MySQL knows the proper table in which to find the conservation_category and common_name columns, and pulls the rows that match.

That works fine, but it's a lot to type. Let's modify this statement to use the USING operator, specifying conservation_status_id just once to make the join. MySQL will understand what to do. Here's that same SQL statement, but with the USING operator:

```
SELECT common_name, conservation_state
FROM birds
JOIN conservation_status
USING(conservation_status_id)
WHERE conservation_category = 'Threatened'
AND common_name LIKE '%Goose%';
```

Now let's modify the SQL statement to include the bird family. To do that, we'll have to add another table, the bird_families. Let's also include Ducks in the list. Try executing the following:

```
SELECT common_name AS 'Bird',
bird_families.scientific_name AS 'Family', conservation_state AS 'Status'
FROM birds
JOIN conservation_status USING(conservation_status_id)
JOIN bird_families USING(family_id)
WHERE conservation_category = 'Threatened'
AND common_name REGEXP 'Goose|Duck'
ORDER BY Status, Bird;
```

```
+-----------------------------+----------+--------------------------+
| Bird                        | Family   | Status                   |
+-----------------------------+----------+--------------------------+
| Laysan Duck                 | Anatidae | Critically Endangered    |
| Pink-headed Duck            | Anatidae | Critically Endangered    |
| Blue Duck                   | Anatidae | Endangered               |
| Hawaiian Duck               | Anatidae | Endangered               |
| Meller's Duck               | Anatidae | Endangered               |
| Red-breasted Goose          | Anatidae | Endangered               |
| White-headed Duck           | Anatidae | Endangered               |
| White-winged Duck           | Anatidae | Endangered               |
| Blue-winged Goose           | Anatidae | Vulnerable               |
| Hawaiian Goose              | Anatidae | Vulnerable               |
| Lesser White-fronted Goose  | Anatidae | Vulnerable               |
| Long-tailed Duck            | Anatidae | Vulnerable               |
| Philippine Duck             | Anatidae | Vulnerable               |
| Swan Goose                  | Anatidae | Vulnerable               |
| West Indian Whistling-Duck  | Anatidae | Vulnerable               |
| White-headed Steamer-Duck   | Anatidae | Vulnerable               |
+-----------------------------+----------+--------------------------+
```

We gave two JOIN clauses in this SQL statement. It doesn't usually matter which table is listed where. For instance, although bird_families is listed just after the join for the conservation_statustable, MySQL determined that bird_families is to be joined to the birds table. Without using JOIN, we would have to be more emphatic in specifying the join points, and we would have to list them in the WHERE clause. It would have to be entered like this:

```
SELECT common_name AS 'Bird',
bird_families.scientific_name AS 'Family', conservation_state AS 'Status'
FROM birds, conservation_status, bird_families
WHERE birds.conservation_status_id = conservation_status.conservation_status_id
AND birds.family_id = bird_families.family_id
AND conservation_category = 'Threatened'
AND common_name REGEXP 'Goose|Duck'
ORDER BY Status, Bird;
```

That's a very cluttered WHERE clause, making it difficult to see clearly the conditions by which we're selecting data from the tables. Using JOIN clauses is much tidier.

Incidentally, the SQL statement with two JOIN clauses used a regular expression—the REGEXP operator in the WHERE clause—to specify that the clause find either Goose or Duck. We also added an ORDER BY clause to order first by Status, then by Bird name.

In this example, though, there's little point in listing the bird family name, because the birds are all of the same family. Plus, there may be similar birds that we might like to have in the list, but that don't have the words Goose or Duck in their name. So let's change that in the SQL statement. Let's also order the results differently and list birds from the least endangered to the most endangered. Enter the following:

```
SELECT common_name AS 'Bird from Anatidae',
conservation_state AS 'Conservation Status'
FROM birds
JOIN conservation_status AS states USING(conservation_status_id)
JOIN bird_families USING(family_id)
WHERE conservation_category = 'Threatened'
AND bird_families.scientific_name = 'Anatidae'
ORDER BY states.conservation_status_id DESC, common_name ASC;
```

Bird from Anatidae	Conservation Status
Auckland Islands Teal	Vulnerable
Blue-winged Goose	Vulnerable
Eaton's Pintail	Vulnerable
Hawaiian Goose	Vulnerable
Lesser White-fronted Goose	Vulnerable
Long-tailed Duck	Vulnerable
Marbled Teal	Vulnerable
Philippine Duck	Vulnerable
Salvadori's Teal	Vulnerable
Steller's Eider	Vulnerable
Swan Goose	Vulnerable
West Indian Whistling-Duck	Vulnerable
White-headed Steamer-Duck	Vulnerable
Bernier's Teal	Endangered
Blue Duck	Endangered
Brown Teal	Endangered
Campbell Islands Teal	Endangered
Hawaiian Duck	Endangered
Meller's Duck	Endangered
Red-breasted Goose	Endangered
Scaly-sided Merganser	Endangered
White-headed Duck	Endangered
White-winged Duck	Endangered
White-winged Scoter	Endangered
Baer's Pochard	Critically Endangered
Brazilian Merganser	Critically Endangered
Crested Shelduck	Critically Endangered
Laysan Duck	Critically Endangered
Madagascar Pochard	Critically Endangered
Pink-headed Duck	Critically Endangered

An obvious change to this example is the elimination of bird_families.scientif
ic_name from the list of selected columns, so only two columns appear in the output.
Another change, which is cosmetic, is to provide the alias states to the conserva
tion_status table so we could refer to the short alias later instead of the long name.

Finally, the ORDER BY clause orders the output by conservation_status_id, because
that value happens to be in the order of severity in the conservation_status table. We

want to override the default order, which puts the most threatened species first, so we add the DESC option to put the least threatened first. We're still ordering results secondarily by the common name of the birds, but using the actual column name this time instead of an alias. This is because we changed the alias for the common_name column from Birds to Birds from Anatidae, because all the results are in that family. We could have used 'Birds from Anatidae' in the ORDER BY clause, but that's bothersome to type.

Let's look at one more basic example of a JOIN. Suppose we wanted to get a list of members located in Russia (i.e., where country_id has a value of ru) who have reported sighting a bird from the Scolopacidae family (shore and wader birds like Sandpipers and Curlews). Information on bird sightings is stored in the bird_sightings table. It includes GPS coordinates recorded from a bird list application on the member's mobile phone when they note the sighting. Enter this SQL statement:

```
SELECT CONCAT(name_first, ' ', name_last) AS Birder,
common_name AS Bird, location_gps AS 'Location of Sighting'
FROM birdwatchers.humans
JOIN birdwatchers.bird_sightings USING(human_id)
JOIN rookery.birds USING(bird_id)
JOIN rookery.bird_families USING(family_id)
WHERE country_id = 'ru'
AND bird_families.scientific_name = 'Scolopacidae'
ORDER BY Birder;
```

```
+--------------------+-------------------+----------------------------+
| Birder             | Bird              | Location of Sighting       |
+--------------------+-------------------+----------------------------+
| Anahit Vanetsyan   | Bar-tailed Godwit | 42.81958072; 133.02246094  |
| Elena Bokova       | Eurasian Curlew   | 51.70469364; 58.63746643   |
| Elena Bokova       | Eskimo Curlew     | 66.16051056; -162.7734375  |
| Katerina Smirnova  | Eurasian Curlew   | 42.69096856; 130.78185081  |
+--------------------+-------------------+----------------------------+
```

This SQL statement joins together four tables, two from the birdwatchers database and two from the birds database. Look closely at this SQL statement and consider the purpose of including each of those four tables. All of them were needed to assemble the results shown. Incidentally, we used the CONCAT( ) function to concatenate together the member's first and last name for the Birder field in the results.

There are other types of joins besides a plain JOIN. Let's do another SELECT using another type of JOIN. For an example of this, we'll get a list of Egrets and their conservation status. Enter the following SQL statement:

```
SELECT common_name AS 'Bird',
conservation_state AS 'Status'
FROM birds
LEFT JOIN conservation_status USING(conservation_status_id)
WHERE common_name LIKE '%Egret%'
```

```
ORDER BY Status, Bird;
```

```
+----------------------+-----------------+
| Bird                 | Status          |
+----------------------+-----------------+
| Great Egret          | NULL            |
| Cattle Egret         | Least Concern   |
| Intermediate Egret   | Least Concern   |
| Little Egret         | Least Concern   |
| Snowy Egret          | Least Concern   |
| Reddish Egret        | Near Threatened |
| Chinese Egret        | Vulnerable      |
| Slaty Egret          | Vulnerable      |
+----------------------+-----------------+
```

This SELECT statement is like the previous examples, except that instead of using a JOIN, we're using a LEFT JOIN. This type of join selects rows in the table on the left (i.e., birds) regardless of whether there is a matching row in the table on the right (i.e., conservation_status). Because there is no match on the right, MySQL returns a NULL value for columns it cannot reconcile from the table on the right. You can see this in the results. The Great Egret has a value of NULL for its Status. This is because no value was entered in the conservation_status_id column of the row related to that bird species. It would return NULL if the value of that column is NULL, blank if the column was set to empty (e.g., ' '), or any value that does not match in the right table.

Because of the LEFT JOIN, the results show all birds with the word Egret in the common name even if we don't know their conservation status. It also indicates which Egrets need to set the value of conservation_status_id. We'll need to update that row and others like it. An UPDATE statement with this same LEFT JOIN can easily do that. We'll show a couple in the next section.

Updating Joined Tables

If you want to use the UPDATE statement to change the data in multiple tables, or change data in a table based on criteria from multiple tables, you can use the JOIN clause. The syntax of the JOIN clause for UPDATE is the same as it is for SELECT. So let's go straight to some practical examples. We'll start with the example at the end of the previous subsection.

Let's use UPDATE with LEFT JOIN to locate rows in the birds table that don't have a value in conservation_status_id. We could update all of the rows, but let's do only rows for one bird family, *Ardeidae* (i.e., Herons, Egrets, and Bitterns). First, execute this SELECT statement to test our joins and WHERE clause:

```
SELECT common_name,
conservation_state
FROM birds
LEFT JOIN conservation_status USING(conservation_status_id)
```

```
JOIN bird_families USING(family_id)
WHERE bird_families.scientific_name = 'Ardeidae';
```

If you're working from the data from the MySQL Resources site, you should have over 150 rows in the results. You'll notice that many of the rows have nothing in the `com mon_name` field. That's because there are many bird species for which there are scientific names, but no common names. Those rows also have no value for the `conserva tion_status_id`. There are also a few rows for bird species that do have common names.

Let's add another row to the `conservation_status`, one for an unknown state. We'll set these unknown rows to that state. Enter these two SQL statements:

```
INSERT INTO conservation_status (conservation_state)
VALUES('Unknown');

SELECT LAST_INSERT_ID();
```

```
+-------------------+
| LAST_INSERT_ID()  |
+-------------------+
|                 9 |
+-------------------+
```

In the first SQL statement here we entered only a value for `conservation_state`. The defaults for the other columns are fine. We'll use the UPDATE statement to set the rows for the birds in *Ardeidae* to this new state, so we want to know the `conservation_sta tus_id` for it. To get that value, we issue a SELECT statement with the `LAST_IN SERT_ID( )` function. It returns the identifier generated from the previous SQL statement entered, which added a row for the current client connection (i.e., just us). Let's use that number to set the `conservation_status_id` in the birds table for bird species in *Ardeidae*. If your identification number is different, use what you received in the following SQL statement:

```
UPDATE birds
LEFT JOIN conservation_status USING(conservation_status_id)
JOIN bird_families USING(family_id)
SET birds.conservation_status_id = 9
WHERE bird_families.scientific_name = 'Ardeidae'
AND conservation_status.conservation_status_id IS NULL;
```

This UPDATE statement should have changed almost 100 rows on your server. The joins here are the same as we used in the previous SELECT statement, in which we discovered that we did not have a conservation status set for the Great Egret. Notice in the WHERE clause here that one of the conditions is that `conservation_status.conservation_sta tus_id` has a value of NULL. We could have removed the LEFT JOIN to the `conserva tion_status` table and then updated simply all of the rows for the *Ardeidae* birds that have a NULL value in the `conservation_status_id` column. But that would not have included any rows that might have other nonmatching values (e.g., a blank column). By including this LEFT JOIN, we updated all of these possibilities. However, it requires the condition that the `conservation_status.conservation_status_id` is NULL, the column from the right table—it will be assumed NULL if not matched.

Because the method of joining tables is the same for both the SELECT statement and the UPDATE statement, you can easily test the JOIN clauses and WHERE clause using a SELECT first. When that's successful, you can then execute an UPDATE statement with the same JOIN and WHERE clauses. That's the best procedure to follow to ensure proper updating of data when joining multiple tables.

Deleting Within Joined Tables

Having used JOIN with SELECT and UPDATE statements, let's look at some practical examples using DELETE. In "Deleting in Multiple Tables" on page 150, we saw an example of DELETE with a JOIN. In that example, we wanted to delete the rows where the member Elena Bokova has a *yahoo.com* email address from both the `humans` and the `prize_win ners` tables from the `birdwatchers` database. For that purpose, we constructed a DE LETE statement that worked fine, but there was potentially a problem with it. Here is that SQL statement again:

```
DELETE FROM humans, prize_winners
USING humans JOIN prize_winners
WHERE name_first = 'Elena'
AND name_last = 'Bokova'
AND email_address LIKE '%yahoo.com'
AND humans.human_id = prize_winners.human_id;
```

Compared to the JOIN clauses we've been using, the syntax here may look strange. This is how it works with a DELETE statement. Tables from which data is deleted are listed in the FROM clause, while tables used in the WHERE clause to provide filters to determine which rows to delete are listed in a USING clause. The clause "USING humans JOIN prize_winners" just tells the server that those two tables provide the columns in the WHERE clause.

 Don't confuse a USING clause, which has JOIN subclauses, with the USING operator, which can be used in a JOIN clause.

As the preceding DELETE SQL statement is constructed, if MySQL finds a row in the `humans` table where the name and email information match, there has to be a matching row in the `prize_winners` table for the `human_id`. If there's not a row in both, MySQL won't delete the row in the `humans` table and no error will be returned—you might not realize it failed. To allow for this possibility, we could use a LEFT JOIN like so:

```
DELETE FROM humans, prize_winners
USING humans LEFT JOIN prize_winners
ON humans.human_id = prize_winners.human_id
WHERE name_first = 'Elena'
AND name_last = 'Bokova'
AND email_address LIKE '%yahoo.com';
```

Notice that for this syntax we moved the valuation of the human_id columns to the USING clause, adding a LEFT JOIN and an ON operator to replace that condition in the WHERE clause. That's necessary because if there's not a match in the other table, the WHERE clause won't include that row in the results to be deleted. With the LEFT JOIN, all of the rows in both the humans and the prize_winners tables that match the criteria given to it will be deleted, and any rows found in the humans table for which there isn't a match in the prize_winners table, but which match the criteria of the WHERE clause will be deleted also. This prevents what are known as orphaned rows.

For general maintenance, we should check occasionally to see if there are rows in the prize_winners table that don't have matching rows in the humans table, and then delete them. Someone might have had us delete their account, but we may have forgotten to remove entries for them in related tables. To handle that possibility, we could use RIGHT JOIN instead of LEFT JOIN. We could enter something like this:

```
DELETE FROM prize_winners
USING humans RIGHT JOIN prize_winners
ON humans.human_id = prize_winners.human_id
WHERE humans.human_id IS NULL;
```

In this DELETE statement, we listed only the prize_winners table in the FROM clause because that's the only one from which we want to delete rows. It's a good policy not to list tables that are not to be affected in the FROM clause of a DELETE statement, even if you think there's no possible way that there is a row that would be deleted in the other tables.

Because we put the humans table first in the USING clause and the prize_winners table second, we're doing a RIGHT JOIN so that columns from the table on the right (prize_winners) will be deleted even if there is no value in the table on the left. If we reversed the order of the tables, we would then need a LEFT JOIN for this task.

It's worth focusing for a moment on the final clause of the previous DELETE statement, a WHERE clause checking for NULLs in one column. As we saw earlier, a LEFT JOIN or RIGHT JOIN can return rows where there was nothing in the column you're doing the join on. The results contain NULL for the missing value. So in the WHERE clause here, we're using that as the condition for finding the orphaned rows in the prize_winners table.

There are many contortions to the JOIN clause. The basic JOIN syntaxes that we covered in "Selecting a Basic Join" on page 157 are worth learning well; they will be the ones you will use primarily. You will sometimes have a need for using a LEFT JOIN or a RIGHT JOIN. Let's move on to a related topic that can be valuable in many situations: subqueries.

Subqueries

A subquery is a query within another query, a SELECT statement within another SQL statement. A subquery returns a single value, a row of data, a single column from several rows, or several columns from several rows. These are known respectively as scalar, column, row, and table subqueries. I'll refer to these distinctions later in this chapter.

Although the same results can be accomplished by using the JOIN clause and sometimes the UNION, depending on the situation, subqueries are a cleaner approach. They make a complex query more modular, which makes it easier to create and to troubleshoot problems. Here are two generic examples of subqueries (we also used a few subqueries in Chapter 8):

```
UPDATE table_1
SET col_5 = 1
WHERE col_id =
  SELECT col_id
  FROM table_2
  WHERE col_1 = value;

SELECT column_a, column_1
FROM table_1
JOIN
  (SELECT column_1, column_2
   FROM table_2
   WHERE column_2 = value) AS derived_table
USING(col_id);
```

In the first example, the SELECT statement is an inner query. The UPDATE statement is referred to as the main or outer query. In the second example, the SELECT within parentheses is the inner query and the SELECT outside of the parentheses is the outer query. An outer query containing a subquery can be a SELECT, INSERT, UPDATE, DELETE, DO, or even a SET statement. There are some limitations, though. An outer query cannot generally select data or modify data from the same table of an inner query. This doesn't apply though if the subquery is part of a FROM clause.

These generic examples may be confusing. Generic examples aren't usually easy to follow. I'd rather present first the syntax for subqueries, but there is no syntax per se for the use of subqueries—other than the syntax inherent in the SQL statements used for the inner and outer queries. Subqueries are rather a method of constructing combinations of SQL statements. As such, you need only to make sure of two basic factors with subqueries.

The first factor of which you need to be mindful is how a subquery is contained within an outer query, where you position it. For instance, if you construct an outer query which is an UPDATE statement, you could place a subquery in the WHERE clause to provide a set of values to which a column is equal (e.g., as in the first generic example). Or you might locate a subquery in the FROM clause of an outer, SELECT statement (e.g., as in the second generic example). These are where subqueries may be positioned. You can have multiple subqueries within an outer query, but they will be positioned generally within the FROM clause or the WHERE clause.

The second factor is whether the results returned from a subquery are in keeping with the expectations of the outer query. For instance, in the first generic example, the UP DATE clause has a WHERE clause that expects a single value from the subquery. If the subquery returns several values, a row of columns, or a table of results, it will confuse MySQL and cause an error. So you need to be sure that the subquery you construct will return the type of values required by the outer query as you constructed it.

You'll better understand these factors as we look at examples of them. As mentioned at the start of this section, the different types of subqueries are scalar, column, row, and table subqueries. In the following subsections, we'll look at each of these types, along with examples of them.

Scalar Subqueries

The most basic subquery is one that returns a single value, a scalar value. This type of subquery is particularly useful in a WHERE clause in conjunction with an = operator, or in other instances where a single value from an expression is permitted. Let's look at simple example of this. Let's get a list of bird families that are members of the *Galliformes* bird order (i.e., Grouse, Partridges, Quails, and Turkeys). This can be done easily with a JOIN in which we join the birds and bird_families tables together based on the order_id for *Galliformes*. We'll use instead a scalar subquery to get the order_id we need. Enter this in mysql:

```
SELECT scientific_name AS Family
FROM bird_families
WHERE order_id =
  (SELECT order_id
   FROM bird_orders
   WHERE scientific_name = 'Galliformes');
```

```
+-----------------+
| Family          |
+-----------------+
| Megapodiidae    |
| Cracidae        |
| Numididae       |
| Odontophoridae  |
| Phasianidae     |
+-----------------+
```

The inner query (i.e., the subquery here) returns one value, the order_id. That's used to complete the WHERE clause of the outer query. That was pretty simple. Let's look at another example of a scalar subquery.

We had an example earlier in this chapter, in the section related to using a JOIN, in which we selected members from Russia who had sighted birds of the family *Scolopacidae*. To thank members in Russia for using our telephone application for recording sightings, we're going to give a one-year premium membership to one of those members. Enter this hefty SQL statement in mysql:

```
UPDATE humans
SET membership_type = 'premium',
membership_expiration = DATE_ADD(IFNULL(membership_expiration,
  CURDATE()), INTERVAL 1 YEAR)
WHERE human_id =
  (SELECT human_id
   FROM
     (SELECT human_id, COUNT(*) AS sightings, join_date
      FROM birdwatchers.bird_sightings
      JOIN birdwatchers.humans USING(human_id)
      JOIN rookery.birds USING(bird_id)
      JOIN rookery.bird_families USING(family_id)
      WHERE country_id = 'ru'
      AND bird_families.scientific_name = 'Scolopacidae'
      GROUP BY human_id) AS derived_1
   WHERE sightings > 5
   ORDER BY join_date ASC
   LIMIT 1);
```

The most inner query here is basically the same as the one in the example mentioned earlier. The difference is that here we're not selecting the names involved. Instead, we're selecting the human_id and the join_date (i.e., the date that the member joined). With the GROUP BY clause, we're grouping members based on the human_id to get a count with the COUNT( ) function. Put another way, we're counting the number of entries of each human_id in the bird_sightings table for the bird family and member country we specified. That subquery will return a table of results; it's a table subquery. We'll talk more about that type of subquery later in this chapter.

The query wrapped around the most inner query, which is also a subquery, selects only rows where the number of sightings is more than five. It orders the rows with newer members first based on the date the members joined—we want the newest Russian member reporting several Curlews and the like to be awarded a year of premium membership. This subquery is limited to one row with one column. It's a scalar query.

The main query in the preceding example is using the single value from the scalar query to determine which member to give one year of premium membership. If we hadn't added the LIMIT to the scalar query, it would have returned more than one value—it then wouldn't have been a scalar query. Based on the operator in the WHERE clause of its outer query, MySQL would have returned an error message like this:

```
ERROR 1242 (ER_SUBSELECT_NO_1_ROW)
SQLSTATE = 21000
Message = "Subquery returns more than 1 row"
```

As with all subqueries, there's always a way to get the same results without a subquery, using JOIN or some other method to bring results together in complex ways. To some extent, it's a matter of style which method you decide to use. I generally prefer subqueries, especially when using them in applications I develop in PHP or Perl. They're easier for me to decipher months or years later when I want to make changes to a program I've written.

Column Subqueries

In the preceding subsection, we discussed instances in which one scalar value was obtained in a WHERE clause. However, there are times when you may want to match multiple values. For those situations, you will need to use the subquery in conjunction with an operator such as IN, which is used to specify a comma-separated list of values. Let's look at an example of this.

In one of the examples in the previous subsection, we used a scalar subquery to get a list of bird families for the bird order *Galliformes*. Suppose that we also want the common name of one bird species from each family in the order; we want to randomly select a bird name from each. To do this, we will create a subquery that will select a list of bird family names for the order. Enter the following SQL statement:

```
SELECT * FROM
  (SELECT common_name AS 'Bird',
   families.scientific_name AS 'Family'
   FROM birds
   JOIN bird_families AS families USING(family_id)
   JOIN bird_orders AS orders USING(order_id)
   WHERE common_name != ''
   AND families.scientific_name IN
     (SELECT DISTINCT families.scientific_name AS 'Family'
      FROM bird_families AS families
      JOIN bird_orders AS orders USING(order_id)
```

```
     WHERE orders.scientific_name = 'Galliformes'
        ORDER BY Family)
    ORDER BY RAND()) AS derived_1
GROUP BY (Family);
```

```
+-------------------------------+-----------------+
| Bird                          | Family          |
+-------------------------------+-----------------+
| White-crested Guan            | Cracidae        |
| Forsten's Scrubfowl           | Megapodiidae    |
| Helmeted Guineafowl           | Numididae       |
| Mountain Quail                | Odontophoridae  |
| Gray-striped Francolin        | Phasianidae     |
+-------------------------------+-----------------+
```

In this example, we have two subqueries, a subquery within a subquery, within an outer query. The most inner subquery is known as a nested subquery. The subqueries here are executed before the outer query, so the results will be available before the WHERE clause of the outer query is executed. In that vein, the nested subquery will be executed before the subquery in which it is contained. In this example, the nested query is contained within the parentheses of the IN operator—the most indented query. That SQL statement selects the bird family name where the name of the order is *Galliformes*. The DISTINCT flag by the alias Family instructs MySQL to return only one entry for each distinct family name. If we had manually entered that information, it would look like this: *('Cracidae','Megapodiidae','Numididae','Odontophoridae','Phasianidae')*. This subquery is a multiple-field or column subquery.

The inner subquery in the preceding example is a table subquery. It selects a list of all birds that are in the list of bird families provided by its subquery. We could just select one bird for each family at this level using a GROUP BY clause to group by the Family name to get one bird species per family. But that would select the first rows found and the results would be the same every time. We want to select randomly each time this SQL statement is executed. To do that, we're selecting all of the birds for each bird family and then using ORDER BY RAND( ) to randomly order the rows of the results table. Then we're wrapping that in another query, the outer query to GROUP BY the bird family. That will give us one entry for each bird family.

Row Subqueries

Row subqueries retrieve a single row of data that is then used by the outer query. It's used in a WHERE clause to compare one row of columns to one row of columns selected in the subquery. Let's consider an example of this and then we'll discuss it more. Suppose another bird-watcher site closes, this one in Eastern Europe. They send us their database, which contains a table with the names of their members, and another table with information members provided related to birds they spotted. We put both of these tables in the birdwatchers database to import into our tables. In the process of importing these members into our humans table, we discover people who are already members of our site. That's OK: we know how to avoid importing the duplicates. Now we want to import the table of birds spottings. Because there were duplicate members, maybe those members have logged information on birds they saw in the wild on this Eastern European site. So we want to check that each entry is not a duplicate and then import it. Look at this SQL statement:

```
INSERT INTO bird_sightings
(bird_id, human_id, time_seen, location_gps)
VALUES
  (SELECT birds.bird_id, humans.human_id,
   date_spotted, gps_coordinates
   FROM
     (SELECT personal_name, family_name, science_name, date_spotted,
      CONCAT(latitude, '; ', longitude) AS gps_coordinates
      FROM eastern_birders
      JOIN eastern_birders_spottings USING(birder_id)
      WHERE
          (personal_name, family_name,
           science_name, CONCAT(latitude, '; ', longitude) )
        NOT IN
          (SELECT name_first, name_last, scientific_name, location_gps
           FROM humans
           JOIN bird_sightings USING(human_id)
           JOIN rookery.birds USING(bird_id) ) ) AS derived_1
   JOIN humans
   ON(personal_name = name_first
      AND family_name = name_last)
   JOIN rookery.birds
   ON(scientific_name = science_name) );
```

This looks very complicated and can be difficult to understand or construct correctly. Let's discern the major elements here. Look first at the subquery in parentheses, the nested subquery. We're selecting data from tables in our database: the names of each person, the bird species and where the member sighted it. This nested subquery is contained within the WHERE clause of another subquery, a row subquery. Notice that a list of columns from the tables of the row subquery is given in parentheses. So the condition of the WHERE clause is that the values of those columns for each row of the joined tables are compared to the values of the columns for each row from joined tables in its subquery. The outer query inserts the relevant values into the bird_sightings table.

The preceding example is certainly an odd one and seemingly, unnecessarily complex. But there are times when a row query like this can be useful. To put our example more simply, if there's a row with the same human name who spotted the same bird species at the exact same map coordinates, don't import it. If all of those values are not the same, then insert it into the bird_sightings table. There are other ways, though, you can accomplish this task. For instance, you might do this in stages with multiple SQL statements and a temporary table. You could also do it in stages within a program using one of the languages like Perl and an API like the Perl DBI. But it's good to know you have the option of doing it within one SQL statement if that's what you want.

Table Subqueries

A subquery can be used to generate a results set, a table from which an outer query can select data. That is to say, a subquery can be used in a FROM clause as if it were another table in a database. It is said to be a derived table.

There are a few rules related to table subqueries. Each derived table must be assigned an alias—any unique name is fine. You can use the keyword AS for assigning an alias. Each column in a subquery that is in part of a FROM clause must have a unique name. For instance, if you select the same column twice in a subquery, you have to assign at least one of them an alias that is unique. A subquery contained in a FROM clause cannot generally be a correlated subquery; it cannot reference the same table as the outer query.

For an example of a table subquery, let's use the example near the beginning of this chapter that used a UNION. In that example, we had two SELECT statements which counted the number of rows for birds in two bird families: *Pelecanidae* and *Ardeidae*. With a UNION, the results were merged into one results set. That was a bulky method. We can do better with a table subquery. The subquery we'll use will select just the bird family name for each bird of the two families that we wanted to count. That may seem silly, to list the bird family name multiple times, especially when we already know the name of the bird families we want to count. But that's how we can count them and use the name for our results set. MySQL won't display the names multiple times—that will go on behind the scenes. It will display only one entry per family because of the GROUP BY clause. Enter the following:

```
SELECT family AS 'Bird Family',
COUNT(*) AS 'Number of Birds'
FROM
  (SELECT families.scientific_name AS family
   FROM birds
   JOIN bird_families AS families USING(family_id)
   WHERE families.scientific_name IN('Pelecanidae','Ardeidae')) AS derived_1
GROUP BY family;
```

```
+-------------+-----------------+
| Bird Family | Number of Birds |
+-------------+-----------------+
| Ardeidae    |             157 |
| Pelecanidae |              10 |
+-------------+-----------------+
```

This a much better way to form this unified results set than using a UNION. We could add more bird family names to the WHERE clause in the subquery to get more rows in the results set, instead of having to copy the SELECT statement for each family we add.

You can see in this example that a table subquery is the same as a table in the FROM clause. We can even give it an alias (e.g., derived_1) as we can with a normal table. The subquery returns a table of results (i.e., the bird family names). The GROUP BY clause tells MySQL to group the results based on the family field, the alias in the subquery for the scien tific_name column of the bird_families table. We used that same alias to select that field in the column list of the outer query. When a column in a subquery is set to an alias, you have to use the alias; the column name becomes inaccessible outside the subquery when an alias is given.

Performance Considerations with Subqueries

Performance problems can occur with subqueries if they are not well constructed. There can be a performance drain when a subquery is placed within an IN( ) operator as part of a WHERE clause of the outer query. It's generally better to use instead the = operator, along with AND for each *column*=*value* pair. For situations in which you suspect poor performance with a subquery, try reconstructing the SQL statement with JOIN and compare the differences between the two SQL statements using the BENCHMARK( ) function. For ideas on improving subquery performance, Oracle has tips on their site for Optimizing Subqueries (*http://bit.ly/optimizing_subqueries*).

Summary

Many developers prefer subqueries—I do. They're easier to construct and decipher when you have problems later. If you work on a database that is very large and has a huge amount of activity, subqueries may not be a good choice because they can sometimes affect performance. For small databases, though, they're fine. You should learn to use subqueries and learn how to work without them (i.e, use JOIN) so you can handle any situation presented to you. You cannot be sure which method your next employer and team of developers may being using. It's best to be versatile.

As for learning to use JOIN, that's hardly optional. Very few developers don't use JOIN. Even if you prefer subqueries, they still call for JOIN. You can see this in almost all of the examples of subqueries in this chapter. You may rarely use UNION. But there's not much to learn there. However, you should be proficient in using JOIN. So don't avoid them; practice manually entering SQL statements that use them. The act of typing them helps.

Exercises

The goal of the following exercises is to give you practice assembling tables using JOIN and creating subqueries. In the process of doing these exercises, think about how tables and data come together. Try to envision each table as a separate piece of paper with a list of data on it, and how you might place them on a desk to find information on them in relation to each other. In such a scenario, you might tend to place your left index finger at one point on a page on the left and your right index finger on a point on another page on your right. That's a join. Where you point on each are the join points. As you type the SQL statements in these exercises, think of this scene and say aloud what you're doing, what you're telling MySQL to do. It helps to better understand the joining of tables and creating of subqueries.

1. In the birdwatchers database, there is a table called bird_sightings in which there are records of birds that members have seen in the wild. Suppose we have a contest in which we will award a prize based on the most sightings of birds from the order *Galliformes*. A member gets one point for each sighting of birds in this order.

   Construct an SQL statement to count the number of entries from each member. There should be two fields in the results set: one containing the human_id with Birder as the alias; and the second field containing the number of entries with Entries as its alias. To accomplish this, join the bird_sightings table to birds, bird_families, and bird_orders. Remember that these tables are in a different database. You will have to use the COUNT( ) function and a GROUP BY clause. Do all of this with JOIN and not with subqueries. Your results should look like the following:

   ```
   +--------+---------+
   | Birder | Entries |
   +--------+---------+
   |     19 |       1 |
   |     28 |       5 |
   +--------+---------+
   ```

   When you have successfully constructed this SQL statement, modify it to join in the humans table. In the column list, replace the field for human_id with the first and last name of the member. Use the CONCAT( ) function to put them together into a single field (with a space in between the names), with the same alias. Once you make the needed changes and execute it, the results should look like this, but the number of names and points may be different:

   ```
   +--------------+--------+
   | Birder       | Points |
   +--------------+--------+
   | Elena Bokova |      4 |
   | Marie Dyer   |      8 |
   +--------------+--------+
   ```

2. In the preceding exercises, you were asked to count the number of bird species the members sighted from the *Galliformes*. So that the contest is more fun, instead of giving one point for each bird species in that order, give a point for only one bird species per bird family in the bird order. That means that a member doesn't get more points for sighting the same bird species multiple times. A member also doesn't get more points for spotting several birds in the same family. Instead, the member has to look through bird guides to find a species for each species and then go looking for one from each in their area. This should make the contest more of an adventure for the members.

   To allow for the change to the contest, you will need to modify the SQL statement you constructed at the end of the previous exercise. First, you will need to add a DISTINCT to the start of the column list in the outer query. You'll need to remove the CONCAT( ) and GROUP BY. When you've done that, execute the SQL statement to make sure you have no errors. You should get a results set that shows multiple entries for some members. Next, place the whole SQL statement inside another SQL statement to make it a subquery. The new, outer query should include CONCAT( ) and GROUP BY so that it can count the single entries from each family for each member. It should return results like this:

   ```
   +---------------+--------+
   | Birder        | Points |
   +---------------+--------+
   | Elena Bokova  |      1 |
   | Marie Dyer    |      5 |
   +---------------+--------+
   ```

3. There are five families in the *Galliformes* bird order. For the contest described in the last two exercises, the most points that a member could achieve therefore is 5. Change the SQL statement you entered at the end of the previous exercise to list only members who have 5 points. To do this, you will need to wrap the previous SQL statement inside another, creating a nested query. When you execute the full SQL statement, the results should look like this:

   ```
   +------------+--------+
   | Birder     | Points |
   +------------+--------+
   | Marie Dyer |      5 |
   +------------+--------+
   ```

## PART IV

Built-In Functions

MySQL has many built-in functions that can be used to manipulate data contained within columns. With these functions, you can format data, extract text, or create search expressions. In and of themselves, functions do not affect data within columns. Instead, they manipulate data within results of queries. However, when used properly within SQL statements such as UPDATE, they can be a tool for changing data within columns. Incidentally, functions can be used for processing plain text or numbers—they don't require that data come from a column.

There are three major groupings of functions: string functions; date and time functions; and numeric or arithmetic functions. String functions are functions that relate to formatting and converting text, as well as finding and extracting text from columns. These are covered in Chapter 10.

Date and time functions are covered in Chapter 11. These functions can be used for formatting date and time values, as well as extracting specific values from a given date or time. They can also be used to get date and time values from the system to use for inserting or updating data in columns of a table.

The numeric or arithmetic functions are used for mathematical or statistical calculations on data. They are covered in Chapter 12.

These three chapters will include the most popular and more useful functions from these three major groups of functions, but not all functions from these categories. As part of learning and developing MySQL and MariaDB, you should be aware of these functions, and learn them well.

## CHAPTER 10

String Functions

A string is a value that can contain alphabetical characters, digits, and other characters (e.g., the ampersand, the dollar sign). Although a string can contain numbers, they are not considered numeric values. It's a matter of context and perspective. For instance, postal codes in the United States are all digits, but you shouldn't store them as integers because the postal code for 02138 would become 2138. You should use a string to store the postal code.

To make the handling of strings easier, MySQL provides many built-in functions. You can format text for nicer results, make better expressions in a WHERE clause, or otherwise extract and manipulate data from a string or column. Therefore, in this chapter, we'll go through several string functions, grouping them by similar features, and provide examples of how they might be used.

Basic Rules for Using Functions

There are a few things to remember when using functions. String functions also have some conventions of their own. Some of these rules can be different depending on how your server is configured:

- The basic syntax of a function is to a keyword immediately followed by arguments in parentheses. You cannot generally have a space between the keyword and the opening parenthesis like you can with operators in SQL statements (e.g., IN ( ) within a WHERE clause).

- Some functions take no arguments, such as NOW( ), which returns the current date or time. Other functions accept a particular number of arguments. Arguments are generally separated by commas, and some arguments can be augmented with keywords.

- When you pass text as an argument to a string function, put the text in single or double quotes.

- When giving a column as an argument, you generally don't use single quotes around the column name—if you do, MySQL will think you mean the literal text given. You can use backticks around the column name if the name is a reserved word or contains a character that might cause other problems.

- If by chance a string function tries to return a value that is larger (i.e., more characters) than allowed by the system settings (set by the `max_allowed_packet` configuration option), MySQL will return NULL instead.

- Some arguments to string functions represent positions within the strings. The first character in a string is numbered 1, not 0. Some functions let you count back from the end of the string, using negative integers. In these arguments, -1 refers to the last character.

- Some string functions call for a character length as an argument. If you give a fractional value to these functions, MySQL will round that value to the nearest integer.

Formatting Strings

Several string functions can format or reconstitute text for a better display. They allow you to store data in columns in a raw form or in separate components and then create the display you want when you retrieve the data.

For instance, in the humans table, we are able to store each member's title, first name, and last name in separate columns because we can put them together when needed. Breaking apart the names allows us to sort easily based on last name or first name. You'll see how this is done in the next subsection.

Concatenating Strings

The `CONCAT( )` function is very useful for pasting together the contents of different columns, or adding some other text to the results retrieved from a column. This is probably the most used string function—we've already used it in several examples in previous chapters. Within the parentheses of the function, in a comma-separated list, you give the strings, columns, and other elements that you want to merge together into one string.

Let's look at an example of how it might be used within a SELECT statement. Suppose we want to get a list of a few members and birds that they've seen. We could enter an SQL statement like this:

```
SELECT CONCAT(formal_title, '. ', name_first, SPACE(1), name_last) AS Birder,
    CONCAT(common_name, ' - ', birds.scientific_name) AS Bird,
```

```
time_seen AS 'When Spotted'
FROM birdwatchers.bird_sightings
JOIN birdwatchers.humans USING(human_id)
JOIN rookery.birds USING(bird_id)
GROUP BY human_id DESC
LIMIT 4;
```

```
+----------------------+-----------------------------------------+--------------------+
| Birder               | Bird                                    | When Spotted       |
+----------------------+-----------------------------------------+--------------------+
| Ms. Marie Dyer       | Red-billed Curassow - Crax blu...| 2013-10-02 07:39:44|
| Ms. Anahit Vanetsyan | Bar-tailed Godwit - Limosa lap...| 2013-10-01 05:40:00|
| Ms. Katerina Smirnova| Eurasian Curlew - Numenius arq...| 2013-10-01 07:06:46|
| Ms. Elena Bokova     | Eskimo Curlew - Numenius borea...| 2013-10-01 05:09:27|
+----------------------+-----------------------------------------+--------------------+
```

The first field displayed by this SQL statement is not a single column from the table, but a CONCAT( ) function that merges the bird-watcher's title, first name, and last name. We added a period in quotes after the title, as we've decided to store the titles without a period. We used quote marks to add spaces where needed. For the second field, we concatenated the common name of each bird species with the scientific name, and put spaces and a hyphen between them.

Without CONCAT( ), we might be tempted to combine text in one column that really should be separated. For instance, we might put the common and scientific names of bird species in one column. Keeping values in separate columns makes a database more efficient and flexible. String functions like CONCAT( ) alleviate the need to do otherwise.

A less common concatenating function is CONCAT_WS( ). It puts together columns with a separator between each. The first argument is the element you want to use as a separator (e.g., a space) and the rest of the arguments are the values to be separated. This can be useful when making data available for other programs.

For instance, suppose we have embroidered patches made with the name of the Rookery site on them and we want to mail one to each premium member. To do this, we use an advertising and marketing agency that will handle the mailing. The agency needs the names and addresses of members, and would like that data in a text file, with the values of each field separated by vertical bars. To do this, we'll run mysql on the command line, passing a single statement to it:

```
mysql -p --skip-column-names -e \
"SELECT CONCAT_WS('|', formal_title, name_first, name_last,
street_address, city, state_province, postal_code, country_id)
FROM birdwatchers.humans WHERE membership_type = 'premium'
AND membership_expiration > CURDATE();" > rookery_patch_mailinglist.txt
```

This example uses mysql with several options. The --skip-column-names option tells MySQL not to display the column headings—we want just the data separated by bars. The -e option says that what follows within quotes is to be executed. We then put the

SQL statement within double quotes. The first argument to CONCAT_WS( ) is the vertical bar that the company wants as a separator. The remaining arguments are the columns to be strung together. After the closing double quotes, we use > to redirect the results to a text file that we'll email to the agency. There is a potential problem with the SQL statement we used. If a column has a NULL value, nothing will be exported and no bar will be put in the file to indicate an empty field. Here's an example of how the text file would look:

```
Ms|Rusty|Osborne|ch
Ms|Elena|Bokova|ru
```

We have only four fields for these members, although we told MySQL to export eight fields. If these two records were in the midst of thousands of records, they would cause errors that might not be obvious when imported. Although it's more cumbersome, we should wrap each column name in an IFNULL( ) function. Then we can give a value to display if the column is NULL, such as the word *unknown* or a blank space. Here's the same example again, but with the IFNULL( ) function:

```
mysql -p --skip-column-names -e \
"SELECT CONCAT_WS('|', IFNULL(formal_title, ' '), IFNULL(name_first, ' '),
IFNULL(name_last, ' '), IFNULL(street_address, ' '),
IFNULL(city, ' '), IFNULL(state_province, ' '),
IFNULL(postal_code, ' '), IFNULL(country_id, ' '))
FROM birdwatchers.humans WHERE membership_type = 'premium'
AND membership_expiration > CURDATE();" > rookery_patch_mailinglist.txt
```

It looks daunting and excessive, but it's simple to MySQL. The new contents of the text file follow:

```
Ms|Rusty|Osborne| | | | |ch
Ms|Elena|Bokova| | | | |ru
```

That's a manageable data file. When the results are like this, the marketing company can import all of the records without errors and then contact us to try to get the missing information. They can add it to their system without having to reimport the text file.

Setting Case and Quotes

Occasionally, you might want to convert the text from a column to either all lowercase letters or all uppercase letters. For these situations, there are LOWER( ) and UPPER( ), which can also be spelled LCASE( ) and UCASE( ), respectively. In the example that follows, the output of the first column is converted to lowercase and the second to uppercase:

```
SELECT LCASE(common_name) AS Species,
UCASE(bird_families.scientific_name) AS Family
FROM birds
JOIN bird_families USING(family_id)
WHERE common_name LIKE '%Wren%'
```

```
ORDER BY Species
LIMIT 5;
```

```
+-----------------------------+-----------------+
| Species                     | Family          |
+-----------------------------+-----------------+
| apolinar's wren             | TROGLODYTIDAE   |
| band-backed wren            | TROGLODYTIDAE   |
| banded wren                 | TROGLODYTIDAE   |
| bar-winged wood-wren        | TROGLODYTIDAE   |
| bar-winged wren-babbler     | TIMALIIDAE      |
+-----------------------------+-----------------+
```

The QUOTE( ) function takes a string and returns it enclosed in single quotes. But it does a good deal more: it makes it input-safe by marking certain characters that could cause trouble in SQL statements or other programming languages. These characters are single quotes, backslashes, null (zero) bytes, and Ctrl-Z characters. The QUOTE( ) function precedes each of these with a backslash so that they won't be interpreted in some way or (in the case of a single quote) cause SQL to prematurely terminate the string.

In the following example, we're selecting a list of bird species named for a *Prince* or *Princess*:

```
SELECT QUOTE(common_name)
FROM birds
WHERE common_name LIKE "%Prince%"
ORDER BY common_name;
```

```
+----------------------------------+
| QUOTE(common_name)               |
+----------------------------------+
| 'Prince Henry\'s Laughingthrush' |
| 'Prince Ruspoli\'s Turaco'       |
| 'Princess Parrot'                |
+----------------------------------+
```

Notice in the results that because of the QUOTE( ) function, the strings returned are enclosed in single quotes, and any single quotes within the strings are escaped with a backslash. This can prevent errors if the value is passed to another program.

Trimming and Padding Strings

One of the problems with allowing the public to enter data into a website is that they're not always careful. They do things like adding spaces before and after the text. There are a few functions for trimming any leading or trailing spaces from the values of a column. The LTRIM( ) function eliminates any leading spaces to the left. For columns with spaces on the right, RTRIM( ) will remove them. A more versatile trimming function, though, is TRIM( ). With it, you can trim both left and right spaces.

These trim functions can be useful for cleaning data with the UPDATE statement. Let's look at an example of their use. In these SQL statements, we'll use LTRIM( ) and RTRIM( ) to eliminate both leading and trailing spaces:

```
UPDATE humans
SET name_first = LTRIM(name_first),
name_last = LTRIM(name_last);

UPDATE humans
SET name_first = RTRIM(name_first),
name_last = RTRIM(name_last);
```

In this example, we trimmed the leading spaces with the first UPDATE and the trailing spaces with the second one. Notice that we set the value of the columns to the same values, but with the strings trimmed. We can combine these functions into one SQL statement like so:

```
UPDATE humans
SET name_first = LTRIM( RTRIM(name_last) ),
name_last = LTRIM( RTRIM(name_last) );
```

You can always combine functions like this for a more dynamic result. In this case, though, the TRIM( ) function is a better alternative. Here's the same SQL statement using it:

```
UPDATE humans
SET name_first = TRIM(name_first),
name_last = TRIM(name_last);
```

The TRIM( ) function also offers more options. You can specify something other than spaces to remove. For instance, suppose we receive a small table with bird sightings from another bird-watcher club, as we did in "Row Subqueries" on page 170. However, in this table, the scientific names of bird species are within double quotes. If we wanted to insert that data into our bird_sightings table, we could use the same SQL query as we did before, with the addition of the TRIM( ) function. Here is the relevant excerpt, the last lines on which we join their table to our birds table:

```
...
JOIN rookery.birds
ON(scientific_name = TRIM(BOTH '"' FROM science_name) ) );
```

It may be difficult to see, but we're enclosing the character that we want trimmed—a double quote—within single quotes. The keyword BOTH isn't actually necessary because it's the default—that's why we didn't specify it in the previous example. If you don't want to remove the string given from one end or the other, you can specify LEADING or TRAILING, thus making TRIM( ) work like LTRIM( ) or RTRIM( ). The default string to trim is a space, as we have seen.

When displaying data in web forms and other such settings, it's sometimes useful to pad the data displayed with dots or some other filler. This can be necessary when dealing with VARCHAR columns where the width varies. Padding the results of a column selected can help the user to see the column limits. There are two functions that may be used for padding: LPAD( ) and RPAD( ). There is also SPACE( ), which pads the string with spaces:

```
SELECT CONCAT(RPAD(common_name, 20, '.' ),
RPAD(Families.scientific_name, 15, '.'),
Orders.scientific_name) AS Birds
FROM birds
JOIN bird_families AS Families USING(family_id)
JOIN bird_orders AS Orders
WHERE common_name != ''
AND Orders.scientific_name = 'Ciconiiformes'
ORDER BY common_name LIMIT 3;
```

```
+-----------------------------------------------+
| Birds                                         |
+-----------------------------------------------+
| Abbott's Babbler....Pellorneidae...Ciconiiformes |
| Abbott's Booby......Sulidae........Ciconiiformes |
| Abbott's Starling...Sturnidae......Ciconiiformes |
+-----------------------------------------------+
```

Notice how all the bird families and orders are aligned vertically. This is because we padded each value out to its maximum width using RPAD( ). The first argument was the column to read, the second was the total size of the resulting string we want, and the third was a period so that periods apear for columns that have less text. This happens to work because MySQL uses a fixed-width font. We could uses spaces instead of dots for a similar effect. For web display, we might use   as padding element for non-breaking spaces.

Extracting Text

There are a few functions for extracting a piece of text from a string. You indicate the point from which to start selecting text and how much text you want. There are four such functions: LEFT( ), MID( ), RIGHT( ), and SUBSTRING( ). The SUBSTRING_INDEX( ) function is also related. We'll look at each one here.

Let's look at the LEFT( ), MID( ), and RIGHT( ) functions first. Suppose our marketing agency acquires a table called prospects containing a list of people who are known to be bird-watchers. Each person's title and first and last name is stored in a column called prospect_name, with email addresses in another column. The prospect_name column is a fixed character length data type, CHAR(54). The marketing agency tells us that the title is contained in the first four characters, the first name in the next 25, and the last name in the remaining 25. For the titles, they're using only *Mr.* and *Ms.* with a space after each—hence the first four characters—but we will extract just the first two

characters for our tables. Let's see how that column looks by executing a simple SE
LECT to retrieve four names:

```
SELECT prospect_name
FROM prospects LIMIT 4;
```

```
+-----------------------------------------------------------+
| prospect_name                                             |
+-----------------------------------------------------------+
| Ms. Caryn-Amy           Rose                              |
| Mr. Colin               Charles                           |
| Mr. Kenneth             Dyer                              |
| Ms. Sveta               Smirnova                          |
+-----------------------------------------------------------+
```

As you can see, the data is a fixed width for each element. Normally, with a CHAR column,
MySQL would not store the trailing spaces. Whoever created this table enforced the
rigid format (4, 25, and 25 characters) by executing SET sql_mode =
'PAD_CHAR_TO_FULL_LENGTH'; before inserting data into the column.

With an INSERT INTO...SELECT statement and a few functions, we can extract and separate the data we need and put these prospects in a new table we created that we call
membership_prospects. Let's execute the SELECT first to test our organization of the
functions before we insert the data:

```
SELECT LEFT(prospect_name, 2) AS title,
MID(prospect_name, 5, 25) AS first_name,
RIGHT(prospect_name, 25) AS last_name
FROM prospects LIMIT 4;
```

```
+-------+---------------------------+----------------------------+
| title | first_name                | last_name                  |
+-------+---------------------------+----------------------------+
| Ms    | Caryn-Amy                 | Rose                       |
| Mr    | Kenneth                   | Dyer                       |
| Mr    | Colin                     | Charles                    |
| Ms    | Sveta                     | Smirnova                   |
+-------+---------------------------+----------------------------+
```

In the example's LEFT( ) function, the starting point for extracting data is the first character. The number we gave as an argument (i.e., 2), is the number of characters we want
to extract starting from the first. The RIGHT( ) function is similar, but it starts from the
last character on the right, counting left. The MID( ) function is a little different. With
it, you can specify the starting point (i.e., the fifth character in our example) and how
many characters you want (i.e., 25 characters).

The SUBSTRING( ) function is synonymous with MID( ) and their syntax is the same. By
default, if the number of characters to capture isn't specified, it's assumed that all the
remaining ones are to be extracted. This makes these functions work like the LEFT( )

function. If the second argument to SUBSTRING( ) or MID( ) is a negative number, the function will start from the end of the string, making it like the RIGHT( ) function.

Because the SUBSTRING( ) function is so versatile, we can use it to accomplish all the text extraction in the previous example. The equivalent SELECT would look like this:

```
SELECT SUBSTRING(prospect_name, 1, 2) AS title,
SUBSTRING(prospect_name FROM 5 FOR 25) AS first_name,
SUBSTRING(prospect_name, -25) AS last_name
FROM prospects LIMIT 3;
```

This example shows three ways to use SUBSTRING( ):

SUBSTRING(prospect_name, 1, 2) AS title
> This has the same syntax we have used for other functions in this section: three arguments to specify the column with the text, the starting point for extracting text, and the number of characters to extract.

SUBSTRING(prospect_name FROM 5 FOR 25) AS first_name
> This shows a different, wordier syntax. The starting point here is 5 and the number of characters to extract is 25.

SUBSTRING(prospect_name, -25) AS last_name
> This specifies a starting point of −25 characters. Because it doesn't specify how many to extract, MySQL takes the remaining characters from that starting point.

You can use whatever style you prefer.

The SUBSTRING_INDEX( ) is similar to the previous functions, but looks for elements that separate data within a string. For example, suppose the prospect_name column was constructed differently. Suppose that instead of having fixed width for the title and names, the text had vertical bars between them. This would be odd for data in a column, but it is possible. Here's how we could separate the same column containing the vertical bar character as the separator (the first and third third lines using SUBSTRING_INDEX( ) are fairly understandable, but the second one is more complex):

```
SELECT SUBSTRING_INDEX(prospect_name, '|', 1) AS title,
SUBSTRING_INDEX( SUBSTRING_INDEX(prospect_name, '|', 2), '|', -1) AS first_name,
SUBSTRING_INDEX(prospect_name, '|', -1) AS last_name
FROM prospects WHERE prospect_id = 7;
```

The second argument to SUBSTRING_INDEX( ) tells MySQL how to break the string into the pieces of text we want. In our example, we use '|' to specify the vertical bar. The number in the third argument tells how many elements to take. So in the first line here we're saying to get the first element. In the third line, because it has a negative sign in front of the number, we're saying to count from the end and get one element there. In the second line, we're using SUBSTRING_INDEX( ) twice, one call embedded inside the other. The inner call extracts the first two elements. Using those results, we then use an outer call to extract its first element starting from the end.

Using SUBSTRING( ) is much nicer, but you need to know the starting point and how many characters to take. In our vertical bar example, we'd need to know exactly where the vertical bars are in each name. To do that, you will need to use other functions to search strings. Those are covered in the next section.

Searching Strings and Using Lengths

MySQL and MariaDB do not have comprehensive functions for searching string based on patterns. Yes, there's the REGEXP operator that permits some pattern matching. But this isn't as robust and isn't fine tuned as easily as the capabilities offered by programming languages like PHP and Perl. But there are a few functions that assist in searching strings. We'll look at some of them in this section.

Locating Text Within a String

MySQL and MariaDB have a few built-in functions that can find characters within a string. These functions return the location where the search parameter was found.

The LOCATE( ) function returns the numeric starting point just left of the first occurrence of a given substring in a given string. It does not search beyond this point. Let's look at an example. Suppose we want a list of Avocet birds—they're a type of shore birds that is part of the *Recurvirostridae* family. We could enter something like this:

```
SELECT common_name AS 'Avocet'
FROM birds
JOIN bird_families USING(family_id)
WHERE bird_families.scientific_name = 'Recurvirostridae'
AND birds.common_name LIKE '%Avocet%';
```

```
+-------------------+
| Avocet            |
+-------------------+
| Pied Avocet       |
| Red-necked Avocet |
| Andean Avocet     |
| American Avocet   |
+-------------------+
```

Now suppose we want to eliminate the word *Avocet* from the names returned. There are a few ways we might do that: one way is to use the LOCATE( ) function to find the word *Avocet*, and extract all text before it with the SUBSTRING( ) function:

```
SELECT
SUBSTRING(common_name, 1, LOCATE(' Avocet', common_name) ) AS 'Avocet'
FROM birds
JOIN bird_families USING(family_id)
WHERE bird_families.scientific_name = 'Recurvirostridae'
AND birds.common_name LIKE '%Avocet%';
```

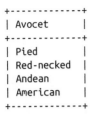

```
+-------------+
| Avocet      |
+-------------+
| Pied        |
| Red-necked  |
| Andean      |
| American    |
+-------------+
```

That's a cumbersome example, but it shows you how you can use LOCATE( ) in conjunction with other functions to get what you want from a string. Let's look at another example.

Earlier in this chapter, in "Trimming and Padding Strings" on page 183, we had some examples involving merging data from another bird-watcher group. That included using the TRIM( ) function to remove quotes from around the scientific names of birds spotted by people in that group. Let's use that column again, but assume that it doesn't have quotes. Instead, the bird species is given with its bird family in this format: *bird species - bird family*. For this, we can use the LOCATE( ) function to locate the hyphen and then the SUBSTRING( ) to get the family name for the JOIN clause in that earlier example. Here's just the excerpt from the JOIN clause:

```
...
JOIN rookery.birds
ON(scientific_name = SUBSTRING(science_name, LOCATE(' - ', science_name) + 3 ) );
```

Let's pull this apart to understand it better. First, let's focus on the inner function, the LOCATE( ). The search parameter it's given is a hyphen surrounded by spaces. The science_name column is the string to search. This function will return the position in the string where the search parameter is found. We're adding 3 to that because the search parameter is three characters long—in other words, LOCATE( ) gives us the point *before* the separator and we want to get the substring *after* the end of the separator. So the results of LOCATE( ) + 3 is given as the starting point for the SUBSTRING( ) function. Because we're not specifying how many characters we want, MySQL will extract the remaining characters. That will give us the scientific name of the bird in the table we're joining to birds.

The POSITION( ) function works like LOCATE( ), except that it takes the keyword IN instead of a comma between the substring you're searching for and the containing string:

```
POSITION(' - ' IN science_name)
```

In addition, LOCATE( ) accepts an optional argument to indicate the starting point for the search, which is not available in POSITION( ).

Another function for searching a string is FIND_IN_SET( ). If you have a string that contains several pieces of data separated by commas, this function tells you which element in that set of data contains the search pattern you give it. To understand this better, suppose that we want to get a list of members from Russia, but ordered by the date when the members joined. We would enter this:

```
SELECT human_id,
CONCAT(name_first, SPACE(1), name_last) AS Name,
join_date
FROM humans
WHERE country_id = 'ru'
ORDER BY join_date;
```

```
+----------+--------------------+------------+
| human_id | Name               | join_date  |
+----------+--------------------+------------+
|       19 | Elena Bokova       | 2011-05-21 |
|       27 | Anahit Vanetsyan   | 2011-10-01 |
|       26 | Katerina Smirnova  | 2012-02-01 |
+----------+--------------------+------------+
```

Now suppose that we want to know the position of the member *Anahit Vanetsyan* in the list of Russian members. We can see easily from the results just shown that she is the third member from Russia to join. That's because there are very few results here. Imagine if the results contained hundreds of names. We could use FIND_IN_SET( ) with a subquery to determine this:

```
SELECT FIND_IN_SET('Anahit Vanetsyan', Names) AS Position
  FROM
    (SELECT GROUP_CONCAT(Name ORDER BY join_date) AS Names
    FROM
      ( SELECT CONCAT(name_first, SPACE(1), name_last) AS Name,
        join_date
        FROM humans
        WHERE country_id = 'ru')
      AS derived_1 )
    AS derived_2;
```

```
+----------+
| Position |
+----------+
|        2 |
+----------+
```

This is a pretty complex SQL statement. The innermost SELECT is essentially the query we saw earlier, but returning just the full name and join date for each Russian person. These results are fed to GROUP_CONCAT, which produces a single huge string containing all the names. The outermost SELECT finds the name we want and returns its position.

When you put a SELECT statement inside parentheses and derive a table from it that you will use with an outer statement, you must give that derived table a name using AS. For naming simplicity, we've named the derived tables in this chapter derived_1 and derived_2. Almost any unique name is fine.

The statement can be useful if we associate it with a user profile page on the Rookery website. We might want to use it to show members where they rank in different lists, such as most sightings of birds or most sightings of birds in a particular category.

FIND_IN_SET( ) returns 0 if the string is not found in the set or if the string list is empty. It returns NULL if the value of either argument is NULL.

String Lengths

There will be times you want to know how long a string is. There are a few functions that return the character length of a string. This can be useful when adjusting formatting or making other decisions related to a string, and they are commonly used with functions like LOCATE( ) and SUBSTRING( ).

The CHAR_LENGTH( ) or CHARACTER_LENGTH( ) function returns the number of characters in a string. This could be helpful when different rows have different-length strings in a particular column.

For instance, suppose we want to display on the Rookery website a list of the birds most recently sighted by members, as recorded in the bird_sightings table. We'll include the common and scientific name and other information about the bird species. Suppose that we want to also include the comments that the member entered when they recorded the sighting. Because this column can contain a lot of text, we want to know how many characters it contains when displaying it. If there's too much (i.e., more than 100 characters), we'll limit the text and include a link on the web page to view all of the text. To check the length, we could construct an SQL statement like this that would be part of a program:

```
SELECT IF(CHAR_LENGTH(comments) > 100), 'long', 'short')
FROM bird_sightings
WHERE sighting_id = 2;
```

Here we're using CHAR_LENGTH( ) to count the number of characters in the comments column for the row selected. We're using the IF( ) function to determine whether the character length of the comments is greater than 100 characters. If it is, the function will return the word long. If not, it will return short. If this SQL statement was used in an API script, the value in the WHERE clause for the sighting_id could be dynamically replaced for each bird sighting.

CHAR_LENGTH( ) understands the character set in current use, as we touched on in "Creating a Database" on page 46. Characters that take up multiple bytes—usually present in Asian languages—are still considered one character. In contrast, the LENGTH( ) function returns the number of bytes in a given string. Note that there are eight bits to a byte and that Western languages normally use one byte for each letter. If you want to count the number of bits, use the BIT_LENGTH( ) function.

As an example, suppose we notice that the comments column of the bird_sightings table contains some odd binary characters. They have been entered into the column through the mobile application we provide to members. To narrow the list of rows that have these odd characters so that we can remove them, we can execute the following SQL statement:

```
SELECT sighting_id
FROM bird_sightings
WHERE CHARACTER_LENGTH(comments) != LENGTH(comments);
```

This will give us the sighting_id for the rows in which the number of characters does not equal the number of bytes in the comments column.

Comparing and Searching Strings

The previous subsection used the output of CHAR_LENGTH( ) as input to an IF( ) statement so that we had a choice of what to return. In this subsection, we'll look at some functions that compare strings, which can also be handy when used with a logical function such as IF( ) or in a WHERE clause.

Let's consider a situation where we might use one of these functions—specifically, the STRCMP( ) function. The name of the function, in the manner much loved by computer programmers, is a compressed version of "string compare."

Email addresses are critical for communicating with members so we decide to require new members to enter their email address twice during the registration process to ensure accuracy. However, in case the connection is lost in the process or the joining member does not correct a problem with their email address, we want to keep both addresses until they do. So we'll add a row to the humans table to store whatever information they give us, and then store both email addresses in another table to compare them. For that comparison, we could use the STRCMP( ) function in an SQL statement.

This scenario is the kind of situation that you would automate with an API program, a program you would create to interface with MySQL or MariaDB. It would store the SQL statements needed for processing the information the new member enters from the website. To start the process related to checking the email, we might create a table that will store the member's identification number and the two email addresses. We could do that like so:

```
CREATE TABLE possible_duplicate_email
(human_id INT,
email_address1 VARCHAR(255),
email_address2 VARCHAR(255),
entry_date datetime );
```

Now when new members register, after their information has been stored in the `hu mans` table, our web interface can store conditionally the two email addresses provided in the `possible_duplicate_email` table. It might look like this:

```
INSERT IGNORE INTO possible_duplicate_email
(human_id, email_address_1, email_address_2, entry_date)
VALUES(LAST_INSERT_ID(), 'bobyfischer@mymail.com', 'bobbyfischer@mymail.com')
WHERE ABS( STRCMP('bobbyrobin@mymail.com', 'bobyrobin@mymail.com') ) = 1 ;
```

For the email addresses, I've displayed the plain text. But in a more realistic example, this SQL statement might be embedded in a PHP script and would refer to variables (e.g., $email_1 and $email_2) where the email addresses are here.

Using the `STRCMP( )` in the `WHERE` clause, if the email addresses match, `STRCMP( )` returns 0. If the addresses don't match, it will return 1 or -1. It returns -1 if the first value is alphabetically before the second. To allow for that possibility, we put it inside of `ABS( )`, which changes the value to the absolute value—it makes negative values positive. So, if the two email addresses don't match, the statement will insert the addresses into the `possible_duplicate_email` table for an administrator to review. Incidentally, that would normally return an error message, but `IGNORE` flag tells MySQL to ignore errors.

Another comparison function is `MATCH( ) AGAINST( )`, which searches for a string and returns matching rows from the table. It even ranks the rows by relevance, but that is beyond the scope of this chapter. Among the complications of `MATCH( ) AGAINST( )`, it works only on columns that have been indexed with a special `FULLTEXT` index. To test this function, we'll first add a `FULLTEXT` index to the `bird_sightings` table, basing it on the `comments` column because that's a `TEXT` column:

```
CREATE FULLTEXT INDEX comment_index
ON bird_sightings (comments);
```

Now you can use `MATCH( ) AGAINST( )`. It is commonly found in `WHERE` clauses as a condition to find columns containing a given string. Text in the given string, which is delimited by spaces or quotes, is parsed into separate words. Small words (i.e., three characters or fewer) are generally ignored. Here is an example:

```
SELECT CONCAT(name_first, SPACE(1), name_last) AS Name,
common_name AS Bird,
SUBSTRING(comments, 1, 25) AS Comments
FROM birdwatchers.bird_sightings
JOIN birdwatchers.humans USING(human_id)
JOIN rookery.birds USING(bird_id)
WHERE MATCH (comments) AGAINST ('beautiful');
```

```
+---------------------+-------------------+-----------------------------+
| Name                | Bird              | Comments                    |
+---------------------+-------------------+-----------------------------+
| Elena Bokova        | Eskimo Curlew     | It was a major effort get   |
| Katerina Smirnova   | Eurasian Curlew   | Such a beautiful bird. I    |
+---------------------+-------------------+-----------------------------+
```

In the `WHERE` clause, we're able now to match the `comments` column against the string `beautiful`. The `comments` column from the `birdwatchers.bird_sightings` is combined in the results with three other columns: `common_name` from `rookery.birds` and `name_first` and `name_last` from `birdwatchers.humans`.

We're using the `SUBSTRING` function to limit the amount of text displayed. This cuts off the text abruptly. You could use the `CONCAT( )` function to append ellipses to indicate there is more text. You might also use the `IF( )` function to determine whether there is more text before appending ellipses. There are other functions you can use for locating the `beautiful` within the column so that you can display only the text around it. We'll cover that kind of function later in this chapter.

Replacing and Inserting into Strings

If you want to insert or replace certain text from a column (but not all of its contents), you could use the `INSERT( )` function. Don't confuse this with the `INSERT` statement. The syntax of this function consists of the string or column into which you want to insert text, followed by the position in which to insert text. You may specify also how much text to delete from that point, if you want. Finally, you give the text to insert. Let's look at some examples of this function.

We'll start with a simple example. Suppose that on a page of the Rookery site, we are thinking of adding some text to the common names of bird species with the word *Least* in their name. We want to explain that it means *Smallest*, so that uninformed birders don't think it means these birds are the least important. To test this, we enter this SQL statement:

```
SELECT INSERT(common_name, 6, 0, ' (i.e., Smallest)')
AS 'Smallest Birds'
FROM birds
WHERE common_name LIKE 'Least %' LIMIT 1;
```

```
+-----------------------------+
| Smallest Birds              |
+-----------------------------+
| Least (i.e., Smallest) Grebe |
+-----------------------------+
```

The first argument is the column containing the string we're manipulating. The second argument is the starting point for inserting text. Based on the `WHERE` clause, we're looking for common names that start with *Least*. That's 5 characters. We add 1 to that because the starting point for INSERT is 1. The third argument specifies how many characters after the starting point should be replaced. In this case, we're just inserting text, not replacing any.

The SQL statement uses INSERT( ) to change the results set, not the data in the table. So we could use the INSERT( ) function to display the common names like this to new members for the first month who have identified themselves as new to bird-watching. We would have to construct a more complex SQL statement to check who is new, but this example shows you how to insert text within a string. Let's look now at an example in which we will replace data using INSERT( ).

Suppose we discover that parts of some of the common bird species names are abbreviated in the birds table (e.g., *Great* is abbreviated as *Gt.*). We prefer not to have any abbreviations for the common names. Before changing the data, we'll execute a SELECT statement to test our use of the INSERT( ) function:

```
SELECT common_name AS Original,
INSERT(common_name, LOCATE('Gt.', common_name), 3, 'Great') AS Adjusted
FROM birds
WHERE common_name REGEXP 'Gt.' LIMIT 1;
```

```
+-------------------+---------------------+
| Original          | Adjusted            |
+-------------------+---------------------+
| Gt. Reed-Warbler  | Great Reed-Warbler  |
+-------------------+---------------------+
```

We've already reviewed the arguments of the INSERT( ) function in the previous example. The extra twist here is in the second argument, which contains the LOCATE( ). We're using that function to determine the position in the string where text is to be replaced. In the previous example, we assumed that the common name would start with the string we wanted to modify. In this case, we're not assuming the position of the string within the column. Instead, we're letting MySQL find it for us.

Another difference in this example is the third element: we're telling the function to replace three characters (i.e., the length of *Gt.*) from the starting point with the text given for the fourth argument (i.e., *Great*). Although the text we're adding is more than three characters, it's fine because when we update the table later, we're updating a column with plenty of space to hold the results.

If LOCATE( ) does not find the string we give it, it returns 0. A value of 0 for the position in the INSERT( ) function negates it and returns the value of common_name unchanged. So with this usage of INSERT( ), because of the inclusion of LOCATE( ) for the starting location, the WHERE clause is unnecessary—except to see that it works where we want it to.

Now that we've verified that our combination of functions works correctly, we can update the data by entering the following SQL statement:

```
UPDATE birds
SET common_name = INSERT(common_name, LOCATE('Gt.', common_name), 3, 'Great')
WHERE common_name REGEXP 'Gt.';
```

There is an alternative to using INSERT( ) for replacing text in a string. In the previous example, we had to use the LOCATE( ) function to determine the location of the text where we wanted to insert text and we had to tell it how many characters to replace. A simpler function for replacing text is REPLACE( ). We could use this function to replace all occurrences of *Gt.* with *Great* in the common_name column. Let's test that with a SELECT statement like so:

```
SELECT common_name AS Original,
REPLACE(common_name, 'Gt.', 'Great') AS Replaced
FROM birds
WHERE common_name REGEXP 'Gt.' LIMIT 1;
```

```
+-----------------+--------------------+
| Original        | Replaced           |
+-----------------+--------------------+
| Gt. Reed-Warbler | Great Reed-Warbler |
+-----------------+--------------------+
```

This works much better. We can use the REPLACE( ) with the arguments we have here and enter the following UPDATE to change the data in the table:

```
UPDATE birds
SET common_name = REPLACE(common_name, 'Gt.', 'Great');

Query OK, 8 rows affected (0.23 sec)
Rows matched: 28891  Changed: 8  Warnings: 0
```

Notice that we didn't include the WHERE clause, but the results message says that only eight rows were changed. This is because there were only eight rows that contained *Gt.* in the common_name column. Updating data in a table with that many rows is intimidating and dangerous without a WHERE clause. That's why it's good to use them and to test the parameters with a SELECT statement first.

Converting String Types

There may be times when you will have to work with tables created by people who might not have made the best choices for column data types. Sometimes you can alter the tables, but sometimes you may not be allowed to do so. For manipulating data from such tables or for importing data from them, you can use the CAST( ) or CONVERT( ) functions to change the data type of columns. The effect just takes place within your SQL statement, not the database itself. Let's look at some examples of how and why you might use these two functions, which are basically synonymous except for a minor syntax difference.

Suppose we're given a table containing images of birds in a particular area, showing female, male, and juvenile color patterns. One of the columns contains numbers for ordering birds based loosely on the type of bird and the date when usually seen in the area. This column isn't a numeric data type like INT, but is CHAR. When we sort the data based on this column, MySQL will sort the rows lexically, not numerically. Here's an example of how that might look:

```
SELECT sorting_id, bird_name, bird_image
FROM bird_images
ORDER BY sorting_id
LIMIT 5;
```

```
+------------+-----------------+----------------------------+
| sorting_id | bird_name       | bird_image                 |
+------------+-----------------+----------------------------+
| 11         | Arctic Loon     | artic_loon_male.jpg        |
| 111        | Wilson's Plover | wilson_plover_male.jpg     |
| 112        | Wilson's Plover | wilson_plover_female.jpg   |
| 113        | Wilson's Plover | wilson_plover_juvenile.jpg |
| 12         | Pacific Loon    | pacific_loon_male.jpg      |
+------------+-----------------+----------------------------+
```

Notice that the rows with a sorting_id starting with 11*n* are listed before one with the value of 12. That's because MySQL is reading the data as characters and not numbers. The two Loons should be together, before the Plovers are listed.

We can use the CAST( ) function to cast the values taken from sorting_id into the INT data type:

```
SELECT sorting_id, bird_name, bird_image
FROM bird_images ORDER BY CAST(sorting_id AS INT) LIMIT 5;
```

```
+------------+-----------------+----------------------------+
| sorting_id | bird_name       | bird_image                 |
+------------+-----------------+----------------------------+
| 11         | Arctic Loon     | artic_loon_male.jpg        |
| 12         | Pacific Loon    | pacific_loon_male.jpg      |
| 111        | Wilson's Plover | wilson_plover_male.jpg     |
| 112        | Wilson's Plover | wilson_plover_female.jpg   |
| 113        | Wilson's Plover | wilson_plover_juvenile.jpg |
+------------+-----------------+----------------------------+
```

That worked correctly. Let's suppose now that we don't want to use sorting_id, but instead the gender_age column. This is an ENUM column specifying that the image file is for a male, female, or juvenile. The color patterns of most birds deviate based on these factors. Let's see how the results will look if we sort based on this column:

```
SELECT bird_name, gender_age, bird_image
FROM bird_images
WHERE bird_name LIKE '%Plover%'
ORDER BY gender_age
```

```
LIMIT 5;
```

```
+------------------+------------+-----------------------------+
| bird_name        | gender_age | bird_image                  |
+------------------+------------+-----------------------------+
| Wilson's Plover  | male       | wilson_plover_male.jpg      |
| Snowy Plover     | male       | snowy_plover_male.jpg       |
| Wilson's Plover  | female     | wilson_plover_female.jpg    |
| Snowy Plover     | female     | snowy_plover_female.jpg     |
| Wilson's Plover  | juvenile   | wilson_plover_juvenile.jpg  |
+------------------+------------+-----------------------------+
```

Notice that the rows are grouped together based on the gender_age column, but those values are not in alphabetical order (i.e., *female* rows should be before *male* rows). This is because of how the enumerated values are listed in the gender_age column:

```
SHOW COLUMNS FROM bird_images LIKE 'gender_age' \G
```

```
*************************** 1. row ***************************
  Field: gender_age
   Type: enum('male','female','juvenile')
   Null: YES
    Key:
Default: NULL
  Extra:
```

To MySQL, the value of male for the gender_age column is stored as 1, and female as 2. This controls the order of the display, even though the values are rendered as text. If we use though the CAST( ) or the CONVERT( ) function in the ORDER BY clause, MySQL will sort the results based on their rendered values and not their column values. Here's how that would look:

```
SELECT bird_name, gender_age, bird_image
FROM bird_images
WHERE bird_name LIKE '%Plover%'
ORDER BY CONVERT(gender_age, CHAR)
LIMIT 5;
```

```
+------------------+------------+-----------------------------+
| bird_name        | gender_age | bird_image                  |
+------------------+------------+-----------------------------+
| Wilson's Plover  | female     | wilson_plover_female.jpg    |
| Snowy Plover     | female     | snowy_plover_female.jpg     |
| Wilson's Plover  | juvenile   | wilson_plover_juvenile.jpg  |
| Snowy Plover     | juvenile   | snowy_plover_juvenile.jpg   |
| Wilson's Plover  | male       | wilson_plover_male.jpg      |
+------------------+------------+-----------------------------+
```

Notice that for the CONVERT( ) function, a comma is used to separate the string given from the data type instead of the AS keyword. The data type given as the second argument can be BINARY, CHAR, DATE, DATETIME, SIGNED [INTEGER], TIME, or UNSIGNED [INTEGER].

BINARY converts a string to a binary string. You can add also `CHARACTER SET` to use a different character set from the default for the value given. To convert the character set of a given string to another, you have to use the `USING` option, like so:

```
SELECT bird_name, gender_age, bird_image
FROM bird_images
WHERE bird_name LIKE '%Plover%'
ORDER BY CONVERT(gender_age USING utf8)
LIMIT 5;
```

Compressing Strings

Some column data types allow large amounts of data. For instance, the `BLOB` column can store plenty. To reduce the size of tables that use this column data type, you can compress the data it contains when inserting the data. The `COMPRESS( )` function compresses a string and the `UNCOMPRESS( )` function decompresses a compressed string. If you want to use them, MySQL has to have been compiled with a compression library (i.e., `zlib`). If it wasn't, a NULL value will be returned when using `COMPRESS( )`. Let's look at some examples of their use.

The humans table has a column for `birding_background` which is a `BLOB`. Members can write as much as they like about themselves, which could result in pages of information on their experiences and education as bird-watchers. This could potentially slow down queries and updates if many members do this. So we decide to use `COMPRESS( )` to compress the member's background when inserting it into the humans table. Here's how that might look:

```
INSERT INTO humans
(formal_title, name_first, name_last, join_date, birding_background)
VALUES('Ms', 'Melissa', 'Lee', CURDATE(), COMPRESS("lengthy background..."));
```

This SQL statement inserts a new member's information into the humans table—it has more columns than shown here, but we're trying to keep this example simple. The statement uses the `COMPRESS( )` function to compress the background information given (which isn't much for this simple example). You would normally get such data from an API variable using something like PHP to store text entered by the user through a web page. So instead of the text shown here, you would use a variable (e.g., `$birding_back ground`).

To see how the data looks in the compressed form, we could do this:

```
SELECT birding_background AS Background
FROM humans
WHERE name_first = 'Melissa' AND name_last = 'Lee' \G

*************************** 1. row ***************************
Background:    x#####/iTHJL##/######## Z######
```

Notice that the results are not normal text. The `mysql` client substitutes a hash sign (#) for binary values. In order to see the text contained in this compressed format, we would use `UNCOMPRESS( )`. It returns NULL if the string is not compressed or if MySQL wasn't compiled with `zlib`:

```
SELECT UNCOMPRESS(birding_background) AS Background
FROM humans
WHERE name_first = 'Melissa' AND name_last = 'Lee' \G

*************************** 1. row ***************************
Background: lengthy background...
```

For small amounts of text like this, compression takes more space than the plain text. But for large amounts of text, it will save plenty of space. So use it sparingly and where appropriate.

Summary

There are more string functions available in MySQL and MariaDB. A few of the functions mentioned here have aliases or close alternatives. There are also functions for converting between ASCII, binary, hexadecimal, and octal strings. And there are also string functions related to text encryption and decryption that were not mentioned. However, I think this chapter has given you a good collection of common string functions that will assist you in building more powerful SQL statements and formatting results to be more attractive.

Exercises

String functions are very necessary to developing databases in MySQL and MariaDB. You need to know them well. To become an expert, you need to practice using them, so be sure to complete all of the following exercises.

1. One of the most commonly used string functions is `CONCAT( )`. Construct a `SELECT` statement to query the humans table. Use the `CONCAT( )` function to merge together values from the `name_first` column with the `name_last` column. Use the `SPACE( )` function to put a space between them in the results. Give that field an alias of Full Name—and remember to put quotes around this alias, as it contains a space. Limit the results to four people. Execute it to be sure it has no errors.

   Add a `WHERE` clause to that `SELECT` statement. For the condition of the `WHERE` clause, copy the `CONCAT( )` you just assembled. List rows where the name is in a set of the following names: Lexi Hollar, Michael Zabalaoui, and Rusty Johnson.

   After you successfully execute the `SELECT` with that `WHERE` clause, add an `ORDER BY` clause to sort the data based on the concatenated name. Do it without using `CONCAT( )`.

2. Construct a SELECT statement that selects, from the `birds` table, the `common_name` and the `scientific_name`. Use a string function to change the `scientific_name` to all lowercase letters. Use the CONCAT( ) function to put them into one field, with a space after the common name, followed by the scientific name in parentheses— for example, *African Desert Warbler (sylvia deserti).* Don't use the SPACE( ) function. Instead, put the spaces and parentheses within single quote marks within the CONCAT( ). Give the resulting field an alias of `Bird Species`. Limit the results to 10 rows.

   After you've successfully executed that SQL statement, modify that statement to join in the `bird_families` and the `bird_orders` tables. The JOIN statement was covered extensively in "Unifying Results" on page 153. Then add the `scientific_name` columns from both of these tables to the fields returned.

   Execute this modified statement to make sure your joins are correct. When they are, move the `scientific_name` columns for the two additional tables into the CONCAT( ). Using the RPAD( ) function, put dots after the bird species name, before the bird family and the bird order names. The results for a field will look like this:

   ```
   Speckled Warbler (pyrrholaemus sagittatus)...Acanthizidae...Passeriformes
   ```

   This will probably require you to use CONCAT( ) twice. Use a WHERE clause to list only Warblers. Limit the results to 10 rows.

3. Construct another SELECT statement to list all of the common names of bird species from the `birds` table, where the common name contains the word *Shrike*. When you execute that statement you should see some names with a hyphen after the word *Shrike*. Add the REPLACE( ) function to the SELECT statement to replace those hyphens with a space in the results, and then execute the SQL statement again.

4. Some of the names of the birds in the results from the SELECT statement in the previous exercise have more than one hyphen (e.g., *Yellow-browed Shrike-Vireo*). Redo that SQL statement to replace only the hyphens after the word *Shrike* (e.g., to look like this: *Yellow-browed Shrike Vireo*). In order to do this, use LOCATE( ) with REPLACE( ). You will need to use LOCATE( ) twice: one within another.

5. True Shrikes are of the *Laniidae* family. Construct another SELECT to select the common bird names with the word *Shrike*, but belonging to *Laniidae*. This will require a join to the `bird_families` table. Use one of the substring functions like SUBSTRING( ) to extract the words before *Shrike*. To do this, you will need to use LOCATE( ) or a similar function. Then use CONCAT( ) to display that value extracted after *Shrike* with a comma and space in between. The results for each field should look like this: `Shrike, Rufous-tailed`. Give the field an alias of `Shrikes`.

6. The humans table contains entries in which the member used either all lowercase letters or all uppercase letters to enter their first and last names (e.g., `andy oram` and `MICHAEL STONE`). Use UPDATE to change the names to title case (i.e., the first letter capital and the rest lowercase). First experiment with SELECT to make sure

you have the functions organized properly. Use the UCASE( ) and LCASE( ) functions to set the cases. You will need to use SUBSTRING( ) or a similar function a few times, and CONCAT( ) a couple of times.

## CHAPTER 11

Date and Time Functions

For many of us, there is a morning and an afternoon in each day. Days are measured in either two 12-hour blocks or one 24-hour block. There are 12 months in a year, with each month consisting of 30 or 31 days, except for one month which usually contains 28 days, but once every four years it contains 29. While this all may be rather natural or at least familiar to humans, putting it in terms a computer can manipulate can make it seem very unnatural and frustrating. However, the recording and manipulating of date and time in a database is a very common requirement.

For storing dates and times, known as *temporal data*, one needs to know which type of column to use in a table. More important is knowing how to record chronological data and how to retrieve it in various formats. Although this seems to be basic, there are many built-in time functions that can be used for more accurate SQL statements and better formatting of data. In this chapter, we will explore these various aspects of date and time functions in MySQL and MariaDB.

Date and Time Data Types

Because dates and times are ultimately just strings containing numbers, they could be stored in a regular character column. However, there are data types designed specifically for dates and times. By using temporal data type columns, you can make use of several built-in functions offered by MySQL and MariaDB. So before we start learning about the date and time functions, let's look at the data types that are available for recording date and time.

There are five temporal data types in MySQL and MariaDB: DATE for storing dates, TIME for storing time, DATETIME and TIMESTAMP for both date and time, and YEAR for a year:

DATE
>   This records the date only, in the format *yyyy-mm-dd*. You may prefer a different format (e.g., *02-14-2014* for St. Valentine's Day), but you can't change how the date

is stored—at least not without changing the source code of MySQL. But other functions discussed in this chapter let you display the date in the format you like.

This data type has a limit to the range of dates it will accept. It allows dates from as early as `1000-01-01` to as late as `9999-12-31`. That's far into the future, but you wouldn't use this for recording historical dates in the first millennium.

TIME

This records time in the format *hhh:mm:ss*. It accepts times ranging from `-838:59:59` to `838:59:59`. If you give it a time outside of that range or in some way not valid, it records the time as all zeros.

You may be wondering how you could have a time in which you need three digits for the hour. This is so that you can record how much time has elapsed for an event or when comparing two times, rather than just recording the time of day. For instance, you might want to note that something took 120 hours to complete. You could do this with two columns, one for recording the start time and the other the end time, and then compare them as needed. But this data type allows you to record the difference in one column, rather than recalculate each time you want that result.

DATETIME

This records a combination of date and time in the format *yyyy-mm-dd hh:mm:ss*. It accepts dates and times from `1000-01-01 00:00:00` to `9999-12-31 23:59:59`. That's the same range as DATE, but with the addition of the full range of a 24-hour day. As of version 5.6 of MySQL, fractions of a second are possible.

TIMESTAMP

This is similar to DATETIME, but more limited in its range of allowable time. Despite the name, it's not limited to time, but covers a range of dates from `1970-01-01 00:00:01` UTC to `2038-01-19 03:14:07` UTC. It's meant for relatively current dates and corresponds to the "epoch" chosen by the designers of the Unix operating system. As of version 5.6 of MySQL, fractions of a second are possible.

Although you can set the value of a column manually using this data type, whenever you insert a row or update a row without specifying an explicit value, MySQL automatically updates the column's value to the current date and time. That can be very convenient for some applications such as logging, but can cause you problems if you're unaware of it or don't allow for it. This is only for the first column in a table which uses TIMESTAMP. For subsequent TIMESTAMP columns, you would have to specify a couple of options to have the same effect: ON UPDATE CURRENT_TIME STAMP and ON INSERT CURRENT_TIMESTAMP.

YEAR

This records just a year in a column, in the format *yyyy*. It could be set to two digits (by defining the column as YEAR(2) with an explicit number), but that's deprecated and causes problems. So don't record years in two-digit formats with this data type.

This data type is also meant for birth years; it allows years from 1901 to 2155. If you give it an invalid value or a year outside of the allowed range, it records the year as 0000.

 Given some of the limitations of these data types, you may need to use a nontemporal data type for dates outside of the allowed ranges. You could use the INT data type to store each component of a date, or CHAR data type to store dates in a fixed width. For instance, you might have one INT column for storing the month, another for the day, and one CHAR(4) column to store years before the 20th century.

That can work generally, but it can be a problem when you try to do a calculation with these data types. Suppose you want to store *February 15* in two INT columns: 2 in my_month and 15 in my_day. If you were to add 20 days to the value of my_day, you would get an invalid date of *February 35*. To deal with this, you would have to construct a complex SQL statement to adjust the my_day and the my_month columns. Plus, you'd have to update the column you create for the year value when a date change pushes the values into a different year. You'd have similar problems if you tried to use INT to store times. All of this complexity is eliminated by using temporal data types for columns, so that you can use date functions provided with MySQL and MariaDB. These types have built-into complex calculations so that you don't have to worry about that.

Now that you're familiar with the temporal data types in MySQL and MariaDB (and hopefully, appreciate them), let's look at some examples of how you might use them with date and time functions. For some of the examples in this chapter, we'll use the tables we've already created, which have columns with these data types.

Current Date and Time

The most basic date and time functions are those related to the current date and time. They may be used for recording the current date and time in a column, for modifying results based on the current date and time, or for displaying the date and time in a results set. Let's start with the simplest one, NOW( ), which determines what time it is when you execute the statement. Enter the first line shown here in mysql (an example of the results follow):

```
SELECT NOW( );
```

```
+---------------------+
| NOW( )              |
+---------------------+
| 2014-02-08 09:43:09 |
+---------------------+
```

As you can see, that returns the date and time on a server in a format that matches the format of the DATETIME data type So if you have a column in a table that uses that data type, you can use the NOW( ) function to conveniently insert the current date and time into the column. The bird_sightings table has a column that uses the DATETIME data type, the time_seen column. Here's an example of how we might enter a row into that table using NOW( ):

```
INSERT INTO bird_sightings
(bird_id, human_id, time_seen, location_gps)
VALUES (104, 34, NOW( ), '47.318875; 8.580119');
```

This function can also be used with an application, or with a script for a web interface so that the user can record bird sightings without having to enter the time information.

 There are a few synonyms for the NOW( ) function: CURRENT_TIME STAMP( ), LOCALTIME( ), and LOCALTIMESTAMP( ). They return the exact same results. Synonyms such as these are provided so that MySQL and MariaDB will conform to functions in other SQL database systems. This way, if you have an application that uses another database (e.g., PostgreSQL, Sybase, Oracle), you can more easily replace it with MySQL without having to change the code in your applications.

The NOW( ) function returns the date and time at the start of the SQL statement containing it. For most purposes, this is fine: the difference between the time at the start and at the completion of an SQL statement is usually minimal and irrelevant. But you may have a situation in which an SQL statement takes a long time to execute, and you want to record the time at a certain point in that process. The SYSDATE( ) function records the time at which the function is executed, not the end of the statement. To see the difference, we can introduce the SLEEP( ) function to tell MySQL to pause execution for a given number of seconds. Here's a simple example showing the difference between NOW( ) and SYSDATE( ):

```
SELECT NOW(), SLEEP(4) AS 'Zzz', SYSDATE(), SLEEP(2) AS 'Zzz', SYSDATE();
```

```
+---------------------+-----+---------------------+-----+---------------------+
| NOW()               | Zzz | SYSDATE()           | Zzz | SYSDATE()           |
+---------------------+-----+---------------------+-----+---------------------+
| 2014-02-21 05:44:57 |   0 | 2014-02-21 05:45:01 |   0 | 2014-02-21 05:45:03 |
+---------------------+-----+---------------------+-----+---------------------+
```

```
1 row in set (6.14 sec)
```

Notice that the difference between the time returned for NOW( ) and for the first SYSDATE( ) is four seconds, the amount given with the first execution of SLEEP( ). The time between the two executions of SYSDATE( ) is two seconds, the amount given with SLEEP( ) the second time. Notice also that the message after the results shows it took a

tad more than six seconds to execute this SQL statement. You probably won't use SYS
DATE( ) often—maybe never. It's useful primarily when you execute very complex SQL
statements or for more advanced usage (e.g., within stored procedures and triggers).
Let's move on to more common usage of functions related to the current date and time.

If the data type for a column is not DATETIME, you can still use the NOW( ) to get and store
the values you need. For instance, if the time_seen column had a data type of DATE and
you entered the preceding INSERT statement, you'd get a warning saying *data truncated
for column*. However, it would still store the date correctly. A similar effect would occur
on a TIME column: you'd get a warning, but the time would be recorded correctly. It's
better, though, to use the correct function. For DATE columns, use CURDATE( ). For TIME
columns, use CURTIME( ). The following example compares these temporal functions:

```
SELECT NOW( ), CURDATE( ), CURTIME( );
```

```
+---------------------+------------+------------+
| NOW( )              | CURDATE( ) | CURTIME( ) |
+---------------------+------------+------------+
| 2014-02-08 10:23:32 | 2014-02-08 | 10:23:32   |
+---------------------+------------+------------+
```

All three of these functions and their synonyms use formats readable or easily understandable by humans. There are, however, built-in functions that return the Unix time,
which is the number of seconds since the "epoch" mentioned earlier. These can be useful
when comparing two temporal values. The following example shows the equivalent of
NOW( ) as a TIMESTAMP:

```
SELECT UNIX_TIMESTAMP( ), NOW( );
```

```
+-------------------+---------------------+
| UNIX_TIMESTAMP( ) | NOW( )              |
+-------------------+---------------------+
|        1391874612 | 2014-02-08 10:50:12 |
+-------------------+---------------------+
```

This returns the number of seconds since since January 1, 1970. Let's test that. Here's a
simple calculation to determine the number of years since the start of 1970, and a more
complicated way of determining it:

```
SELECT (2014 - 1970) AS 'Simple',
UNIX_TIMESTAMP( ) AS 'Seconds since Epoch',
ROUND(UNIX_TIMESTAMP( ) / 60 / 60 / 24 / 365.25) AS 'Complicated';
```

```
+--------+---------------------+-------------+
| Simple | Seconds since Epoch | Complicated |
+--------+---------------------+-------------+
|     44 |          1391875289 |          44 |
+--------+---------------------+-------------+
```

This was run near the start of the year 2014 so we used the ROUND( ) function to round down the number of years for a simple comparison. It's good to do exercises like this to confirm and to better know functions like this one. It helps you to understand and trust them.

Let's look at a more meaningful example in which you might want to use Unix time. Suppose you want to know how many days ago our bird-watchers spotted a particular bird, a *Black Guineafowl* (bird_id 309). To do this, we can use a join like so:

```
SELECT CONCAT(name_first, SPACE(1), name_last) AS 'Birdwatcher',
ROUND((UNIX_TIMESTAMP( ) - UNIX_TIMESTAMP(time_seen)) / 60 / 60 / 24)
    AS 'Days Since Spotted'
FROM bird_sightings JOIN humans USING(human_id)
WHERE bird_id = 309;
```

```
+-------------+--------------------+
| Birdwatcher | Days Since Spotted |
+-------------+--------------------+
| Marie Dyer  |                129 |
+-------------+--------------------+
```

In this example, we used CONCAT( ) to put together the bird-watcher's first and last name. We issued the first UNIX_TIMESTAMP( ) with no argument, so it used the current date and time. The second UNIX_TIMESTAMP( ) specifies a column (time_seen) containing the date our bird-watchers spotted each bird. The function changed the value to a Unix timestamp so that we could do a comparison

There are other ways and other functions that may be used to compare dates and times. We'll look at those later in this chapter. Let's look next at how to extract the date and time components.

Extracting Date and Time Components

Temporal data types store more information than you may sometimes want. There will be situations in which you don't want a full date or a time to the second. Because of this, there are functions that will extract any component of a temporal value you may want, as well as some common permutations. Let's look first at some basic functions for extracting just the date and just the time, then we'll look at ones for each component.

A DATETIME column, as the name implies, contains both the date and the time. If you want to extract just the date from such a value, you can use the DATE( ) function. To extract just the time, use TIME( ). Let's look at an example of these two. We'll again select the time_seen value for sightings of a *Black Guineafowl*:

```
SELECT CONCAT(name_first, SPACE(1), name_last) AS 'Birdwatcher',
time_seen, DATE(time_seen), TIME(time_seen)
FROM bird_sightings
JOIN humans USING(human_id)
```

```
WHERE bird_id = 309;
```

```
+-------------+---------------------+-----------------+-----------------+
| Birdwatcher | time_seen           | DATE(time_seen) | TIME(time_seen) |
+-------------+---------------------+-----------------+-----------------+
| Marie Dyer  | 2013-10-02 07:39:44 | 2013-10-02      | 07:39:44        |
+-------------+---------------------+-----------------+-----------------+
```

That was easy: DATE( ) returned just the date from time_seen and TIME( ) just the time. However, you may want to extract just one component of a date or time. You can do this with all of the temporal data types, as long as the column contains the component you want—you can't get the hour from a YEAR column.

To extract only the hour of a time saved in a column, the HOUR( ) function could be used. For the minute and second, there's MINUTE( ) and SECOND( ). These may be used with DATETIME, TIME, and TIMESTAMP columns. Let's see how the results from them might look. Enter the following in mysql:

```
SELECT CONCAT(name_first, SPACE(1), name_last) AS 'Birdwatcher',
time_seen, HOUR(time_seen), MINUTE(time_seen), SECOND(time_seen)
FROM bird_sightings JOIN humans USING(human_id)
WHERE bird_id = 309 \G
```

```
*************************** 1. row ***************************
     Birdwatcher: Marie Dyer
       time_seen: 2013-10-02 07:39:44
 HOUR(time_seen): 7
MINUTE(time_seen): 39
SECOND(time_seen): 44
```

These functions will allow you to use, assess, and compare each component of the time for a column. You can break apart a date, as well.

To extract the year, month, and day, you could use the YEAR( ), MONTH( ), and DAY( ) functions. You have to give a date value as the argument for each function. This can be a column that contains a date, or a string value that contains a date (e.g., '2014-02-14', including the quotes). It cannot be a number, unless the number is properly ordered. For instance, the numeric value 20140214 is acceptable, but not 2014-02-14 (without quotes) or 2014 02 14 (with spaces). Here's the same SQL statement as before, but using these functions instead:

```
SELECT CONCAT(name_first, SPACE(1), name_last) AS 'Birdwatcher',
time_seen, YEAR(time_seen), MONTH(time_seen), DAY(time_seen),
MONTHNAME(time_seen), DAYNAME(time_seen)
FROM bird_sightings JOIN humans USING(human_id)
WHERE bird_id = 309 \G
```

```
*************************** 1. row ***************************
     Birdwatcher: Marie Dyer
       time_seen: 2013-10-02 07:39:44
 YEAR(time_seen): 2013
```

```
      MONTH(time_seen): 10
        DAY(time_seen): 2
  MONTHNAME(time_seen): October
   DAYNAME(time_seen): Wednesday
```

This example has a couple of other date functions: MONTHNAME( ) to get the name of the
month for the date; and DAYNAME( ) to get the name of the day of the week for the date.
Using all of these functions, you can put together nicer looking results or easily check
date information. Let's look at how you might use the date and time functions to reorder date results. Here's an example that retrieves a list of endangered birds spotted by
the members of the site:

```
SELECT common_name AS 'Endangered Bird',
CONCAT(name_first, SPACE(1), name_last) AS 'Birdwatcher',
CONCAT(DAYNAME(time_seen), ', ', MONTHNAME(time_seen), SPACE(1),
   DAY(time_seen), ', ', YEAR(time_seen)) AS 'Date Spotted',
CONCAT(HOUR(time_seen), ':', MINUTE(time_seen),
   IF(HOUR(time_seen) < 12, ' a.m.', ' p.m.')) AS 'Time Spotted'
FROM bird_sightings
JOIN humans USING(human_id)
JOIN rookery.birds USING(bird_id)
JOIN rookery.conservation_status USING(conservation_status_id)
WHERE conservation_category = 'Threatened' LIMIT 3;
```

```
+---------------------+---------------+---------------------------+-----------+
| Endangered Bird     | Birdwatcher   | Date Spotted              | Time      |
+---------------------+---------------+---------------------------+-----------+
| Eskimo Curlew       | Elena Bokova  | Tuesday, October 1, 2013  | 5:9 a.m.  |
| Red-billed Curassow | Marie Dyer    | Wednesday, October 2, 2013 | 7:39 a.m. |
| Red-billed Curassow | Elena Bokova  | Wednesday, October 2, 2013 | 8:41 a.m. |
+---------------------+---------------+---------------------------+-----------+
```

This is a very cluttered SQL statement. Yes, because it involves using JOIN a few times,
it's lengthy as one would expect. But using CONCAT( ) twice with so many date and time
functions clutters it unnecessarily. Notice that 5:9 is displayed for the hours and minutes,
instead of 5:09. That's because the function, MINUTE( ) doesn't pad with zeroes. We could
fix that by using the LPAD( ) function, but that would be more clutter. We complicated
the statement even further by using the IF( ) function to label the time morning or
evening (i.e., a.m. or p.m.).

There's a cleaner, easier way to reformat dates and times using date and time formatting
functions, which are described in the next section. Meanwhile, you can reduce the
number of date and extraction functions to a single one: EXTRACT( ).

The EXTRACT( ) function can be used to extract any component of a date or time. The
syntax is simple and a little verbose: EXTRACT(*interval* FROM *date_time*). The intervals given are similar to the names of the date and time extraction functions we've
already reviewed: MONTH for month, HOUR for hour, and so on. There are also some

combined ones such as YEAR_MONTH and HOUR_MINUTE. For a list of intervals allowed with EXTRACT( ) and similar date and time functions, see Table 11-1.

Table 11-1. Date and time intervals and formats

INTERVAL	Format for given values
DAY	dd
DAY_HOUR	'dd hh'
DAY_MICROSECOND	'dd.nn'
DAY_MINUTE	'dd hh:mm'
DAY_SECOND	'dd hh:mm:ss'
HOUR	hh
HOUR_MICROSECOND	'hh.nn'
HOUR_MINUTE	'hh:mm'
HOUR_SECOND	'hh:mm:ss'
MICROSECOND	nn
MINUTE	mm
MINUTE_MICROSECOND	'mm.nn'
MINUTE_SECOND	'mm:ss'
MONTH	mm
QUARTER	qq
SECOND	ss
SECOND_MICROSECOND	'ss.nn'
WEEK	ww
YEAR	yy
YEAR_MONTH	'yy-mm'

Let's look at a simple example of this function by redoing the example that queried for the bird-watchers who saw the *Black Guineafowl*. Here it is again with EXTRACT( ):

```
SELECT time_seen,
EXTRACT(YEAR_MONTH FROM time_seen) AS 'Year & Month',
EXTRACT(MONTH FROM time_seen) AS 'Month Only',
EXTRACT(HOUR_MINUTE FROM time_seen) AS 'Hour & Minute',
EXTRACT(HOUR FROM time_seen) AS 'Hour Only'
FROM bird_sightings JOIN humans USING(human_id)
LIMIT 3;
```

```
+---------------------+--------------+------------+---------------+-----------+
| time_seen           | Year & Month | Month Only | Hour & Minute | Hour Only |
+---------------------+--------------+------------+---------------+-----------+
| 2013-10-01 04:57:12 |       201310 |         10 |           457 |         4 |
| 2013-10-01 05:09:27 |       201310 |         10 |           509 |         5 |
| 2013-10-01 05:13:25 |       201310 |         10 |           513 |         5 |
+---------------------+--------------+------------+---------------+-----------+
```

As you can see, when you use EXTRACT( ) with single intervals, it works fine as a consistent substitute for the other temporal extraction functions. Asking for HOUR_MINUTE doesn't produce very nice results, because there is no colon between the hour and minute (for instance, 4:57 is shown as 457). When you use EXTRACT( ) with combined intervals, it returns results combined together with no formatting. That may be what you want sometimes, but other times you might want to format a date or time. Once again, you'll need the date and time formatting functions in the next section.

Formatting Dates and Time

In the first section of this chapter, we looked briefly at the temporal data types in MySQL and MariaDB, including the formats in which dates and times are stored. I mentioned that if you don't like those formats, there are built-in functions that may be used to return temporal data in different formats. The most useful is the DATE_FORMAT( ) function, and a similar one, TIME_FORMAT( ). You can use these to format date and time values taken from a column, a string, or another function. With these two functions, you can specify the format you want with simple formatting codes. Let's redo the SQL statement from the example at the end of the previous section, using these functions:

```
SELECT common_name AS 'Endangered Bird',
CONCAT(name_first, SPACE(1), name_last) AS 'Birdwatcher',
DATE_FORMAT(time_seen, '%W, %M %e, %Y') AS 'Date Spotted',
TIME_FORMAT(time_seen, '%l:%i %p') AS 'Time Spotted'
FROM bird_sightings
JOIN humans USING(human_id)
JOIN rookery.birds USING(bird_id)
JOIN rookery.conservation_status USING(conservation_status_id)
WHERE conservation_category = 'Threatened' LIMIT 3;
```

```
+---------------------+--------------+----------------------------+-----------+
| Endangered Bird     | Birdwatcher  | Date Spotted               | Time      |
+---------------------+--------------+----------------------------+-----------+
| Eskimo Curlew       | Elena Bokova | Tuesday, October 1, 2013   | 5:09 AM   |
| Red-billed Curassow | Marie Dyer   | Wednesday, October 2, 2013 | 7:39 AM   |
| Red-billed Curassow | Elena Bokova | Wednesday, October 2, 2013 | 8:41 AM   |
+---------------------+--------------+----------------------------+-----------+
```

This is still a hefty SQL statement, but the portions related to formatting the date and time is more straightforward. With the DATE_FORMAT( ) and the TIME_FORMAT( ) functions, you give the column to format as the first argument and then provide a string in quotes that contains formatting codes and text to lay out how you want the date and time formatted. Incidentally, the DATE_FORMAT( ) function will return times in addition to dates. So there's really no need to use TIME_FORMAT( ). It's just a matter of style.

The problems we had in the previous two examples (i.e., lack of padding for minutes, no colon, and the need for IF( ) to indicate morning or evening), doesn't exist here. We took care of all of that by using the '%l:%i %p' formatting codes. If we were willing to include the seconds, we could replace those three formatting codes with just '%r'. Table 11-2 shows a list of formatting codes and what they return.

Table 11-2. Date and time formatting codes

Code	Description	Results
%a	Abbreviated weekday name	(Sun…Sat)
%b	Abbreviated month name	(Jan…Dec)
%c	Month (numeric)	(1…12)
%d	Day of the month (numeric)	(00…31)
%D	Day of the month with English suffix	(1st, 2nd, 3rd, etc.)
%e	Day of the month (numeric)	(0…31)
%f	Microseconds (numeric)	(000000…999999)
%h	Hour	(01…12)
%H	Hour	(00…23)
%i	Minutes (numeric)	(00…59)
%I	Hour	(01…12)
%j	Day of the year	(001…366)
%k	Hour	(0…23)
%l	Hour	(1…12)
%m	Month (numeric)	(01…12)
%M	Month name	(January…December)
%p	AM or PM	AM or PM
%r	Time, 12-hour	(hh:mm:ss [AP]M)
%s	Seconds	(00…59)
%S	Seconds	(00…59)
%T	Time, 24-hour	(hh:mm:ss)
%u	Week, where Monday is the first day of the week	(0…52)
%U	Week, where Sunday is the first day of the week	(0…52)
%v	Week, where Monday is the first day of the week; used with `%x'	(1…53)
%V	Week, where Sunday is the first day of the week; used with `%X'	(1…53)
%w	Day of the week	(0=Sunday…6=Saturday)
%W	Weekday name	(Sunday…Saturday)

Code	Description	Results
%x	Year for the week, where Monday is the first day of the week (numeric, four digits); used with `%v`	(yyyy)
%X	Year for the week, where Sunday is the first day of the week (numeric, four digits); used with `%V`	(yyyy)
%y	Year (numeric, two digits)	(yy)
%Y	Year (numeric, four digits)	(yyyy)
%%	A literal `%`	

Different places in the world prefer various standards for formatting the date and time. In the next section, we'll look at this and how to adjust to the time zones of other regions.

Adjusting to Standards and Time Zones

There a few standards for formatting the date and time. For instance, the last day of December and the year could be written numerically as *12-31-2014* or *31-12-2014*. Which standard you will use on a server may be based on where you're located in the world, or your employer and client preferences, or some other factor. To get the date format for a particular standard, you can use GET_FORMAT( ). Enter the following to try this:

```
SELECT GET_FORMAT(DATE, 'USA');
```

```
+-------------------------+
| GET_FORMAT(DATE, 'USA') |
+-------------------------+
| %m.%d.%Y                |
+-------------------------+
```

As the name implies, GET_FORMAT( ) checks for a particular place or locale and returns the string that can be used in DATE_FORMAT( ) to produce the desired format. It might be a bit surprising that the U.S. format uses periods instead of hyphens to separate elements of the date. In GET_FORMAT, the first argument indicates whether you want the date, the time, or both (i.e., DATE, TIME, or DATETIME). The second argument specifies the date or time standard, and can be one of the following:

- EUR for Europe
- INTERNAL for the format in which time is stored, without punctuation
- ISO for ISO 9075 standard
- JIS for Japanese Industrial Standard
- USA for United States

The ISO standard (yyyy-mm-dd hh:mm:ss) is the default for displaying the date and time in MySQL.

Enter this simple example that uses GET_FORMAT( ):

```
SELECT GET_FORMAT(DATE, 'USA'), GET_FORMAT(TIME, 'USA');
```

```
+------------------------+------------------------+
| GET_FORMAT(DATE, 'USA') | GET_FORMAT(TIME, 'USA') |
+------------------------+------------------------+
| %m.%d.%Y                | %h:%i:%s %p             |
+------------------------+------------------------+
```

Try running GET_FORMAT for various standards in order to become familiar with the different layouts—or check the documentation (*http://bit.ly/get_format*). After you've done that, execute the following SQL statement to see how this function works in conjunction with DATE_FORMAT( ):

```
SELECT DATE_FORMAT(CURDATE(), GET_FORMAT(DATE,'EUR'))
    AS 'Date in Europe',
DATE_FORMAT(CURDATE(), GET_FORMAT(DATE,'USA'))
    AS 'Date in U.S.',
REPLACE(DATE_FORMAT(CURDATE(), GET_FORMAT(DATE,'USA')), '.', '-')
    AS 'Another Date in U.S.';
```

```
+----------------+--------------+----------------------+
| Date in Europe | Date in U.S. | Another Date in U.S. |
+----------------+--------------+----------------------+
| 18.02.2014     | 02.18.2014   | 02-18-2014           |
+----------------+--------------+----------------------+
```

Because I don't agree that U.S. dates should use periods, the last field shows how to use the REPLACE( ) function to replace the periods with dashes. GET_FORMAT( ) isn't a function you'll use often, but it's good to know about it. A more useful and somewhat similar function is CONVERT_TZ( ).

CONVERT_TZ( ) converts a time to a given time zone. Before we can convert to a given time zone, though, we need to know which time zone our server is using. We can determine this by entering the following from the mysql client:

```
SHOW VARIABLES LIKE 'time_zone';
```

```
+---------------+--------+
| Variable_name | Value  |
+---------------+--------+
| time_zone     | SYSTEM |
+---------------+--------+
```

This shows that my server is using the filesystem time, which is probably the same time zone where it's located. Suppose the server we use for our bird-watching site is located in Boston, Massachusetts, which is in the U.S. Eastern Time Zone. If a member enters information in the morning about a bird sighting in Rome, Italy, which is in the Central European Time Zone, we don't want them to see the time in Boston after they save the entry. We would want the time adjusted for the time zone in which the bird was sighted. Otherwise people in the United States might think that Italians often see birds during the night and nocturnal birds such as owls during the day. So we'll use CONVERT_TZ( ) to adjust the times appropriately.

The syntax for CONVERT_TZ( ) requires three arguments: the date and time to convert, the time zone from whence the time came, and the time zone to which to convert. Let's look at an example:

```
SELECT common_name AS 'Bird',
CONCAT(name_first, SPACE(1), name_last) AS 'Birdwatcher',
DATE_FORMAT(time_seen, '%r') AS 'System Time Spotted',
DATE_FORMAT(CONVERT_TZ(time_seen, 'US/Eastern', 'Europe/Rome'), '%r')
  AS 'Birder Time Spotted'
FROM bird_sightings
JOIN humans USING(human_id)
JOIN rookery.birds USING(bird_id)
JOIN rookery.conservation_status USING(conservation_status_id) LIMIT 3;
```

Bird	Birdwatcher	System Time Spotted	Birder Time Spotted
Whimbrel	Richard Stringer	04:57:12 AM	10:57:12 AM
Eskimo Curlew	Elena Bokova	05:09:27 AM	11:09:27 AM
Marbled Godwit	Rusty Osborne	05:13:25 AM	11:13:25 AM

Notice that the time zones on the system are six hours earlier than the converted times. Of course, this is assuming that everyone is located in the same time zone as Rome. What we could do is add a column to the humans table to include the time zone in which the user is located or prefers. When a user registers, we can guess at their time zone based on what their web browser tells us or some other clever method. But then we could give the user an option of choosing another time zone in case we guessed wrong. However you determine and store the time zone, you would modify the preceding SQL statement to change the time to which CONVERT_TZ( ) converts to that value.

Notice that the time zones we're giving for CONVERT_TZ( ) are not limited to three-character code (e.g., *CET* for Central European time). They're based on the time zone names in MySQL, which include *CET*. If you ran the preceding SQL statement and it returned null values for the field containing CONVERT_TZ( ), it may be because the time zone information hasn't been loaded. When MySQL or MariaDB are installed, on Unix-type systems you will find the time zone files in the */usr/share/zoneinfo* directory. If you get a listing of that directory, you'll see the names that may be used for the time zone arguments in CONVERT_TZ( ). For instance, you will see a directory named *US*. Within it will be a file named *Eastern*. It's from these two pieces of information that we get the value *US/Eastern*. To install the time zone file, enter the following, changing the file path to wherever the time zone files are located:

```
mysql_tzinfo_to_sql /usr/share/zoneinfo | mysql -p -u root mysql
```

If your server runs on Windows, you may have to go to Oracle's site to download time zone tables (*http://dev.mysql.com/downloads/timezones.html*). That web page will provide some instructions on installing the package you download. After you've installed the time zone files, try the previous SQL statement again to be sure everything was installed properly.

Rather than use the time zone where our web server happens to be located, we could use some other time zone. We could change the time zone for the server, without having to relocate it or change the filesystem clock. We could set the server to a more global time zone such as Greenwich Mean Time (GMT or UTC). Because birdwatching has some roots in England thanks to botanists like Joseph Banks and Charles Darwin, let's use GMT. To set the time zone, we can use the SET statement like so:

```
SET GLOBAL time_zone = 'GMT';
```

If we wanted to set only the time zone for the current session, we wouldn't include the GLOBAL flag. It would be better to set this value globally in the server's configuration file (i.e., *my.cnf* or *my.ini*) so it isn't reset when the server is rebooted. To do that, add this line to the [mysqld] section:

```
default-time-zone='GMT'
```

If you use that method, instead of using SET, you'll have to restart the server for it to take effect. Once you've done that, run the SHOW VARIABLES statement again to see the results.

Setting the time zone on a server, knowing the user's time zone, and adjusting times using CONVERT_TZ( ) helps the user to feel he is part of the community of a website. Otherwise, the times shown will make the user feel like he is an outsider. So learn to use CONVERT_TZ( ) so that your sites and services will be part of the global community.

Adding and Subtracting Dates and Time

MySQL and MariaDB include several built-in functions that may be used to change a given date or time. You can use them to change a date to a future one by adding time, or change a date to a past one by subtracting time. The main functions that do this, or perhaps the most popular ones, are DATE_ADD( ) and DATE_SUB( ). The syntax for both of these is the same: the first argument is the date to be modified and the second argument is the amount of time. The amount of time is presented with the keyword INTERVAL, followed by a count of intervals, followed by the date or time factor (e.g., INTERVAL 1 DAY).

Let's look at an example using DATE_ADD( ). Suppose we want to extend the membership of all of our members who live in the United Kingdom by three months. To do this, we would enter the following:

```
UPDATE humans
SET membership_expiration = DATE_ADD(membership_expiration, INTERVAL 3 MONTH)
WHERE country_id = 'uk'
AND membership_expiration > CURDATE( );
```

In this example, we're adding three months to the current membership_expiration, but just for members who are in the U.K., but not for those whose membership has already expired. Notice that we're using a simpler operator, in this case the greater-than sign (>), to compare two day values in the WHERE clause. Notice also how we had to set the membership_expiration column equal to the modified value of itself. Date and time functions don't change the value of columns simply by being executed. You have to use them in conjunction with other methods for them to affect stored data. For a list of intervals allowed with DATE_ADD( ) and similar date and time functions, see Table 11-1.

Let's look at another example using DATE_SUB( ). Suppose a member named *Melissa Lee* renewed her membership for two years, but meant to renew it for only one year. You could enter the following SQL statement to make that adjustment:

```
UPDATE humans
SET membership_expiration = DATE_SUB(membership_expiration, INTERVAL 1 YEAR)
WHERE CONCAT(name_first, SPACE(1), name_last) = 'Melissa Lee';
```

Because there may be more than one *Melissa Lee* in our database, we should have first determined her human_id and used that in the WHERE clause.

DATE_ADD( ) is a very useful function so let's look at some more examples using it. First, let's redo the previous example to use DATE_ADD( ) instead of DATE_SUB( ). You would enter it like this:

```
UPDATE humans
SET membership_expiration = DATE_ADD(membership_expiration, INTERVAL -1 YEAR)
WHERE CONCAT(name_first, SPACE(1), name_last) = 'Melissa Lee';
```

This is exactly the same as the previous example, except that we're using DATE_ADD( ) and we changed the count of the interval to a negative number to indicate that one year should be subtracted and not added, despite the name of the function.

Let's look at another example with DATE_ADD( ). Suppose one of the members of our site recorded a bird sighting in the bird_sightings table, but for some reason the day and time is off. She lets us know that the entry in time_seen should be set to one day and two hours later. After we have determined the sighting_id, we can execute this SQL statement to update the date and time:

```
UPDATE bird_sightings
SET time_seen = DATE_ADD(time_seen, INTERVAL '1 2' DAY_HOUR)
WHERE sighting_id = 16;
```

In this example, the argument for the interval count is a combination of two intervals, DAY_HOUR for both DAY and HOUR. We list the counts in the same order, and put them within quotes. If we want to subtract the intervals (i.e., one day and two hours earlier), we would put a negative sign within the quotes before one of the values. Incidentally, you can't do a combination of subtracting and adding within the same DATE_ADD( ). You'd have to do either two passes at the column, or embed one call within the other. Table 11-1 lists other acceptable combined intervals.

When we use DATE_ADD( ) and similar functions to have MySQL calculate a new date or time, it goes through a process behind the scenes to determine the new result that is requested. Basically, it counts the number of seconds between dates and times, and then returns the new date and time. There may be situations in which you want to determine the method of those calculations, when you want more control over those calculations. For those situations, there are the TIME_TO_SEC( ) and SEC_TO_TIME( ) functions.

The TIME_TO_SEC( ) function converts a time to seconds so that a calculation may be performed easily. If you give it a date and time value, it uses only the time portion. Let's look at a very simple example of this to see what the results from it mean:

```
SELECT TIME(NOW()),
TIME_TO_SEC(NOW()),
TIME_TO_SEC(NOW()) / 60 /60 AS 'Hours';
```

```
+---------------------+--------------------+------------+
| NOW()               | TIME_TO_SEC(NOW()) | Hours      |
+---------------------+--------------------+------------+
| 2014-02-18 03:30:00 |              12600 | 3.50000000 |
+---------------------+--------------------+------------+
```

For the first field here, we're getting the current time. Notice that the time portion is exactly 3:30 a.m. For the second field, we're using TIME_TO_SEC( ) to get the number of seconds for that time: three and a half hours into the day. The third field is a calculation to confirm that: 12,600 seconds equals 3.5 hours.

Conversely, if you know the number of seconds that have elapsed since the start of an event—whether it be the start of a day or an action—you can use the SEC_TO_TIME( ) function to give you a time. Suppose you have two events and you want to know how much time elapsed between them. For instance, we might have a bird identification test online. The user would be presented with an image of a bird and asked to identify it. We would record the time when the image is displayed. When the user enters the correct identification, that time is recorded in another column in the same table. We could use SEC_TO_TIME( ) to get the difference between the two times, but in a time format (i.e., hh:mm:ss). Let's create an example of that by first creating a table to record each bird-watcher's test results:

```
CREATE TABLE bird_identification_tests
(test_id INT AUTO_INCREMENT KEY,
 human_id INT, bird_id INT,
 id_start TIME,
 id_end TIME);
```

There's not much to this table: we just want to record the human_id for the member, the bird_id for the image presented to the member, and then the start and completion times. We don't care about the date, just how long it took the member to identify the bird. Let's insert some data into that table, just one row of data so that we'll be able to try the SEC_TO_TIME( ) function:

```
INSERT INTO bird_identification_tests
VALUES(NULL, 16, 125, CURTIME(), NULL);
```

Notice that we didn't provide a value for the id_end column. That will be set when the member completes the identification. We're simulating this scenario, but if we were doing this for a site, we would embed this INSERT statement in a script that's executed when the user is shown a bird image. Another script containing an UPDATE statement would be executed when the user identifies the bird. So, to continue this simulation, wait a bit and then enter this SQL statement to set the time for the id_end column:

```
UPDATE bird_identification_tests
SET id_end = CURTIME();
```

We've now updated the one row in the table by setting the value of the id_end column to the current time. Now we can execute a SELECT using the SEC_TO_TIME( ) function to see how that function works:

```
SELECT CONCAT(name_first, SPACE(1), name_last)
    AS 'Birdwatcher',
common_name AS 'Bird',
SEC_TO_TIME( TIME_TO_SEC(id_end) - TIME_TO_SEC(id_start) )
    AS 'Time Elapsed'
FROM bird_identification_tests
JOIN humans USING(human_id)
JOIN rookery.birds USING(bird_id);
```

```
+-------------+-------------------+--------------+
| Birdwatcher | Bird              | Time Elapsed |
+-------------+-------------------+--------------+
| Ricky Adams | Crested Shelduck  | 00:01:21     |
+-------------+-------------------+--------------+
```

As nice as this SQL statement is, a problem arises when the two times are in different days, such as when the bird-watcher starts the test before midnight and finishes after midnight. Then the value of id_end is less than id_start, occurring seemingly before the event started. To allow for that possibility, you have to construct a much more complex SQL statement to include the IF( ) function to test for that rare occurrence. But that doesn't allow for when someone starts the test and waits to respond until more than 24 hours later. For that, you might want to cancel the session using other methods than those provided by MySQL. But there may be situations in which you will be comparing times that you will expect to be more than a day apart. For those situations, you would do better to use the DATETIME data type along with other functions for comparing dates and times. Those are covered in the next section.

Let's look at one more function related to adding and subtracting dates. The PERI OD_ADD( ) function takes a date as the first argument and adds a specified number of months given as the second argument. It can be used also to subtract months from a date, if the count given for the second argument is a negative value.

PERIOD_ADD( ) is a bit of an oddball in this chapter because it takes a string as an argument instead of a date, and returns a string in the same format. The string consists of a year as either two or four digits, followed by a month as two digits (e.g., April 2014 could be either 1404 or 201404). Let's try out this function with the birdwatchers database.

Suppose we want a count of bird sightings recorded by each member, but just for the previous quarter. This seems like it would be simple to do, just by using QUARTER( ) in the WHERE clause of a SELECT statement. Such an SQL statement might look like this:

```
SELECT CONCAT(name_first, SPACE(1), name_last) AS 'Birdwatcher',
COUNT(time_seen) AS 'Sightings Recorded'
FROM bird_sightings
JOIN humans USING(human_id)
WHERE QUARTER(time_seen) = (QUARTER(CURDATE()) - 1)
AND YEAR(time_seen) = (YEAR(CURDATE( )) - 1)
GROUP BY human_id LIMIT 5;

Empty set (0.14 sec)
```

An empty set was returned. This is because the result of QUARTER(CURDATE()) is 1, because I happened to execute this example during the first quarter of the year. So, QUARTER(CURDATE()) - 1 equals 0. Because all of the rows will have a date in quarters 1 through 4 (i.e., QUARTER(time_seen)), none will match. If I entered this statement during a different quarter, it would return results for the wrong quarter (the previous one).

Therefore, we have to adjust this SQL statement. We can do this by using PERI OD_ADD( ) a couple of times, along with a few other date functions we covered earlier. Here's how we could get the list of people and the number of sightings they recorded for last quarter, regardless of the quarter in which it's executed:

```
SELECT CONCAT(name_first, SPACE(1), name_last) AS 'Birdwatcher',
COUNT(time_seen) AS 'Sightings Recorded'
FROM bird_sightings
```

```
JOIN humans USING(human_id)
WHERE CONCAT(QUARTER(time_seen), YEAR(time_seen)) =
CONCAT(
   QUARTER(
      STR_TO_DATE(
         PERIOD_ADD( EXTRACT(YEAR_MONTH FROM CURDATE()), -3),
                           '%Y%m') ),
   YEAR(
      STR_TO_DATE(
         PERIOD_ADD( EXTRACT(YEAR_MONTH FROM CURDATE()), -3),
                           '%Y%m') ) )
GROUP BY human_id LIMIT 5;

+--------------------+--------------------+
| Birdwatcher        | Sightings Recorded |
+--------------------+--------------------+
| Richard Stringer   |                  1 |
| Rusty Osborne      |                  1 |
| Elena Bokova       |                  3 |
| Katerina Smirnova  |                  3 |
| Anahit Vanetsyan   |                  1 |
+--------------------+--------------------+
```

I indented this SQL statement plenty to make it easier to read. We're using EXTRACT( ) to extract the year and month from the CURDATE( ) and to put it in the format we need for PERIOD_ADD( ) (i.e., yyyymm). The first time we use PERIOD_ADD( ), it's getting the number of the previous quarter. The second time we use this function, it's getting the year of that previous quarter. We use STR_TO_DATE to convert the result of PERI OD_ADD to a date.

Then we're using CONCAT( ) to put the quarter and year together. We'll compare that to the quarter and year we'll concatenate from time_seen. This process would be simpler if EXTRACT( ) had an option of YEAR_QUARTER. Then we wouldn't need to determine the date of the previous quarter twice, extract the year and month separately, and concatenate them. Sometimes we push the limits of MySQL and MariaDB. But they occasionally add new features and options. For now, there are ways to accomplish what you want with more complex SQL statements.

Comparing Dates and Times

We've seen, in a few examples in this book, some ways to compare values containing dates and times. Several functions are designed specifically for this task. The most straightforward ones are DATEDIFF( ) and TIMEDIFF( ). With these, you can easily compare two dates or times. Let's look at some examples of how you might use them.

The humans table contains a column holding the date in which a person's membership expires, membership_expiration. Suppose that we want to display the number of days until their membership expires on the member's profile page, to remind them. For that requirement, we can use the DATEDIFF( ) function in an SQL statement similar to the following:

```
SELECT CURDATE() AS 'Today',
DATE_FORMAT(membership_expiration, '%M %e, %Y')
   AS 'Date Membership Expires',
DATEDIFF(membership_expiration, CURDATE())
   AS 'Days Until Expiration'
FROM humans
WHERE human_id = 4;
```

```
+------------+-----------------------------+-----------------------+
| Today      | Date Membership Expires     | Days Until Expiration |
+------------+-----------------------------+-----------------------+
| 2014-02-13 | September 22, 2013          |                  -144 |
+------------+-----------------------------+-----------------------+
```

Notice that the result here from DATEDIFF( ) is a negative amount. That's because the date contained in membership_expiration is a date before the current date, the date when CURDATE( ) was executed. If you swapped the two values given for DATEDIFF( ), the results would be positive. If you want to know only the number of days apart the two dates are, and don't care which comes first, you can use ABS( ) with DATEDIFF( ) to get the absolute value no matter how you order them. Incidentally, although you may give values in date and time formats, only the date portions are used for determining the difference.

Similar to DATEDIFF( ), you can get the difference between time values using the TIME DIFF( ) function. Before looking at an example of it, let's create a new table that uses dates and times. Suppose we've decided to organize and sponsor birding events, outings in which bird-watchers will go together to look for interesting birds. To store that information, we'll create a table called birding_events in the birdwatchers database:

```
CREATE TABLE birding_events
(event_id INT AUTO_INCREMENT KEY,
 event_name VARCHAR(255),
 event_description TEXT,
 meeting_point VARCHAR(255),
 event_date DATE,
 start_time TIME);
```

For the examples in this section, the column in this table with which we're mostly concerned is start_time. Let's add a birding event to birding_events by entering the following:

```
INSERT INTO birding_events
VALUES (NULL, 'Sandpipers in San Diego',
"Birdwatching Outing in San Diego to look for Sandpipers,
Curlews, Godwits, Snipes and other shore birds.
Birders will walk the beaches and surrounding area in groups of six.
A light lunch will be provided.",
```

```
"Hotel del Coronado, the deck near the entrance to the restaurant.",
 '2014-06-15', '09:00:00');
```

Now we can try using TIMEDIFF( ). Enter the following to determine how many days
and how much time until the start of the event:

```
SELECT NOW(), event_date, start_time,
DATEDIFF(event_date, DATE(NOW())) AS 'Days to Event',
TIMEDIFF(start_time, TIME(NOW())) AS 'Time to Start'
FROM birding_events;
```

```
+---------------------+------------+------------+--------------+---------------+
| NOW()               | event_date | start_time |Days to Event| Time to Start |
+---------------------+------------+------------+--------------+---------------+
| 2014-02-14 06:45:24 | 2014-06-15 | 09:00:00   |          121 | 02:14:36      |
+---------------------+------------+------------+--------------+---------------+
```

The event will start in 121 days, 2 hours, 14 minutes, and 36 seconds from the time this
SQL statement was executed. That's correct, but the results displayed for *Time to Start*
seem more like a time of day, rather than a count of hours, minutes, and seconds remaining. Let's use DATE_FORMAT( ) for a nicer display. Let's also use CONCAT( ) to put the
number of days together with the time remaining:

```
SELECT NOW(), event_date, start_time,
CONCAT(
   DATEDIFF(event_date, DATE(NOW())), ' Days, ',
   DATE_FORMAT(TIMEDIFF(start_time, TIME(NOW())), '%k hours, %i minutes'))
   AS 'Time to Event'
FROM birding_events;
```

```
+---------------------+------------+-----------+-----------------------------+
| NOW()               | event_date |start_time| Time to Event                |
+---------------------+------------+-----------+-----------------------------+
| 2014-02-14 06:46:25 | 2014-06-15 | 09:00:00 | 121 Days, 2 hours, 13 minutes |
+---------------------+------------+-----------+-----------------------------+
```

You have to carefully check the parentheses on that statement to execute it successfully.
We embed NOW( ) in the DATE( ) and TIME( ) functions. These in turn are embedded in
DATEDIFF( ) and TIMEDIFF( ) to get the difference from the date and time stored in the
database. TIMEDIFF( ) is embedded in DATE_FORMAT( ), and all those functions are embedded in CONCAT( ).

After looking at these results, we decide that it would be much simpler if we change the
table to use a single column to record the date and time of the event. I said in the first
section of this chapter that we would cover some examples of how to change temporal
data types for a column. Let's do that now. Let's create a new column, event_date
time, using the DATETIME data type:

```
ALTER TABLE birding_events
ADD COLUMN event_datetime DATETIME;
```

That adds the new column to contain the date and time. Now let's update the table to combine them into event_datetime:

```
UPDATE birding_events
SET event_datetime = CONCAT(event_date,SPACE(1), start_time);
```

The CONCAT( ) function merges the date and time together as a string. MySQL will automatically convert that string into a date, and then set the value of event_date time to a date and time value. Let's execute a SELECT statement to see how the data looks now:

```
SELECT event_date, start_time, event_datetime
FROM birding_events;

+------------+------------+---------------------+
| event_date | start_time | event_datetime      |
+------------+------------+---------------------+
| 2014-06-15 | 09:00:00   | 2014-06-15 09:00:00 |
+------------+------------+---------------------+
```

The UPDATE worked fine. Let's try now to get the formatting we want for the time remaining until the event, but from the new column. Enter the following:

```
SELECT NOW(), event_datetime,
CONCAT(DATEDIFF(event_datetime, NOW() ), ' Days, ',
     TIME_FORMAT( TIMEDIFF( TIME(event_datetime), CURTIME() ),
                  '%k hours, %i minutes') )
  AS 'Time to Event'
FROM birding_events;

+---------------------+---------------------+------------------------------+
| NOW()               | event_datetime      | Time to Event                |
+---------------------+---------------------+------------------------------+
| 2014-02-14 05:48:55 | 2014-06-15 09:00:00 | 121 Days, 3 hours, 11 minutes |
+---------------------+---------------------+------------------------------+
```

That looks fine and it's much better than having the date and time in separate columns. We can now alter birding_events to drop the two columns for date and time that we no longer need:

```
ALTER TABLE birding_events
DROP COLUMN event_date,
DROP COLUMN start_time;
```

We've successfully completed the process of migrating the date and time from two columns into one. You probably would have initially chosen to create one column instead of two, as we did in these examples. But you won't always choose though the best temporal data type for a column. That's why I wanted to walk you through the process of how to migrate between temporal data types: to prepare you for what to do when you don't make the best choice the first time.

Summary

We've covered almost all of the date and time functions in MySQL and MariaDB in this chapter. There are only a few more. We skipped the aliases (e.g., ADDDATE( ) for DATE_ADD( ), SUBDATE( ) for DATE_SUB( )). There are also a few other functions for specialized needs, which you can learn as you need them. You've learned plenty in this chapter, and the information here should come in handy for many years.

The primary reason we went through so many date and time functions is because the date and time is a major part of most cultures: when something has happened, when something will happen, making appointments, and how much time has passed are common concerns when people interact with one another. This information is therefore a significant component of a database. I want you to be familiar with the temporal functions and to have a firm grasp on what tools are available. To that end, work through the exercises in the following section. You'll retain more of what you learned in this chapter if you do.

Exercises

Here are some exercises to practice using date and time functions and a few of the string functions that we covered in Chapter 10. Some require you to use UPDATE to change the date values in tables. By updating data with date and time functions, you will gain a better understanding of the potential of these functions. The UPDATE statement is covered in Chapter 8.

1. Construct an SQL statement to select a list of members from the humans table who live in the United Kingdom. Select first and last names, concatenating them. Include the date they joined and when their membership expires. Use the DATE_FORMAT( ) function to format the result for each date to look like this: Sun., Feb. 2, 1979. Be sure to include all of the punctuations (i.e., the comma and the periods after the abbreviations, but not at the end, and the comma). Refer to Table 11-2 for the formatting codes.

   When you're finished, execute the SQL statement to check the results are correct. If they're not, modify the statement until you get the right results.

2. Execute the SELECT statement to get a list of members and their expiration dates, ordering the results by membership_expiration. Then use the UPDATE statement to change the values in the membership_expiration column of the humans table. Use the ADDDATE( ) function to extend the membership of all members by 1 month and 15 days, but only for those whose membership has not yet expired as of June 30, 2014. Refer to Table 11-1 to find the interval codes you will need. You will also need to use a string in the WHERE clause. When finished, execute SELECT again and

compare the results to the previous ones to confirm you were successful in changing the expiration dates for the correct members.

When you've finished extending the memberships, use DATESUB( ) to change mem bership_expiration to five days less for those same members as you did before. When that's done, execute SELECT again and compare the results to the previous results.

Change the expiration date one more time, but this time use ADD_DATE( ) to change the expiration date to 10 days less. Remember, this will require you to use a negative value. After you've done that, execute SELECT again to check the results.

3. In "Adjusting to Standards and Time Zones" on page 214, we created a new table called bird_identification_tests. We added one row of data to it for testing. For this exercise, insert at least five more rows into that table. Make entries for two other human_id values and a few other bird_id values. While doing this, as shown in the example in that same section, enter a time value for id_start using CURTIME( ), but enter NULL for id_end. Then run an UPDATE statement after each INSERT to set the time for id_end, using CURTIME( ) again so that the times will be different. Wait a short amount of time between the INSERT and the UPDATE for each row.

After you've entered several more rows to bird_identification_tests, construct a SELECT statement using the TIMEDIFF( ) function to compare the difference in the times of id_start and id_end for each row. Be sure to put the columns in the correct order within TIMEDIFF( ) so that the results do not show negative values. Include the first name of each person in the SQL statement. You'll need to use JOIN to do that (covered in "Joining Tables" on page 156).

4. Put together another SELECT statement to get common_name from the birds table, and the id_start and id_end columns from the birdwatchers table. Use the TIME DIFF( ) function to compare the differences in time between the two columns containing times. When you join the two tables, remember to adjust the JOIN to reflect that they are in separate databases. When that's finished, execute the SELECT statement to be sure it's constructed properly. Then add a GROUP BY clause to group by bird_id, and wrap TIMEDIFF( ) in AVG( ) to get the average time. Give that field an alias of Avg. Time or something similar. Run that statement to see the results. The results for the average time field should include a number with four decimal places, all zeros (e.g., 219.0000 for 2 minutes, 19 seconds).

Next, redo the SELECT statement to convert the average time from a number with four decimal places to the TIME format. To do this, first use the TRIM( ) function with the TRAILING option and give it a string of .0000 to trim that string from the end of the average time. Run the SELECT to see the results of that addition. Then, wrap all of that in LPAD( ) to make sure there's enough zeros to conform to this format: *hhmmss*. Run the SELECT statement again to see the improvements in the results. Both of these string functions were covered in "Trimming and Padding Strings" on page 183.

Finally, use STR_TO_DATE( ) to convert the padded number (e.g., 000219) to a time. Refer to Table 11-2 to get the formatting codes for the *hhmmss* format. If you provide only formatting codes for time elements, STR_TO_DATE( ) will return only time information, which is what we want for this exercise. Execute the SELECT when you're finished to make sure it's correct. Make corrections until you get it to work.

5. Redo the SELECT you constructed successfully at the end of the previous exercise. Put what you assembled for the average time field into DATE_FORMAT( ). Change the format to display like this: 01 minute(s), 21 seconds. When finished, execute the SQL statement. For extra points, use a string function to remove the leading zero for minutes, and when they occur, for the seconds. Use the IF( ) function to set minute or minutes as needed, and second and seconds.

Aggregate and Numeric Functions

Databases will always include numbers: there's always something to value, count, or calculate. And you may want to round the results from those numbers to conform to personal preferences. There are numeric and arithmetic functions to do these things in MySQL and MariaDB. Some are known as *aggregate* functions. We will cover almost all of the aggregate and many numeric functions in this chapter. We won't cover the more advanced functions related to statistics, or the mathematical functions related to calculus and geometry. Instead, we will cover the most useful and most used functions and leave the others for you to learn later on your own as you need them.

Aggregate Functions

Statistics can provide us with useful information about a database. If a database includes information about the activities of an organization, we can determine some statistical information about those activities. If a database includes numeric values associated with items an organization sells or tracks, statistics can provide us with information for making decisions about those items.

In our birdwatchers database, we can use aggregate functions to understand the behavior of our members in relation to our bird-watchers website, the events they attend, and other activities. For our rookery database, we can ascertain some information about birds using aggregate functions. That can be useful to our members related to searching for birds in the wild, as well as their concerns for the well-being of birds. We can ascertain information about where birds are seen in the wild by our members.

In this section, we will look at aggregate functions that will help us to determine this kind of information. In order to aggregate data together to calculate statistical values of sorts, we sometimes must use the GROUP BY clause. Some of the aggregate functions, such as the COUNT( ) function we've used in earlier chapters for counting rows in a table, do not require this clause, at least under certain conditions. We'll start with COUNT( )

and then look at functions for simple statistics, such as determining an average for a set of numbers.

Counting Values

One of the simplest calculations we can do is to count. We learn it as children as an introduction to mathematics. So let's start with counting, the COUNT( ) function.

Suppose we want to know how many birds are in the birds table. To do that, enter the folowing in mysql:

```
SELECT COUNT(*)
FROM birds;
```

```
+-----------+
| COUNT(*)  |
+-----------+
|     28891 |
+-----------+
```

Notice that we didn't have to include the GROUP BY clause for this simple SQL statement. That's because we wanted MySQL to count all of the rows in the table. We didn't need GROUP BY because we didn't want it to separate the rows into separate groups—there's just one group here. Notice also that we're giving COUNT( ) an asterisk as the argument. That's a wildcard to tell MySQL that we want to count all of the rows found. Because we don't have a WHERE clause, all of the rows will be selected.

Many of the bird species lack common names. So the common_name column in birds is blank for these species. COUNT( ) has a special convention: if you pass a column name instead of an asterisk as its argument, it counts only the columns that are not NULL. Let's change that data and then see how it might look. Enter these two SQL statements:

```
UPDATE birds
SET common_name = NULL
WHERE common_name = '';
```

```
SELECT COUNT(common_name)
FROM birds;
```

```
+--------------------+
| COUNT(common_name) |
+--------------------+
|               9553 |
+--------------------+
```

That's the number of birds with a common name in the table. We could have gotten the same results with a WHERE clause, and without having modified the data as we did. This lets us select only rows where the common_name does not equal ' '. We've changed those values to NULL, though, so let's use the WHERE clause to see how that would look based on NULL values. Enter the following:

```
SELECT COUNT(*) FROM birds
WHERE common_name IS NULL;
```

```
+----------+
| COUNT(*) |
+----------+
|    19338 |
+----------+
```

This gave us a different number. That's because we're counting the rows where the common_name is NULL—we used the operator IS NULL. Before, we counted the rows where the common_name was not NULL. We can count those with the WHERE clause like so:

```
SELECT COUNT(*) FROM birds
WHERE common_name IS NOT NULL;
```

```
+----------+
| COUNT(*) |
+----------+
|     9553 |
+----------+
```

That's the answer we got before. It just required us to use the IS NOT NULL operator.

As useful as all of this may be, let's get some more interesting results. Let's count the number of birds within each family of birds. To do that, we have to use the GROUP BY clause. We'll enter the following to get a count of the number of birds in each family:

```
SELECT COUNT(*)
FROM birds
GROUP BY family_id;
```

```
+----------+
| COUNT(*) |
+----------+
|        5 |
|        6 |
|      248 |
|      119 |
|      168 |
|       39 |
|      223 |
|      ... |
+----------+
```

```
227 rows in set (0.15 sec)
```

In this example, we told MySQL to GROUP BY the family_id. So it sorted the rows by the family_id and counted the number of rows for each group. Because the results here would take up 227 rows, I've removed some of the results to save space. This SQL statement did what we asked, but it's not very useful or interesting. It would be better to get the name of the bird families to go with these counts. To do this, we'll have to use a JOIN to include the bird_families table. Here's how we would do that:

```
SELECT bird_families.scientific_name AS 'Bird Family',
COUNT(*) AS 'Number of Species'
FROM birds JOIN bird_families USING(family_id)
GROUP BY birds.family_id;
```

```
+---------------------+-------------------+
| Bird Family         | Number of Species |
+---------------------+-------------------+
| Gaviidae            |                 6 |
| Anatidae            |               248 |
| Charadriidae        |               119 |
| Laridae             |               168 |
| Sternidae           |                39 |
| Caprimulgidae       |               223 |
| Sittidae            |                92 |
| ...                 |                   |
+---------------------+-------------------+
```

225 rows in set (0.17 sec)

That's nicer looking, and the results are more interesting. I've shortened the results again, but notice that we now have only 225 rows. That's because we have some rows in the birds table in which the family_id is NULL. When using a database, watch for discrepancies like this; don't ignore them just because you weren't looking for problems. They can help you catch problems you overlooked.

Let's modify the SELECT statement to show the number of rows in birds that do not have matching values in bird_families. We'll do this with a LEFT JOIN (covered in "Joining Tables" on page 156, which included examples, but let's apply that concept again here):

```
SELECT bird_families.scientific_name AS 'Bird Family',
COUNT(*) AS 'Number of Species'
FROM birds LEFT JOIN bird_families USING(family_id)
GROUP BY birds.family_id;
```

```
+---------------------+-------------------+
| Bird Family         | Number of Species |
+---------------------+-------------------+
| NULL                |                 4 |
| NULL                |                 1 |
| Gaviidae            |                 6 |
| Anatidae            |               248 |
```

```
| Charadriidae      |               119 |
| Laridae           |               168 |
| Sternidae         |                39 |
| Caprimulgidae     |               223 |
| Sittidae          |                92 |
| ...               |                   |
+-------------------+-------------------+
```

225 rows in set (0.17 sec)

Some of these rows may have a `family_id` of NULL, and one may have a `family_id` not contained in `bird_families`. To resolve this problem, we would run a SELECT to list rows where the `bird_id` is not included in `bird_families`. But this is getting away from learning about aggregate functions. Let's assume that we've found the rows with missing data and fixed them so that we can move on.

In the results for the last two examples, you may have noticed that the names of the bird families are not listed alphabetically. That's because GROUP BY orders rows based on the columns by which it is grouping (i.e., `family_id`). If we want to order the results based on the family name, the `scientific_name` in the `bird_families` table, we'd have to change the GROUP BY clause to group by that column. Try entering this:

```sql
SELECT bird_families.scientific_name AS 'Bird Family',
COUNT(*) AS 'Number of Species'
FROM birds LEFT JOIN bird_families USING(family_id)
GROUP BY bird_families.scientific_name;
```

```
+-------------------+-------------------+
| Bird Family       | Number of Species |
+-------------------+-------------------+
| Acanthisittidae   |                 9 |
| Acanthizidae      |               238 |
| Accipitridae      |               481 |
| Acrocephalidae    |               122 |
| Aegithalidae      |                49 |
| Aegithinidae      |                20 |
| Aegothelidae      |                21 |
| Alaudidae         |               447 |
| ...               |                   |
+-------------------+-------------------+
```

That's better. What would be nicer is if those results also showed the total number of birds at the bottom. We can get that from a separate SQL statement, but to get the total in the same results set, we would add WITH ROLLUP to the GROUP BY clause like so:

```sql
SELECT bird_families.scientific_name AS 'Bird Family',
COUNT(*) AS 'Number of Species'
FROM birds JOIN bird_families USING(family_id)
GROUP BY bird_families.scientific_name WITH ROLLUP;
```

```
+--------------------+--------------------+
| Bird Family        | Number of Species  |
+--------------------+--------------------+
| Acanthisittidae    |                  9 |
| Acanthizidae       |                238 |
| Accipitridae       |                481 |
| Acrocephalidae     |                122 |
| Aegithalidae       |                 49 |
| Aegithinidae       |                 20 |
| Aegothelidae       |                 21 |
| Alaudidae          |                447 |
| ...                |                    |
| NULL               |              28891 |
+--------------------+--------------------+
```

The total is on the last line and is equal to the count we did in the first example of this section. In the results here, the NULL value for the first field doesn't refer to rows that don't have a value for family_id. Instead, this is the total line. MySQL just doesn't have a value to put in that field as a label, so it uses NULL. We can tweak that, though, to give it a label. While we're doing that, let's include counts by orders of birds. Enter the following:

```
SELECT IFNULL( bird_orders.scientific_name, '') AS 'Bird Order',
IFNULL( bird_families.scientific_name, 'Total:') AS 'Bird Family',
COUNT(*) AS 'Number of Species'
FROM birds
JOIN bird_families USING(family_id)
JOIN bird_orders USING(order_id)
GROUP BY bird_orders.scientific_name, bird_families.scientific_name
WITH ROLLUP;
```

```
+--------------------+--------------------+--------------------+
| Bird Order         | Bird Family        | Number of Species  |
+--------------------+--------------------+--------------------+
| Anseriformes       | Anhimidae          |                  3 |
| Anseriformes       | Total:             |                  3 |
| Apodiformes        | Apodidae           |                316 |
| Apodiformes        | Hemiprocnidae      |                 16 |
| Apodiformes        | Trochilidae        |                809 |
| Apodiformes        | Total:             |               1141 |
| Caprimulgiformes   | Aegothelidae       |                 21 |
| Caprimulgiformes   | Caprimulgidae      |                224 |
| Caprimulgiformes   | Nyctibiidae        |                 17 |
| Caprimulgiformes   | Podargidae         |                 26 |
| ...                |                    |                    |
|                    | Total:             |              28890 |
+--------------------+--------------------+--------------------+
```

Besides adding another field to get the number of birds within an order of birds, we used the IFNULL( ) function to wrap the fields for the bird order counts and family counts. This function tells MySQL that if the value for the field will be NULL, it should be replaced with the value or string given—else it should return the count. Because the statement calculates first the primary totals (i.e., the totals for each family of birds), and then calculates the secondary totals (i.e., the totals for each order of birds), this works.

The results in the previous example aren't marvelous, but you can easily use this method in conjunction with a script that will display these results on a web page. You can use an API to check for a value of *Total:* in the second field and then adjust for that. You could instead do these simple calculations in an API script, rather than have MySQL do them. However, sometimes it's better to do calculations at the database system level. I have found often that better SQL statements make for tighter and easier to maintain API scripts. All right; enough of that. Let's move on to more aggregate functions, besides just counting the number of rows.

Calculating a Group of Values

In Chapter 11, we created a new table, `bird_identification_tests`, for recording fun tests members could do online to try their skills at identifying birds. Suppose we want to tell the member how long it takes them on average to identify birds. A simple calculation would be to get the total time elapsed (i.e., subtracting `id_end` from `id_start`) for each row and then adding those differences together to get the sum of all rows. We would then divide that sum by the number of rows. To get the sum, we can use the `SUM( )` function.

Before we jump too far ahead, though, let's look at some entries for one of the members to remember and know what to do. We'll use the `TIMEDIFF( )` function to determine the difference between the time the test started and when it ended (covered in the section "Comparing Dates and Times" on page 222). Enter the following:

```
SELECT common_name AS 'Bird',
TIME_TO_SEC( TIMEDIFF(id_end, id_start) )
    AS 'Seconds to Identify'
FROM bird_identification_tests
JOIN humans USING(human_id)
JOIN rookery.birds USING(bird_id)
WHERE name_first = 'Ricky' AND name_last = 'Adams';
```

```
+--------------------+---------------------+
| Bird               | Seconds to Identify |
+--------------------+---------------------+
| Crested Shelduck   |                  81 |
| Moluccan Scrubfowl |                 174 |
| Indian Pond-Heron  |                 181 |
+--------------------+---------------------+
```

Because we need the total number of seconds for each test in order to add the values together to get to an average, we used `TIME_TO_SEC( )` to convert the results from `TIMEDIFF( )` (e.g., to convert from 121, for 1 minute and 21 seconds, to 81 seconds). We

did this extra step just to see how these values come more easily together with SUM( )
and to better understand the time functions in the following SQL statement:

```
SELECT CONCAT(name_first, SPACE(1), name_last)
    AS 'Birdwatcher',
SUM(TIME_TO_SEC( TIMEDIFF(id_end, id_start) ) )
    AS 'Total Seconds for Identifications'
FROM bird_identification_tests
JOIN humans USING(human_id)
JOIN rookery.birds USING(bird_id)
WHERE name_first = 'Ricky' AND name_last = 'Adams';
```

```
+-------------+----------------------------------+
| Birdwatcher | Total Seconds for Identifications |
+-------------+----------------------------------+
| Ricky Adams |                              436 |
+-------------+----------------------------------+
```

That gives us the correct number of seconds that Ricky Adams spent identifying three
birds. Notice that this is another aggregate function that doesn't require the GROUP BY
clause. Now let's change the SQL statement to calculate the average time (e.g., *426*
seconds divided by *3 entries*). To do this, we'll use an absurdly complex and inefficient
method. We'll create a subquery to get each value to calculate the average. You don't
have to enter this one. Just look it over:

```
SELECT Identifications, Seconds,
(Seconds / Identifications) AS 'Avg. Seconds/Identification'
FROM
  ( SELECT human_id, COUNT(*) AS 'Identifications'
    FROM bird_identification_tests
    JOIN humans USING(human_id)
    JOIN rookery.birds USING(bird_id)
    WHERE name_first = 'Ricky' AND name_last = 'Adams')
      AS row_count
  JOIN
  ( SELECT human_id, CONCAT(name_first, SPACE(1), name_last)
      AS 'Birdwatcher',
    SUM(TIME_TO_SEC(TIMEDIFF(id_end, id_start)))
      AS 'Seconds'
    FROM bird_identification_tests
    JOIN humans USING(human_id)
    JOIN rookery.birds USING(bird_id) )
      AS second_count
  USING(human_id);
```

```
+-----------------+---------+-----------------------------+
| Identifications | Seconds | Avg. Seconds/Identification |
+-----------------+---------+-----------------------------+
|               3 |     436 |                    145.3333 |
+-----------------+---------+-----------------------------+
```

That was a lot of work for something that should be simple—and it can be. Let's change that to use AVG( ):

```
SELECT CONCAT(name_first, SPACE(1), name_last)
    AS 'Birdwatcher',
AVG( TIME_TO_SEC( TIMEDIFF(id_end, id_start)) )
    AS 'Avg. Seconds per Identification'
FROM bird_identification_tests
JOIN humans USING(human_id)
JOIN rookery.birds USING(bird_id)
WHERE name_first = 'Ricky' AND name_last = 'Adams';
```

```
+-------------+--------------------------------+
| Birdwatcher | Avg. Seconds per Identification |
+-------------+--------------------------------+
| Ricky Adams |                       145.3333 |
+-------------+--------------------------------+
```

That was much easier, and without any subqueries. If we remove the WHERE clause, we would get the average time for all of the members. Let's do that and change the formatting of the time to minutes and seconds, not just the average of total seconds. We'll use SEC_TO_TIME( ) to do that, reversing the results of TIME_TO_SEC( ) now that we've calculated the average. Enter this on your server:

```
SELECT CONCAT(name_first, SPACE(1), name_last)
    AS 'Birdwatcher',
COUNT(*) AS 'Birds',
TIME_FORMAT(
    SEC_TO_TIME(AVG( TIME_TO_SEC( TIMEDIFF(id_end, id_start)))),
    '%i:%s' )
    AS 'Avg. Time'
FROM bird_identification_tests
JOIN humans USING(human_id)
JOIN rookery.birds USING(bird_id)
GROUP BY human_id LIMIT 3;
```

```
+----------------+-------+-----------+
| Birdwatcher    | Birds | Avg. Time |
+----------------+-------+-----------+
| Rusty Osborne  |     2 | 01:59     |
| Lexi Hollar    |     3 | 00:23     |
| Ricky Adams    |     3 | 02:25     |
+----------------+-------+-----------+
```

This time we included more members—but limited the results to three—and include the number of birds that each member identified. We also formatted the average time better. We can see that Ricky Adams took much longer on average than Lexi Hollar. It may be that Lexi is quicker or that Ricky was distracted when he was identifying birds.

Because we used the LIMIT clause, we can't determine the longest and quickest average times from these results. To know that, we need to remove the LIMIT and then make the SQL statement a subquery of another in which we will add an ORDER BY clause. Essentially, the inner SELECT returns a list with each bird-watcher and their average time, which the outer SELECT puts in the order we want:

```
SELECT Birdwatcher, avg_time AS 'Avg. Time'
FROM
  (SELECT CONCAT(name_first, SPACE(1), name_last) AS 'Birdwatcher',
   COUNT(*) AS 'Birds',
   TIME_FORMAT( SEC_TO_TIME( AVG(
                 TIME_TO_SEC( TIMEDIFF(id_end, id_start)))
                 ),'%i:%s' ) AS 'avg_time'
   FROM bird_identification_tests
   JOIN humans USING(human_id)
   JOIN rookery.birds USING(bird_id)
   GROUP BY human_id) AS average_times
ORDER BY avg_time;
```

```
+--------------------+-----------+
| Birdwatcher        | Avg. Time |
+--------------------+-----------+
| Lexi Hollar        | 00:23     |
| Geoffrey Dyer      | 00:25     |
| Katerina Smirnova  | 00:48     |
| Rusty Osborne      | 01:59     |
| Ricky Adams        | 02:25     |
| Anahit Vanetsyan   | 03:20     |
+--------------------+-----------+
```

Now we know that Lexi is the quickest and Anahit was the slowest. We had to use a subquery because you can't generally put a GROUP BY and an ORDER BY clause in the same SQL statement. You have to do what we did here instead.

If we don't want to know the names of who had the minimum average and who had the maximum, we could use the MAX( ) and MIN( ) functions. Let's redo the previous SQL statement to include those aggregate functions. Try this on your server:

```
SELECT MIN(avg_time) AS 'Minimum Avg. Time',
MAX(avg_time) AS 'Maximum Avg. Time'
FROM humans
JOIN
 (SELECT human_id, COUNT(*) AS 'Birds',
  TIME_FORMAT(
    SEC_TO_TIME( AVG(
      TIME_TO_SEC( TIMEDIFF(id_end, id_start)))
        ), '%i:%s' ) AS 'avg_time'
  FROM bird_identification_tests
  JOIN humans USING(human_id)
  JOIN rookery.birds USING(bird_id)
  GROUP BY human_id ) AS average_times;
```

```
+-------------------+-------------------+
| Minimum Avg. Time | Maximum Avg. Time |
+-------------------+-------------------+
| 00:23             | 03:20             |
+-------------------+-------------------+
```

Comparing these results to the previous ones, we can see that they are correct. If we want to see the minimum and maximum time for each person, instead of the averages, we could do this:

```
SELECT CONCAT(name_first, SPACE(1), name_last) AS 'Birdwatcher',
TIME_FORMAT(SEC_TO_TIME(
            MIN(TIME_TO_SEC( TIMEDIFF(id_end, id_start)))
            ),%i:%s' )  AS 'Minimum Time',
TIME_FORMAT(SEC_TO_TIME(
            MAX(TIME_TO_SEC( TIMEDIFF(id_end, id_start)))
            ), '%i:%s' ) AS 'Maximum Time'
FROM bird_identification_tests
JOIN humans USING(human_id)
JOIN rookery.birds USING(bird_id)
GROUP BY Birdwatcher;
```

```
+-------------------+--------------+--------------+
| Birdwatcher       | Minimum Time | Maximum Time |
+-------------------+--------------+--------------+
| Anahit Vanetsyan  | 00:20        | 08:48        |
| Geoffrey Dyer     | 00:09        | 00:42        |
| Katerina Smirnova | 00:22        | 01:02        |
| Lexi Hollar       | 00:11        | 00:39        |
| Ricky Adams       | 01:21        | 03:01        |
| Rusty Osborne     | 01:50        | 02:08        |
+-------------------+--------------+--------------+
```

This shows an alphabetic list of members and each one's minimum and maximum time to identify a bird. Essentially, once you group items by the bird-watcher, you can run aggregate functions such as AVG( ) and MAX( ) on them. We removed the field counting the number of identifications they made.

We could play with this more to see which birds take the longest to identify and which take the least amount of time. We could mark ones that are most difficult to identify for more advanced members. Some members may have a low average time if it were not for one bird that was particularly difficult to identify. For those entries, we could use the aggregate functions for more advanced statistical calculations to remove them, functions like STDDEV( ) and VARIANCE( ). As a beginner, you probably won't need to know them. Just know that they exist in case one day you do.

Before moving on, let's look at one more example using MIN( ) and MAX( ), an example that uses values other than time values. The bird_sightings table contains information on birds that our members saw in the field. It includes the GPS coordinates where each bird was seen: the location_gps column. This column contains two 11-digit numbers:

the latitude and the longitude on the globe. Because birds tend to migrate between north and south, suppose we want to know the farthest north and south that birds were seen. We could use SUBSTRING( ) to extract the latitude, the MAX( ) function to determine which value is farthest north, and MIN( ) to determine which is the farthest south. We would do this like so:

```
SELECT common_name AS 'Bird',
MAX(SUBSTRING(location_gps, 1, 11)) AS 'Furthest North',
MIN(SUBSTRING(location_gps, 1, 11)) AS 'Furthest South'
FROM birdwatchers.bird_sightings
JOIN rookery.birds USING(bird_id)
WHERE location_gps IS NOT NULL
GROUP BY bird_id LIMIT 3;
```

```
+-----------------+----------------+----------------+
| Bird            | Furthest North | Furthest South |
+-----------------+----------------+----------------+
| Eskimo Curlew   | 66.16051056    | 66.16051056    |
| Whimbrel        | 30.29138551    | 30.29138551    |
| Eurasian Curlew | 51.70469364    | 42.69096856    |
+-----------------+----------------+----------------+
```

In these results, because there was only one sighting of the first two birds, the values for both fields are the same. But for the *Eurasian Curlew*, you can see that it shows the farthest north and south that the bird was seen by our members.

Concatenating a Group

There is one more aggregate function that I want to cover before finishing with them. The GROUP_CONCAT( ) function is not used much, but it can be handy for particular situations. It's used to concatenate together the values for a group into a comma-separated list. Without it, you would need to do a subquery and use CONCAT_WS( ) to concatenate the results of a field.

To list the bird families for a particular order of birds, we could issue a simple SELECT statement. Now suppose we want a list of bird orders and bird families together, but we want one of the fields in the results to contain all of the bird families for each bird order. That would be cumbersome to do without GROUP_CONCAT( ). Let's see what it can do for us, using this supposition. Enter the following on your server:

```
SELECT bird_orders.scientific_name AS 'Bird Order',
GROUP_CONCAT(bird_families.scientific_name)
AS 'Bird Families in Order'
FROM rookery.bird_families
JOIN rookery.bird_orders USING(order_id)
WHERE bird_orders.scientific_name = 'Charadriiformes'
GROUP BY order_id \G
```

```
*************************** 1. row ***************************
          Bird Order: Charadriiformes
Bird Families in Order:

Charadriidae,Laridae,Sternidae,Burhinidae,Chionidae,Pluvianellidae,
Dromadidae,Haematopodidae,Ibidorhynchidae,Recurvirostridae,
Jacanidae,Scolopacidae,Turnicidae,Glareolidae,Pedionomidae,
Thinocoridae,Rostratulidae,Stercorariidae,Alcidae
```

I limited the results to one particular family to save space here. To get lists of orders for all families, just remove the WHERE clause:

```
SELECT bird_orders.scientific_name AS 'Bird Order',
GROUP_CONCAT(bird_families.scientific_name SEPARATOR ', ')
AS 'Bird Families in Order'
FROM rookery.bird_families
JOIN rookery.bird_orders USING(order_id)
GROUP BY order_id \G
```

If you tried that, you saw that the SEPARATOR clause of the GROUP_CONCAT( ) added a comma and a space after each family name.

Numeric Functions

Numeric functions are functions that change numbers in some way. They don't do a calculation, per se. That would be arithmetic functions. Instead, they help you simplify the numeric result of a query. You might want to round a number up or down, or get the absolute value. These actions can be done easily with numeric functions. We'll look at them in this section.

Rounding Numbers

Computers are very precise, so when we ask them to do a calculation, they will sometimes return a number with many decimal places. That may not matter to you, especially if the number is not displayed and used just by other functions for processing, either now or later. However, as humans, we tend to be more comfortable with rounded numbers. We're usually not as precise as computers. To that end, there are a few numeric functions that may be used for rounding.

In "Dynamic Columns" on page 68, we created some tables with dynamic columns in MariaDB. These included surveys of members about their bird-watching preferences. Let's use those tables and the data they contain to test some numeric functions. If you didn't create those survey tables or if you aren't using MariaDB, you won't be able to participate in these examples.

To start, let's look at one of the SQL statements we used in that section. We'll run it again, but with more data from my site:

```
SELECT IFNULL(COLUMN_GET(choices, answer AS CHAR), 'total')
AS 'Birding Site', COUNT(*) AS 'Votes'
FROM survey_answers
JOIN survey_questions USING(question_id)
WHERE survey_id = 1
AND question_id = 1
GROUP BY answer WITH ROLLUP;
```

```
+---------------+-------+
| Birding Site  | Votes |
+---------------+-------+
| forest        |    30 |
| shore         |    42 |
| backyard      |    14 |
| total         |    86 |
+---------------+-------+
```

This shows us the number of votes from members for the types of locations they prefer for watching birds. Let's calculate the percentages to go with these results. To do this, we need first to count the number of votes for all of the choices. We could put that in a subquery, but let's keep it simpler by executing a SELECT statement first to get that value. We'll create a user-defined variable in which to temporarily store that number. A user variable is temporary and will last only for the current client session. It can be accessed only by the user that creates it. You would use the SET statement to create a user variable. The variable name must start with @, followed by the equals sign, and then a value, an expression, or an SQL statement that will determine the value of the user-defined variable. Let's create one now for our example. Enter the following on your MariaDB server:

```
SET @fav_site_total =
(SELECT COUNT(*)
FROM survey_answers
JOIN survey_questions USING(question_id)
WHERE survey_id = 1
AND question_id = 1);

SELECT @fav_site_total;
```

```
+-----------------+
| @fav_site_total |
+-----------------+
|              86 |
+-----------------+
```

Because I added plenty more rows to the survey_answers table, this result is now higher than previously. You'll see that the total is correct in the results of the next example. Let's use the variable we created as the denominator for calculating the percentage of votes for each choice:

```
SELECT COLUMN_GET(choices, answer AS CHAR)
  AS 'Birding Site',
COUNT(*) AS 'Votes',
```

```
(COUNT(*) / @fav_site_total) AS 'Percent'
FROM survey_answers
JOIN survey_questions USING(question_id)
WHERE survey_id = 1
AND question_id = 1
GROUP BY answer;
```

```
+--------------+-------+---------+
| Birding Site | Votes | Percent |
+--------------+-------+---------+
| forest       |    30 | 0.3488  |
| shore        |    42 | 0.4884  |
| backyard     |    14 | 0.1628  |
+--------------+-------+---------+
```

In this example, we're dividing the number of votes for each choice by the variable containing the total number of votes. That gives us numbers with four decimal places. Let's change those numbers to read as percentages by multiplying them by 100 and using the ROUND( ) function to get rid of the decimals. We'll use CONCAT( ) to paste a percent sign to the end of the number:

```
SELECT COLUMN_GET(choices, answer AS CHAR)
   AS 'Birding Site',
COUNT(*) AS 'Votes',
CONCAT( ROUND( (COUNT(*) / @fav_site_total) * 100), '%')
   AS 'Percent'
FROM survey_answers
JOIN survey_questions USING(question_id)
WHERE survey_id = 1
AND question_id = 1
GROUP BY answer;
```

```
+--------------+-------+---------+
| Birding Site | Votes | Percent |
+--------------+-------+---------+
| forest       |    30 | 35%     |
| shore        |    42 | 49%     |
| backyard     |    14 | 16%     |
+--------------+-------+---------+
```

Notice that the ROUND( ) function rounded the first two numbers up and the last one down. That's how rounding goes. Let's change the results to show one decimal place:

```
SELECT COLUMN_GET(choices, answer AS CHAR)
AS 'Birding Site',
COUNT(*) AS 'Votes',
CONCAT( ROUND( (COUNT(*) / @fav_site_total) * 100, 1), '%') AS 'Percent'
FROM survey_answers
JOIN survey_questions USING(question_id)
WHERE survey_id = 1
AND question_id = 1
GROUP BY answer;
```

```
+---------------+-------+---------+
| Birding Site  | Votes | Percent |
+---------------+-------+---------+
| forest        |    30 | 34.9%   |
| shore         |    42 | 48.8%   |
| backyard      |    14 | 16.3%   |
+---------------+-------+---------+
```

The ROUND( ) function rounded up and down to the first decimal place based on the true value, which includes multiple decimal places. Suppose we want to be conservative and round all values down, or all values up. For that, we need other functions.

Rounding Only Down or Up

To round only down, use the FLOOR( ) function. To round only up, use the CEILING( ) function. Let's use the previous example to see how we would round down the results:

```
SELECT COLUMN_GET(choices, answer AS CHAR)
  AS 'Birding Site',
COUNT(*) AS 'Votes',
CONCAT( FLOOR( (COUNT(*) / @fav_site_total) * 100), '%')
  AS 'Percent'
FROM survey_answers
JOIN survey_questions USING(question_id)
WHERE survey_id = 1
AND question_id = 1
GROUP BY answer;
```

```
+---------------+-------+---------+
| Birding Site  | Votes | Percent |
+---------------+-------+---------+
| forest        |    30 | 34%     |
| shore         |    42 | 48%     |
| backyard      |    14 | 16%     |
+---------------+-------+---------+
```

In this example, we replaced ROUND( ) with FLOOR( ) so that the results would be rounded down. The FLOOR( ) function doesn't allow for specifying the number of decimal places. Instead, it rounds down to the integer value.

If we want to round only up, we would use the CEILING( ) function like so:

```
SELECT COLUMN_GET(choices, answer AS CHAR)
AS 'Birding Site',
COUNT(*) AS 'Votes',
CONCAT( CEILING( (COUNT(*) / @fav_site_total) * 100), '%') AS 'Percent'
FROM survey_answers
JOIN survey_questions USING(question_id)
WHERE survey_id = 1
AND question_id = 1
GROUP BY answer;
```

```
+---------------+-------+---------+
| Birding Site  | Votes | Percent |
+---------------+-------+---------+
| forest        |    30 | 35%     |
| shore         |    42 | 49%     |
| backyard      |    14 | 17%     |
+---------------+-------+---------+
```

That rounded up all of the values. If a value has no decimal places, it wouldn't change the value.

Truncating Numbers

If we don't want to round a number up or down, but we just want to eliminate the extra decimal places, we can use TRUNCATE( ). Let's see how that looks with the same SQL statement we've been modifying:

```
SELECT COLUMN_GET(choices, answer AS CHAR)
  AS 'Birding Site',
COUNT(*) AS 'Votes',
CONCAT( TRUNCATE( (COUNT(*) / @fav_site_total) * 100, 1), '%')
  AS 'Percent'
FROM survey_answers
JOIN survey_questions USING(question_id)
WHERE survey_id = 1
AND question_id = 1
GROUP BY answer;
```

```
+---------------+-------+---------+
| Birding Site  | Votes | Percent |
+---------------+-------+---------+
| forest        |    30 | 34.8%   |
| shore         |    42 | 48.8%   |
| backyard      |    14 | 16.2%   |
+---------------+-------+---------+
```

As the name of the function implies, it truncated the value after the number of decimal places specified (i.e., 1 in this example).

Eliminating Negative Numbers

Sometimes when we're working with numbers in functions, we get them in the wrong order and the result is a number with a negative sign. If we're trying to find only the difference between two numbers, we can use ABS( ) to return the absolute value, the value without a negative sign. Absolute values are also important for certain mathematical calculations.

We'll try this function by using part of some examples from the previous section, where we determined the total number of seconds each member took to identify birds. This time we'll just calculate a total for all rows, not grouping by human_id:

```
SELECT
SUM( TIME_TO_SEC( TIMEDIFF(id_start, id_end) ) )
    AS 'Total Seconds for All',
ABS( SUM( TIME_TO_SEC( TIMEDIFF(id_start, id_end) ) ) )
    AS 'Absolute Total'
FROM bird_identification_tests;
```

```
+------------------------+----------------+
| Total Seconds for All | Absolute Total |
+------------------------+----------------+
|                  -1689 |           1689 |
+------------------------+----------------+
```

There's not much to this function and example. The first field has a negative sign because we put the id_start before the id_end within TIMEDIFF( ). We could just reverse the order, but there will be situations in which you won't know which value will be greater than the other. For this, you may need ABS( ).

In other situations, you want to know whether a value is positive or negative. For this, you can use the SIGN( ) function. It returns a value of 1 if the argument given results in a positive number, -1 if results in a negative number, and 0 if it's given a value of zero.

As an example, let's go back to our bird identification tests. Suppose we want a list of birds that members identified in less time than the average. We calculated the minimum average earlier in "Calculating a Group of Values" on page 235. We'll reuse part of that SQL statement, but save the results to a user-defined variable and use that variable to compare each row in bird_identification_tests so we can list only rows in which the time it took to identify the bird was less than average. Set up that variable and test it by entering this on your server:

```
SET @min_avg_time =
(SELECT MIN(avg_time) FROM
  (SELECT AVG( TIME_TO_SEC( TIMEDIFF(id_end, id_start)))
    AS 'avg_time'
  FROM bird_identification_tests
  GROUP BY human_id) AS average_times);

SELECT @min_avg_time;
```

```
+---------------+
| @min_avg_time |
+---------------+
|       23.6667 |
+---------------+
```

That's about right. We had a value of 23 seconds before, but that's because we rounded it with `TIME_FORMAT( )`. This is more accurate. Let's use that variable now to do a comparison using `SIGN( )` in the `WHERE` clause. Enter this on your server:

```
SELECT CONCAT(name_first, SPACE(1), name_last)
    AS 'Birdwatcher',
common_name AS 'Bird',
ROUND(@min_avg_time - TIME_TO_SEC( TIMEDIFF(id_end, id_start) ) )
    AS 'Seconds Less than Average'
FROM bird_identification_tests
JOIN humans USING(human_id)
JOIN rookery.birds USING(bird_id)
WHERE SIGN( TIME_TO_SEC( TIMEDIFF(id_end, id_start) - @min_avg_time)) = -1;
```

```
+-------------------+------------------------+---------------------------+
| Birdwatcher       | Bird Identified        | Seconds Less than Average |
+-------------------+------------------------+---------------------------+
| Lexi Hollar       | Blue Duck              |                         3 |
| Lexi Hollar       | Trinidad Piping-Guan   |                        13 |
| Geoffrey Dyer     | Javan Plover           |                        15 |
| Katerina Smirnova | Blue Duck              |                         2 |
| Anahit Vanetsyan  | Great Crested Grebe    |                         4 |
+-------------------+------------------------+---------------------------+
```

The use of `SIGN( )` in the `WHERE` clause selects rows in which the member took less than the average time. That's a function that would be difficult to duplicate in MySQL by any other method.

Summary

Although we didn't cover all of the aggregate and numeric functions, we covered most of them—including the ones that are used most often. We primarily skipped the statistics functions. We didn't cover many arithmetic functions, but those are pretty straightforward (e.g., `POWER(2, 8)` returns 2 to the eighth power, or 256), or they're specialized (e.g., `PI( )` returns π, or 3.141593). What's important is that you feel comfortable with aggregate functions and using the `GROUP BY` clause—you'll use them often—and that you have a firm grasp on the numeric functions covered in this chapter. Several other numeric functions exist, in case you ever need them. If you want to learn about these other functions, you can check the MySQL documentation (*http://bit.ly/group_by*) or the MariaDB documentation (*http://bit.ly/mariadb_docs*).

Exercises

Numeric functions are pretty easy, once you know what each does. You probably didn't have any trouble following the sections on them in this chapter. Aggregate functions, though, can be a little bothersome. Therefore, while some exercises in this section require you to use numeric functions, most include aggregate functions. Some call for you to combine numeric and aggregate functions. These should help you to retain what you learned in this chapter. There aren't many exercises for this chapter, though, so it shouldn't take you much time to complete all of them.

1. Construct a simple SELECT statement that counts the number of rows in the birds table where the common_name contains the word Least. Execute that to make sure you did it correctly. Next, modify that SQL statement to count the rows in which the common_name contains the word Great. You'll do this by using the LIKE operator in the WHERE clause.

2. In "Calculating a Group of Values" on page 235, we covered how to group columns for counting. Combine the two SQL statements you constructed in the previous exercise and make one SQL statement using GROUP BY to produce one field in the results that shows the number of birds with a common_name containing Least and another field that shows the number of birds that are Great.

3. In some of the examples in this chapter (see "Counting Values" on page 230), we had MySQL count the number of birds in each species and in each bird family. For this exercise, you may want to refer to those examples.

   Construct a SELECT statement to query the birds table, with three fields in the results set: the name of the bird species, the number of birds in that species, and the percentage that species represents of the total number of species. Let MySQL calculate the total number of species; don't enter that value manually in the SQL statement.

   After you've successfully executed this SQL statement, modify the SQL statement using one of the numeric functions to round to one decimal place the field that contains the percentage value.

4. Do the previous exercise again, but this time create another SELECT statement that retrieves only the total number of bird species. With the SET statement, create a user variable to store that value taken by MySQL from the SELECT statement. You may give any name you want for that variable.

   Now change the SELECT statement you created in the previous exercise, but use the variable you created for determining the percentage of total birds in the table. Once you have it executed correctly, exit the mysql client and log back in.

   Run the same SQL statement to create the user variable and the second SQL statement for this exercise again. Notice the time it takes to execute in the results statement. Then execute again the SELECT statement from the previous exercise, the one that doesn't use a user variable. Notice how long it took to execute compared to the SELECT statement that uses a user variable.

5. In the humans table, the membership_expiration column contains date values. Put together a SELECT statement in which you determine the number of months after the date 2014-01-01 until each member's membership will expire. If you're not sure

how to do this, refer to "Comparing Dates and Times" on page 222. Use the SIGN( ) function in the WHERE clause to determine whether a membership has expired. List only unexpired memberships. This was covered in "Eliminating Negative Numbers" on page 245. Remember to use the IF NOT NULL operator in the WHERE clause to exclude those members who don't have a paid membership (i.e., no expiration date). Label the field as Months to Expiration.

6. Modify the SQL statement you created for the previous exercise. Don't exclude expired memberships this time—but still exclude those without a paid membership. Use the CONCAT( ) function to append " - expired" to the number of months remaining or past due. Don't append the text if the membership hasn't expired. You'll have to use the IF( ) function to test that for the field containing the number of months. You'll also have to use the ABS( ) function to remove the negative sign from the value.

7. Based on the SQL statement you constructed in the previous exercises, create a new one to determine the average number of months until expiration for all paid members in one field, and the average number of months past expiration, based on the date of 2014-01-01. You will need to use the AVG( ) function to calculate these averages. Once you have that working, add fields to determine the minimum and maximum number of months, using MIN( ) and MAX( ), and the GROUP BY clause.

## PART V

Administration and Beyond

In this final part, we will cover some administrative activities of MySQL and MariaDB. These are activities that are not necessarily related to the development of databases, but are still related to the management of data. Some of these are routine activities and some are only occasionally performed. And we'll cover some aspects that go beyond MySQL and MariaDB.

First, in Chapter 13, we'll cover the management of user accounts and their privileges. We covered this briefly at the start of this book, but in this chapter we will discuss it in more depth. We'll go through how to be more precise about which privileges are given to each user and for which databases and tables.

In Chapter 14, we'll discuss how to make backups of databases. This is a very important administrative duty. Related to that, we will cover the less routine administrative activity of restoring a backup. When this is needed, it's usually critical and urgent. You're always encouraged to complete the exercises at the end of each chapter, but because this chapter covers such an important topic, the exercises here are particularly essential.

Chapter 15 explains the administrative task of importing large amounts of data. The bulk importing of data from another database or from another format (e.g., from a spreadsheet or a text file containing comma-separated values) may not be something you will do often. However, knowing how to do it when needed can be very useful and save you plenty of time and frustration.

The book concludes with Chapter 16, which briefly covers a few APIs. These include examples for connecting and querying MySQL and MariaDB with PHP and a few other programming languages. Almost all databases are interfaced with an API, as it allows for greater control and security–and doesn't require users to know anything about using a database.

## CHAPTER 13

User Accounts and Privileges

We've addressed user accounts and privileges a few times up until this point, but in this chapter we're going to thoroughly discuss this crucial topic. Given the importance of security in any data-related activity, some readers might feel that this topic should have been covered thoroughly at the beginning of the book, and there's some logic to support that approach. But it's much more interesting to work with databases first before spending a lot of time on the less exciting administrative tasks such as user privileges and security. Plus, it's easier to understand the importance of user privileges, and to think about the various ways to set privileges, after you have a firm understanding of tables and other elements of a database. You're now ready to consider user accounts and related topics, and will have a better appreciation of what's covered here than you would have if we had explored this subject earlier in the book.

We'll start by looking at the basics of creating a user account and granting privileges. Then we'll go through the details of restricting access and granting privileges for various database components. Once you understand these ways to restrict access, we'll look at what privileges to give some common administrative user accounts. We'll then look at how to revoke privileges and delete user accounts, as well as how to change passwords and rename user accounts.

User Account Basics

In this book, I have used the term *user account* several times instead of just *user*. This was done to distinguish a person from the combination of a username and the location or host from which the user may access the MySQL or MariaDB server.

For instance, the *root* user has full access to all databases and all privileges, but only when connecting from the localhost. The *root* user is not allowed to access the server through a remote host, such as through the Internet. That would be a major security vulnerability. At a minimum, access and privileges are based on the combination of the user and its host, which is called the user account.

As the *root* user, you can create a user account with the CREATE USER statement. Here's an example using this SQL statement to create a user account for a woman named Lena Stankoska:

```
CREATE USER 'lena_stankoska';
```

In this example, we're just creating the user account without giving it any privileges. To see the privileges a user account has, use the SHOW GRANTS statement like this:

```
SHOW GRANTS FOR 'lena_stankoska';
```

```
+--------------------------------------------+
| Grants for lena_stankoska@%                |
+--------------------------------------------+
| GRANT USAGE ON *.* TO 'lena_stankoska'@'%' |
+--------------------------------------------+
```

Notice that these results are in the form of an SQL statement. Instead of using the CREATE USER statement, you can enter a GRANT statement exactly as shown in the results. Let's pull apart the results here, but a bit in reverse order.

The user is *lena_stankoska* and the host is the wildcard, %. The wildcard was used because we didn't specify a host when we created the user. Any privileges that will be granted to this user account will be permitted from any host. This is not a good idea. You should always specify a host. For our examples, to start, we'll use localhost. We'll look at setting the host in the next section.

The *.* part in the results says that usage is granted for all databases and tables—the part before the period refers to databases, and the part after the period refers to tables. In order to limit usage to a specific database or table, you would have to change that part to *database.table*. We'll look at that in a bit.

Once you create a user account, you would generally then give it privileges. If you want to give an existing user account all privileges to be able to use all SQL statements from the localhost, you would execute the GRANT statement like this:

```
GRANT ALL ON rookery.*
TO 'lena_stankoska'@'localhost';

SHOW GRANTS FOR 'lena_stankoska'@'localhost';
```

```
+---------------------------------------------------------------------+
| Grants for lena_stankoska@localhost                                 |
+---------------------------------------------------------------------+
| GRANT USAGE ON *.* TO 'lena_stankoska'@'localhost'                  |
| GRANT ALL PRIVILEGES ON `rookery`.* TO 'lena_stankoska'@'localhost' |
+---------------------------------------------------------------------+
```

Notice that the results of the SHOW GRANTS statement for the *lena_stankoska@localhost* user account now shows two rows: one similar to the result shown previously, but with the host as localhost, and the new SQL statement we executed. This user account now has all of the privileges allowed on the rookery database, except the ability to give privileges to others. We'll cover that one and the many privileges that may be given to a user account later in this chapter.

Because we didn't specify a password for this user account, it can be accessed without a password. That makes this user account a high security risk: it can allow anyone who gets on to the server to do almost anything to the database, and it doesn't require a password. Because we created it only to see how granting and showing privileges works, let's remove it. We'll create this user account again later.

User accounts are removed through the DROP USER statement. However, removing the user accounts for Lena isn't as straightforward as you might think. When we executed the CREATE USER statement and didn't specify a host, we created one user account—one with the wildcard for the host. When we executed the GRANT statement to give privileges to the same user, but with the host of localhost, a second user account was created. To understand this better, let's look at what is stored in the user table in the mysql database. That's where this user account information is stored. Execute the following SQL statement from your server:

```
SELECT User, Host
FROM mysql.user
WHERE User LIKE 'lena_stankoska';
```

```
+----------------+-----------+
| User           | Host      |
+----------------+-----------+
| lena_stankoska | %         |
| lena_stankoska | localhost |
+----------------+-----------+
```

As you can see here, there are two user accounts, although we sought to create only one. If you had not understood before the distinction between a user and a user account, I hope you do now.

 Although you may be able to access the user account privileges directly in the mysql database, you should never use that method to make changes to user account data. Although the examples so far have been simple, there are situations in which user permissions will affect several tables in the mysql database. If you attempt to insert, update, or delete a user account in the user table using the INSERT, UPDATE, or DELETE statements instead of the appropriate user account statements described in this chapter, you may not make the changes the way you want and may orphan entries in other tables.

To eliminate both of the user accounts that we created for Lena, we will have to execute the DROP USER statement twice, like this:

```
DROP USER 'lena_stankoska'@'localhost';
DROP USER 'lena_stankoska'@'%';
```

This eliminates both user accounts for Lena. We'll create more user accounts for her in the next sections. In doing so, though, we will look more closely at how to restrict access of user accounts, rather than give her all privileges and access from anywhere and without a password.

Restricting the Access of User Accounts

As a database administrator, you may give users full access to databases from anywhere, or you can limit them based on various aspects of the connection and the database. Put simply, you can restrict user access and privileges based on the username and host, the database components (e.g., tables) the user account may access, and the SQL statements and functions that may be used on those database components. We'll address these restrictions in this section.

Username and Host

When you create user accounts, consider both who needs access and from where. First, let's define *who*. This can represent a person or a group of people. You can give an individual a username—which might be related to their actual name, such as *lena_stankoska* for Lena Stankoska—or define a username to a group of people, such as *sales_dept* for the Sales Department. You could also create a user account based on a function or use. In that case, one person might have several user accounts.

If Lena Stankoska is a database administrator of the rookery and birdwatchers databases, she might have multiple usernames, perhaps all from the localhost, for example, *lena_stankoska*, for personal use; *admin_backup*, for when she makes backups; *admin_restore*, for when she restores backups; and *admin_import*, if she regularly imports large amounts of data.

Let's first create the personal accounts for Lena Stankoska. We'll create the administrative accounts later. For her personal username, *lena_stankoska*, let's give her two user accounts: one from localhost and another from a remote location. We'll give her more privileges when she's logged into the localhost, but less when she accesses the server remotely—from her home if she has a static IP address. Let's create for her *lena_stankoska@localhost* and *lena_stankoska@lena_stankoska_home*.

The hostname for a user account can be a name that a DNS can translate to an IP address or it can be an actual IP address. The DNS could be the server's external DNS, which translates Internet domain names to an IP address. Or you can use the bind system and put the name in the server's hosts file (e.g., */etc/hosts* on a Linux system). If you do that, you'll have to restart MySQL for it to take effect.

Let's create these two personal user accounts for Lena. Enter the following SQL statements on your server:

```
CREATE USER 'lena_stankoska'@'localhost'
IDENTIFIED BY 'her_password_123';

GRANT USAGE ON *.* TO 'lena_stankoska'@'lena_stankoska_home'
IDENTIFIED BY 'her_password_123';
```

These examples used the CREATE USER and the GRANT statements to create the user accounts. If you enter GRANT and specify a username that doesn't exist, it automatically creates the user—and remember that each combination of user and hostname is a unique user account. However, it's recommended that you start with CREATE USER to create the user account and then grant privileges. We added the IDENTIFIED BY clauses in each of these SQL statements to set the passwords for each user account.

Let's see how one of Lena's user accounts looks at this point. Enter the following on your server:

```
SHOW GRANTS FOR 'lena_stankoska'@'localhost' \G

*************************** 1. row ***************************
Grants for admin_backup@localhost:
        GRANT USAGE ON *.* TO 'lena_stankoska'@'localhost'
        IDENTIFIED BY PASSWORD ' *B1A8D5415ACE5AB4BBAC120EC1D17766B8EFF1A1'
```

Notice that the password is encrypted in the results. There isn't a way within MySQL to retrieve the password in plain text, to decrypt it. Also notice that the encrypted password is preceded by the PASSWORD keyword. If you don't want to enter someone's password with clear text as we did in the earlier commands, you could encrypt the password on a different computer with the PASSWORD( ) function and then copy the results to the server using the GRANT statement. You would do that like this:

```
SELECT PASSWORD('her_password_123');

+------------------------------------------+
| PASSWORD('its_password_123')             |
+------------------------------------------+
| *B1A8D5415ACE5AB4BBAC120EC1D17766B8EFF1A1 |
+------------------------------------------+
```

The encrypted text is identical to the one in the results of the earlier SHOW GRANTS statement. If your server is logging all transactions, you may want to encrypt passwords on your personal computer by this method and use the results for entering the passwords on your server so no one else will know the password for a user account. Starting with MySQL version 5.6, any SQL statement that contains the reserved word PASSWORD will not be logged.

At this point, Lena can log into the server with any one of these user accounts—one allows her to do so only from home, and the other four only when logging in from the server. But she can't access any database, other than the default ones (i.e., `test` and *information_schema*) and not always those. This allows her to do anything she wants in the `test` database, including creating tables and selecting, updating, and deleting data. She can't access or even see the other databases, and she can't create another database. She is greatly limited with these user accounts. Let's proceed to the next section to learn more about what a user account may access and then give Lena access to more than the `test` database.

SQL Privileges

Lena needs more than access to the databases to be able to perform her duties. We have to grant her the privileges to execute various tasks, such as reading and writing data on the `rookery` and `birdwatchers` databases. At this point, we need to give the *lena_stankoska@localhost* user account the SELECT, INSERT, and UPDATE privileges for both of our databases. To give a user account multiple privileges, list the privileges in a comma-separated list. Enter this on the server:

```
GRANT SELECT, INSERT, UPDATE ON rookery.*
TO 'lena_stankoska'@'localhost';

GRANT SELECT, INSERT, UPDATE ON birdwatchers.*
TO 'lena_stankoska'@'localhost';

SHOW GRANTS FOR 'lena_stankoska'@localhost \G

*************************** 1. row ***************************
Grants for lena_stankoska@localhost:
GRANT USAGE ON *.*
TO 'lena_stankoska'@'localhost'

*************************** 2. row ***************************
Grants for lena_stankoska@localhost:
GRANT SELECT, INSERT, UPDATE ON `birdwatchers`.*
TO 'lena_stankoska'@'localhost'

*************************** 3. row ***************************
Grants for lena_stankoska@localhost:
GRANT SELECT, INSERT, UPDATE ON `rookery`.*
TO 'lena_stankoska'@'localhost'
```

Some privileges cover more than one SQL statement. For a list of privileges, see Table 13-1.

Although we gave *lena_stankoska@localhost* enough privileges to manipulate data on our two databases, we didn't give it the ability to delete data. To add privileges to a user account, you don't have to list again all of the privileges it already has. Just execute the

GRANT statement with the new privileges and the system will add them to the user account's privileges list. Do that like so:

```
GRANT DELETE ON rookery.*
TO 'lena_stankoska'@'localhost';

GRANT DELETE ON birdwatchers.*
TO 'lena_stankoska'@'localhost';

SHOW GRANTS FOR 'lena_stankoska'@localhost \G

*************************** 1. row ***************************
Grants for lena_stankoska@localhost:
GRANT USAGE ON *.*
TO 'lena_stankoska'@'localhost'

*************************** 2. row ***************************
Grants for lena_stankoska@localhost:
GRANT SELECT, INSERT, UPDATE, DELETE ON `birdwatchers`.*
TO 'lena_stankoska'@'localhost'

*************************** 3. row ***************************
Grants for lena_stankoska@localhost:
GRANT SELECT, INSERT, UPDATE, DELETE ON `rookery`.*
TO 'lena_stankoska'@'localhost'
```

Now Lena can manipulate data in all of the basic ways on our two databases, but only from the localhost. She still can't do anything from home. We'll give her privileges from home later.

Table 13-1. Privileges for GRANT and REVOKE statements

Privilege	Description
ALL [PRIVILEGES]	Grants all of the basic privileges. Does not include the GRANT OPTION.
ALTER	Allows use of the ALTER TABLE statement, but requires also the CREATE and INSERT privileges. DROP is also needed to rename a table. This is a security risk: someone could rename a table to get access to it.
ALTER ROUTINE	Allows user account to alter or drop stored routines. This includes the ALTER FUNCTION and ALTER PROCEDURE statements, as well as the DROP FUNCTION and DROP PROCEDURE statements.
CREATE	Allows use of the CREATE TABLE statement. Needs INDEX privilege to define indexes.
CREATE ROUTINE	Allows user account to create stored routines. This includes the CREATE FUNCTION and CREATE PROCEDURE statements. Gives the user has ALTER ROUTINE privileges to any routine he creates.
CREATE TEMPORARY TABLES	Allows the CREATE TEMPORARY TABLES statement to be used.
CREATE USER	Allows the user account the ability to execute several user account management statements: CREATE USER, RENAME USER, REVOKE ALL PRIVILEGES, and the DROP USER statements.
CREATE VIEW	Permits the CREATE VIEW statement.

Privilege	Description
DELETE	Allows the DELETE statement to be used.
DROP	Permits the user to execute DROP TABLE and TRUNCATE statements.
EVENT	Allows the user account to create events for the event scheduler. It allows the use of the CREATE EVENT, ALTER EVENT, and the DROP EVENT statements.
EXECUTE	Allows the execution of stored procedures, the EXECUTE statement.
FILE	Allows the use of SELECT...INTO OUTFILE and LOAD DATA INFILE statements to export and import to and from a filesystem. This is a security risk. It can be limited to specific directories with the secure_file_priv variable.
INDEX	Grants the use of the CREATE INDEX and DROP INDEX statements.
INSERT	Permits the use of INSERT statements. It's required to execute ANALYZE TABLE, OPTIMIZE TABLE, and REPAIR TABLE statements.
LOCK TABLES	Allows the use of LOCK TABLES statements for tables for which the user has SELECT privileges.
PROCESS	Allows the use of the SHOW PROCESSLIST and SHOW ENGINE statements.
RELOAD	Allows the FLUSH statement to be issued.
REPLICATION CLIENT	Allows the user to query master and slave servers for status information, the SHOW MASTER STATUS and SHOW SLAVE STATUS statements, as well as the SHOW BINARY LOGS statement.
REPLICATION SLAVE	Required for replication slave servers, this allows binary log events to be read from the master server.
SELECT	Allows the use of the SELECT statement.
SHOW DATABASES	Permits the use of the SHOW DATABASES statement for all databases, not just the ones for which the user has privileges.
SHOW VIEW	Allows the use of the SHOW CREATE VIEW statement.
SHUTDOWN	Allows the use of the shutdown option with the mysqladmin utility.
SUPER	Grants use of CHANGE MASTER TO, KILL, PURGE BINARY LOGS, and SET GLOBAL statements, and the debug option with the command-line utility mysqladmin.
TRIGGER	This privilege allows the user account the ability to create and drop triggers, using the CREATE TRIGGER and the DROP TRIGGER statements.
UPDATE	Allows the UPDATE statement to be used.
USAGE	Included to create a user without privileges, or to modify an existing one without affecting the existing privileges.

Database Components and Privileges

Now we'll turn to the parts of the database a user account can access. A user account can be given access to all of the databases on a server, or limited to specific databases, specific tables, and even specific columns. Let's first see how to limit user accounts to specific databases, and then how to limit user accounts to tables and columns.

We've given Lena more restrictions when she's at home than when she's at work. Of course, if she really wants access to more information at home, she can first log into the server at the operating system level using ssh and then log into MySQL from there using her *lena_stankoska@localhost* user account. This may be fine, because we can more easily control security at the operating system level, and we're assuring that sensitive data isn't being passed unencrypted through the Internet by adding extra restrictions to the home account. But on the operating system level, if you want, you can restrict use of ssh to prevent Lena from getting around security.

Restricting to specific databases

In order to limit the *lena_stankoska@lena_stankoska_home* user account to the rookery database, we would have to do something like this:

```
GRANT USAGE ON rookery.*
TO 'lena_stankoska'@'lena_stankoska_home'
IDENTIFIED BY 'her_password_123';

SHOW GRANTS FOR 'lena_stankoska'@'lena_stankoska_home' \G

*************************** 1. row ***************************
Grants for lena_stankoska@lena_stankoska_home:
    GRANT USAGE ON *.* TO 'lena_stankoska'@'lena_stankoska_home'
    IDENTIFIED BY PASSWORD '*B1A8D5415ACE5AB4BBAC120EC1D17766B8EFF1A1'
```

Here we're limiting this user account's access on the server to the rookery database. However, we can see from the results of the SHOW GRANTS statement that she still has global usage. If she were to access the server from her home to get a list of databases, this is what she'd see:

```
mysql --user lena_stankoska --password='her_password_123' \
    --host rookery.eu --execute='SHOW DATABASES'

+--------------------+
| Database           |
+--------------------+
| information_schema |
| test               |
+--------------------+
```

She still can't see the rookery database. This is because she can't do anything on that database. She can't even execute a SHOW TABLES statement or a SELECT statement for that database. To do that, we need to give her privileges other than hollow access to the rookery database. Let's start by giving her the SELECT privilege for the rookery database. We'll do that by executing the following:

```
GRANT SELECT ON rookery.*
TO 'lena_stankoska'@'lena_stankoska_home';

SHOW GRANTS FOR 'lena_stankoska'@'lena_stankoska_home';
```

```
+-----------------------------------------------------------------------+
| Grants for lena_stankoska@lena_stankoska_home                         |
+-----------------------------------------------------------------------+
| GRANT USAGE ON *.* TO 'lena_stankoska'@'lena_stankoska_home'          |
| IDENTIFIED BY PASSWORD '...'                                          |
| GRANT SELECT ON `rookery`.* TO 'lena_stankoska'@'lena_stankoska_home' |
+-----------------------------------------------------------------------+
```

You can't specify just the database name in the GRANT statement; you have to specify a table too. That's why we added .* to refer to all tables in the rookery database.

In the results, notice that there is still the row granting global usage for this user account. Following that is an entry related to the rookery database. To make the results fit on the page here, I replaced the password with an ellipsis. Lena can now access the rookery database from her home, although she can only select data. Here's what she sees from her home when she executes SHOW DATABASES and a SELECT statement to get a list of Avocet birds from the command line:

```
mysql --user lena_stankoska --password='her_password_123' --host rookery.eu \
    --execute="SHOW DATABASES; \
            SELECT common_name AS 'Avocets'
            FROM rookery.birds \
            WHERE common_name LIKE '%Avocet%';"
```

```
+--------------------+
| Database           |
+--------------------+
| information_schema |
| rookery            |
| test               |
+--------------------+
+--------------------+
| Avocets            |
+--------------------+
| Pied Avocet        |
| Red-necked Avocet  |
| Andean Avocet      |
| American Avocet    |
| Mountain Avocetbill |
+--------------------+
```

Restricting to specific tables

At this point, Lena has sufficient access to the two databases when at her office. However, although she can select data on the rookery database from home, she can't access the birdwatchers databases from home. Let's give her the SELECT privilege for that database, but only for certain tables.

If we want to give Lena access only to the bird_sightings table in the birdwatchers database from home, we would enter the following:

```
GRANT SELECT ON birdwatchers.bird_sightings
TO 'lena_stankoska'@'lena_stankoska_home';

SHOW GRANTS FOR 'lena_stankoska'@'lena_stankoska_home';
```

```
+--------------------------------------------------------------------+
| Grants for lena_stankoska@lena_stankoska_home                      |
+--------------------------------------------------------------------+
| GRANT USAGE ON *.* TO 'lena_stankoska'@'lena_stankoska_home'       |
| IDENTIFIED BY PASSWORD '...'                                       |
| GRANT SELECT ON `rookery`.* TO 'lena_stankoska'@'lena_stankoska_home' |
| GRANT SELECT ON `birdwatchers`.`bird_sightings`                    |
| TO 'lena_stankoska'@'lena_stankoska_home'                          |
+--------------------------------------------------------------------+
```

Now Lena can see only that one table in the birdwatchers database. Here is what happens if she executes the following from her home computer:

```
mysql --user lena_stankoska --password='her_password_123' --host rookery.eu \
    --execute="SHOW TABLES FROM birdwatchers;"
```

```
+-----------------------+
| Tables_in_birdwatchers |
+-----------------------+
| bird_sightings        |
+-----------------------+
```

To give her access to more tables in the birdwatchers database, we could execute a GRANT statement for each table. That can be tedious with a database that has many tables, to give her access to many of them but not all. But there's no simple way around it. I have requested while writing this chapter that a feature be added to MariaDB to specify multiple tables in a single GRANT statement. So maybe one day there will be an easy way to do it with MariaDB. For now, you can either manually enter the GRANT statement many times, or you can create a short script to do it.

For example, suppose that we want to give Lena access to all of the tables in the bird watchers database, except ones with personal and sensitive information. The tables to exclude would be the humans table and the two tables containing information about children, the birder_families and birding_events_children tables. Here's how such a shell script might look:

```
#!/bin/sh

mysql_connect="mysql --user root -pmy_pwd"
```

```
results=`$mysql_connect --skip-column-names \
        --execute 'SHOW TABLES FROM birdwatchers;'`

items=$(echo $results | tr " " "\n")

for item in $items
do

  if [ $item = 'humans' ] ||
     [ $item = 'birder_families' ] ||
     [ $item = 'birding_events_children' ]
  then
    continue
  fi

  `$mysql_connect --execute "GRANT SELECT ON birdwatchers.$item \
                      TO 'lena_stankoska'@'lena_stankoska_home'"`
done

exit
```

This simple shell script gets a list of tables using the SHOW TABLES statement. The script then goes through the list to execute a GRANT statement for each table name in the results, but skipping the three sensitive tables.

At this point, Lena can do plenty from her office and check on things from her home. If she needs to do more than this, it will probably be because she is performing an administrative task like making a backup or importing large amounts of data. When she does those tasks, she'll use one of the three administrative user accounts we created for her. Let's give those three accounts the necessary privileges so that Lena can perform the tasks required of her.

Restricting to specific columns

To give a user account access only to specific columns, issue a GRANT statement listing all of the columns permitted for the table within parentheses, in a comma-separated list after the privilege for which they apply. This will make more sense when you see an example. If you're granting many privileges, this can be an excessively long SQL statement.

In the previous section, as a security precaution, we didn't give Lena access to the humans table in the birdwatchers database from home. Suppose we changed our mind about that. Suppose we want her to have access to most of the humans table when she works at home, but not to the contact information of our clients (e.g., email addresses). Looking at the columns in the humans table, we decide she needs access to the human_id column to be able to join to other tables, and the formal_title, name_first, and name_last columns, as well as membership_type. The other columns either contain sensitive information or are unnecessary for her duties.

Based on the list of columns we want to permit Lena to access from home, let's enter the following:

```
GRANT SELECT (human_id, formal_title, name_first,
name_last, membership_type)
ON birdwatchers.humans
TO 'lena_stankoska'@'lena_stankoska_home';
```

Now Lena can access the humans table from home to get the names of members, as well as the type of membership each has.

Administrative User Accounts

Earlier, I mentioned that we need to create three administrative accounts for Lena to use in performing her duties as a database administrator from the localhost: *admin_backup*, *admin_restore*, and *admin_import*. These are common administrative user accounts that you may need to create and use. You'll use them in examples and exercises in Chapter 14 (which covers backing up and restoring), and Chapter 15 (importing data). In this section, we'll create these administrative user accounts and look at the privileges needed for them, as well as another one for granting privileges to other user accounts.

User Account for Making Backups

The *admin_backup* user account will be used with the mysqldump utility to make backups of the rookery and birdwatchers databases. This is covered in Chapter 14. Just a few privileges are needed to accomplish these tasks:

- At a minimum, it will need the SELECT privilege to read our two databases. You should limit an administrative account to the databases it needs to backup. In particular, you should not let it have SELECT privileges for the mysql database, because that contains user passwords.
- To lock the tables when making a backup, the LOCK TABLES privilege is required.
- If a database contains views and triggers, which we didn't cover in this book, the user account will need the SHOW VIEW and TRIGGER privileges, respectively.

Based on those considerations, let's create the *admin_backup@localhost* user account and give it the SELECT and LOCK TABLES privileges, but only for the rookery and birdwatchers databases. Do that by executing the following SQL statement:

```
CREATE USER 'admin_backup'@'localhost'
IDENTIFIED BY 'its_password_123';

GRANT SELECT, LOCK TABLES
ON rookery.*
```

```
TO 'admin_backup'@'localhost';

GRANT SELECT, LOCK TABLES
ON birdwatchers.*
TO 'admin_backup'@'localhost';
```

This allows Lena to use this `admin_restore` account to make backups of our databases. We created another account for restoring data, so let's give that account the privileges it needs.

User Account for Restoring Backups

Although you could create one administrative user account for both making backups and restoring them, you might want to use separate user accounts for those tasks. The main reason is that the task of making backups is usually one handled by scripts that run automatically. But the task of restoring data is generally run manually and can overwrite or destroy data on a live server. You might not want the user account with those privileges to be the same one for which you use in a script containing its password. For our examples in this chapter, let's give the *admin_restore@localhost* user account the privileges needed for restoring data to our databases:

- At a minimum, a user account for restoring a dump file needs the `INSERT` privilege to insert data into tables.
- It should also have the `LOCK TABLES` privilege to lock the tables while inserting data.
- It will need the `CREATE` privilege to create tables and `INDEX` to create indexes.
- Because a dump file can include SQL statements to alter tables to set the collation, the `ALTER` privilege may be needed.
- Depending on the method Lena uses to restore tables, she might also want to restore them to temporary tables. For that, she will need the `CREATE TEMPORARY TABLES` privilege. Temporary tables are dropped when the client connection is closed.
- If a database has views and triggers, the `CREATE VIEW` and `TRIGGER` privileges are required.

For our database usage, we won't need `CREATE VIEW` or `TRIGGER`, but we will need the other privileges. Create the *admin_restore@localhost* user account and give it the necessary privileges by entering the following on your server:

```
CREATE USER 'admin_restore'@'localhost'
IDENTIFIED BY 'different_pwd_456';

GRANT INSERT, LOCK TABLES, CREATE,
CREATE TEMPORARY TABLES, INDEX, ALTER
ON rookery.*
TO 'admin_restore'@'localhost';
```

```
GRANT INSERT, LOCK TABLES, CREATE,
CREATE TEMPORARY TABLES, INDEX, ALTER
ON birdwatchers.*
TO 'admin_restore'@'localhost';
```

With those privileges, Lena should have what she needs to restore any of the data in the rookery and birdwatchers databases.

User Account for Bulk Importing

The last administrative user we need to create for Lena is *admin_import*. She'll use this user account to import large data text files into our databases. This is covered in Chapter 15. For this method of importing data, she'll use the LOAD DATA INFILE statement. That requires just the FILE privilege.

 The FILE privilege is a security risk because it has the ability to read data from any file on the server to which MySQL has rights. This is why it is especially important that this privilege be given only to a user account designated for importing files. The password for that user account should be given only to someone who is trusted. You can restrict the directory from which files may be loaded with the secure_file_priv variable. That will minimize the security risk to the filesystem. You can also revoke this privilege when it's not in use and grant it again when needed to minimize risk to the databases.

The FILE privilege cannot be given for specific databases or components. It's a global privilege. If we give it to the *admin_import@localhost* user account, it can import data into any database—and it can export data from any database, including the mysql database. So be careful who gets this privilege and never allow it with a remote host. Still, create *admin_import@localhost* and give it this privilege by entering the following on the server:

```
CREATE USER 'admin_import'@'localhost'
IDENTIFIED BY 'another_pwd_789';

GRANT FILE ON *.*
TO 'admin_import'@'localhost';
```

We have created all of Lena's administrative user accounts and set each one with the necessary privileges (no more and no less) for her to perform her duties related to our databases. Let's create one more administrative user account, though, that may be of use to you.

User Account to Grant Privileges

Another user account that you might need is one for creating other users. You could use *root* for that, but to continue the policy of using limited administrative user accounts for separate functions, we should create a separate user account for user and privilege maintenance. Besides, this task might be given to someone who we don't want to have complete control over our database system.

To create a user account with the ability to create other user accounts and grant those other user accounts privileges, the GRANT statement has to include the GRANT OPTION clause. This clause allows the user to grant the same privileges it has to other users—but only the precise privileges granted in this GRANT statement. If we limit the privileges in the GRANT statement to our two databases, the user account cannot grant privileges to other databases. For instance, execute the following on your server to create this user account and give it the GRANT OPTION for our two databases:

```
GRANT ALL PRIVILEGES ON rookery.*
TO 'admin_granter'@'localhost'
IDENTIFIED BY 'avocet_123'
WITH GRANT OPTION;

GRANT ALL PRIVILEGES ON birdwatchers.*
TO 'admin_granter'@'localhost'
IDENTIFIED BY 'avocet_123'
WITH GRANT OPTION;
```

This creates the *admin_granter@localhost* user account, which has the privilege of granting privileges on the rookery and birdwatchers databases to other user accounts.

This user account's privileges are still fairly limited if we want it to be used to manage other user accounts. Suppose we want this user account to create and drop user accounts for our databases. To do that, we need to grant the CREATE USER privilege globally to *admin_granter@localhost*. So that this user account can execute the SHOW GRANTS statement, it will also need the SELECT privilege on the mysql database. This is another security risk, so be careful who gets this privilege. Enter these two SQL statements to give this user account these two additional privileges:

```
GRANT CREATE USER ON *.*
TO 'admin_granter'@'localhost';

GRANT SELECT ON mysql.*
TO 'admin_granter'@'localhost';
```

Now the *admin_granter@localhost* user account has the privileges to perform its tasks of managing user accounts on our databases. Let's test it by entering the first line in the following example from the command line to log into MySQL, then the following SQL statements from within the mysql client:

```
mysql --user admin_granter --password=avocet_123

SELECT CURRENT_USER() AS 'User Account';

+------------------------+
| User Account           |
+------------------------+
| admin_granter@localhost |
+------------------------+

CREATE USER 'bird_tester'@'localhost';

GRANT SELECT ON birdwatchers.*
TO 'bird_tester'@'localhost';

SHOW GRANTS FOR 'bird_tester'@'localhost';

+----------------------------------------------------------------+
| Grants for bird_tester@localhost                               |
+----------------------------------------------------------------+
| GRANT USAGE ON *.* TO 'bird_tester'@'localhost'                |
| GRANT SELECT ON `birdwatchers`.* TO 'bird_tester'@'localhost'  |
+----------------------------------------------------------------+

DROP USER 'bird_tester'@'localhost';
```

That worked well. We logged in with the *admin_granter@localhost* user account and used the CURRENT_USER( ) to confirm the user account. Then we created a user with the SELECT privilege on the birdwatchers database. We were able to execute SHOW GRANTS to verify this and then successfully issued DROP USER to delete the user account. We can give this user account to someone on our staff whose responsibility will be to manage user accounts for our databases.

Revoking Privileges

So far in this chapter we have been giving privileges to user accounts. But there may also be times when you want to revoke a privilege that you gave to a user account. Maybe you gave a privilege by mistake, or you've changed your mind about which tables you want the user account to have access, or changed your policy about which tables you want to protect.

The REVOKE statement revokes all or certain privileges that were granted to a user account. There are two forms of syntax to do this: one to revoke all privileges and another for specific privileges. Let's look at examples for both syntaxes.

Suppose we have a user, Michael Stone, who is taking a leave of absence for a few months, and there is no chance he will access the database while he's gone. We could delete his user account, but instead we decide to revoke his user account privileges. We'll add them back when he returns. To do this, we would enter something like this:

```
REVOKE ALL PRIVILEGES
ON rookery.*
FROM 'michael_stone'@'localhost';

REVOKE ALL PRIVILEGES
ON birdwatchers.*
FROM 'michael_stone'@'localhost';
```

The syntax is similar to the GRANT statement that grants all privileges. The main difference is that instead of an ON clause, there's a FROM to revoke privileges from a user account.
Although Michael may have had privileges for only certain tables in the two databases,
this removes them all. We don't have to remove the specific privileges with multiple SQL
statements for each table. To give privileges again to the user account, though, we may
have to use the GRANT statement many times as we would for a new user account.

The second syntax can be used to revoke only some privileges. The specific privileges
have to be given in a comma-separated list after the keyword REVOKE. The privileges for
REVOKE are the same as for GRANT (see Table 13-1). You can specify one table per REVOKE
statement, or revoke privileges on all tables of a database by putting an asterisk in as the
table name. To revoke privileges for specific columns, list them within parentheses in a
comma-separated list—the same as with the GRANT statement. Let's look at an example
of this second syntax.

To keep security tight, suppose we have a policy of removing any privileges not needed
by user accounts. When we granted privileges to the *admin_restore@localhost* user account, we included the ALTER privilege. Suppose we have found that ALTER is never
needed. We can revoke it like so:

```
REVOKE ALTER
ON rookery.*
FROM 'admin_restore'@'localhost';

REVOKE ALTER
ON birdwatchers.*
FROM 'admin_restore'@'localhost';
```

Deleting a User Account

The DROP USER statement deletes a user account. Let's look at an example of how this is
done. Suppose Michael Stone tells us that he won't return from his leave of absence
because he has found a new job. We would execute the following to delete his user
account:

```
DROP USER 'michael_stone'@'localhost';
```

If you use an older version of MySQL (i.e., before 5.0.2), you must first revoke all privileges before you drop the user account. This requires executing `REVOKE ALL ON *.* FROM 'user'@'host'` and then `DROP USER 'user'@'host'`.

Some users, like Lena, may have more than one personal user account. So we should check to see whether there are any other accounts associated with Michael Stone. Unfortunately, there isn't a `SHOW USERS` statement. Instead, we'll have to check the user table in the `mysql` database like this:

```
SELECT User, Host
FROM mysql.user
WHERE User LIKE '%michael%'
OR User LIKE '%stone%';
```

```
+----------------------+-------------+
| User                 | Host        |
+----------------------+-------------+
| mstone               | mstone_home |
| michael_zabbalaoui   | localhost   |
+----------------------+-------------+
```

It seems that Michael Stone has another user account related to his home IP address. After confirming that it's his user account, we'll drop it like so:

```
DROP USER 'mstone'@'mstone_home';
```

When you drop a user account, if the user account is logged in and has active sessions running, it won't stop the sessions. The active sessions will continue for the user account until the user exits or they've been idle so long that they end. However, you can shut down a user's activities sooner. First, you will need to get the process identifier for the session. You can do this be executing the following:

```
SHOW PROCESSLIST;
...

*************************** 4. row ***************************
      Id: 11482
    User: mstone
    Host: mstone_home
      db: NULL
 Command: Query
    Time: 78
   State: init
    Info: SELECT * FROM `birds`
Progress: 0.000
```

These are trimmed results, but we can see that *mstone@mstone_home* has an active connection even though we've dropped this user account. We're concerned that he's selecting data from our databases from his home, even though he no longer works for us and isn't intending on returning. We can kill this process by executing the following:

```
KILL 11482;
```

Notice that we used the process identification number from the results of the SHOW PROCESSLIST statement. The SHOW PROCESSLIST statement requires the PROCESS privilege, and the KILL statement requires the user account to have the SUPER privilege to execute it. Now that that session has been killed and his user accounts have been dropped, he can no longer access our databases. For good measure, we should remove his account from our server at the operating system level, a topic beyond the scope of this book.

Changing Passwords and Names

For better security, it's a good idea to change the passwords for user accounts regularly, especially for accounts with administrative privileges. How to change passwords is covered in the next subsection. A user may ask, or you may want to rename a user account. This isn't done as often, although it could be another security precaution. However, when you change a name or a password, you should be mindful of whether the user account name and password are incorporated into any scripts, in particular ones that run automatically to make backups of the databases. You'll have to change them in those scripts, as well.

Setting a User Account Password

In the examples throughout this chapter, we have created user accounts without passwords or given them passwords when creating the user accounts. You will occasionally need to change the password for a user account, and actually should do so regularly for good security. To do this, use the SET PASSWORD statement with the PASSWORD( ) function to encrypt the password given.

 As of version 5.6, you can force a user to change their password by expiring it. For this, you would use the ALTER USER statement with the PASSWORD EXPIRE clause like this:

```
ALTER USER 'admin_granter'@'localhost' PASSWORD EXPIRE;
```

The next time the user tries to log in or execute an SQL statement, he will receive an error message instructing him to change his password. He'll have to use the SET PASSWORD statement to do that, before any other SQL statements can be executed.

Let's change the password for the *admin_granter@localhost* user account:

```
SET PASSWORD FOR 'admin_granter'@'localhost' = PASSWORD('some_pwd_123');
```

That's not a very good password. Let's change the password to something more complicated, such as *P1ed_Avoce7-79873*. For an extra security measure, we'll use our personal computer to encrypt that password before logging onto the server to set it in MySQL. From a local computer, we'll execute the following from the command line, assuming MySQL is running on it:

```
mysql -p --skip-column-names --silent \
    --execute="SELECT PASSWORD('P1ed_Avoce7-79873')"

*D47F09D44BA0456F55A2F14DBD22C04821BCC07B
```

The result returned by the statement is the encrypted password. We'll copy that, log into the server, and use it to change the password for *admin_granter@localhost*, like so:

```
SET PASSWORD FOR 'admin_granter'@'localhost' =
'*D47F09D44BA0456F55A2F14DBD22C04821BCC07B';
```

This will immediately update the privileges cache for the new password. Try that on your server and then see whether you can log in with the *P1ed_Avoce7-79873* password.

 If you forget the *root* password, there's an easy way to reset it. First, create a simple text file with this text, each SQL statement on one line:

```
UPDATE mysql.user SET Password=PASSWORD('new_pwd') WHERE User='root';
FLUSH PRIVILEGES;
```

Name this file something like *rt-reset.sql* and put it in a protected directory. Then start MySQL from the command line using the --init-file option like so:

```
mysqld_safe --init-file=/root/rt-reset.sql &
```

Once it's started, log into MySQL to confirm the password has changed. You can change it again, if you want. Then delete the *rt-reset.sql* file, and if you want, restart MySQL without the --init-file option.

Renaming a User Account

A username can be changed with the RENAME USER statement. This SQL statement can change the username and the host for the user account. The user account that you use to rename another user account needs to have the CREATE USER privilege, as well as the UPDATE privilege for the mysql database.

In order to see how the RENAME USER statement works, let's rename the *lena_stankoska@lena_stankoska_home* user account to *lena@stankoskahouse.com*, assuming she is the owner of that domain and will access our databases from it. Do that by entering the following:

```
RENAME USER 'lena_stankoska'@'lena_stankoska_home'
TO 'lena'@'stankoskahouse.com';
```

When you do this, all of the privileges related to *lena_stankoska@lena_stankoska_home* will be changed for the new username and host. Let's check that by executing the following:

```
SHOW GRANTS FOR 'lena'@'stankoskahouse.com';
```

```
+--------------------------------------------------------------------------+
| Grants for lena@stankoskahouse.com                                       |
+--------------------------------------------------------------------------+
| GRANT USAGE ON *.* TO 'lena'@'...' IDENTIFIED BY PASSWORD '...'          |
| GRANT SELECT ON `rookery`.* TO 'lena'@'...'                              |
| GRANT SELECT ON `birdwatchers`.`eastern_birders_spottings` TO 'lena'@'...' |
| GRANT SELECT ON `birdwatchers`.`membership_prospects` TO 'lena'@'...'    |
| GRANT SELECT ON `birdwatchers`.`survey_answers` TO 'lena'@'...'          |
| GRANT SELECT ON `birdwatchers`.`surveys` TO 'lena'@'...'                 |
| GRANT SELECT ON `birdwatchers`.`survey_questions` TO 'lena'@'...'        |
| GRANT SELECT ON `birdwatchers`.`eastern_birders` TO 'lena'@'...'         |
| GRANT SELECT ON `birdwatchers`.`prospects` TO 'lena'@'...'              |
| GRANT SELECT ON `birdwatchers`.`prize_winners` TO 'lena'@'...'           |
| GRANT SELECT ON `birdwatchers`.`possible_duplicate_email` TO 'lena'@'...' |
| GRANT SELECT ON `birdwatchers`.`birdwatcher_prospects_import` TO 'lena'@'...'|
| GRANT SELECT (membership_type, human_id, name_last, formal_title, name_first)|
|        ON `birdwatchers`.`humans` TO 'lena'@'...'                        |
| GRANT SELECT ON `birdwatchers`.`bird_identification_tests` TO 'lena'@'...' |
| GRANT SELECT ON `birdwatchers`.`birdwatcher_prospects` TO 'lena'@'...'   |
| GRANT SELECT ON `birdwatchers`.`bird_sightings` TO 'lena'@'...'          |
| GRANT SELECT ON `birdwatchers`.`birding_events` TO 'lena'@'...'          |
| GRANT SELECT ON `birdwatchers`.`random_numbers` TO 'lena'@'...'          |
+--------------------------------------------------------------------------+
```

This user account has many entries in the grants tables. This is because we gave it some privileges based on the tables and one based on columns, in addition to privileges at the database level. What's important here is that all of these privileges have been changed for the user account when we renamed it and changed the host for it.

User Roles

Creating multiple user accounts for one person is a bit tiresome. Imagine if you were the administrator for an organization with many users similar to Lena Stankoska. You would have to create a few user accounts for each of them. If a user needed certain privileges for a short period of time, perhaps covering for someone on vacation, you would have to grant them extra privileges and later revoke the privileges. It can be plenty of work to manage user accounts like these, leading eventually to sloppy security policies (e.g., granting too many privileges) and ineffective controls (e.g., poor monitoring of user accounts). There's a better way to do this.

An alternative method, called *user roles*, was introduced in version 10.0.5 of MariaDB. It's not available in MySQL. User roles allow you to a create a higher-level concept, a *role*, and grant it to specific user accounts. The user accounts would have their normal privileges for daily use, but when they need to perform an unusual task requiring special privileges, they can temporarily assume the role you've created for them. When they're done, they can unassume the role. It's very convenient. Let's look at an example of how you would do this.

Earlier, we created for Lena a user account called `admin_import` with the `FILE` privilege for her to be able to execute the `LOAD DATA INFILE` statement. She'll use this to import data from text files into our databases. This SQL statement and the process involved is covered in Chapter 15. Suppose there are two other users—Max Mether and Ulf Sandberg—who occasionally need to do this task. Rather than create extra user accounts for Max and Ulf, in addition to Lena, we could give Max and Ulf the password for *admin_import*. But that would be an unprofessional security method. Instead, we'll use the `CREATE ROLE` statement to create a role that we'll name, *admin_import_role* and then grant that role to Max and Ulf.

Enter the following if you have MariaDB installed on your server:

```
CREATE ROLE 'admin_import_role';

GRANT FILE ON *.*
TO 'admin_import_role'@localhost;
```

The first SQL statement creates the role. The next uses the `GRANT` statement to grant the `FILE` privilege that this role will need to import files into the databases. Now let's grant this role to Max and Ulf—assuming they already have user accounts. We would enter this on the MariaDB server:

```
GRANT 'admin_import_role' TO 'max'@localhost;
GRANT 'admin_import_role' TO 'ulf'@localhost;
```

Now Max and Ulf can assume the role of *admin_import_role* when they need it. Max, for instance, would enter the following while he's logged into MariaDB to do this:

```
SET ROLE 'admin_import_role';

LOAD DATA INFILE

...

SET ROLE NONE;
```

As you can see here, Max set his role to *admin_import_role* and then executed the `LOAD DATA INFILE` statement—I removed the details of that SQL statement and any others he might execute so that we can focus just on the user role. Then Max set his role to `NONE` to unassume the role.

One drawback with roles is that they may be used only for the current session. This makes it difficult to use with an external utility such as mysqldump. If you run the mysql client from the command line to set the role for your user account and then exit mysql or open a different terminal to execute the mysqldump, the dump would be in a new client session and wouldn't have the assumed role. So you wouldn't have the privileges you need.

User roles work well and are much easier than creating many user accounts and setting passwords and privileges for each. They're ideal for granting someone a role temporarily. They make the management of user accounts and privileges easier for you as an administrator. For users, they will need to enter only one username and password for all of their activities. They will need only to assume a role when necessary. Of course, you will have to rely on each user to assume the role only when necessary, and to reset the role to NONE afterward.

Summary

When you first start as a database administrator, you may have a tendency to create a minimal number of user accounts—you may even try to use only the *root* user account. However, you should learn not to use *root* and to instead use various user accounts. You should also learn to give each person at least one personal user account—try not to allow sharing of user accounts, if practical. Additionally, learn to give access only to databases and tables that are needed by each user account and only the privileges needed. This may be tedious, but it's a good security practice—not just to protect sensitive data, but to protect data from being lost and schema being changed or deleted inadvertently.

There are several options related to user accounts and security that we did not discuss. Some options limit the number of connections at a time or per hour for a user account. There are several functions for encrypting and decrypting strings that may be used for passwords. You probably won't need these often, especially not as a newcomer to MySQL and MariaDB. However, you can find more information on them in my book, *MySQL in a Nutshell*, or on the MySQL Resources site (*http://mysqlresources.com*).

Exercises

Although you can easily refer back to this chapter for the syntax for using CREATE USER, GRANT, REVOKE, and DROP USER, you should try to learn them well without having to do so every time. The SHOW GRANTS statement can help you to remember the syntax. Still, if you know these SQL statements well, you will be more likely to tweak user account privileges. Otherwise, you might resort to using the same user accounts for everyone in your database department and giving each user account all privileges. The exercises here are therefore intended to make you more familiar and comfortable with these SQL statements. However, you will need to discipline yourself to always maintain good policies about managing user accounts and privileges.

1. Log onto your server and use the CREATE USER statement to create an administrative user account with the username admin_boss and the host localhost.

   Then use the GRANT statement to give this account ALL privileges on the *rookery* and birdwatchers databases, and the SUPER privilege to be able to change server settings. Also give the account the GRANT OPTION rights, covered in "User Account to Grant Privileges" on page 268. You may have to use the GRANT statement more than once. Be sure to use the IDENTIFIED BY clause at least once to set the password for the user account.

   When you've finished creating this user account, exit MySQL and try to log in again with the admin_boss user account to be sure the password was entered correctly. Try using this user account instead of root for now on.

2. While logged into the server as *admin_boss*, use the GRANT statement to create a user named *sakari* for the localhost. Assign the user account only the SELECT, INSERT, and UPDATE privileges on the rookery and birdwatchers databases. Be sure to give the user account a password. Do all of this in one GRANT statement. When you're finished, exit MySQL.

   Log into MySQL with the *sakari@localhost* user account you created. Execute the SHOW DATABASES statement to make sure you see only the two default databases and our two databases. Execute a SELECT to get a list of rows from the humans table in the birdwatchers database. Use the INSERT statement to insert one row with minimal data. Then use the UPDATE statement to change the data in at least one column for the row you added. You should be able to do all of this. If you can't, log in as *admin_boss* and use SHOW GRANTS to see how the permissions look for *sakari@localhost*. Fix whatever is wrong or missing and test the user account again.

   Now try to delete the row you added with DELETE, while logged in with the *sakari@localhost* user account—not *admin_boss*. You shouldn't be able to do that with this user account.

3. While logged into the server as admin_boss, use the REVOKE statement to revoke the INSERT and UPDATE privileges from the *sakari@localhost* user account you created in the second exercise. When finished, exit MySQL.

   Log into MySQL with the *sakari@localhost* user account. Try to use the INSERT statement to insert another row in the humans table. You shouldn't be able to do this. If *sakari* still has the user privilege, log back into MySQL with *admin_boss* and determine what you did wrong when you executed the REVOKE statement and fix it. Then try again to insert a row using *sakari*.

4. Log into the server with *admin_boss* and change the password for the *sakari@localhost* user account (this was covered in "Changing Passwords and Names" on page 272). When finished, log out of MySQL.

Log in with *sakari*, using the new password. Then press the up arrow key on your keyboard a few times. Check whether you can you see the *sakari@localhost* password in one of the entries. If so, this means that other users may also be able to see the password. Exit MySQL when finished checking.

From the command line using the `mysql` client on your personal computer—preferably not on the server—execute the `SET` statement, using the `PASSWORD( )` function to get an encrypted password for *sakari@localhost*. Set a different password. For an example of how to do this, refer to "Changing Passwords and Names" on page 272.

Log into the server with *admin_boss* and change the password for *sakari@localhost* using the encrypted password without the `PASSWORD( )` function and plain text this time. Then log out and back in as `sakari` with the new password. Press the up arrow a few times to see that it shows the new password encrypted and not in plain text this time.

5. Log into the server with *admin_boss* and use the `DROP USER` statement to drop the *sakari@localhost* user account. Then log out and try logging in as *sakari*. You shouldn't be able to do that.

CHAPTER 14

Backing Up and Restoring Databases

A database is often the culmination of the work of many people, sometimes thousands of people. The organization creating the database employs developers and administrators. Then there are people who contribute content, and who may be employees or members of the organization. But much of the content of a database can come from other people, such as clients, and unknown people providing content through a website. The amount of data can be enormous. It's not unusual for even a small site to accumulate thousands of rows of data. A large site could easily have millions of rows of data. All of this content—all of this work from hundreds or thousands of people—can be lost easily, through something as simple as the failure of a hard drive on the server. Because of this, it's essential to make backups regularly and correctly: too many and too much depend on it.

If you're going to be a database administrator, you will need to understand how to make backups and restore them. You will need to develop a plan of what will be backed up, as well as when and where. In addition, you will need to check occasionally that backups are not failing. You shouldn't wait until you need to restore data to find that the backups haven't been working. And you will need practice restoring backups so that you will be ready when you need to quickly restore them. We will cover all of this in this chapter.

Making Backups

One of the best utilities you can use to make backup copies of data in MySQL or MariaDB is mysqldump. It's included with both servers and it costs you nothing. You probably already have it installed on your server. Best of all, it doesn't require you to shut down MySQL services to make a backup, although you might restrict access to the backup utility for better consistency of data. There are other backup utilities (e.g., MySQL Enterprise Backup and Percona XtraBackup), some with a GUI and some that are more comprehensive. You can learn about other types of backups and tools in the book *MySQL Troubleshooting* (O'Reilly) by Sveta Smirnova. However, mysqldump is the most popular one, and as a new administrator, you should know how to use it, even if you later will use one of the commercial releases. We will use this utility for the examples in this chapter.

The `mysqldump` utility works very simply: it queries the server for the schema and data of each database and table and exports all of this to a text file. The default text file it creates, which is known as a *dump file*, includes the SQL statements necessary to reconstruct the databases and data. If you were to open a dump file generated by `mysqldump`, you would see `CREATE TABLE` statements and a multitude of `INSERT` statements. That may seem cumbersome, but it's simple and manageable.

The `mysqldump` utility offers many options. You can make a backup of all of the databases, or only specific ones. You can also back up just specific tables. In this section, we'll look at many of the available options and go through some examples of combinations for common uses.

Backing Up All Databases

The simplest way to make a backup is to dump all of the databases with all of the tables and their data. You can do this easily with `mysqldump`. Try executing something like the following at the command line on your server, using the administrative user you created in Chapter 13. You'll have to change the path given from */data/backups/*, to a path on your server. Or you can omit it and the dump file will be created in the current directory:

```
mysqldump --user=admin_backup \
          --password --lock-all-tables
          --all-databases > /data/backups/all-dbs.sql
```

The options used here include the following:

`--user=admin_backup`

Tells the utility to act as the user named *admin_backup* when interacting with the MySQL server. I showed how to create this user in "Restricting the Access of User Accounts" on page 256, so create a special user with the right privileges now if you have not already done so. Although you might be tempted to use the *root* user for backups, you should always use a special administrative user, as we're doing here. The user just needs the proper permissions to lock tables and read data from all the databases and tables.

`--password`

Tells the utility that the user needs to be prompted for a password, which will have to be typed in on the next line when asked. This acts the same way as the `mysql` client. If the backup is to be executed by `cron` through a shell script, this option can be changed to `--password=my_pwd`, where *my_pwd* is the password. That means, though, that the password will be in *crontab* in plain text. This is a good example of why you shouldn't use the *root* user.

`--lock-all-tables`

Makes MySQL lock all of the tables before performing the backup. The lock won't be released until the process is finished. For a busy database with many users, locking all of the tables for a lengthy period of time can create problems. We'll look at alternatives in a bit.

`--all-databases`

Specifies that all of the databases are to be exported. In the next subsection, in which we will backup only some databases, we'll replace this option with another so that we may specify the databases to backup.

The greater-than sign in the command line shown here is a shell redirect of the standard output (STDOUT) to the path and filename given after it. Set the path and filenames to suit your system and preferences.

The resulting dump file will generally contain separate INSERT statements for each row or each table. To bundle INSERT statements into one statement for each table in the dump file, include the `--extended-insert` option. This will make a smaller dump file. Additionally, the combined INSERT statements will execute faster when you have to restore a database. If your server generates extended inserts in a dump file by default, but you prefer them as separate statements, use the `--skip-extended-insert` option.

The INSERT statements don't include the column names—it just lists the values in the same order as the columns. If you want the column names included, though, you would add the `--complete-insert` option.

You can put the options in any order after the mysqldump command. You just have to put any values you want to pass to an option immediately after it. The only other order requirement is the final piece, the shell redirect—but that's actually a shell operator and isn't part of the mysqldump command. Basically, the ordering of options is very much like any command.

MySQL utilities used to offer shorter, single-hyphen options, such as `-u` for `--user`. But the short names are being deprecated and may not be available in the future.

When making backups of InnoDB or other transactional tables with mysqldump, it's best to include the `--single-transaction` option. This will keep the data more consistent. It won't change between the tables until the dump is finished. However, that option will cancel the `--lock-tables` option. This means that a backup of MyISAM tables in the same database could be inconsistent. You can avoid this potential problem by either using the same storage engine for all of the tables in a database, or making separate backups of InnoDB tables and MyISAM tables.

Backing up all of the databases at once with mysqldump may result in one large dump file. For smaller databases and as part of a regular routine, this is fine and managable. However, for larger databases, this method could take much longer to complete the backup, disrupting traffic while tables are locked, and later it may make restoration bothersome. Instead, you can construct a more adept backup method. For instance, it might be useful to perform a separate backup for each large database, leaving several smaller dump files. You could also back up larger and more active databases during slower traffic times so that you don't diminish database and web services. We'll discuss later how to specify which databases to back up and some backup strategies. For now, let's take some time to become familiar with dump files.

There's a security concern about making backups of all of the databases, as it could include the user table in the mysql database. This table contains usernames and passwords. You can eliminate it from a backup by adding --ignore-table=mysql.user to the mysqldump at the command line when creating the dump file. To make a backup occasionally of just the mysql.user, though, you might use a different user account for the backup and write the dump files to a protected directory or somewhere safe.

Understanding Dump Files

After the mysqldump command in the previous section has finished running, use a simple text editor to open the dump file that it generated. Scroll through the file to examine the contents. You'll notice quite a few things: the utility annotates the dump file, sets certain variables, then lists CREATE DATABASE, CREATE TABLE, and many INSERT statements. Let's review a few of those entries so you'll have a better understanding of dump files. This will be useful later when you need to restore a database.

First, let's look at the header. Here's an example of the first few lines in a dump file generated by mysqldump using the settings from the previous example:

```
-- MySQL dump 10.14  Distrib 5.5.39-MariaDB, for Linux (i686)
--
-- Host: localhost    Database: rookery
-- ------------------------------------------------------
-- Server version       5.5.39-MariaDB
```

The first line of the dump file lists the version of mysqldump that was used and the distribution of MySQL, or in this case, MariaDB, and on which operating system the command was executed. Next, we see that the dump was executed while logged into the server, from the local host. On the same line, we find the name of the first database to be backed up. The next line, after some dashes for nicer formatting, is the version number of MariaDB—that was given in the line showing the distribution, but here it's more clearly listed.

Next in the dump file come a batch of SET statements that look something like Example 14-1.

Example 14-1. Conditional SET commands in dump file

```
/*!40101 SET @OLD_CHARACTER_SET_CLIENT=@@CHARACTER_SET_CLIENT */;
/*!40101 SET @OLD_CHARACTER_SET_RESULTS=@@CHARACTER_SET_RESULTS */;
/*!40101 SET @OLD_COLLATION_CONNECTION=@@COLLATION_CONNECTION */;
/*!40101 SET NAMES utf8 */;
/*!40103 SET @OLD_TIME_ZONE=@@TIME_ZONE */;
/*!40103 SET TIME_ZONE='+00:00' */;
/*!40014 SET @OLD_UNIQUE_CHECKS=@@UNIQUE_CHECKS, UNIQUE_CHECKS=0 */;
/*!40014 SET @OLD_FOREIGN_KEY_CHECKS=@@FOREIGN_KEY_CHECKS, FOREIGN_KEY_CHECKS=0 */;
/*!40101 SET @OLD_SQL_MODE=@@SQL_MODE, SQL_MODE='NO_AUTO_VALUE_ON_ZERO' */;
/*!40111 SET @OLD_SQL_NOTES=@@SQL_NOTES, SQL_NOTES=0 */;
```

The way these SET statements are enclosed between /* and */, they may seem to be comments that won't be processed. However, they're SQL statements or tokens that will will executed conditionally based on the version of MySQL or MariaDB that is installed on the server. That's why the lines start with /*! and not just /*. Within the dump file, comment lines are prefaced instead with --.

You can reduce the size of the dump file by including one or more of the following options when running mysqldump:

--skip-add-drop-table
   Leave out DROP TABLE statements that clean up old tables.

--skip-add-locks
   Dump without first locking each table.

--skip-comments
   Suppress comments in the file.

--skip-disable-keys
   Suppress commands that manipulate the indexes in the tables.

--skip-set-charset
   Suppress SET NAMES statements that control the character set in use.

--compact
   Use all of the previous options in this list.

Some of the options in the preceding list have potentially risky consequences. For instance, if you don't set the character set, you may end up with the wrong one, and if you don't lock the tables while the server is running, it could make changes while you're dumping and end up with an inconsistent table in the backup.

Because a dump file may be used to copy databases from one server to another, and not just for backup and recovery on the same server, the conditional statements are used to check that the server for which the SQL statements in the dump file will be executed. This is necessary so that there won't be any problems when starting to execute the SQL statements that create tables and insert data. When the dump file is executed, it will restore or re-create the databases and tables exactly as they were at the time of the dump.

Let's look back at the first SET command:

```
/*!40101 SET @OLD_CHARACTER_SET_CLIENT=@@CHARACTER_SET_CLIENT */;
```

This line starts by specifying that the command will be executed only if the version of MySQL or MariaDB is at least 4.01.01. mysqldump makes sure in this way that it won't try to invoke a feature on old versions of databases that don't support the feature. It's assumed that once a feature is supported, all future versions of the server will continue to support it. The SQL statement that follows saves the current value of the CHARACTER_SET_CLIENT global variable. If you look back at Example 14-1, you'll see that the subsequent lines save CHARACTER_SET_RESULTS and COLLATION_CONNECTION as well. The fourth line then sets all three variables to utf8 with NAMES—that's an abbreviation for these three variables.

If you skip to the very end of the dump file, you'll see a similar batch of SQL statements that look like this:

```
/*!40103 SET TIME_ZONE=@OLD_TIME_ZONE */;

/*!40101 SET SQL_MODE=@OLD_SQL_MODE */;
/*!40014 SET FOREIGN_KEY_CHECKS=@OLD_FOREIGN_KEY_CHECKS */;
/*!40014 SET UNIQUE_CHECKS=@OLD_UNIQUE_CHECKS */;
/*!40101 SET CHARACTER_SET_CLIENT=@OLD_CHARACTER_SET_CLIENT */;
/*!40101 SET CHARACTER_SET_RESULTS=@OLD_CHARACTER_SET_RESULTS */;
/*!40101 SET COLLATION_CONNECTION=@OLD_COLLATION_CONNECTION */;
/*!40111 SET SQL_NOTES=@OLD_SQL_NOTES */;

-- Dump completed on 2014-09-14  6:13:40
```

These conditional SQL statements reverse the first batch of conditional SQL statements. They use the variables that were created at the start to set the global variables back to their old settings. You'll see many conditional statements like these throughout the dump file. This resetting of key characteristics makes it important to lock tables when restoring a dump file, so that the results of such SET statements won't affect any data changes that users might make during the restoration of a database.

Let's go back to the start of the dump file and look at the lines that follow the initial conditional SQL statements. You should see something like this:

```
--
-- Current Database: `rookery`
--

CREATE DATABASE /*!32312 IF NOT EXISTS*/ `rookery`
```

```
/*!40100 DEFAULT CHARACTER SET latin1 COLLATE latin1_bin */;

USE `rookery`;
```

The first three lines present a header comment so that when you review the dump file, you will know that this is the start of the section related to the `rookery` database. The first SQL statement, reasonably enough, is a `CREATE DATABASE` statement. It can look a bit confusing because it contains a couple of conditional components, which are related to the version of MySQL or MariaDB on which the statement will later be executed. Let's look at one of those components.

In this SQL statement, `IF NOT EXISTS` will be executed if the server is running at least version 3.23.12 of MySQL. That's quite an old version of MySQL, but this option was introduced in that version and release of MySQL and hasn't changed since. It's unlikely that a server anywhere in the world is still using such an early version, but this is the nature of `mysqldump`, to be ready for any conflict. More important is the option itself. If the `rookery` database already exists, it won't be created with this `CREATE DATABASE` statement and it won't be overwritten. Incidentally, if you want to create a dump file without `CREATE DATABASE` and without `CREATE TABLE` statements, you can add the `--no-create-info` option when running `mysqldump`.

The last SQL statement in the previous snippet switches the default database to use to `rookery`. You may wonder why the utility uses the `USE` statement instead of just including the database name in the subsequent SQL statements (e.g., it doesn't have statements like, `INSERT INTO `rookery`.`bird_families`...`). That would seem to me more dependable of a method, but the method used has an advantage. When executing a dump table, if you want to create a new database on the same server, but with all of the tables and data the same, you can simply edit the `USE` statement in the dump file and change the database name (e.g., change `rookery` to `rookery_backup`) in one place. Then the original will be preserved and you'll have an identical copy. We'll talk more about this later. Let's look at what's next in the dump file.

The next section of the dump file deals with the first table of the `rookery` database. As the following excerpt shows, it's the table structure of the `bird_families` table:

```
--
-- Table structure for table `bird_families`
--

DROP TABLE IF EXISTS `bird_families`;

/*!40101 SET @saved_cs_client     = @@character_set_client */;
/*!40101 SET character_set_client = utf8 */;

CREATE TABLE `bird_families` (
  `family_id` int(11) NOT NULL AUTO_INCREMENT,
  `scientific_name` varchar(100) COLLATE latin1_bin DEFAULT NULL,
  `brief_description` varchar(255) COLLATE latin1_bin DEFAULT NULL,
```

```
   `order_id` int(11) DEFAULT NULL,
   PRIMARY KEY (`family_id`),
   UNIQUE KEY `scientific_name` (`scientific_name`)
 ) ENGINE=MyISAM AUTO_INCREMENT=334 DEFAULT CHARSET=latin1 COLLATE=latin1_bin;

 /*!40101 SET character_set_client = @saved_cs_client */;
```

The first SQL statement here may concern you. It should. It's a DROP TABLE statement that will delete the bird_families table. No data ought to be lost because the following SQL lines will re-create the table and insert data into it from the time the dump file was created. However, if there have been changes to the data in the bird_families table since the dump file was created, those changes will be lost when the table is restored to its previous state. For such a situation, there are other methods you can resort to besides the bulk clobbering of tables. One method uses the suggestion made previously to alter the USE statement to point all schema and data statements to a different, temporary database. Then you can attempt to merge the old and new data together. Depending on the situation, you might be able to do this by changing the INSERT to a REPLACE statement. Another method would be to remove the DROP TABLE statement and change the name of CREATE TABLE statement that follows to create a new table name. We'll cover such techniques later in this chapter in "Restoring Backups" on page 292.

The IF EXISTS option ensures that a restore will drop the table only if it exist. If this statement was omitted, a restore would probably try to run the statement when the table didn't exist, and thus generate an error that could abort the restore.

After the DROP TABLE statement, there are more conditional SQL statements for variables related to the table and the client. These are followed by the CREATE TABLE statement, which matches the results of a SHOW CREATE TABLE statement for the table. This section ends by returning the variable changed to its previous setting.

Now the bird_families table is ready for the data. The next set of entries in the dump file are:

```
--
-- Dumping data for table `bird_families`
--

LOCK TABLES `bird_families` WRITE;

/*!40000 ALTER TABLE `bird_families` DISABLE KEYS */;

INSERT INTO `bird_families` VALUES

...

/*!40000 ALTER TABLE `bird_families` ENABLE KEYS */;

UNLOCK TABLES;
```

After the comment appears a LOCK TABLES statement to lock the bird_families table. It includes the WRITE option so that the data in the table cannot be changed during the restoration of the table. Users can't read the table either. Another thought may have occurred to you now: mysqldump is write-locking tables one at a time, as needed. That may be what you want, making other tables available for reading and writing when they're not being dumped. However, this may cause a problem with the consistency of the data.

For example, suppose during backup is at the point where it has preserved the contents of the humans table but not the bird_sightings table in the birdwatchers database. At this point, you decided to delete someone from the humans table along with entries in the bird_sightings table for that person. After that, mysqldump backs up the bird_sightings table. If you were later to restore the entire birdwatchers database, you would have an entries in the bird_sightings table for a person who isn't listed in the humans table.

If a database isn't very active, the previous scenario is unlikely. However, if you want to be assured of the consistency of your data, when executing the mysqldump utility, you could add the --lock-tables option. This locks all tables in a database before backing it up, and leaves them locked until the backup of the database is completed. When making a backup of multiple databases, this option still locks only the tables in one database at a time, releasing them before starting the next database. If you're concerned about consistency between databases—that is to say, if data in one database depends on data in another database—use the --lock-all-tables option to lock all of the tables in all of the databases until the dump is completed.

In the previous excerpt, the LOCK TABLES statement is followed by a conditional statement (i.e., ALTER TABLE...DISABLE KEYS) to alter the bird_families table so as to disable the keys. This can save time when the table is restored. When the INSERT statement that follows—truncated in the example to save space—is executed, data will be inserted much faster if MySQL doesn't have to index all of the data as it's inserted. Instead, another ALTER TABLE statement will be executed conditionally to enable the keys again. When that occurs, the table will be indexed. This method uses a special algorithm that is generally much faster when performed for the entire table at once, rather than when each row is inserted.

 Conditional components like DISABLE KEYS are included if the --disable-keys option is set by default on the server. If you don't see them in the dump files created by mysqldump, it isn't set by default on your system. It can be added when mysqldump is executed at the command line, or it can be added to the MySQL configuration file under the [mysqldump] heading.

The last line of the previous excerpt issues an UNLOCK TABLES statement to unlock the tables that were locked at the start of this section of the dump file.

In summary, the basic pattern for each table is to establish the table structure and then address the data. To establish the table structure, the dump file generally contains SQL statements to drop the table, set related temporary variables, re-create the table, and then restore the variables. To deal with the data when it re-creates the table, it locks the table, disables the keys, inserts all of the data, and then re-enables the keys and unlocks the table. This pattern is repeated for each table in the database. When the command has finished dumping all of the tables in the database, it will proceed to the next database, and continue until it has finished all of the databases, because in this example it was instructed to make a backup of all of the databases.

The contents of a dump file created by mysqldump can vary depending on the version of the utility and the default settings. It also can vary depending on the databases it's dumping and what instructions are given with the options at the command line. However, this review of an example of a dump file should give you a good sense of how to read one. Let's return now to making backups with mysqldump.

Backing Up Specific Databases

Before we concerned ourselves so much with the contents of the dump file, we were experimenting with making backups, learning how to back up all databases on the server. However, you may want to export only one database, or only specific ones. Let's see how to do that.

To export only one database and not all, instead of using the --all-databases option, use the --databases option followed by the name of the database. Try making a backup of just the rookery database by entering the following on your server from the command line:

```
mysqldump --user=admin_backup --password --lock-tables \
        --verbose --databases rookery > rookery.sql
```

This is basically the same as the example that dumped all of the databases, except that we've specified the database to be exported, rookery. As mentioned before, you may want to make separate backups of databases to reduce the load on a busy server and to make restoration more manageable. Incidentally, if for some reason you want to make a backup of a database's schema without the data, you can use the --no-data option. The command would then dump only the database and table schemas and not the rows of data.

You may have noticed in the previous example that we added the --verbose option. This option instructs the utility to display messages regarding each major step in the process of querying the database and creating the dump file. For our database, running this command produces messages like this:

```
-- Connecting to localhost...
-- Retrieving table structure for table bird_families...
-- Sending SELECT query...
-- Retrieving rows...
-- Retrieving table structure for table bird_images...
...
-- Disconnecting from localhost...
```

Sometimes these messages can be useful, especially when there are problems, to know which tables are dumped successfully and when problems occur.

To export multiple databases, just enter them after the `--databases` option, separated by spaces—not commas as you might think. Try executing the following on your server to back up the `rookery` and the `birdwatchers` databases:

```
mysqldump --user=admin_backup --password --lock-tables \
          --databases rookery birdwatchers > rookery-birdwatchers.sql
```

This will dump the `rookery` and the `birdwatchers` databases into one file named *rookery-birdwatchers.sql*. Because those two databases are related and there aren't any other databases associated with them, this can be useful. We can copy this line into *crontab* or some other scheduling utility on the server to run automatically each day. However, each command that runs will overwrite the dump file from the previous day. If something happens and data is deleted accidentally, but we don't discover it for a few days, we won't be able to restore that data from the backup. To allow for this possibility, we need to create a new dump file each day with a unique name so we don't overwrite the previous dump files. Unless we intend to initiate the backups manually, we need to be creative and automate the process. We can accomplish this twist with a shell script.

Creating Backup Scripts

To automate many aspects of making backups of databases, it's useful to create a set of scripts that will execute the `mysqldump` for the databases you want with the settings that you prefer. It's not too difficult to do this. You don't need to be very advanced in programming if you want to do only a few simple things, such as varying the output slightly each time.

Let's use the problem presented at the end of the previous section for an example backup script. The solution is to change the name of the dump file each day to include the current date so that there will a unique dump file for each day. Here's an example of a very simple shell script that may be run on a Linux or Mac system to do this:

```
#!/bin/sh

my_user='admin_back'
my_pwd='my_silly_password'

db1='rookery'
```

```
db2='birdwatchers'

date_today=$(date +%Y-%m-%d)

backup_dir='/data/backup/'
dump_file=$db1-$db2-$date_today'.sql'

/usr/bin/mysqldump --user=$my_usr --password=$my_pwd --lock-tables \
                --databases $db1 $db2 > $backup_dir$dump_file

exit
```

This script will execute the `mysqldump` with the same options as in our previous example. It starts by setting variables with the username, password, and the names of the databases. It then uses the `date` command to get the numerical values for the year, month, and day and saves them with dashes in another variable (`date_today`). It uses the variables for the database names (i.e., `$db1` and `$db2`), combined with `$date_today` to assemble the name of the dump file (e.g., *rookery-birdwatchers-2014-10-25.sql*). All of these variables are then used in the `mysqldump` command.

Because the username and password are included in the script, it can be run automatically and daily by *cron* without user intervention. It will create a dump file with a new name every day. This script is by no means flawless and definitely not in good form. It doesn't allow for errors. If the backup fails, it doesn't notify the administrator that there was a problem. It also doesn't address older backup files. A good script could remove the older dump files after a certain amount of time. Of course, having an automated script delete files can be a little disturbing. This script is provided only to give you an idea and starting point for constructing your own backup scripts. The ones that you create and use should be much more complex and allow for many possibilities, handle errors, and provide some sort of reporting.

Backing Up Specific Tables

For very large and active databases, you may want to back up the data for individual tables rather than the whole database. You could back up the entire database weekly, perhaps and then do daily backups for tables whose data changes often. For most databases, developing a strategy like this can be prudent.

Take our two databases. The data in the `rookery` tables will rarely change: new species of birds aren't discovered daily, and bird families and orders are rarely changed. Once we have all of the details for each bird in each table entered, there will hardly be any changes. Conversely, if our site is very active, almost all of the tables in the `birdwatchers` database will have new rows and changes frequently, so we would want to back up all of its tables every day. A reasonable strategy, then, is to back up the whole `rookery` database once a week and all of the `birdwatchers` database each day.

Still, suppose our boss is overly concerned about losing any data entered by our members. Suppose he insists that we make a backup of the humans table twice a day, once at noon and again at midnight. We could write a shell script like the one in previous section to vary the filenames to include the date and just add a bit more to indicate the time during the day when the dump was made (e.g., *birdwatchers-humans-2014-09-14-midday.sql* and *birdwatchers-humans-2014-09-14-midnight.sql*). The only other change is to create a mysqldump command to back up just one table, humans. Try executing the following on your server from the command line:

```
mysqldump --user=admin_backup --password --lock-tables \
      --databases birdwatchers --tables humans > birdwatchers-humans.sql
```

This is similar to the previous examples, but with the addition of the --tables option followed by the table name. If you want to make a backup for more than one table in the same database, you would just list them after the --tables option, each table name separated by a space. But this example is wordier than necessary. Because we're backing up tables in only one database, we don't need the --databases option. We also don't need the --tables because mysqldump assumes that any nonreserved words after the database name are the names of tables. So the previous example can be entered like this:

```
mysqldump --user=admin_backup --password --lock-tables \
      birdwatchers humans > birdwatchers-humans.sql
```

Although this command is simpler, the previous one makes it easier to discern what is a database name and what is a table name.

Let's add another table to the example here, but from another database. Suppose that our boss wants us also to backup the birds table in the rookery database. This possibility is not allowed with mysqldump: you can't list two databases with the --tables option. You would have to run mysqldump twice. This would create two dump files. If you want one dump file containing both tables, you could do something like this:

```
mysqldump --user=admin_backup --password --lock-tables \
      --databases rookery --tables birds > birds-humans.sql

mysqldump --user=admin_backup --password --lock-tables \
      --databases birdwatchers --tables humans >> birds-humans.sql
```

Here we're executing mysqldump twice, but the second time we're setting the redirect (i.e., >>) to append to the dump file instead of creating a fresh one. The dump file will have a comment in the middle of it saying that the dump is completed and then another starting header for the second dump. Because those are just comments, they will have no effect if you use the combined dump file to restore the two tables. Nor will modifying variables twice using SET during the execution of the combined dump file. So it's fine to append to a dump file like this.

The mysqldump utility is easy to use and very powerful. We've touched on many options that may be used with it. However, there are many more options. You can find these on-line on the MySQL and MariaDB websites or in my book, *MySQL in a Nutshell* (*http://bit.ly/mysql-nutshell-2e*) (O'Reilly).

One of the problem with dump files, though, is that you can clobber your databases when you use them to restore data if you're not careful. Therefore, you should practice restoring dump files on a test database or a test server. Do this often so that you will be comfortable with making and restoring backups. Don't wait until you've lost data and feel panic to restore it, because you might make unrecoverable errors or even find out that you haven't been backing up your data properly. Develop these skills in advance and in a safe and controlled way. To learn how to restore dump files, see the next section on restoring data from backups.

Restoring Backups

If data is lost in MySQL, but you've been using mysqldump to make regular backups of the data, you can use the dump files to restore the data. This is the point of the back-ups, after all. Restoring a dump file made with mysqldump is just a matter of using the mysql client to execute all of the SQL statements contained in the dump file. You can restore all of the databases, a single database, individual tables, or even specific rows of data. We'll cover all of these in this section.

Restoring a Database

Let's look at how to restore an entire database. To be safe, as part of experimenting, we'll make a fresh backup of the rookery database and then restore it. Execute the following from the command line on your server:

```
mysqldump --user=admin_backup --password --lock-tables \
        --databases rookery > rookery.sql
```

Before proceeding, check the contents of the dump file. Make sure it contains the SQL statements for restoring the rookery database. If everything looks OK, delete the rookery database from the server. This may seem scary, but you just made a good back-up. There will come a time when a database is deleted or corrupted unintentionally. So it's better to develop confidence in your ability to restore a database with a test database like rookery. To get rid of the database, you can execute the following from the command line:

```
mysql --user=admin_maintenance --password --execute "DROP DATABASE rookery;"
```

Here we're using the mysql client at the command line to execute the DROP DATABASE statement. You could have done this from within the mysql client, though. It's done here on the command line with the --execute option. You'll have to specify an administrative user that has privileges to drop a database. Here we're using the *admin_restore* user we created in the previous chapter. After you've dropped the rookery database, execute

SHOW DATABASES statement with the mysql client to confirm that rookery has been deleted.

We're now ready to restore the rookery database. To do this, execute the following from the command line:

```
mysql --user=admin_restore --password  < rookery.sql
```

This uses the mysql client from the command line to execute the SQL statements contained in the *rookery.sql* dump file. Notice that we're using a less-than sign, the redirect for the standard input (STDIN) in the shell, to tell mysql to extract the contents of the dump file as an input source. The command will create the rookery database and all of its tables and insert all of the data into those tables. Log into MySQL, switch to the rookery database, and execute the SHOW TABLES statement to see that all of the tables are there. Execute a few SELECT statements to see that the data is there. It's important to do this so that you'll feel more confident about your ability to restore a database.

Restoring a Table

The problem with restoring from a dump file of a whole database is that you may overwrite tables that you wish you hadn't. For instance, suppose a table was dropped by accident and you want to restore it. The other tables in the database may be fine. If the latest dump file is several hours old and the other tables have been changed since the last update, you wouldn't want to overwrite those tables. That would delete any new rows or updates since the dump file was created. If you have a backup strategy of making backups of tables separately, restoring one table would be simple. But that might be cumbersome to maintain. There are, however, a few ways of limiting a restoration to one table using a dump file that contains an entire database. Let's look at those methods.

Modifying a dump file

As we saw in "Understanding Dump Files" on page 282, a database dump file is a simple text file containing SQL statements to create a database and then separate sections that restore each table, including its data. One way to restore a table from a database dump file is to modify the dump file. You could eliminate all of the SQL statements except the ones needed to restore the table you want.

Suppose you have a dump file that contains only the rookery database and you need to restore the conservation_status table because some of the data has been deleted or changed by mistake. You can make a copy of the *rookery.sql* dump file, open the copy with a plain-text editor, and delete the sections that create the other tables. Leave in the opening and closing lines that set the variables, as well as the section for the conserva tion_status table. A similar method would be to open the dump file in a text editor and then copy and paste the parts you need into a new text document: the opening and closing lines and the section for the `conservation_status` table. Either of these methods would result in the same dump file that you could use to restore the table.

Here is an example of how such a trimmed dump file might look:

```
-- MySQL dump 10.14  Distrib 5.5.39-MariaDB, for Linux (i686)
--
-- Host: localhost    Database: rookery
-- ------------------------------------------------------
-- Server version       5.5.39-MariaDB

/*!40101 SET @OLD_CHARACTER_SET_CLIENT=@@CHARACTER_SET_CLIENT */;
/*!40101 SET @OLD_CHARACTER_SET_RESULTS=@@CHARACTER_SET_RESULTS */;
/*!40101 SET @OLD_COLLATION_CONNECTION=@@COLLATION_CONNECTION */;
/*!40101 SET NAMES utf8 */;
/*!40103 SET @OLD_TIME_ZONE=@@TIME_ZONE */;
/*!40103 SET TIME_ZONE='+00:00' */;
/*!40014 SET @OLD_UNIQUE_CHECKS=@@UNIQUE_CHECKS, UNIQUE_CHECKS=0 */;
/*!40014 SET @OLD_FOREIGN_KEY_CHECKS=@@FOREIGN_KEY_CHECKS,FOREIGN_KEY...=0*/;
/*!40101 SET @OLD_SQL_MODE=@@SQL_MODE, SQL_MODE='NO_AUTO_VALUE_ON_ZERO' */;
/*!40111 SET @OLD_SQL_NOTES=@@SQL_NOTES, SQL_NOTES=0 */;


--
-- Current Database: `rookery`
--

CREATE DATABASE /*!32312 IF NOT EXISTS*/ `rookery`
/*!40100 DEFAULT CHARACTER SET latin1 COLLATE latin1_bin */;

USE `rookery`;

--   [ snip ]


--
-- Table structure for table `conservation_status`
--

DROP TABLE IF EXISTS `conservation_status`;
/*!40101 SET @saved_cs_client     = @@character_set_client */;
/*!40101 SET character_set_client = utf8 */;

CREATE TABLE `conservation_status` (
  `conservation_status_id` int(11) NOT NULL AUTO_INCREMENT,
  `conservation_category` char(10) COLLATE latin1_bin DEFAULT NULL,
  `conservation_state` char(25) COLLATE latin1_bin DEFAULT NULL,
  PRIMARY KEY (`conservation_status_id`)
) ENGINE=MyISAM AUTO_INCREMENT=10
  DEFAULT CHARSET=latin1 COLLATE=latin1_bin;
/*!40101 SET character_set_client = @saved_cs_client */;


--
-- Dumping data for table `conservation_status`
```

```
--

LOCK TABLES `conservation_status` WRITE;
/*!40000 ALTER TABLE `conservation_status` DISABLE KEYS */;

INSERT INTO `conservation_status` VALUES
(1,'Extinct','Extinct'),
(2,'Extinct','Extinct in Wild'),
(3,'Threatened','Critically Endangered'),
(4,'Threatened','Endangered'),
(5,'Threatened','Vulnerable'),
(6,'Lower Risk','Conservation Dependent'),
(7,'Lower Risk','Near Threatened'),
(8,'Lower Risk','Least Concern'),
(9,NULL,'Unknown');
/*!40000 ALTER TABLE `conservation_status` ENABLE KEYS */;

UNLOCK TABLES;

--  [ snip ]

/*!40103 SET TIME_ZONE=@OLD_TIME_ZONE */;

/*!40101 SET SQL_MODE=@OLD_SQL_MODE */;
/*!40014 SET FOREIGN_KEY_CHECKS=@OLD_FOREIGN_KEY_CHECKS */;
/*!40014 SET UNIQUE_CHECKS=@OLD_UNIQUE_CHECKS */;
/*!40101 SET CHARACTER_SET_CLIENT=@OLD_CHARACTER_SET_CLIENT */;
/*!40101 SET CHARACTER_SET_RESULTS=@OLD_CHARACTER_SET_RESULTS */;
/*!40101 SET COLLATION_CONNECTION=@OLD_COLLATION_CONNECTION */;
/*!40111 SET SQL_NOTES=@OLD_SQL_NOTES */;

-- Dump completed on 2014-09-15  6:48:27
```

This dump file will restore the conservation_status table. I added a couple of comment lines with [snip] to indicate that this is where I cut lines of text from the original dump file. I also added some hard returns so that the lines would fit on the printed page. Otherwise, this is exactly the way a dump file would look if we had backed up only the conservation_status table.

This method works, but it can be tedious and you might accidentally delete a line you shouldn't or include a line you shouldn't. Other methods to restore just one table are covered in the next sections.

Restoring with a temporary database

Another way to restore a single table from a dump file that contains a database with many tables is simply to change the name of the database in the dump file. The dump file generally contains a CREATE DATABASE statement. If you change the name of the database to a unique name that's not already used on the server, a new database will be created on the server when the dump file is run. Then you can copy the table you want from this temporary database within MySQL to the original database. When you're finished, you can delete the temporary database. Let's look at an example.

Returning to the previous scenario, suppose that you have a dump file containing the rookery database, from which you need to restore only the conservation_status table. So that you can participate, if you don't have a current dump file of rookery, use mysqldump to make one.

First, run SHOW DATABASES on the server to see the names of the database so that you don't by chance give the temporary database a name that's already in use. Next, open the dump file in a text editor and look for the lines near the top that creates the database. Edit that section to change the name of the database. Here's how that section of the dump file might look after you edit it:

```
--
...
-- Current Database: `rookery`
--

CREATE DATABASE /*!32312 IF NOT EXISTS*/ `rookery_backup`
/*!40100 DEFAULT CHARACTER SET latin1 COLLATE latin1_bin */;

USE `rookery_backup`;
...
```

In this excerpt, you can see that I changed the name of rookery to rookery_backup in two places: the CREATE DATABASE statement and the USE statement. That's all that you need to change. You can save the dump file now and execute it. Using an administrative user that has the CREATE privilege, enter something like this from the command line:

```
mysql --user=admin_restore --password < rookery.sql
```

Once you've executed this, there should be a new database called rookery_backup. Log into MySQL through the mysql client and set the default database to rookery_backup. Run the SHOW TABLES statement and a couple of SELECT statements. You'll see that the tables and data are all there. Now you're ready to restore the table you need.

There are a couple of ways you can restore a table at this point. Let's try both. First, let's delete the conservation_status table in the rookery database. To do this, execute the following within the mysql client:

```
DROP TABLE rookery.conservation_status;
```

Now create a new conservation_status table in rookery. You can do this based on the backup copy by using a CREATE TABLE...LIKE statement, covered in "Essential Changes" on page 61. Enter the following on your server:

```
CREATE TABLE rookery.conservation_status
LIKE rookery_backup.conservation_status;
```

Next, you need to copy the data from the backup table to the newly created table. You can do that by entering this SQL statement on your server:

```
INSERT INTO rookery.conservation_status
SELECT * FROM rookery_backup.conservation_status;
```

The `INSERT...SELECT` syntax is covered in "Other Possibilities" on page 104. It will insert into the original database's table all of the rows selected from the backup table. When that's finished, execute a `SELECT` statement to see that all of the data is in the `conservation_status` table. If everything is fine, delete the temporary database by entering the following on your server:

```
DROP DATABASE rookery_backup;
```

This method of restoring a single table works nicely. For a large database, though, it could take a long time to temporarily import the entire database into MySQL. However, if you have a database this large, you should make backups based on tables or batches of tables to make restoration more manageable. This method requires `CREATE` and `DROP` privileges, which allow the user account to create new databases and drop them.

There is another method for restoring a single table that doesn't require editing the dump file. That method is explained in the next section.

Using a limited user account

A simple way to restore only one table is to create a temporary user account that has only privileges for the table you want to restore. When you run the dump file, the SQL statements for other tables will fail and not be executed—only the table for which the user account has privileges will be restored. To create such a user account, you need the `GRANT OPTION` privilege. As root, you will have that privilege. Let's go through the steps involved in this method, using the previous example in which we want to restore the `conservation_status` table.

 There is a risk in this method. If you're not precise about what privileges you grant the user account, or if you restore data from the dump file inadvertently using the root user account instead of the limited user account, you will overwrite all of the databases that were backed up to the dump file. So be careful.

Before you start to restore your data, delete the `conservation_status` table and change some data in one of the other tables so that you can see how well this method works. You can run something like the following from the command line, using the `admin_boss` user account you should have created in the Chapter 13 exercises:

```
mysql --user=admin_boss --password \
      --execute "DROP TABLE rookery.conservation_status;
```

```
INSERT INTO rookery.birds (common_name,description)
VALUES('Big Bird','Large yellow bird found in New York');

SELECT LAST_INSERT_ID();"
```

That should delete the conservation_status table. To test our restore, we've also added a row to the birds table, which we want to make sure has not been lost when we do our restore. The last statement returns the bird_id for the row inserted. Log into MySQL and verify that the conservation_status table has been deleted and use the SELECT statement to view the row inserted into birds, where the bird_id equals the number you were given when you executed the command. If everything looks as it should, you're ready to proceed.

Now you need to create the limited administrative user. Enter the GRANT statement on your server like this:

```
GRANT SELECT
ON rookery.* TO 'admin_restore_temp'@'localhost'
IDENTIFIED BY 'its_pwd';

GRANT ALL ON rookery.conservation_status
TO 'admin_restore_temp'@'localhost';
```

These two SQL statements grant the temporary with the necessary SELECT privilege on all of the tables in the rookery database, and ALL privileges for the conservation_sta tus table. When you restore the database dump file containing all of the tables in the rookery database, using the *admin_restore_temp* user account, only conservation_sta tus will be replaced.

When you execute the dump file with this user account, MySQL will generate errors when it tries to replace the other tables. Normally, that might stop execution of the dump file. To overlook the errors and to proceed with the restoration of data for tables for which no errors are generated, use the --force option with the mysql client.

Let's restore the table now. Enter the following at the command line:

```
mysql --user admin_restore_temp --password --force < rookery.sql
```

This should work without a problem. To verify that the conservation_status table has been restored, log into MySQL and check. Then execute the SELECT statement again to see whether the row you entered for Big Bird from the command line in the birds table is still there. If it is, that means the birds table wasn't overwritten when you restored the dump file. Everything else should be fine.

Restoring Only Rows or Columns

You'll rarely need to restore an entire database or even an entire table. It's not often that a database or a table is dropped, or that the data in all of the rows in a table are changed accidentally. It's more common that someone deletes a single row in a table or data in a single column and can't undo what they did. In such a situation, if the table has many other rows that were changed correctly since the last backup was made, you wouldn't want to restore the whole table to fix one small mistake. Instead, you will want to restore only one row or column.

This can be done easily using the method covered in "Restoring with a temporary database" on page 295. That section described how to modify the dump file for the rookery database so that MySQL imports the database into a new, temporary database (rookery_backup). If you use that method, you can then use the INSERT...SELECT statement with a WHERE clause to select only the row or rows you want to restore. Let's walk through this process.

Suppose that someone accidentally deleted one of the members (e.g., Lexi Hollar) and the email address of another member (e.g., Nina Smirnova) from the humans table in the birdwatchers table. To be able to follow along and to set the stage, make a backup of just the birdwatchers database, delete the entry for Lexi Hollar, and Nina Smirnova's email address by executing the following from the command line:

```
mysqldump --user=admin_backup --password --lock-tables \
        --databases birdwatchers > birdwatchers.sql

mysql --user=admin_maintenance --password \
      --execute "DELETE FROM birdwatchers.humans
                WHERE name_first = 'Lexi'
                AND name_last = 'Hollar';

                UPDATE birdwatchers.humans
                SET email_address=''
                WHERE name_first = 'Nina'
                AND name_last = 'Smirnova'"
```

After executing this, log into MySQL to confirm there is no member with the name Lexi Hollar and no email address for Nina Smirnova in the humans table. You should do this even though you may be logically satisfied that these changes were made. It's good to go through the motions to build more confidence in the restoration process.

Now let's import the birdwatchers database into a temporary table. Edit the *birdwatchers.sql* dump file you just created and look for the SQL statements that reference the database—there should be only the CREATE DATABASE statement and the USE statement. Change the database name wherever it occurs to birdwatchers_backup, assuming that this name doesn't already exist on your server. When you've done that, save the dump file and exit it. From the command line, execute the following to import it:

```
mysql --user=admin_maintenance --password < birdwatchers.sql
```

When you've finished importing the database, log into MySQL and run SHOW DATABASES to see that it has been created. Now you're ready to restore the data in the humans table. Execute the following from within the mysql client:

```
REPLACE INTO birdwatchers.humans
SELECT * FROM birdwatchers_backup.humans
WHERE name_first = 'Lexi' AND name_last = 'Hollar';

UPDATE birdwatchers.humans
SET email_address = 'bella.nina@mail.ru'
WHERE name_first = 'Nina' AND name_last = 'Smirnova';
```

That will restore the row for the member that was deleted, restore the email address for the other member, and have no effect on the other rows or other tables in the database. You'll notice I used the REPLACE statement instead of the INSERT statement. If MySQL finds a row that matches the WHERE clause and that has the same human_id, it will replace the row with the matching row from the backup table. Otherwise, it will insert a new row. Either way, it will restore the row with the same value for the human_id column. That means that any other tables that reference that row will have the correct human_id. Incidentally, if you want to generate a dump file that uses REPLACE instead of INSERT statements, you can do so using the --replace option with mysqldump.

When you're finished, you can use the DROP DATABASE statement to remove the bird watchers_backup database.

This method is very useful in restoring rows and columns, especially when you want to restore data to accommodate someone without disturbing other users. It doesn't usually take long to do and it's simple. You can restore rows based on whatever criteria you give in the WHERE clause. This is a skill you should learn well if you want to be a good database administrator: users will herald you as their hero when you recover data without much trouble or disruption.

Recovering from a Binary Log

In the previous few sections, we looked at how to restore databases and tables. Most of those are broad methods of restoring data. Sometimes you need more precision, as in the previous section, where we restored a single row and a single column. You would use that method when you have specific rows to restore and the lost data is contained in one of your dump files. However, suppose you want to restore data that was created some time *after* the last backup. This may sound impossible, but it just requires care and an understanding of MySQL's binary log. You can use the binary logs to restore data that was created after the most recent dump file was created, up to a specific point in time. This is referred to as *point-in-time recovery*.

To do point-in-time recoveries, you will have to enable the binary logs. You can't wait until you need them; you have to enable the binary logs before a problem occurs. To check that it's enabled, execute the following from the mysql client:

```
SHOW BINARY LOGS;

ERROR 1381 (HY000): You are not using binary logging
```

If you get the error message shown here, you will need to enable binary logging.

 Enabling the binary log does add a security vulnerability. All of the SQL statements executed on the server that modify the data will be recorded in the binary log. This may include sensitive information (e.g., credit card numbers, if your server records them) and passwords. So be sure that you protect the log files and the directory where they are stored, and preferably don't log changes to the `mysql` table. That's where passwords for user accounts are stored, so it's good not to log it. Use the `--binlog-ignore-db` option to omit databases from the log.

To enable binary logs, edit the configuration file for MySQL (*my.cnf* or *my.ini*, depending on your system). In the [`mysqld`] section, add the following lines:

```
log-bin
binlog-ignore-db=mysql
```

The `log-bin` option requires no equals sign or value. The second line here tells MySQL to ignore any changes to the `mysql` database. When you've added these entries to the configuration file, restart MySQL for it to take effect. Once that's done, log into MySQL and check again whether binary logs are enabled. This time, we'll use the SHOW MASTER STATUS statement:

```
SHOW MASTER STATUS;
```

```
+-------------------------+----------+--------------+------------------+
| File                    | Position | Binlog_Do_DB | Binlog_Ignore_DB |
+-------------------------+----------+--------------+------------------+
| mysqlresources-bin.000001 |   245  |              | mysql            |
+-------------------------+----------+--------------+------------------+
```

Here you can see the name of the current binary log file and verify that it's ignoring changes to the `mysql` table.

Now that MySQL is recording all of the SQL statements in the binary log, point-in-time recovery is possible. To be able to experiment with this, log into MySQL and insert many rows of data into a table. To make this easier, you may download two dump files from the MySQL Resources site (*http://mysqlresources.com/files*) called *birds-simple.sql* and *birds-simple-transactions.sql*. The *birds-simple.sql* dump file will add the `birds_sim ple` table with data to `rookery`. The *birds-simple-transactions.sql* file will insert many rows of data in `birds_simple`, change several rows with a single SQL statement—simulating an accident—and then insert more rows. For the example that follows, we will restore everything up until the offending SQL statement and all transactions after it—skipping the bad statements. To participate in the examples, download those two dump files and execute the following from the command line in the directory where you've placed them:

```
mysql --user=admin_maintenance --password --database=rookery < birds-simple.sql
```

```
mysql --user=root --password --silent \
     --execute="SELECT COUNT(*) AS '' FROM rookery.birds_simple;"
```

If you didn't get an error message, the second line should return the number of rows contained in the birds_simple table. It should be about 28,892. You may have noticed that I added the --database option, setting it to rookery. When I generated the dump file, I dumped only the birds_simple table. As a result, the dump file does not contain a USE statement and the table name isn't prefaced with rookery. So the SQL statements are not specific to any database. By adding it at the command line like I did here, you can make MySQL execute all SQL statements contained in the dump file in that database.

Let's move on to messing with the birds_simple table. Process the *birds-simple-transactions.sql* file, which will add and delete many rows:

```
mysql --user=admin_maintenance --password \
     --database=rookery < birds-simple-transactions.sql
```

```
mysql --user=root --password --silent \
     --execute="SELECT COUNT(*) AS '' FROM rookery.birds_simple;"
```

The count of the number of rows should now be about 296 fewer. The *birds-simple-transactions.sql* dump file contains a couple of DELETE statements that delete a lot of rows based on the WHERE clause. There are also a couple of INSERT statements that add more rows to the same table.

Now we're ready to go through the steps to restore based on a point in time. To restore everything to a specific point in time, we need to start from the last good backup. In this case, we'll start by restoring the *birds-simple.sql* dump file:

```
mysql --user=admin_maintenance --password \
     --database=rookery < birds-simple.sql
```

That should have restored the birds_simple back to where it was at the time that dump file was generated. If you want, log into MySQL and get a count of the number of rows in the birds_simple table. It should be back to 28,892.

The next step is to get the SQL statements that were executed on the server for the rookery database since the time of the dump file. That can be a bit of a bother to determine on a very active database. Therefore, if you intend to use mysqldump in conjunction with mysqlbinlog, you should have mysqldump flush the logs when it performs the backup. I did this when I created the *birds-simple.sql* dump file by including the --flush-logs option. So now we need to restore data from the beginning of the current log file to the point at which the DELETE statements were run. We can determine that point in time from the binary logs.

We'll use the `mysqlbinlog` utility to extract all of the transactions from the current binary log and save them to a text file. We'll then examine that text file to find the exact point in which the erroneous SQL statements were run.

Finding information in the binary log

To get the information, we need to know the name of the binary log file that contains these SQL statements, as well as where to find that log file. We'll run the `SHOW MASTER STATUS` to get the filename. Its location will be the data directory, which we can determine by executing the `SHOW VARIABLES` statement. Enter both of those as you see here:

```
SHOW MASTER STATUS;
```

```
+---------------------------+----------+---------------+------------------+
| File                      | Position | Binlog_Do_DB  | Binlog_Ignore_DB |
+---------------------------+----------+---------------+------------------+
| mysqlresources-bin.000002 | 7388360  |               | mysql            |
+---------------------------+----------+---------------+------------------+
```

```
SHOW VARIABLES WHERE Variable_Name LIKE 'datadir';
```

```
+---------------+-------------+
| Variable_name | Value       |
+---------------+-------------+
| datadir       | /data/mysql/ |
+---------------+-------------+
```

The results from the first SQL statement show the name of the current binary log file (i.e., *mysqlresources-bin.000002*). The name changed since we last checked our server because `mysqldump` flushed the logs when the dump file was made. The results of the second SQL statement in the previous listing shows that the data directory is */data/ mysql/*. Check the contents of that directory to make sure that *mysqlresources-bin. 000002* is there. Assuming it is there, we're now ready to extract the transactions we need from the binary log. Enter the following from the command line:

```
mysqlbinlog --database=rookery \
            /data/mysql/mysqlresources-bin.000002 > recovery-research.txt
```

Here you can see that I've included the `--database` option to instruct `mysqlbinlog` to extract only transactions for the `rookery` database. If we didn't do this, we would get transactions for other databases. On this particular server, there are over two dozen databases, some of them large and very active. To make restoration simpler and avoid overwriting data in other databases, it's best to limit the results to only what is needed.

Next, we specify the path and name of the binary file. This is followed by a redirect to have the system write the results from `mysqlbinlog` to a text file (*recovery-research.txt*).

Extracting and executing information from the binary log

When `mysqlbinlog` has finished creating a text file for us, we'll open the file with a simple text editor and search for the DELETE statements. Because we know that there were only two DELETE statements that occurred together, this will be easy to fix. Here's an excerpt from the output of the binary log showing these two transactions:

```
# at 1258707
#140916 13:10:24 server id 1 end_log_pos 1258778
Query   thread_id=382 exec_time=0 error_code=0
SET TIMESTAMP=1410887424/*!*/;
SET @@session.sql_mode=0/*!*/;

BEGIN
/*!*/;

# at 1258778
#140916 13:10:24 server id 1 end_log_pos 1258900
Query   thread_id=382 exec_time=0 error_code=0
use `rookery`/*!*/;
SET TIMESTAMP=1410887424/*!*/;

DELETE FROM birds_simple WHERE common_name LIKE '%Blue%'
/*!*/;

# at 1258900
#140916 13:10:24 server id 1 end_log_pos 1258927 Xid = 45248

COMMIT/*!*/;


...


# at 1284668
#140916 13:10:28 server id 1 end_log_pos 1284739
Query   thread_id=382 exec_time=0 error_code=0
SET TIMESTAMP=1410887428/*!*/;
SET @@session.sql_mode=0/*!*/;
BEGIN
/*!*/;

# at 1284739
#140916 13:10:28 server id 1 end_log_pos 1284862
Query   thread_id=382 exec_time=0 error_code=0
SET TIMESTAMP=1410887428/*!*/;
DELETE FROM birds_simple WHERE common_name LIKE '%Green%'
/*!*/;

# at 1284862
#140916 13:10:28 server id 1 end_log_pos 1284889 Xid = 45553
COMMIT/*!*/;
```

This may seem very confusing, but it's not too bad when you understand how binary log entries are organized and a few things about transactions.

Binary log entries always start with two comment lines for a header—comments start with a hash sign (i.e., #). The first comment line contains the position number of the entry after the word at. This is the number we need to restore to a specific point. The second comment line of the header provides the time of the entry and other information. A binary log entry ends with /*!*/;.

A transaction is a set of SQL statements that are executed together and are generally related. Transactions are used with transactional tables (e.g., InnoDB) and not non-transactional tables (e.g., MyISAM). Any SQL statements contained within a transaction can be undone or rolled back if they're not yet committed. The binary log uses transactions so that when data is restored, it can be restored properly. This will make more sense as we look at the components of a transaction in the excerpt shown.

Transactions always start with a BEGIN statement and end generally with a COMMIT statement, which commits the SQL statements between the two—they can't be rolled back or otherwise undone once they are committed. Near the start of the excerpt from the binary log, you can see a BEGIN statement, followed soon after by the first DELETE statement. Therefore, the DELETE is in the midst of a transaction.

The position number for the entry containing the first DELETE is 1258778. However, we need to go back to the entry containing the BEGIN before it so that we can get the whole transaction. Let's look at the header for that entry:

```
# at 1258707
#140916 13:10:24 server id 1 end_log_pos 1258778 Query thread_id=382
```

The position number for that entry is 1258707. The date and time of the entry is 140916 13:10:24 (i.e., 2014 September 16 at 1:10 p.m. and 24 seconds). We now know the position number and time for the transaction that contains the first DELETE. You may notice that the same line has a number following end_log_pos. That's the position number for the next log entry (1258778), which is the entry for the DELETE. Don't let that confuse you. Position numbers are based on positions in the file; they're not from an incremental counter.

We want to restore the binary log from the beginning until the start of the transaction containing the first DELETE, which means until position 1258707. We could edit the text file that we created with mysqlbinlog (i.e., *recovery-research.txt*) and delete the transactions that we don't want, and then just execute the file with the mysql client. However, there's an easier and better way to do this. We can have the mysqlbinlog export the transactions again, but have it stop just before position 1258707. To do this, enter the following at the command line:

```
mysqlbinlog --database=rookery  --stop-position="1258707" \
            /data/mysql/mysqlresources-bin.000002 |
            mysql --user=admin_maintenance --password
```

This will extract the same log entries, starting from the beginning of the same binary log file, but stopping at the position we gave it.

At this point, we've restored all of the transactions up until the DELETE statements—but not including them. Now we need to restore all of the transactions starting from the transaction immediately after the transaction containing the second DELETE statement.

Looking at the binary log excerpt for the COMMIT for that transaction for the second DELETE statement, we see that the end_log_pos has a value of 1284889. That is the position of the start of the next transaction. We want to restore from that point forward. As for where we want to stop restoring, we don't need to specify a position number for it. Instead, we'll use the option --to-last-log to indicate that we want to install to the end of the log. This may be further than the end of the log file, if the logs have been flushed and more log files were added. Given these two factors, execute the following:

```
mysqlbinlog --database=rookery  --start-position="1284889" --to-last-log \
            /data/mysql/mysqlresources-bin.000002 |
            mysql --user=admin_maintenance --password
```

This will restore all of the remaining log entries, but omitting the DELETE statements. This method is very precise in that it utilizes exact positions in the binary log for specific transactions. You may also perform a point-in-time recovery using starting and ending times. To do that, use the --start-datetime and --stop-datetime options with mysqlbinlog. Looking back at the binary log excerpts, you could do the following to accomplish the same point-in-time recovery that we made:

```
mysqlbinlog --database=rookery --stop-datetime="140916 13:10:24" \
            /data/mysql/mysqlresources-bin.000002 |
            mysql --user=admin_maintenance --password
```

```
mysqlbinlog --database=rookery --start-datetime="140916 13:10:29" --to-last-log \
            /data/mysql/mysqlresources-bin.000002 |
            mysql --user=admin_maintenance --password
```

Our first invocation of mysqlbinlog gives it the date and time we noted earlier for the stop point just before the first DELETE statement. Our second invocation specifies one second past the time of the transaction for the second DELETE statement as the start point for restoring data. This will work just fine, but using position numbers is more precise, because plenty can happen in a second.

A similar method of making backups with the binary logs is to use MySQL replication. With replication, you would have another server, a slave that has been continuously reading the binary log of the main or master server. The slave can use the binary log entries to maintain an exact duplicate of the databases on the master. When you want to make a backup, you need only stop the slave from replicating the master and make a backup of the databases on the slave. When you're finished, begin replicating again, and within seconds the slave is current again. This topic is beyond the scope of this book. However, my book *MySQL Replication: An Administrator's Guide to Replication in MySQL* (A Silent Killdeer Publishing, 2010) explains replication and how to resolve problems with MySQL.

Developing a Backup Policy

Knowing how to make backups of databases and how to restore them is fine. But these skills will be of no use unless you put a system in place to make backups regularly and effectively. The value of backups is greatly diminished if you can't restore them without clobbering databases in the process, without causing more loss of data, or if you can't quickly restore them. To be effective as a database administrator, you should develop a backup policy and and adhere to it.

A backup policy should be in writing, even if it's only for your use, and it should cover a variety of aspects of making backups and being able to restore them. You'll have to develop your own unique policy according to your situation, based on the value of the databases, the sensitivity of the information, and other factors. For instance, if you have a database for your personal website, a database for which you earn nothing, that no one else depends upon, and one that you change rarely, your policy might be to make a complete backup once a week and keep backups for at least a month. However, if you're the database administrator for a large site with millions of rows of data in many tables, a database that thousands of people use every day and your employer uses to store credit card numbers from transactions amounting to a significant amount of revenues, your backup policy will be much more elaborate. You will address security, the effect that making a backup has on user traffic, and how quickly data can be restored when needed. For our purposes, we'll develop a backup policy that is somewhere in between these two extremes to give you a sense of what you should consider.

The first step is to take inventory of the databases and tables for which you're responsible. Let's use the two databases that we have been using for the examples throughout this book. However, so that the scenario is more meaningful, let's suppose that a couple of years have passed and the bird-watchers website has attracted many more members. Based on that, I've arbitrarily increased the row counts for most of the tables, and eliminated temporary tables. Table 14-1 lists the tables, grouped by database and sorted alphabetically, along with an assessment of each table.

Table 14-1. Assessment of databases for backup policy

Table	Row Count	Changing	Active	Sensitive
rookery				
bird_families	229		✓	
bird_images	8			
bird_orders	32		✓	
birds	28,892		✓	
birds_bill_shapes	9			
birds_body_shapes	14			
birds_details	0			
birds_habitats	12			
birds_wing_shapes	6			
habitat_codes	9			
birdwatchers				
bird_identification_tests	3,201	✓	✓	
bird_sightings	12,435	✓	✓	
birder_families	96			✓
birding_events	42	✓		
birding_events_children	34			✓
humans	1822	✓	✓	✓
prize_winners	42		✓	
survey_answers	736			
survey_questions	28			
surveys	16			

This list of tables for the two databases indicates a few factors that we've decided are important to the policy we're developing: the number of rows in each table; whether a table changes often (i.e., its data changes or its schema is altered occasionally); if a table is generally active or the data is accessed often; and if it contains sensitive information. When you develop a backup policy, you may be concerned with other factors. However, for our example here, these concerns will dictate how and when we will backup these two databases.

We won't bother making daily backups of the tables that rarely change. We will make backups of the active tables each day, running *mysqldump* when they are less in use. We will make backups of tables that contain sensitive information (e.g., personal information on members and their children) with a special user account and store them in a more secure directory. We will also make a full backup once a week and store those dump files in the same secure directory for the same reason.

With all of these concerns in mind, we can begin to formulate a schedule for making backups and where they should be located. Table 14-2 groups backups based on each database and then groups tables based on security and usage concerns. For each backup, there is a list of tables, if not all tables. The columns to the right in the table show whether a backup should be made daily or weekly, as well as which days of the week and at what time of the day. The table also indicates whether the backup should be made to a secure directory and whether a copy should be kept off site, in addition to on site.

Table 14-2. Backup schedule

Backup	Frequency	Days	Time	Secure	Off-Site
rookery - full back-up	Weekly	First	8:00	No	Yes
all tables (rookery-yyyy-mmm-dd.sql)					
rookery - bird classification	Daily	Every	9:00	No	No
birds, bird_families, bird_orders (rookery-class-yyyy-mmm-dd.sql)					
birdwatchers - full back-up	Weekly	First	8:30	Yes	Yes
all tables (birdwatchers-yyyy-mmm-dd.sql)					
birdwatchers - people	Daily	Every	9:30	Yes	No
humans, birder_families, birding_events_children (birdwatchers-people-yyyy-mmm-dd.sql)					
birdwatchers - activities	Daily	Every	10:00	No	No
bird_sightings, birding_events, bird_identification_tests, prize_winners, surveys, survey_answers, survey_questions (birdwatchers-activities-yyyy-mmm-dd.sql)					

The first day of the week will be Monday. All times are in G.M.T. Backups containing sensitive information will be made by a special administrator and stored in a secure directory. Some backup files are also stored offsite.

Notice that the plan here is to do a full backup of each of the two databases once a week. You might want to put these backups into one dump file, but I prefer them separate. It makes it easier to restore one later.

The plan also calls for daily backups of the tables that change often, either in content or in structure. Because the other tables change rarely, there's no need to make daily backups of them. However, because the other tables are so small, it's not much of a problem to make backups of them each day as well. For some people, full backups every day is easiest and preferred. But if you have very large databases and security and performance concerns, full backups might not be the best choice. For this example, I want you to see alternative ways in which you might organize a backup schedule.

For the fictitious bird-watchers website, our database contains many members in Europe and the United States. Because bird-watching is a hobby for most people, most of our traffic will be in the evenings. The times here are all Greenwich Mean Time and in the morning. When it's 8:00 a.m. in London, the time of our first backup, it will be midnight in San Francisco. Put another way, when it's late at night for our members that are the furthest West, with the exception of a few we might have in the Pacific, we begin making our backups. This should be a slow traffic time for our databases.

We will keep all backups on site and on two separate servers. We'll use *cron* to copy the dump file automatically to the second server across our internal network. Additionally, we will copy the weekly, full backups to a cloud server like DropBox or Google Drive in case there is a fire or some other catastrophe destroying our servers in the same building.

Now that we have a plan about what and when we will backup, we need a plan to check those backups to make sure they are being performed correctly (see Table 14-3). This will include not only looking to see whether the files are there, but trying to restore them. This has the added advantage of giving us practice restoring databases. As mentioned several times already, when there is an urgent situation in which you need to restore data, you need to be ready and know what to do. It's difficult to become proficient in restoring data during a crisis.

Table 14-3. Backup verification schedule

Back-up	Verify	Restoration Tests			Retention
		Database	Tables	Rows	
rookery - full back-up	Weekly	Monthly	N/A	Semi-monthly	Two months
rookery - bird classification	Weekly	N/A	Semi-monthly	Semi-monthly	One month
birdwatchers - full back-up	Weekly	Monthly	N/A	Semi-monthly	Two months
birdwatchers - people	Weekly	N/A	Semi-monthly	Semi-monthly	One month
birdwatchers - activities	Weekly	N/A	Semi-monthly	Semi-monthly	One month

Backups will be verified on a regular basis. For testing and practicing purposes, databases, tables, and rows will be restored regularly in a test environment.

Let's go through the verification plan in this schedule. Once a week we will inspect all of the dump files made for that week to ensure that the back-ups are being made and contain the tables that we want. To carry out this task, you could look to see whether the files are created and check the file sizes of each. You could also open each with a text editor to see whether it looks correct. You might also use the grep command to extract the table names used with the CREATE TABLE within the dump file. If you want to use grep, you could execute something like the following to get a list of tables the *rookery.sql* dump file would create if executed:

```
grep 'CREATE TABLE' rookery.sql | grep -oP '(?<=CREATE\ TABLE\ \`).*(?=\`)'
```

```
bird_families
bird_images
bird_orders
birdlife_list
birds
birds_bill_shapes
birds_body_shapes
birds_details
birds_habitats
birds_wing_shapes
conservation_status
habitat_codes
```

The next three columns of Table 14-3 are related to testing and practicing restoring data. Once a month, we will try to restore the databases made in the full backups. You could test this by restoring each database to a test server. Then you can execute queries on the live and the test server to compare the results. Just keep in mind that the data will be a little different on the live server.

The other backup dump files are based on tables. These tables change often or are large and critical to our bird-watchers site. So we'll test restoring tables from these dump files twice a month. For all of the backups, we'll try twice a month to restore individual rows. This is the type of restoration we will be most likely to do. It's important that we know how to restore very specific data from all of our dump files. With this much practice, restoring a minor loss of data when needed won't be much trouble for us.

The last column in the table has to do with retention: how long we will retain the dump files. Our plan is to keep the dump files for the full backups for two months and the ones for specific tables only one month. You might not want to keep them that long, or maybe you will want to keep them longer. Some people copy dump files to CDs for each month and then store them for years.

Tables 14-2 and 14-3 basically represent our backup policy. One table lists what we will back up, when, and where. The other lists when we will verify that the backups are performed successfully, when we will perform restoration drills, and how long we will retain the backups. There are other factors you could put into a backup policy and much more detail. However, this should give you a sense of one way you might develop a backup policy.

Summary

By now you probably understand that making backups is important. It can save you from plenty of problems and frustrations. Being skilled in restoring backups can make life as a database administrator easier, and help you to turn major problems into minor ones that can be resolved easily. Developing and adhering to a good backup policy ensures that all of your efforts and skills are brought together in an effective manner.

As mentioned near the start of this chapter, there are quite a few utilities that you can use to make backups of your data, as well as other methods (e.g., replication). Using `mysqldump` is the easiest and in some ways the best. As an administrator, you should know how to use it well and how to restore dump files. To that end, complete the exercises in the next section to get some practice.

Exercises

A few exercises follow to get you more familiar with making backups with `mysqldump`, as well as restoring them. You should try to complete all of the exercises. However, there are a couple that might be too advanced. If you're having difficulty working through them, try again later when you are more experienced.

1. So that you won't cause yourself problems with the other exercises here, make a couple of backups for the first exercise. Using the `mysqldump` utility, make a backup of all of the databases. Then make a backup of both the `rookery` and the `birdwatchers` databases in one dump file. Don't use these two dump files for the remaining exercises. Keep them in case something goes wrong and you need to restore something.

2. Refer to the backup schedule in Table 14-2. It contains a list of backups to be made regularly. There are two full backups and three backups based on tables. Make all five backups in this schedule using `mysqldump` and name the dump files in accordance with the naming pattern shown in the table for each.

3. Write five simple shell scripts, each to make a backup using `mysqldump` for each of the backups listed in Table 14-2. Make it so that the names of the dump files that it creates conform automatically to the naming pattern based on the current date, as shown in Table 14-2. There is a script that can do this in "Creating Backup Scripts" on page 289. You can copy this script and modify it, or you can write your own using a scripting or programming language with which you're comfortable.

   After you write the five scripts, execute them and see whether they create and name the dump files correctly. If it won't cause problems to your server, add lines to *crontab* or another scheduling utility to have the five scripts execute automatically, but at a time not long afterwards. Wait and see if they execute as scheduled. You can remove the entries from *crontab* after you've tried this.

4. Modify the scripts that you created in the previous exercise and have the scripts remove older dump files, ones that are older than the amount of time set in the retention column for each table in Table 14-3. Make copies of the first set of dump files you created with these scripts, but change the names so that the date part of the filenames are further back than the retention period. Make copies for dates that are one and two days within the retention period and dates that are one and two days outside of the retention period.

   Run your scripts again to see whether they delete the dump files with the older names. You may have to try this a few times to get it right, so that the scripts delete the right dump files.

5. Log into MySQL and use the `DROP TABLE` statement to delete the `birds_bill_shapes` and `birds_body_shapes` tables.

   Next, use the dump file you made in the second exercise here to restore these tables from the *rookery.sql* dump file. When you finish, log into MySQL to verify that they were restored and contain the data.

6. Log into MySQL and use the `UPDATE` statement to change the `common_name` in the `birds` table to NULL for any rows where the `common_name` contains the word *Parrot*. There should be about 185 rows.

   Make a copy of the *rookery.sql* dump file. Name it *rookery_temp.sql*. Edit this new dump file to change the name of the database to `rookery_temp`. This method was described in "Restoring Only Rows or Columns" on page 298.

   Next, use the *rookery_temp.sql* dump file to create the `rookery_temp` database on your server. When that's done, restore the Parrot common names in `rookery.birds` from `rookery_temp.birds` using the `UPDATE` statement.

7. If you haven't already, enable binary logging on your server as described in "Recovering from a Binary Log" on page 300. Remember to restart the server once you've set it to be enabled. Use `mysqldump` to make a backup of just the `birds` table in the `rookery` database. Be sure to include the `--flush-logs` option.

   After you've enabled binary logging and made the backup of the table, log into MySQL and execute a `DELETE` statement to delete any birds with the word *Gray*. Then insert a few rows of data into the `birds` table. You can just make up values for the `common_name` column and leave the other columns blank.

   Now use the dump file to restore the `birds` table. Using the point-in-time recovery method described in "Recovering from a Binary Log" on page 300, restore all of the transactions in the binary logs up until the `DELETE` statement that deleted the gray birds with `mysqlbinlog`. This will require you to find the position number in the binary log when the `DELETE` statement was executed.

Next, using the position number for the transaction immediately after the DELETE statement in the binary logs, restore the transactions from that point until the end of the binary logs.

Log into MySQL to see whether you were successful in restoring the data. When you're done, remember to disable binary logging if you don't want to continue logging transactions.

## CHAPTER 15

Bulk Importing Data

You might be asked one day to create a MySQL or MariaDB database that will replace an existing database that uses a different database system—or some other format used for storing data. Or you might be asked to take the data from an application that was not designed for databases, like a spreadsheet. So that you don't have to manually enter the data, there are ways you can import it. This chapter explains how to bulk import data into a database.

When using other applications, export the data from the source application to a format that MySQL can read, such as a text file containing data separated by particular characters. If you're given a large amount of data to import, hopefully it will already be well organized and in a data text file. Then you can use the LOAD DATA INFILE statement to import the data.

This isn't an overly difficult task, but the processing of large amounts of data can be intimidating the first time. It can be a barrier to migrating data to MySQL and MariaDB. There are many nuances to consider for a clean import, which is especially important if you want to automate the process. There may also be restraints to consider when importing data onto a server provided by a web hosting company. We'll cover all of these in this chapter.

Preparing to Import

To import data into MySQL or MariaDB, the data needs to be in a compatible format. Both database systems will accept a simple text file in which the values are delimited in some way. The easiest way to deal with incompatible data in any format is to load it in its original software and to export it to a delimited text file. Most applications can do this. They will usually separate field values by commas and separate records by hard returns, putting each row on a separate line. Some applications will allow you to set the delimiters to your choice. If that's an option, you might use the bar (i.e., |) to separate fields because it won't typically be used within the data, and separate records with a new-line.

For some examples related to the rookery database, let's get a large data text file to use. Cornell University is famous for ornithology. They also publish books on birds through Cornell University Press. One of their publications is *The Clements Checklist of World Birds* by James F. Clements. The list of birds from this publication is on its website (*http://www.birds.cornell.edu/clementschecklist/*) in a spreadsheet and in a comma-separated values (CSV) format. Every August, an updated list is posted on the site for people and organizations to use freely on their own sites and in their databases to promote the study and appreciation of birds.

Suppose we want to compare the latest list to our `birds` table to see whether there are any new species. This may seem intimidating, but it can be done without much trouble. To participate, download the CSV file from Cornell's site or MySQL Resources (*http://mysqlresources.com/files*). For the examples that follow, I downloaded the *Clements-Checklist-6.9-final.csv* file.

 If you use FTP to upload a text file to the server, be sure to upload it in ASCII mode and not binary mode. If the text file was created with a program that uses binary characters or binary hard returns, these will cause problems when loading the data.

After you download the Cornell data text file, open it with a text editor to see how the content looks. You will need to know how the lines and fields are organized and delineated. Some excerpts follow from the Cornell data file that I downloaded:

```
sort 6.9,Clements 6.9 change,2014 Text for website,
Category,Scientific name,English name,Range,
Order,Family,Extinct,Extinction Year,sort 6.8,sort 6.7,page 6.0,,,,,

...

4073,new species,"Walters (1991) and Cibois et al. (2012) proposed
recognition of Prosobonia ellisi Sharpe 1906, with English name
Moorea Sandpiper and range ""extinct;
formerly Moorea (Society Islands)""."",
species,Prosobonia ellisi,Moorea Sandpiper,extinct;
formerly Moorea (Society Islands),
Charadriiformes,Scolopacidae (Sandpipers and Allies)
  ,1,xxxx,,,addition (2014),,,,,

...
```

```
6707,new species,"Robb et al. (2013) describe a new species of owl, Omani Owl
(Strix omanensis), from the Arabian Peninsula, with range
""central Al Hajar mountains, northern Oman"".
Position Omani Owl immediately following Hume's Owl (Strix butleri).",
species, inStrix omanensis,Omani Owl,"central Al Hajar mountains, northern Oman",
Strigiformes,Strigidae (Owls),,,,,addition (2014),,,,,

...
```

The CSV file contains about 32,000 lines, but I've listed here just a few lines of interest as a sample. I put hard returns within each record to make them easier to discuss. Each record in the original file, though, is on one long line without breaks.

The first record gives the field names. Some of the names are a bit confusing, as they refer to earlier versions of the Clements list for continuity with earlier lists. The first field, sort 6.9, is an identification number for each row. The sort 6.8 and sort 6.7 fields you see further down are the identification numbers from those earlier lists. There are several more fields, but for the examples in this chapter we care only about the Clements 6.9 change, Scientific name, English name, Order, and Family fields.

The Clements 6.9 change field indicates the type of change for the bird since the last Clements list. For the purpose of the scenario we're concerned about now, we want the *new species* changes.

The two records containing data are the ones that we want to import. Record 4073 is related to a new species that was added to the Clements list, the *Prosobonia ellisi* or *Moorea Sandpiper*. Unfortunately, this bird is extinct. Ornithologists collect information on all known birds, even extinct ones. For good form, we'll add it to the birds table, even though none of our birdwatchers will see one. Record 6707 shows another new species, the *Strix omanensis* or *Omani Owl*. Fortunately, this owl from the Arabian Peninsula isn't extinct.

Before begining an import, you will need to put the CSV file on the server and in a directory accessible by MySQL. It's a good security habit to put data files in non public directories. But to keep it simple, for our purposes, we'll use the */tmp* directory to hold temporarily the data text files for importing.

The next task in preparing to import the *Clements-Checklist-6.9-final.csv* file is to create a table into which to import it. It contains more rows and more columns than we need, but importing 32,000 lines from a CSV file will take only seconds. So the size is not a problem.

We could import the data directly into an existing table, but it's best to create a new table that we'll use only for the import. We can execute an INSERT INTO...SELECT statement later to copy the data from the import table we create into an existing table. Execute the following on your server to create the import table:

```
CREATE TABLE rookery.clements_list_import
(id INT, change_type VARCHAR(255),
col2 CHAR(0), col3 CHAR(0),
scientific_name VARCHAR(255),
english_name VARCHAR(255),
col6 CHAR(0), `order` VARCHAR(255),
family VARCHAR(255),
col9 CHAR(0), col10 CHAR(0),
col11 CHAR(0), col12 CHAR(0),
col13 CHAR(0), col14 CHAR(0),
col15 CHAR(0), col16 CHAR(0), col17 CHAR(0));
```

This CREATE TABLE statement creates a table with one column for each field of a line in the data text file. The columns are in the same order as the fields in the data text file. For the fields that we won't need, we've assigned generic names for the related columns with a data type of CHAR(0)—a fixed character field with a width of 0 characters—so that the data for those fields won't be stored. There's a better way to do this. We could just import the columns we want. But we'll cover that later in this chapter. For this example, we'll use this simple method and focus on the other fields.

For the fields we want, I've assigned names for the columns close to the field names from the data text file and a data type of VARCHAR(255). Notice that we had to put the order field within backticks. That's because the word order is a reserved word (e.g., the ORDER BY clause). We can use it for a column name, as long as we always refer to it in this way. Otherwise it will confuse MySQL and cause an error.

At this point, we have a good data text file to import and we have placed the file in an accessible directory on the server. We have determined how the data is organized in the file. And we have created a table to receive the data. We're now ready to load the data.

Loading Data Basics

To load data into MySQL or MariaDB, you need an administrative user account that has FILE privileges. Let's use the user account, *admin_import* that we created in Chapter 13.

The LOAD DATA INFILE statement loads data from a text file. It's a versatile SQL statement with several options and clauses. We'll look at them throughout this chapter. The following command is the minimum we would enter from the mysql client to load the data from the *Clements-Checklist-6.9-final.csv* file data file from Cornell into the clements_list_import table:

```
LOAD DATA INFILE '/tmp/Clements-Checklist-6.9-final.csv'
INTO TABLE rookery.clements_list_import
FIELDS TERMINATED BY ',';
```

Notice in the SQL statement here that the file path and name are enclosed in quotes. You can use single or double quotes. Notice also the FIELDS clause. In this clause, we define the parameters of the fields, how they are identified. For the CSV file we're importing, fields are deliminated from each other with a comma. For this, we add to the FIELDS clause the TERMINATED BY subclause and a comma within quotes.

There are other subclauses and other clauses, but this is the least required for the LOAD DATA INFILE statement. However, this SQL statement as we've constructed it will cause problems and generate warning messages.

Watching for Warnings

If you ran the LOAD DATA INFILE statement in the previous section, you may have noticed many warnings. The following output shows the message generated by running that SQL statement, and the first few warnings:

```
Query OK, 32187 rows affected, 65535 warnings (0.67 sec)
Records: 32187  Deleted: 0  Skipped: 0  Warnings: 209249

SHOW WARNINGS;

+---------+------+----------------------------------------------------------+
| Level   | Code | Message                                                  |
+---------+------+----------------------------------------------------------+
| Warning | 1366 | Incorrect integer value: 'sort 6.9' for column 'id' at row 1 |
| Warning | 1265 | Data truncated for column 'col2' at row 1                 |
| Warning | 1265 | Data truncated for column 'col3' at row 1                 |
...
```

You can execute the SHOW WARNINGS statement to get a list of the warnings. Because there were 209,249 warnings, I've listed only a few of them here, just the ones for the first row. The warnings for all of the other rows are about the same. Most of these warnings appeared because we have columns using the CHAR data type with a width of 0. This means that any data in the fields that corresponds to those columns will contain more data than it can hold. In such cases, the data is truncated upon being loaded into the table and the server generates a warning for each such column. Let's look at a sample of the data in the table to see more clearly what the warnings are trying to tell us and how well the statement did:

```
SELECT * FROM rookery.clements_list_import LIMIT 2 \G;

*************************** 1. row ***************************
             id: 0
    change_type: Clements 6.9 change
           col2:
           col3:
scientific_name: Scientific name
   english_name: English name
           col6:
```

```
          order: Order
         family: Family
           col9:
          col10:
          col12:
          col13:
          col14:
          col15:
          col16:
          col17:
*************************** 2. row ***************************
             id: 1
    change_type:
           col2:
           col3:
scientific_name: Struthio camelus
   english_name: Ostrich
           col6:
          order: Struthioniformes
         family: Struthionidae (Ostrich)
           col9:
          col10:
          col12:
          col13:
          col14:
          col15:
          col16:
          col17:
```

The LOAD DATA INFILE statement seems to be working well. It has inserted the fields correctly into the columns of the table. The first row, though, contains the field names. We don't need that row, but it won't affect anything for our scenario. Looking at the second row, you can see that the data we want from the text file went into the right columns: we have the scientific and common name of the birds, as well as the name of the order and family to which they belong. For the fields that we don't want, the columns with generic names have no value. That's fine. As I said before, there is a more professional, cleaner way in which we could have loaded the data. We'll cover that method later. Let's proceed with the next step to add new species to the birds table.

Checking the Accuracy of the Import

Before inserting data into the birds table, let's check a little more closely the accuracy of the data loaded into the clements_list_import table. We'll use the SELECT statement to see how the data looks for the rows we want, the new species. Enter the following SQL statement on your server and review the results:

```
SELECT id, change_type,
scientific_name, english_name,
`order`, family
FROM rookery.clements_list_import
```

```
WHERE change_type = 'new species' LIMIT 2 \G

*************************** 1. row ***************************
           id: 4073
  change_type: new species
scientific_name: species
 english_name: Prosobonia ellisi
        order: extinct; formerly Moorea (Society Islands)
       family: Charadriiformes
*************************** 2. row ***************************
           id: 6707
  change_type: new species
scientific_name:  from the Arabian Peninsula
 english_name:  with range ""central Al Hajar mountains
        order: species
       family: Strix omanensis
```

The results here are limited to two rows, but you can remove the LIMIT clause to see all of the rows. There should be 11 in all. These two rows relate to the two records in the excerpt from the *Clements-Checklist-6.9-final.csv* file shown earlier in this chapter. Notice that data isn't getting into the correct columns. To determine where things are going awry, let's look closely at the record for the second row:

```
6707,
new species,
"Robb et al. (2013) describe a new species of owl,
 Omani Owl (Strix omanensis),
 from the Arabian Peninsula,
 with range ""central Al Hajar mountains,
 northern Oman"". Position Omani Owl immediately following
 Hume's Owl (Strix butleri).",
species,
Strix omanensis,
Omani Owl,
"central Al Hajar mountains,
northern Oman",
Strigiformes,
Strigidae (Owls),
,,,,addition (2014),,,,,
```

The text that was inserted in the columns is shown in boldface here. It seems that MySQL was confused by the commas contained within some of the fields. This is because the LOAD DATA INFILE we executed included a FIELDS clause that stipulated that they are terminated by a comma. The result is that text from fields containing commas is being cut into pieces and inserted into the subsequent columns. We can fix this problem by adding more parameters to the FIELDS clause.

Let's delete the data in the clements_list_import table. This is one of the advantages of using a temporary table as we have done: we can delete everything and start anew. Then we'll reload the data. Enter the following two SQL statements on your server:

```
DELETE FROM rookery.clements_list_import;

LOAD DATA INFILE '/tmp/Clements-Checklist-6.9-final.csv'
INTO TABLE rookery.clements_list_import
FIELDS TERMINATED BY ',' OPTIONALLY ENCLOSED BY '"'
IGNORE 1 LINES;
```

The first SQL statement deletes all of the data in `clements_list_import` so that we may start with an empty table. The second SQL statement is the same as the previous LOAD DATA INFILE, except that we've added the ENCLOSED BY subclause to the FIELDS clause to specify that fields are enclosed with double quotes. In addition, we've included the OPTIONALLY option to that subclause to indicate that some fields may not be enclosed within double quotes. That tells MySQL that if it encounters a double quote, to look for a second one and to treat everything inside of the pair of double quotes as data. So if it finds a comma within double quotes, it will not consider it a marker indicating the termination of a field.

It may seem strange that this works, considering there is text outside of the double quotes and more than one pair of double quotes in some fields, but it does work.

 When loading data into a table, it's generally locked and other users are prevented from accessing the table. However, you can include the LOW_PRIORITY option to let other clients read from the table while you are loading it: LOAD DATA LOW_PRIORITY INFILE. The execution of the SQL statement will be delayed until no other clients are reading the table. It works only with tables that use storage engines with table-level locking (e.g., MyISAM), not with row-level locking tables (e.g., InnoDB).

There was another addition to the LOAD DATA INFILE statement we used here. We added the IGNORE clause to the end. This tells MySQL to ignore the number of lines specified, starting from the beginning of the data text file. By specifying that the statement ignore one line, we skip over the first line, which is the line containing the field names that we don't need. If the data text file has more than one line for the header, you can tell it to ignore more than one.

Execute the earlier SELECT statement again:

```
SELECT id, change_type,
scientific_name, english_name,
`order`, family
FROM rookery.clements_list_import
WHERE change_type = 'new species' LIMIT 2 \G

*************************** 1. row ***************************
            id: 4073
   change_type: new species
```

```
scientific_name: Prosobonia ellisi
   english_name: Moorea Sandpiper
          order: Charadriiformes
         family: Scolopacidae (Sandpipers and Allies)
*************************** 2. row ***************************
             id: 6707
    change_type: new species
scientific_name: Strix omanensis
   english_name: Omani Owl
          order: Strigiformes
         family: Strigidae (Owls)
```

It's now loading well. The scientific and common names are in the correct columns, along with the other columns that we want. We're ready to move to the next step.

Selecting Imported Data

Now that we have properly loaded the data from the Cornell data text file into the clements_list_import table, we can use the INSERT INTO...SELECT statement to copy the data we want to the birds table. We're learning and experimenting, so let's create a table identical to the birds table to insert the data from the clements_list_import table. Execute the following on your server:

```
CREATE TABLE rookery.birds_new
LIKE rookery.birds;
```

Now let's select the rows we want from clements_list_import and insert them into birds_new. Execute this on your server:

```
INSERT INTO birds_new
   (scientific_name, common_name, family_id)
SELECT clements.scientific_name, english_name, bird_families.family_id
   FROM clements_list_import AS clements
   JOIN bird_families
      ON bird_families.scientific_name =
      SUBSTRING(family, 1, LOCATE(' (', family) )
   WHERE change_type = 'new species';
```

In this SQL statement, we're inserting only two columns from the clements_list_im port table (i.e., scientific_name and english_name). We're joining the clem ents_list_import table to the bird_families table to get the family_id. To determine the family_id, we have to join on the name of the family. This is included in the family column of the clements_list_import table, but it has extra text in parentheses—common names for some of the birds in the family. So we're using the SUBSTRING( ) and the LOCATE( ) functions to get all of the text from the start of the string until it finds a space followed by an open parenthesis, as in Strigidae (Owls). In the WHERE clause here, we're selecting any change_type that has a value of *new species*.

Let's see how effective the INSERT INTO...SELECT statement was. Execute the following on your server:

```
SELECT birds_new.scientific_name,
common_name, family_id,
bird_families.scientific_name AS family
FROM birds_new
JOIN bird_families USING(family_id);
```

```
+-----------------------+----------------------+-----------+---------------+
| scientific_name       | common_name          | family_id | family        |
+-----------------------+----------------------+-----------+---------------+
| Prosobonia ellisi     | Moorea Sandpiper     |       164 | Scolopacidae  |
| Strix omanensis       | Omani Owl            |       178 | Strigidae     |
| Batrachostomus chaseni | Palawan Frogmouth   |       180 | Podargidae    |
| Erythropitta yairocho | Sulu Pitta           |       217 | Pittidae      |
| Cichlocolaptes maza...| Cryptic Treehunter   |       223 | Furnariidae   |
| Pomarea nukuhivae     | Nuku Hiva Monarch    |       262 | Monarchidae   |
| Pomarea mira          | Ua Pou Monarch       |       262 | Monarchidae   |
| Pnoepyga mutica       | Chinese Cupwing      |       285 | Pnoepygidae   |
| Robsonius thompsoni   | Sierra Madre Gro...  |       290 | Locustellidae |
| Zoothera atrigena     | Bougainville Thrush  |       303 | Turdidae      |
| Sporophila beltoni    | Tropeiro Seedeater   |       322 | Thraupidae    |
+-----------------------+----------------------+-----------+---------------+
```

This looks good. It's shows all 11 new species and we're able to match them to the appropriate bird families. Now we need only run an INSERT INTO...SELECT to copy all of this data into the birds table.

Although there are plenty of records in the CSV data text file, it wasn't too difficult to load the data. There are smoother ways we could have loaded the data. And there are some other clauses, subclauses, and options available for other situations. We'll look at all of these in the next few sections.

Better Loading

Although we have done well at loading a rather large data text file, we could do better. This section covers a few ways we can improve the method of loading data with the LOAD DATA INFILE statement.

Mapping Fields

When we loaded the data from the Cornell CSV data text file, we included many fields containing data in which we had no interest. We dealt with this by creating pointless character columns with no width to store data. That generated many warnings, which we ignored.

There's a better way to address unwanted fields. At the end of the LOAD DATA INFILE statement, you can add a comma-separated list of columns in the table that map to fields in the original input. This list can also include user variables in place of columns. There must be a column or a variable for each field and the columns must match the order of the fields, but the order of columns in the LOAD DATA INFILE can be different from the order the are in the table. So you can import fields into a table in any order you want. Additionally, you can import fields you don't want into a temporary variable multiple times and their data will be discarded; the variable itself disappears when the client session is terminated.

Let's drop the clements_list_import table and re-create it without the generic columns that we don't need. Let's also put the columns in a different order. Enter the following two SQL statements on your server:

```
DROP TABLE rookery.clements_list_import;

CREATE TABLE rookery.clements_list_import
(id INT, scientific_name VARCHAR(255),
english_name VARCHAR(255), family VARCHAR(255),
bird_order VARCHAR(255), change_type VARCHAR(255));
```

Now we have only the columns we want in this import table. We have the family before the bird_order, and we put the change_type last.

Now let's load the data again. This time we'll provide a list of columns and variables to map the fields where we want. We'll direct data from unwanted fields to a temporary variable, @niente. Any name is fine. *Niente* means nothing in Italian. Execute this SQL statement on your server:

```
LOAD DATA INFILE '/tmp/Clements-Checklist-6.9-final.csv'
INTO TABLE rookery.clements_list_import
FIELDS TERMINATED BY ',' OPTIONALLY ENCLOSED BY '"'
IGNORE 1 LINES
(id, change_type, @niente, @niente,
scientific_name, english_name,
@niente, bird_order, family, @niente,
@niente, @niente, @niente, @niente,
@niente, @niente, @niente, @niente);

Query OK, 32180 rows affected (0.66 sec)
Records: 32180  Deleted: 0  Skipped: 0  Warnings: 0
```

The list of columns and variables are in the order of the fields in the CSV data text file. The fields we want to store in the table have the names of the columns with which MySQL is to associate them. They're in a different order from the table, but MySQL will handle them the way we want. The contents of the fields we want are stored in the @niente variable, replacing its value each time. This works fine and without any warnings. Let's select the last two new species from the table to see how the data looks now:

```
SELECT * FROM rookery.clements_list_import
WHERE change_type='new species'
ORDER BY id DESC LIMIT 2 \G
```

```
*************************** 1. row ***************************
         id: 30193
scientific_name: Sporophila beltoni
  english_name: Tropeiro Seedeater
        family: Thraupidae (Tanagers and Allies)
    bird_order: Passeriformes
   change_type: new species
*************************** 2. row ***************************
         id: 26879
scientific_name: Zoothera atrigena
  english_name: Bougainville Thrush
        family: Turdidae (Thrushes and Allies)
    bird_order: Passeriformes
   change_type: new species
```

Your results might be different, depending on which file you downloaded from Cornell's site. We can see here, though, that the data is in the correct columns. We can now simply run the INSERT INTO...SELECT statement to copy the new bird species into the birds_new and then to the birds table—or directly to the birds table if we're feeling confident about our abilities to import data. This is much better than our first pass at loading the data, but we can do better. Let's try loading the data again, but this time let's get rid of those common names in the family column.

Setting Columns

If you want to process the values found in a field before loading them into a column in a table, you can use the SET clause of the LOAD DATA INFILE statement to do that. In the previous examples, we used SUBSTRING( ) in the INSERT INTO...SELECT statement to eliminate common names contained within parentheses from the family column in the clements_list_import table. Let's try loading the data again, but this time let's get rid of those common names when they're loaded into the family column. Delete and load the data again by running these two SQL statements:

```
DELETE FROM rookery.clements_list_import;

LOAD DATA INFILE '/tmp/Clements-Checklist-6.9-final.csv'
INTO TABLE rookery.clements_list_import
FIELDS TERMINATED BY ',' OPTIONALLY ENCLOSED BY '"'
IGNORE 1 LINES
(id, change_type, @niente, @niente,
scientific_name, english_name,
@niente, bird_order, @family, @niente,
@niente, @niente, @niente, @niente,
@niente, @niente, @niente, @niente, @niente)
SET family = SUBSTRING(@family, 1, LOCATE(' (', @family) );
```

This is the same as the previous LOAD DATA INFILE statement, except that we are storing the family name in a variable called @family and we added the SET clause. This clause sets the value of columns in the table into which data is loaded. Here we are setting the value of the `family` column to the value returned by `SUBSTRING( )`, which is extracting a substring from the `@family` variable. Let's see how well that did by selecting just one of the new species, the Treehunter bird:

```
SELECT * FROM rookery.clements_list_import
WHERE change_type='new species'
AND english_name LIKE '%Treehunter%' \G

*************************** 1. row ***************************
           id: 13864
scientific_name: Cichlocolaptes mazarbarnetti
  english_name: Cryptic Treehunter
        family: Furnariidae
    bird_order: Passeriformes
   change_type: new species
```

We can see here that the data is in the correct columns. In addition, the parenthetical text listing common names of birds in the family has been removed. If we want, we can run the `INSERT INTO...SELECT` statement again to copy the data for new species to the `birds` table.

More Field and Line Definitions

Not all data text files will be constructed like the Cornell CSV data text file we used in the examples so far in this chapter. Some files format the fields and lines differently. Let's load a different data text file to learn about other ways to define lines and fields with the `LOAD DATA INFILE` statement.

For the examples in this section, let's refer back to an earlier example ("Extracting Text" on page 185) in which our marketing agency gave us a table in a dump file containing prospects for our site. This time, let's assume the marketing agency gave us a data text file. The text file is named *birdwatcher-prospects.csv* and contains a list of names and email addresses of people who might want to be members of the Rookery site. You can download a copy of this file from the MySQL Resources site (*http://mysqlresour ces.com/files*). Here are the first few lines of that text file:

```
["prospect name"|"prospect email"|"prospect country"]
["Mr. Bogdan Kecman"|"bodgan\@kecman-birds.com"|"Serbia"]
["Ms. Sveta Smirnova"|"bettasveta\@gmail.com"|"Russia"]
["Mr. Collin Charles"|"callincollin\@gmail.com"|"Malaysia"]
["Ms. Sveta A. Smirnova"|"bettasveta\@gmail.com"|"Russia"]
```

The first line lists the name of the fields. Lines start with an opening bracket and end with a closing bracket. Fields are enclosed within double quotes and separated by a vertical bar. The ampersand is preceded with a backslash as an escape character, to indicate that the character that follows it is a literal character. To import the data, we'll have to allow for all of these details so that MySQL knows when a record starts and ends, when a field starts and ends, and how characters are escaped.

Starting, Terminating, and Escaping

Before loading the *birdwatcher-prospects.csv* file, let's create a table in which to import its contents. In addition to columns for each of the three fields in the data text file, we'll add an incremental column as the primary key. Because email addresses are generally taken by individuals, we'll make the column for the prospect's email address a UNIQUE key column. Execute the following SQL statement to create this table:

```
CREATE TABLE birdwatchers.birdwatcher_prospects_import
(prospect_id INT AUTO_INCREMENT KEY,
prospect_name VARCHAR(255),
prospect_email VARCHAR(255) UNIQUE,
prospect_country VARCHAR(255));
```

That creates the import table. Let's load the data from the *birdwatcher-prospects.csv* file into it. Execute the following SQL statement:

```
LOAD DATA INFILE '/tmp/birdwatcher-prospects.csv'
INTO TABLE birdwatchers.birdwatcher_prospects_import
FIELDS TERMINATED BY '|' ENCLOSED BY '"' ESCAPED BY '\\'
LINES STARTING BY '[' TERMINATED BY ']\r\n'
IGNORE 1 LINES
(prospect_name, prospect_email, prospect_country);
```

Although this SQL statement is correct, if you loaded the *birdwatcher-prospects.csv* file, it generated an error and no data was inserted into the table. We'll address that error in the next section. Let's focus now on the subclauses of the FIELDS and LINES clause included in the LOAD DATA INFILE statement here.

First, let's look at the FIELDS clause:

- The TERMINATED BY subclause says that fields end with a vertical bar. The last field doesn't have one, but because we'll let the statement know it's the end of the line, MySQL will then assume the last field has ended.

- The ENCLOSED BY subclause says that each field is positioned between double quotes.

- The ESCAPED BY clause specified the character that's used to escape special characters. The default is a backslash. So there's no need to include this subclause for this data text file, but I wanted you to be aware that it exists.

Let's look now at the LINES clause:

- The `STARTING BY` subclause specifies an opening bracket.
- The `TERMINATED BY` subclause specifies a closing bracket followed by a carriage return and a newline. Normally, a newline is sufficient. But this data text file was created on a MS Windows computer with an application that ends lines this way.

Replacing Data Versus Ignoring Errors

Let's address the error generated by executing the `LOAD DATA INFILE` statement in the previous section. The following error message appeared when that SQL statement was run:

```
ERROR 1062: Duplicate entry 'bettasveta@gmail.com' for key 'prospect_email'
```

This error was caused because there are two identical email addresses for Sveta Smirnova in the data text file and we stipulated that the `prospect_email` be unique. Because of the error, the entire import was rolled back and no data was inserted.

We have a few choices of how to handle such an error. We could modify the table so that the `prospect_email` column allows for duplicate email addresses. Another choice would be to tell MySQL to ignore any errors like this. To do this, we would add the `IGNORE` option to the `LOAD DATA INFILE` statement. Try entering this:

```
LOAD DATA INFILE '/tmp/birdwatcher-prospects.csv'
IGNORE INTO TABLE birdwatchers.birdwatcher_prospects_import
FIELDS TERMINATED BY '|' ENCLOSED BY '"' ESCAPED BY '\\'
LINES STARTING BY '[' TERMINATED BY ']\r\n'
IGNORE 1 LINES
(prospect_name, prospect_email, prospect_country);

Query OK, 4 rows affected, 1 warning (0.02 sec)
Records: 5  Deleted: 0  Skipped: 1  Warnings: 1


SHOW WARNINGS \G

*************************** 1. row ***************************
  Level: Warning
   Code: 1062
Message: Duplicate entry 'bettasveta@gmail.com' for key 'prospect_email'
```

This worked. Notice the results message. It says one row was skipped and there's a warning. The warning in turn says there's a duplicate entry. That's the row it skipped, the second entry for Sveta. Let's execute a `SELECT` statement to see how the row for Sveta looks now:

```
SELECT * FROM birdwatchers.birdwatcher_prospects_import
WHERE prospect_name LIKE '%Sveta%' \G
```

```
*************************** 1. row ***************************
   prospect_id: 16
 prospect_name: Ms. Sveta Smirnova
prospect_email: bettasveta@gmail.com
prospect_country: Russia
```

This shows that the first record for Sveta was inserted into the table, but the second one was not. We know this because the second record included a middle initial for her name. If we prefer that duplicate records replace previous ones, we can replace the IGNORE option with the REPLACE option. The statement would then be entered as follows:

```
LOAD DATA INFILE '/tmp/birdwatcher-prospects.csv'
REPLACE INTO TABLE birdwatchers.birdwatcher_prospects_import
FIELDS TERMINATED BY '|' ENCLOSED BY '"' ESCAPED BY '\\'
LINES STARTING BY '[' TERMINATED BY ']\n'
IGNORE 1 LINES
(prospect_name, prospect_email, prospect_country);

Query OK, 6 rows affected (0.02 sec)
Records: 5  Deleted: 1  Skipped: 0  Warnings: 0

SELECT * FROM birdwatchers.birdwatcher_prospects_import
WHERE prospect_name LIKE '%Sveta%' \G

*************************** 1. row ***************************
   prospect_id: 26
 prospect_name: Ms. Sveta A. Smirnova
prospect_email: bettasveta@gmail.com
prospect_country: Russia
```

Notice how the results message reads this time. It says that no rows were skipped, but one was deleted. That's the replacement of the first entry for Sveta. You can see in the results of the SELECT statement that the record containing her middle initial replaced the one without it.

Importing from Outside MySQL

So far in this chapter, we have covered ways to load from within MySQL. It is possible to import data while not logged into MySQL, per se. At a minimum, you can execute the LOAD DATA INFILE statement through the mysql client with the --execute option. However, there is another client made specifically for importing data, the mysqlimport utility. We'll cover it in this section. This utility, as well as the LOAD DATA INFILE statement, require FILE privileges. But if you don't have this privilege, there is a way around it. First, let's cover how to load a data text file located locally without uploading it to the server.

Importing Local Files

If you are not allowed to upload a data text file to the server, you can use LOAD DATA INFILE to load it locally through the mysql client. For this operation, add the LOCAL option. You don't log onto the server first and start the mysql client on the server with the host as localhost. Instead, you log locally onto the server by entering something like this on your local computer:

```
mysql --user=admin_import --password \
      --host=mysqlresources.com --database=rookery
```

Once you have established the connection through the local client, you can execute the SQL statement like so:

```
LOAD DATA LOCAL INFILE '/tmp/birdwatcher-prospects.csv'
REPLACE INTO TABLE birdwatchers.birdwatcher_prospects_import
FIELDS TERMINATED BY '|' ENCLOSED BY '"' ESCAPED BY '\\'
LINES STARTING BY '[' TERMINATED BY ']\n'
IGNORE 1 LINES
(prospect_name, prospect_email, prospect_country);
```

Basically, the data text file is read by the client and the contents sent to the server to store in the operating system's temporary directory (e.g., /tmp).

This works only if the server and client have been configured to allow the LOCAL option. This requires someone to add local-infile=1 to the MySQL configuration file on both systems. Additionally, the user account must have FILE privileges on the server from the remote location. Normally, this isn't given to a user. But if it's your server, you can allow it. See Chapter 13 for more information on how to do this.

Using mysqlimport

If you regularly receive a data text file in the same format, you might find it useful to create a simple shell script to load the data into MySQL. For such a task, you can use the mysqlimport utility. It will execute the LOAD DATA INFILE statement with any options you include.

For an example of how this utility may be used, let's use one of the recent examples of the LOAD DATA INFILE statement, where we loaded data from the *birdwatcher-prospects.csv* file. For this utility, though, we will have to rename the file to the same as the import table, so the file's name will be *birdwatcher_prospects.csv*. I'll explain this in a moment. For now, try executing the following from the command line on your server:

```
mysqlimport --user='marie_dyer' --password='sevenangels' \
   --replace --low-priority  --ignore-lines='1' \
   --fields-enclosed-by='"' --fields-terminated-by='|' --fields-escaped-by='\\' \
   --lines-terminated-by=']\r\n' \
   --columns='prospect_name, prospect_email, prospect_country' \
     birdwatchers '/tmp/birdwatcher_prospects_import.csv'
```

As you can see, all of the options are the sames as their counterparts, but in lowercase letters and preceded by two hyphens. The order of options doesn't matter, except that the database and filename are last. After the filename, you can list multiple text files separated by spaces, and they will be processed in order by mysqlimport.

The prefix of the filename must be the same as the table—the dot and the extension are ignored. This rule lets the command determine the table into which to load data. Because table names cannot include a hyphen, which could be mistaken for a minus sign, we had to use an underscore.

The mysqlimport utility works the same as LOAD DATA INFILE; in fact, internally it calls that SQL statement. As mentioned, you can include it in a shell script or an entry in crontab to automate the loading of data from a data text file that is periodically replaced on the server.

> You may have noticed that the --lines-starting-by option was not included in the previous example. That's because there is no such option for mysqlimport. Paul Dubois, a famous writer specializing in MySQL software, reported this oversight in 2006. So far, nothing has been done to add that option, which tells us that this is not a well-supported utility. In fact, in testing it on my server, I had difficulty getting it to work. If it works on your server, though, that's fine. If you're constructing a script to load data, you may want instead to use the LOAD DATA INFILE statement as part of an API script (see Chapter 16). Most scripting languages include modules that can be used to convert data text files.

Importing Without FILE Privileges

Some web hosting companies do not allow the use of LOAD DATA INFILE due to security vulnerabilities it would present for them. They block its use by not giving you FILE privileges. If your database is located on a server on which you don't have this privilege, it's possible to get around it, but that requires some extra steps.

First, you will need access to another MySQL server on which you do have FILE privileges. It could be on your own personal computer. We'll call whatever computer you use your *staging server* and the other the *live server*. On the staging server, you will need to create a table identical to the one on the live server into which you want to load the data. You should also create an import table on the live server as we did in earlier examples in this chapter, rather than import directly into the ultimate table.

After you've created tables on the staging and live server, execute the LOAD DATA IN FILE statement on the staging server to load the data from the text file.

Next, export the data from the table on the staging server using the mysqldump utility (this utility was covered extensively in Chapter 14). Be sure to use the --tables option so that you dump only the import table (see "Backing Up Specific Tables" on page 290), and use the `--no-create-info` option so that the utility doesn't include `CREATE DATABASE` and `CREATE TABLE` statements in the dump file.

After you've created the dump file of the table, upload it to the live server. On the live server, use the `mysql` client to process the dump file to insert the rows of data into the import table on that server (this method was covered in "Restoring Backups" on page 292). From there, you can use the `INSERT INTO...SELECT` statement to copy the rows to the appropriate table.

This method is the same as the other methods for loading data, but with the extra steps of loading the data on a staging server and then using `mysqldump` to dump the data and `mysql` to insert the data into the appropriate table on the live server. It's not particularly difficult, just more time consuming.

Bulk Exporting Data

Thus far in this chapter we have looked at how to bulk import data into MySQL and MariaDB from data text files. However, you may be asked to do the opposite, and bulk export data to provide someone with a text file containing data from your MySQL databases. This can be done more easily than importing, so long as you get to decide the layout of the data text file.

The easiest way to bulk export data to a text file is to use the `SELECT` statement with the `INTO OUTFILE` clause. This works similarly to the `LOAD DATA INFILE` statement, with the same subclauses—except that it exports instead of imports data. Let's look at an example.

Suppose we want to give someone a list of birds from the `rookery` database. We want specifically to give them a test file containing a list of birds in the *Charadriiformes*—an order of birds that includes Sea Gulls and Plovers. We want to export the scientific and common name of each bird, and the family name.

We'll do this in stages. First, let's construct a `SELECT` statement to make sure we're exporting the correct data. Execute this from your server:

```
SELECT birds.scientific_name,
IFNULL(common_name, ''),
bird_families.scientific_name
FROM rookery.birds
JOIN rookery.bird_families USING(family_id)
JOIN rookery.bird_orders USING(order_id)
WHERE bird_orders.scientific_name = 'Charadriiformes'
ORDER BY common_name;
```

This `SELECT` statement includes a `JOIN` (covered extensively in Chapter 9). We're joining together the main three tables in the `rookery` database to get the bird names and the family names for the family order that we want. We're ordering the list based on com mon_name. The SELECT...INTO OUTFILE statement will generally convert NULL values to the letter N. So we're using IFNULL( ) to change any null values for the com mon_name to a blank space. That SELECT statement works fine. If you tried it on your server, it should have returned about 718 rows.

To keep anyone receiving the data text from being confused as to what each field represents, let's include a first row containing field names. The easiest way to do this is to just execute SELECT with a set of strings like this:

```
SELECT 'scientific name','common name','family name';
```

These field names don't have to be the same as the columns in the tables for which they will be associated, and don't have to conform to any convention for our purposes. We'll join the results of this SQL statement with the previous one with the UNION, but with the field names first. This was also covered in Chapter 9.

Having tested the SELECT statements, we're now ready to put them together to export data to a text file. Execute the following on your server:

```
( SELECT 'scientific name','common name','family name' )
UNION
( SELECT birds.scientific_name,
  IFNULL(common_name, ''),
  bird_families.scientific_name
  FROM rookery.birds
  JOIN rookery.bird_families USING(family_id)
  JOIN rookery.bird_orders USING(order_id)
  WHERE bird_orders.scientific_name = 'Charadriiformes'
  ORDER BY common_name
  INTO OUTFILE '/tmp/birds-list.csv'
  FIELDS ENCLOSED BY '"' TERMINATED BY '|' ESCAPED BY '\\'
  LINES TERMINATED BY '\n');
```

That should have executed without any problems. Because we've already discussed the SELECT statements in general, let's focus on the INTO OUTFILE clause in the second SELECT statement. First notice that the path for the export file is /tmp. MySQL will generally only write to an accessible directory like this one, one in which everyone on the server has full read and write privileges. Next notice that the subclauses are listed after the file path and name—the opposite of LOAD DATA INFILE. The subclauses, though, are the same.

Here we're enclosing fields with double quotes and separating them with a vertical bar. We're using the backslash as the escape character. For the SELECT...INTO OUTFILE statement, you have to include the ESCAPED BY subclause, because there is no default escape character for this statement. There are two backslashes here because the first escapes the second; a backslash by itself is an escape character in this command. Finally, we're terminating each line with a newline character.

Here are the first few lines of the file generated by the previous SELECT...INTO OUT FILE statement:

```
"scientific name"|"common name"|"family name"
"Charadrius vociferus"|"Killdeer"|"Charadriidae"
"Charadrius montanus"|"Mountain Plover"|"Charadriidae"
"Charadrius alexandrinus"|"Snowy Plover"|"Charadriidae"
"Pluvialis squatarola"|"Black-bellied Plover"|"Charadriidae"
"Pluvialis fulva"|"Pacific Golden Plover"|"Charadriidae"
"Burhinus vermiculatus"|"Water Thick-knee"|"Burhinidae"
"Burhinus oedicnemus"|"Eurasian Thick-knee"|"Burhinidae"
...
```

This works nicely. The first line provides a list of field names. The lines that follow organize the text from the columns we selected. This is an easy and simple way to export data to a text file to give to someone using a different database system.

Summary

Although you may rarely use the LOAD DATA INFILE statement, when you need it and use it, you'll find that it saves you plenty of time. It makes bulk importing of data and migrating to MySQL and MariaDB much easier. Because the layout of data text files can vary so much, you might need a few attempts to load data properly. But as long as you create a temporary import table, you can keep deleting the data and trying again without disturbing anyone else or risking the loss of other data.

The SELECT...INTO OUTFILE statement is an excellent method for sharing data with others. It may become a regularly used tool for you if you work in an organization that shares data with other organizations. So at least be very familiar with it in case your situation calls for it.

Exercises

For the exercises in this chapter, you will need to download the *employees.csv* and *birder-list.csv* files from the MySQL Resources site (*http://mysqlresources.com/files*). You should copy it to the */tmp* directory, or another directory on your server that is accessible by the mysql system user.

I generated the *employees.csv* file by using the SELECT...INTO OUTFILE statement to export data from the employee database. This is a large sample database created originally by the staff at MySQL, and is free for download (*https://launchpad.net/test-db/*).

1. Open the *employees-list.csv* file with a text editor to see how it's formatted. Then create an import table to match it. When you're finished, use the LOAD DATA IN FILE statement to load the list of employees into the import table you created.

2. Open the *birder-list.csv* in a text editor to determine how it's formatted. It contains a list of people who live in Italy and are prospects for our site. Create in the `bird watchers` database an import table with columns with these names and in this order: `id`, `formal_title`, `name_first`, `name_last`, `country`, and `email`. Make the `id` column an automatically incremented key column.

   Construct a `LOAD DATA INFILE` statement to load the data from the *birder-list.csv* file into the import table you create. Be sure to provide a list of column names with this SQL statement. Use the `SET` clause to set the value of `formal_title` when loading the data. Female Italian names generally end with the letter *a*. Male Italian names end generally with the letter *o*, but sometimes with *i*, or *e*. Use these assumptions to have MySQL make a reasonable guess as to the person's title of either Ms. or Mr. when loading the data. When ready, run the `LOAD DATA INFILE` you constructed to load the data into the import table.

   When finished, execute a `SELECT` statement to make sure the data loaded properly. If it didn't, delete the data in the import table and try again until you get it right. Once you've successfully loaded the data, run a `INSERT INTO...SELECT` statement to add the names to the `humans` table.

3. Using the `SELECT...INTO OUTFILE` statement, export a list of birds with the word *Least* in their common name to a text file named *little-birds.csv*. Export the common and scientific name of the birds, as well as the scientific names of the family and order to which they belong. Enclose the fields in double quotes, and separate them with commas. End the lines with a semicolon, but without a line ending (i.e., no \n or \r). This should cause the CSV file to write all of the text to one long line. After you've exported the data, open the file with a text editor to verify that the data is contained on one line.

4. Create a table named `birds_least` in the `rookery` database. It should have four columns: `scientific_name`, `common_name`, `family_name`, and `order_name`. Load this table with data from the *little-birds.csv* you generated in the previous exercise, using the `LOAD DATA INFILE` statement. This may be a little tricky. If you don't do it right, delete the data in the import table and load it again until you get the values in the right columns.

## CHAPTER 16

Application Programming Interfaces

An API allows a programming language to interface easily with a computer software system. The advantage of an API is that you can customize user interfaces to MySQL and MariaDB to suit your needs. Huge websites use APIs to allow the public to interact with their MySQL and MariaDB databases, without the user needing to know anything about the databases they're using or SQL statements.

This chapter covers several APIs that may be used to interface with MySQL and MariaDB, so that you may write customized applications to interface with databases. There are sections for the C API, the Perl DBI, the PHP API, the Connector/Python, and the Ruby API. Many other programming languages have APIs for connecting to MySQL; these are just some of the more popular ones. The section on each API and related libraries includes a basic tutorial on how to connect to MySQL and MariaDB, and how to query a database with the API.

It's unlikely you will need to know more than one API. Instead, you may want to read the section for the programming language you know and use. My preference is the Perl language and the Perl DBI. It's most in line with natural languages such as English and Italian. If you have no preference and would like to learn a MySQL API, though, the PHP API is very popular and has many functions for interacting with MySQL. Plus, PHP is a fairly easy language to learn and you can use snippets of code within web pages and content management systems like Wordpress and Drupal.

It's beyond the scope of this book to include a tutorial on any programming language. I assume you can learn the basics of the language you choose among the many books and online resources available. These examples use basic features of the languages to show you how database access works.

Before skipping ahead to a section about a particular API, you should create a couple of API user accounts that you may use in the examples and in the exercises. The exercises at the end of the chapter are suited to whichever API you prefer, not to one in particular.

Creating API User Accounts

Assuming that the programs that we'll write may be executed by the public, let's create a user account specifically for them (creating users was covered in Chapter 13). We'll call this user account *public_api* and give it only the SELECT privilege for the rookery and birdwatchers databases. Execute the following on your server:

```
CREATE USER 'public_api'@'localhost'
IDENTIFIED BY 'pwd_123';

GRANT SELECT
ON rookery.*
TO 'public_api'@'localhost';

GRANT SELECT
ON birdwatchers.*
TO 'public_api'@'localhost';
```

This creates the *public_api@localhost* user account with the password *pwd_123*. You can give it a more secure and different password. It has access just to our two databases from the localhost. It can only execute SELECT statements and can't change or delete data or do anything else. We'll use this user account for the API programs that we'll create, which retrieve data through a public web page.

For some of the API programs we will write, we'll need another administrative user account, *admin_members*. It will be designated for administering information on members of our site. Create that user account by executing the following SQL statements:

```
CREATE USER 'admin_members'@'localhost'
IDENTIFIED BY 'doc_killdeer_123';

GRANT SELECT, UPDATE, DELETE
ON birdwatchers.*
TO 'admin_members'@'localhost';
```

This administrative user account can select, update, and delete data only on the bird watchers database. It mostly needs access to the humans table, but may sometimes need access to the other tables in the database. It won't use the rookery database, so we're not giving it access to that database.

C API

The C language isn't as popular as it once was, but it's still a standard. In fact, the core software of MySQL is written in C. The C API is provided by MySQL. This section provides a basic tutorial on how to connect to a database and how to query it with C and the C API, the basic components and tasks you need to know to use this API.

Connecting to MySQL

When writing a C program to interact with a database, first we need to prepare variables that will store data on the database connection and the results of a query we intend to execute. Then we will need to establish a connection to the server. To do this easily, we'll include a couple of C header files: *stdio.h* for basic C functions and variables, and *mysql.h* for special MySQL functions and definitions (these two files come with C and MySQL, as well as MariaDB; you shouldn't have to download them if C and MySQL were installed properly on your server):

```
#include <stdio.h>
#include "/usr/include/mysql/mysql.h"
int main(int argc, char *argv[  ])
{
    MYSQL *mysql;
    MYSQL_RES *result;
    MYSQL_ROW row;
...
```

The < and > symbols surrounding *stdio.h* tells C to look for the file in the default location for C header files (e.g., */usr/include*), or in the user's path. Because *mysql.h* may not be in the default locations, the absolute path is given within double quotes. An alternative here would have been <mysql/mysql.h>, because the header file is in a subdirectory of the default C header file directory.

The standard `main` function begins by preparing variables needed for the connection to MySQL. The first line creates a pointer to the MYSQL structure stored in the `mysql` variable. The next line defines and names a results set based on the definitions for MYSQL_RES in *mysql.h*. The results are to be stored in the `result` array, which will be an array of rows from MySQL. The third line of `main` uses the definition for MYSQL_ROW to establish the row variable, which will be used later to contain an array of columns from MySQL.

Having included the header files and set the initial variables, we can now set up an object in memory for interacting with the MySQL server using the `mysql_init( )` function:

```
...
if(mysql_init(mysql) == NULL) {
    fprintf(stderr, "Cannot Initialize MySQL");
    return 1;
}
...
```

The `if` statement here is testing whether a MySQL object can be initialized. If the initialization fails, a message is printed and the program ends. The `mysql_init( )` function initializes the MySQL object using the MYSQL structure declared at the beginning of the `main` function, which is called by convention, `mysql` . If C is successful in initializing the object, it will go on to attempt to establish a connection to the MySQL server:

```
...
if(!mysql_real_connect(mysql,"localhost",
  "public_api","pwd_123","rookery",0,NULL,0))
{
    fprintf(stderr, "%d: %s \n", mysql_errno(mysql), mysql_error(mysql));
    return 1;
}
...
```

The elements of the `mysql_real_connect( )` function here are fairly obvious: first the MySQL object is referenced; next the hostname or IP address; then the username and password; and finally the database to use. For this example, we're using the *public_api@localhost* user account we created in the beginning of this chapter. The three remaining items are the port number, the socket filename, and a client flag, if any. Passing 0 and NULL values tells the function to use the defaults for these.

If the program cannot connect, it prints the error message generated by the server to the standard error stream, along with the MySQL error number (`%d`), and finally a string (`%s`) containing the MySQL error message and then a newline (`\n`). It will get the error number from the `mysql_errno( )` function and the error message from the `mysql_er ror( )` function. If the program can connect without an error, though, it will return 1 to indicate success and continue with the program.

Querying MySQL

The program so far only makes a connection to MySQL. Now let's look at how you can add code to the program to run an SQL statement with the C API.

If the API program has connected to MySQL, it can query the MySQL server with a query function such as `mysql_query( )`. Let's use `SELECT` to get a list of birds from the `birds` table. The code for doing this and displaying the results is as follows:

```
...
if(mysql_query(mysql,"SELECT common_name, scientific_name FROM birds")) {
    fprintf(stderr, "%d:  %s\n",
    mysql_errno(mysql), mysql_error(mysql));
}
else {
    result = mysql_store_result(mysql);
    while(row = mysql_fetch_row(result)){
        printf("\%s - \%s \n", row[0], row[1]);
    }
    mysql_free_result(result);
}
mysql_close(mysql);
return 0;
}
```

Within the `if` statement here, we're using `mysql_query( )` to query MySQL. You could use the `mysql_real_query( )` function instead. It allows the retrieval of binary data, which can be safer, but isn't necessary for this simple example. The `mysql_query( )` function returns 0 if it's successful and nonzero if it's not. So if the SQL statement contained within it doesn't succeed in selecting data from MySQL, an error message will be printed. However, if the query is successful, the `else` statement will then be executed, because the `if` statement will have received a value of 0.

In the `else` statement block, the first line uses the `mysql_store_result( )` function to store the results of the query in the `result` variable.

Before letting go of the data, using `while`, the code loops through each row of the results set. We're using the `mysql_fetch_row( )` function to fetch each row and store it temporarily in the `row` variable. Because we know how the data is organized from the `SELECT` statement, we can use `printf` with its formatting codes to display each column. Notice that each column is extracted with standard array syntax (i.e., `array [n]`).

Once C has gone through each row of the results, it will stop processing and use `mysql_free_result( )` to free the memory for `result`, concluding the `else` statement.

We end this brief program with the `mysql_close( )` function to end the MySQL session and to disconnect from MySQL. The final closing curly brace ends the main function.

Complete Minimal C API Program

It's easier to explain the components of a program step by step as I have done here, but seeing even a small program in pieces can be confusing. So here it is again in its entirety:

```
#include <stdio.h>
#include "/usr/include/mysql/mysql.h"
int main(int argc, char *argv[  ])
{
    MYSQL *mysql;
    MYSQL_RES *result;
    MYSQL_ROW row;

    if(mysql_init(mysql) == NULL) {
        fprintf(stderr, "Cannot Initialize MySQL");
        return 1;
    }

    if(!mysql_real_connect(mysql, "localhost", "public_api",
      "pwd_123", "rookery", 0, NULL, 0)) {
        fprintf(stderr, "%d: %s \n", mysql_errno(mysql), mysql_error(mysql));
        return 1;
    }

    if(mysql_query(mysql,"SELECT common_name, scientific_name FROM birds")) {
```

```
            fprintf(stderr, "%d:   %s\n",
            mysql_errno(mysql), mysql_error(mysql));
    }
    else {
        result = mysql_store_result(mysql);

        while(row = mysql_fetch_row(result)) {
            printf("\%s - \%s \n", row[0], row[1]);
        }
        mysql_free_result(result);
    }
    mysql_close(mysql);
    return 0;
}
```

Compiling with C Includes

You can use any compiler to compile the program we wrote, but I'll show the GNU C
Compiler (gcc) here because it's free software and automatically loaded on some systems. To compile and link the program, enter something like the following from the
command line:

```
gcc -c `mysql_config --cflags` mysql_c_prog.c
gcc -o mysql_c_prog mysql_c_prog.o `mysql_config --libs`
```

When the compiler attempts to compile the program (*mysql_c_prog.c*), it will check for
syntax errors in the code. If it finds any, it will fail to compile and will display error
messages. If it's successful, the resulting compiled program (*mysql_c_prog*) will be ready
to be executed.

Perl DBI

The easiest method of connecting to MySQL with the Perl programming language is to
use the Perl DBI module. This section assumes that you have a basic knowledge of the
Perl language. We'll focus on how to connect to MySQL, run SQL statements, and retrieve data with Perl, rather than the idiosyncrasies of Perl itself. This is meant to be a
simple tutorial for a Perl programmer to get started with the Perl DBI.

For the example in this section, suppose we want to write a program for one of the
administrators to get a list of members and to optionally change the expiration of their
membership. For this, we'll use the `admin_members` user account that's designated for
administering information on members. We created that user account at the start of this
chapter.

Installing

The Perl DBI module is part of the core Perl installation. You can download both Perl and the DBI module from CPAN (*http://www.cpan.org*).

If your server already has Perl installed on it, which most do, you can execute the following from the command line to install the DBI module:

```
perl -MCPAN -e 'install DBI'
```

If you don't have Perl installed already on your server, you can use an installation utility like yum to install the DBI module. If you have yum on your server, enter the following from the command line while logged in as root or an administrative filesystem user:

```
yum install perl perl-mysql
```

Connecting to MySQL

To interface with MySQL, you must first call the DBI module and then connect to MySQL. To make a connection to a database using the Perl DBI, only the following lines are needed in a Perl program to connect to the database:

```
#!/usr/bin/perl -w
use strict;

use DBI;

my $user = 'admin_members';
my $password = 'doc_killdeer_123';
my $host =  'localhost';
my $database = 'birdwatchers';

my $dbh = DBI->connect("DBI:mysql:$database:$host", $user, $password)
          || die "Could not connect to database: " . DBI->errstr;
...
```

The first two lines start Perl and set a useful condition for reducing programming errors (i.e., use strict). The next line calls the DBI module. Then we create a set of variables containing values for logging into MySQL. The next statement, which is spread over two lines, sets up a database handle ($dbh) that specifies the database engine (mysql). We give it the login variables. The rest of the statement relates to what to do if the program is unable to connect to MySQL. If the connection is successful, though, the program will continue on.

Querying MySQL

Making a connection to MySQL does little good unless an SQL statement is executed. Any SQL statement can be executed through an API. The only restrictions are those imposed by the MySQL server on the user account executing the SQL statements within the application. If the user account can execute only SELECT statements, that's all that the application may execute. Let's look at some examples here of how to select and insert data in MySQL through an application.

Selecting data

Continuing the previous example, let's execute a SELECT to get a list of birds from the birds table. Let's allow the user of the Perl program to specify a common name of birds to select, when executing it from the command line. For instance, the user might enter *Avocet* to get a list of Avocet birds. We'll use a LIKE operator in the WHERE clause to allow for some flexibility. Here's how the code for that would look:

```
...
my $search_parameter = shift;

my $sql_stmnt = "SELECT human_id,
                CONCAT(name_first, SPACE(1), name_last) AS full_name,
                membership_expiration
                FROM humans
                WHERE name_last LIKE ?";

my $sth = $dbh->prepare($sql_stmnt);

$sth->execute("%$search_parameter%");
...
```

The first line here sets up a variable, $search_parameter, to store a value from shift, which loads into that variable the value given by the user when executing the program. On the next line of code, we create the $sql_stmnt variable to store the SQL statement. Notice that where we would specify the last name of the member in the WHERE clause, we entered instead a question mark. This is known as a *placeholder*. We will replace the placeholder with $search_parameter two lines later. Placeholders are a good security precaution. For more information on this, see "SQL Injection" on page 364.

After creating the $sql_stmnt variable, we use the prepare( ) function of the database handle in order to prepare the SQL statement to form an SQL statement handle ($sth). Then we use the execute( ) function to execute the statement handle, with the $search_parameter to replace the placeholder. To replace multiple placeholders, you would list them in a comma-separated list within the parentheses of execute( ).

Having connected to MySQL and invoked an SQL statement, what remains is to capture the data results and to display them to the administrator. The fetchrow_array( ) function can be used to fetch the data one row at a time. We'll use that with a while statement. Here's how that would look:

```
...
while(my($human_id,$full_name,$membership_expiration) = $sth->fetchrow_array())
{
    print "$full_name ($human_id) - $membership_expiration \n";
}

$sth->finish();
$dbh->disconnect();
```

The `while` statement executes its block of code repeatedly so long as there are rows to process. The value of each element of each array (i.e., each row) is stored in the two variables `$common_name` and `$scientific_name`—and overwritten by each loop of `while`. Then the variables are printed to the screen with a newline character after each pair.

The second to last line uses `finish( )` to end the SQL statement handle. The last line disconnects the database handle with `disconnect( )`. Alternatively, you can leave open the connection to MySQL so that you can create and execute more statement handles to interface with MySQL.

A better method of retrieving data from MySQL perhaps would be to capture all of the data in memory for later use in the Perl program, thus allowing the connection to MySQL to end before processing the results. Putting MySQL on hold while processing each row as shown earlier can slow down a program, especially when dealing with large amounts of data. It's sometimes better to create a complex data structure (i.e., an array of arrays) and then leave the data structure in memory until needed. To do this, you'd use the `fetchall_arrayref( )` method. It will return the starting location in memory of the array. Here's an example of this:

```
...
my $members = $sth->fetchall_arrayref();

$sth->finish();

foreach my $member (@$members){
    my ($human_id, $full_name, $membership_expiration) = @$member;
    print "$full_name ($human_id) - $membership_expiration \n";
}

$dbh->disconnect();
```

The `fetchall_arrayref( )` fetches all of the rows, stores them in an array in memory, and returns a reference to its location. This is stored in `$members`. Using a `foreach`, we extract each array within the `@$members` array and store it in `$member`. With the block of the `foreach`, we extract each element of the `$member` array and store those values in `$human_id`, `$full_name`, and `$membership_expiration`. We then display them using `print`.

Notice that we executed the `finish( )` to end the statement handle and to free MySQL resources. We could have also put `disconnect( )` immediately after it if we didn't intend to create and execute more SQL statement handles. This would have had no effect on the `foreach` processing the results fetched by `fetchall_arrayref( )`.

Updating data

In the previous examples, we saw how to select data from a table. Let's now look at an example that updates data in a table. We'll change the `$sql_statement` to include an UPDATE statement that will update the date of `membership_expiration` for a member in the humans table. We can do that like this:

```
...
my ($human_id, $membership_expiration) = (shift, shift);

$sql_stmnt = "UPDATE humans
              SET membership_expiration = ?
              WHERE human_id = ?";

$sth = $dbh->prepare($sql_stmnt);
$sth->execute($membership_expiration,$human_id);
...
```

Here we're using `shift` twice to capture two values entered by the user and store them in the `$human_id` and `$membership_expiration` variables. The `$sql_statement` is given two placeholders. We replace those placeholders with the two variables, in the proper order, when we execute the SQL statement through the statement handle (`$sth`) using `execute( )`.

The end result of this bit of code is to update the row related to the given `$human_id` in the humans table. Because this UPDATE privilege is one to which you might not want the public to have access, it would be best to use this program just internally from a known IP address, and to require a password.

A Full Example with Perl DBI

It's easier to explain the components of a program step by step as I have done here, but seeing a program in pieces can be confusing. Combinig these Perl program snippets, we'll create a program and call it *member_adjust_expiration.plx*. Here's how it looks:

```
#!/usr/bin/perl -w use strict;

use DBI;

my $search_parameter = shift || '';
my $human_id = shift || '';
my $membership_expiration = shift || '';
```

```perl
my $user = 'admin_members';
my $password = 'doc_killdeer_123';
my $host = 'localhost';
my $database = 'birdwatchers';

my $dbh = DBI->connect("DBI:mysql:$database:$host", $user, $password)
        || die "Could not connect to database: " . DBI->errstr;

if($search_parameter && !$membership_expiration) {
   my $sql_stmnt = "SELECT human_id,
                    CONCAT(name_first, SPACE(1), name_last) AS full_name,
                    membership_expiration
                    FROM humans
                    WHERE name_last LIKE ?";

   my $sth = $dbh->prepare($sql_stmnt);
   $sth->execute("%$search_parameter%");

   my $members = $sth->fetchall_arrayref();

   $sth->finish();

   print "List of Members - '$search_parameter' \n";

   foreach my $member (@$members){
       my ($human_id, $full_name, $membership_expiration) = @$member;
       print "$full_name ($human_id) - $membership_expiration \n";
   }

}

if($human_id && $membership_expiration) {
   $sth = $dbh->prepare($sql_stmnt);
   $sql_stmnt = "UPDATE humans
                 SET membership_expiration = ?
                 WHERE human_id = ?";

   $sth = $dbh->prepare($sql_stmnt);
   my ($rc) = $sth->execute($email_address,$human_id);

   $sth->finish();

   if($rc) {
     print "Membership Expiration Changed. \n";
   }
   else {
     print "Unable to change Membership Expiration. \n";
   }
}
```

```
$dbh->disconnect();
exit();
```

If this program is executed from the command line, adding the last name of the *Hollar* after the name of the program, it will return the name of Lexi Hollar with her human_id in parentheses, along with the date her membership expires. The following example shows how a user might execute the program, and the results returned from running it with this user value:

member_adjust_expiration.plx *Hollar*

```
List of Members - 'Hollar'
Lexi Hollar (4) - 2013-09-22
```

The program can be run again with a new expiration date for the member like so:

member_adjust_expiration.plx *Hollar 4 2015-06-30*

Notice that the program is expecting three values. If it receives only one value, the member's last name, it executes the SELECT statement and displays the user information. If it receives three values, it will execute the UPDATE statement. Values must be in the correct order and format. The program will display a message indicating whether it's successful in changing the membership expiration date.

You could write this program in more elaborate ways. You could allow the user to select a date, or the number of months or years to add to the expiration date using date functions. You could change it to run through a web interface using the CGI Perl module so that the user can click choices instead of typing them at the command line. However, this simple program gives you a good idea of how to get started writing a Perl API to interface with MySQL.

More Information

To learn about Perl, see *Learning Perl* (O'Reilly) by Randal Schwartz, brian d foy, and Tom Phoenix. For more details on using the Perl DBI with MySQL, see Alligator Descartes and Tim Bunce's *Programming the Perl DBI* (O'Reilly). To learn more about Perl references and other advanced Perl topics, see *Intermediate Perl* (O'Reilly) by Randal Schwartz.

PHP API

One of the most popular programming language and database engine combinations for the Web is PHP with MySQL. This combination works well for many reasons, but primarily the speed, stability, and simplicity that both offer. In addition, PHP scripts can be used easily with HTML to generate web pages. This section provides a basic tutorial on how to connect to MySQL and how to query MySQL with PHP using the PHP API, all within a web page.

Installing and Configuring

There are actually three popular APIs that may be used to connect to MySQL with PHP. It's recommended that you use the mysqli (*MySQL Improved*) extension, which replaces the older mysql extension. We'll use the mysqli API for the programming examples in this section.

On many Linux systems, PHP is already installed. However, you can use an installation utility like yum to install PHP, as well as the PHP API, mysqli. You would do that like this:

```
yum install php php-mysql
```

If you'll be executing PHP code within web pages, which is a very nice feature, you may have to make an adjustment to your web server configuration. If you're using Apache, you may have to add the AddType directive to your Apache configuration to tell the web server to execute code snippets with PHP. You can either put the following line in the web server's configuration file (*httpd.conf*) to make it global, or add it to a *.htaccess* file in the directory where the HTML pages containing the PHP code snippets are located:

```
AddType application/x-httpd-php .html
```

If you add this directive to the *httpd.conf* configuration file, you'll have to restart the Apache web service for it to take effect. You won't have to do that with the *.htaccess* file.

To use PHP with MySQL, you may also have to enable MySQL with PHP by configuring PHP with the --with-mysql=*/path_to_mysql* option. That won't be necessary, though, if you installed the PHP API using yum.

Connecting to MySQL

For PHP code to interface with MySQL, it must first make a connection to MySQL to establish a MySQL client session. This bit of code will do that:

```php
<?php

    $host = 'localhost';
    $user = 'public_api';
    $pw = 'pwd_123';
    $db = 'rookery';

    $connect = new mysqli($host, $user, $pw, $db);

    if (mysqli_connect_errno()) {
        printf("Connect failed: %s\n", mysqli_connect_error());
        exit();
    }

?>
```

We've enclosed the code within <?php...?> tags so that it may be embedded within an HTML web page. If you wanted to create a program that is executed from the command line and not by a web browser, it would have to start with #!/usr/bin/php. For our examples, though, we'll stay with writing code for use in a web page.

The PHP code contained within the <?php...?> tags creates variables containing information the application will need to connect to MySQL and select the default database. After those variables, we're using the mysqli( ) function to connect to MySQL with those variables. We'll refer to that connection with the variable we named $connect. If it's unsuccessful, the script dies with an error message. If the connection is successful, though, we can then query the database. The connection will stay open until we close it.

Querying MySQL

Let's continue with our script by retrieving a list of birds from the birds table. The following snippet would be placed after the previous snippet that connects to MySQL, but within the same web page. It will query the database, fetch rows from the birds table, and display them to the user:

```php
<?php
$sql_stmnt = "SELECT common_name, scientific_name
                FROM birds
                WHERE LOWER(common_name) LIKE LOWER(?)";
$sth = $connect->prepare($sql_stmnt);

$search_parameter = $_REQUEST['birdname'];
$search_parameter = "%" . $search_parameter . "%";

$sth->bind_param('s', $search_parameter);

$sth->execute();
$sth->bind_result($common_name, $scientific_name);

while( $sth->fetch() ) {
  print "$common_name - <i>$scientific_name</i> <br/>";
}

$sth->close();
$connect->close();
?>
```

The first piece of this creates a variable ($sql_stmnt) containing the SQL statement we want to execute. We then prepare that statement with the prepare( ) function in relation to $connect, thus creating a statement handle ($sth).

A user would execute the program we're creating through a query at the end of the web address. For instance, they would add *?birdname=Avocet* to the web address to query for a list of Avocet birds.

A Web Form

A web user wouldn't normally enter a variable name and a search value at the end of a web address in a web browser. Instead, this web page we're building would be preceded by another web page containing an HTML form for the user to enter a search parameter. Here's how that web form would look:

```
<h3>Search Birds Database</h3>
<form action="birds.html" method="post">
<p>Enter a parameter by which to search
the common names of birds in our database:</p>
<input type="text" name="birdname" />
<input type="submit" />
</form>
```

This form on the preceding page calls the web page we're writing, passing the search parameter to it in the proper format.

In the next pair of lines in the example, we're capturing the query request value in a variable we named $search_parameter. Because we intend to use this variable with a LIKE operator, we need to put the % wildcard before and after the variable.

The next line uses bind_param( ) to bind the prepared statement to the $search_pa rameter, specifying first that it's a string value with the 's'. Then we use the exe cute( ) function to execute the completed statement handle.

The bind_result( ) prepares the variables that will be used to parse the array elements, or fields of the results. Calling on the statement handle again, a while statement loops through the results using the fetch( ) function to fetch data one row at a time from the results. Within the while statement block, we're printing the values with HTML tags. When it's finished, we close the statement handle and the connection.

The output of this script is a line for each bird based on the search criteria in the birds table. In this simple example, only a few of the many PHP functions for MySQL are used to get and display data. These snippets are shown here together within a very basic web page:

```
<html>
<body>

<?php
  $search_parameter = $_REQUEST['birdname'];
```

```php
    $host = 'localhost';
    $user = 'public_api';
    $pw = 'pwd_123';
    $db = 'rookery';

    $connect = new mysqli($host, $user, $pw, $db);

    if (mysqli_connect_errno()) {
        printf("Connect failed: %s\n", mysqli_connect_error());
        exit();
    }
?>

<h3>Birds - <?php echo $search_parameter ?></h3>
<p>Below is a list of birds in our database based on your search criteria:</p>

<?php
  $sql_stmnt = "SELECT common_name, scientific_name
                FROM birds
                WHERE common_name LIKE ?";
  $sth = $connect->prepare($sql_stmnt);

  $search_parameter = "%" . $search_parameter . "%";
  $sth->bind_param('s', $search_parameter);
  $sth->execute();
  $sth->bind_result($common_name, $scientific_name);

while($sth->fetch()) {
  print "$common_name - <i>$scientific_name</i> <br/>";
}

$sth->close();
$connect->close();
?>

</body>
</html>
```

This example is almost the same as the two major sections shown previously. We've added opening and closing HTML tags and some with text in between the two PHP code snippets. We also positioned a couple of the lines in different places, but it flows the same. Here's the text returned to the web user when searching for Avocet birds:

```
Birds - "Avocet"
Below is a list of birds in our database based on your search criteria:

Pied Avocet - Recurvirostra avosetta
Red-necked Avocet - Recurvirostra novaehollandiae
Andean Avocet - Recurvirostra andina
American Avocet - Recurvirostra americana
Mountain Avocetbill - Opisthoprora euryptera
```

More Information

If you would like to learn more about using the PHP API mysqli, there's an extensive manual on the PHP site, including a MySQL Improved Extension manual (*http://php.net/manual/en/book.mysqli.php*). You might also like to read Robin Nixon's book, *Learning PHP, MySQL & Javascript* (O'Reilly) to learn more about using PHP within web pages to access MySQL.

Python

To use Python with MySQL, you can you use the MySQL Connector/Python. It's written in Python and needs only the Python libraries to function. It doesn't require any Python modules besides what's already part of the Python standard library. Nor does it require the MySQL client library.

Installing

The first thing you will need to do is install the MySQL Connector/Python on your server. You can do this by using an installation utility like yum on a Linux system. Python and its libraries are probably already installed on your server, but you can try installing them at the same time to be sure. Execute this from the command line:

```
yum install python python-libs mysql-connector-python
```

 This section uses Version 2 of Python, which is still the most common one installed on Linux and Mac systems at the time of this writing. Version 3 is becoming popular, and requires minor syntax changes, but you can read about it elsewhere. If you want to use Version 3, and perhaps another library for connecting Python to MySQL, you will probably need only minor changes to the code shown in this section.

Once you have the connector installed on your server, you can then write and run a Python program to connect to MySQL and query databases. For the example in this section, suppose the database administrator in charge of managing MySQL users has asked us to write a program that would give him a list of user accounts and privileges for each. Let's go through a very simple program to do this.

Connecting to MySQL

To query a database with Python, we will need to establish a connection with MySQL. Here is the beginning part of a Python program to do this:

```
#!/usr/bin/python

import mysql.connector

config = {
    'user': 'admin_granter',
    'password': 'avocet_123',
    'host': 'localhost',
    'database': 'rookery'
}

cnx = mysql.connector.connect(**config)
cur = cnx.cursor(buffered=True)
```

The first line is the required line invoking Python. Next we import mysql.connector, the MySQL Connector/Python. We then create a hash to store the login information we will need for connecting to MySQL. We're using the *admin_granter@localhost* user account because it has the privileges to execute the SHOW GRANTS statement and to query the mysql database, which contains user account information. We created this user in "User Account to Grant Privileges" on page 268.

The final pair of lines of the previous code snippet establishes the connection to MySQL. The first uses the connect( ) call for the MySQL Connector/Python using the values in the config hash, loading its results into the cnx variable. The second creates a cursor object (cur) to use for executing queries on the database.

Querying MySQL

Because there is no SHOW USERS statement, we'll have to query the mysql database to select a list of user accounts from the user table. To do this, we'll first create a variable to store the SELECT statement we want to execute. Then we'll use the execute( ) call to execute it. Here's how this part of the program would look:

```
sql_stmnt =  ("SELECT DISTINCT User, Host FROM mysql.db "
             "WHERE Db IN('rookery','birdwatchers') "
             "ORDER BY User, Host")

cur.execute(sql_stmnt)
```

So as to fit the SELECT statement on the page, we've broken it onto multiple lines. We pass that variable to the execute( ) function to execute the SQL statement. We're now ready to fetch the rows, parse the fields from the results, and display them:

```
for row in cur.fetchall() :
  user_name = row[0]
  host_address =  row[1]
  user_account =  "'" + user_name + "'@'" + host_address + "'"

  print "%s@%s" % (user_name, host_address)
```

```
    cur.close()
    cnx.close()
```

We're using a for statement here to loop through the results of a fetchall( ) call for
the cur cursor object. It takes the values from each row fetched and stores it in an array
we named row. Within the statement block of the for statement, we extract each array
element and store the values temporarily in string variables, in user_name and host_ad
dress. Then we assemble them with some text for nicer formatting and store them in
a variable we named user_account. Its contents will look like lena_stankoska@local
host.

We end this program by displaying the user_account values to the administrator, and
then closing the cursor object and the connection to MySQL.

Sample Python Program

It's easier to discuss a program by breaking it into its components as we've just done,
but it can be confusing to understand how it all comes together. The following listing
combines the preceding snippets, but with some additions that make it a bit more
elaborate:

```
#!/usr/bin/python

import re
import mysql.connector

# connect to mysql
config = {
    'user': 'admin_granter',
    'password': 'avocet_123',
    'host': 'localhost',
    'database': 'rookery'
}

cnx = mysql.connector.connect(**config)
cur = cnx.cursor(buffered=True)

# query mysql database for list of user accounts
sql_stmnt =  "SELECT DISTINCT User, Host FROM mysql.db "
sql_stmnt += "WHERE Db IN('rookery','birdwatchers') "
sql_stmnt += "ORDER BY User, Host"

cur.execute(sql_stmnt)

# loop through list of user accounts
for user_accounts in cur.fetchall() :
  user_name = user_accounts[0]
  host_address =  user_accounts[1]
```

```
          user_account =  "'" + user_name + "'@'" + host_address + "'"

          # display user account heading
          print "\nUser Account: %s@%s" % (user_name, host_address)
          print "-----------------------------------------"

          # query mysql for grants for user account
          sql_stmnt = "SHOW GRANTS FOR " + user_account
          cur.execute(sql_stmnt)

          # loop through grant entries for user account
          for grants in cur.fetchall() :
            # skip 'usage' entry
            if re.search('USAGE', grants[0]) :
              continue

            # extract name of database and table
            dbtb = re.search('ON\s(.*)\.+?(.+?)\sTO', grants[0])
            db = dbtb.group(1)
            tb = dbtb.group(2)

            # change wildcard for tables to 'all'
            if re.search('\*', tb) :
              tb = "all"

            # display database and table name for privileges
            print "database: %s; table: %s" % (db,tb)

            # extract and display privileges for user account
            # for database and table
            privs = re.search('GRANT\s(.+?)\sON', grants[0])
            print "privileges: %s \n" % (privs.group(1))

      cur.close()
      cnx.close()
```

This program does much more than the previous snippets. As a result, I've annotated it at various points to help you understand it. Still, let's go through the key points, especially the additions.

First, the program gets a list of user accounts, storing them in an array named user_ac counts. Using a for statement, it goes through each row of user_accounts to extract each user_account. For each, it prints a heading to display the user account to the administrator. This part is similar to the previous excerpts.

We then put a new SQL statement, SHOW GRANTS, in sql_stmnt for each user_ac count. We execute and then use another for statement to go through the results of a fetchall( ), which we store in a variable we've named grants. If a row from grants contains the word USAGE, we skip displaying that. We then parse out the database and table name, store them in variables named db and tb, and display them. The last pair of lines extracts the list of privileges and displays them.

Some of the results of running this Python program on my system follow:

```
User Account: lena_stankoska@localhost
-------------------------------------------
database: `rookery`; table: all
privileges: SELECT, INSERT, UPDATE, DELETE

database: `birdwatchers`; table: all
privileges: SELECT, INSERT, UPDATE


User Account: public_api@localhost
-------------------------------------------
database: `birdwatchers`; table: all
privileges: SELECT

database: `rookery`; table: all
privileges: SELECT
```

This is a nice way for the administrator to get a list of users and see what privileges they have for particular databases and tables, especially because there isn't a built-in function to do what we want.

More Information

If you would like more information on MySQL Connector/Python, there's an extensive manual on MySQL's site, including a MySQL Connector/Python Developer Guide (*http://bit.ly/mysql-cpdg*). You might also like to read Mark Lutz's book, *Learning Python* (O'Reilly).

Ruby API

The Ruby language has become very popular and can be used to create programs to access a database. There are two MySQL modules for Ruby. The MySQL/Ruby module is built on the MySQL C API. As such, it has the same functions in Ruby as the C API. This is a nice feature if you already know the C API. The other module is the Ruby/MySQL module—this pairing and reverse pairing of the names can be confusing. The Ruby/MySQL module is written in Ruby and is included in Ruby on Rails. For the examples in this section, we will use the former, the MySQL/Ruby module.

Installing and Preparing MySQL/Ruby

Before writing a Ruby program to interface with MySQL, let's install the MySQL/Ruby module, which uses the same functions as the MySQL C API. You can do this by using an installation utility like yum on a Linux system. Execute the following from the command line, while logged in as the *root* or some other administrative filesystem user:

```
yum install ruby ruby-mysql
```

If you can't use yum on your server, you can check MySQL's website to download Ruby modules (*http://dev.mysql.com/downloads/ruby.html*) and to find instructions on installing them.

Once you have Ruby and the MySQL/Ruby module installed on your server, you can then write and run a Ruby program to connect to MySQL and query the databases. Let's go through a very simple program to do this. For this example program, we'll use the *admin_backup@localhost* user account. We created this user account in "Username and Host" on page 256. We will be selecting and inserting data in a database we'll call server_admin. One of the tables in this database will be backup_policies. We'll then insert data into this table related to our backup policies as a reference. We'll log information about the backups, and other server information in that database.

To prepare for the program we're about to write, let's create the server_admin database and the tables we need for it. Create the database and the backup_policies table by executing the following SQL statements:

```
CREATE DATABASE server_admin;

CREATE TABLE backup_policies
(policy_id INT AUTO_INCREMENT KEY,
backup_name VARCHAR(100),
file_format_prefix VARCHAR(25),
frequency ENUM('daily','weekly'),
days ENUM('first','every'), start_time TIME,
secure TINYINT DEFAULT 0,
location ENUM('on-site','off-site','both'),
tables_include VARCHAR(255) );
```

Now that we've created the backup_policies table, let's insert data in it related to our backup policies shown in Table 14-2. We'll execute the following INSERT statement:

```
INSERT INTO backup_policies
(backup_name, file_format_prefix, frequency,
 days, start_time, secure, location, tables_include)
VALUES
('rookery - full back-up', 'rookery-', 2, 1, '08:00:00', 0, 2, "all tables"),
('rookery - bird classification', 'rookery-class-', 1, 2, '09:00:00', 0, 1,
 "birds, bird_families, bird_orders"),
('birdwatchers - full back-up',
 'birdwatchers-', 2, 1, '08:30:00', 1, 2, "all tables"),
('birdwatchers - people', 'birdwatchers-people-', 1, 2, '09:30:00', 1, 1,
 "humans, birder_families, birding_events_children"),
('birdwatchers - activities', 'birdwatchers-activities-', 1, 2, '10:00:00', 0, 1,
```

```
"bird_sightings, birding_events, bird_identification_tests,
 prize_winners, surveys, survey_answers, survey_questions");
```

In addition, we will need another table in the `server_admin` database. We'll call it `backup_reports` and store reports in it that will be generated by the program that we'll create. The SQL statement to create this table is as follows:

```
CREATE TABLE backup_reports
(report_id INT AUTO_INCREMENT KEY,
 report_date DATETIME,
 admin_name VARCHAR(100),
 report TEXT);
```

This is a simple table containing a key, the date of the report, the name of the administrator generating the report, and a `TEXT` column to store the report, which will be generated by the program we'll create in this section. Because we will be using the *admin_backup* user account, we will need to give that account user privileges to access the `server_admin` database. We can do that by executing this SQL statement:

```
GRANT SELECT, INSERT ON server_admin.*
TO 'admin_backup'@'localhost';
```

We're now ready to create the program for the backup administrator.

Connecting to MySQL

To query a database with Ruby, we will need to establish a connection with MySQL. Here's the beginning part of a Ruby program to do this:

```
require 'mysql'

user = 'admin_backup'
password = 'its_password_123'
host = 'localhost'
database = 'server_admin'

begin
    con = Mysql.new host, user, password, database

# Database Queries Here
# ...

rescue Mysql::Error => e
    puts e.errno
    puts e.error

ensure
    con.close if con
end
```

This excerpt of a Ruby program shows how to connect and disconnect from MySQL. The first line is the usual line to invoke Ruby. The next line calls the MySQL module. Then there is a list of variables that we'll use for connecting to the server. The names of these variables are not important.

This is followed by a `begin` statement that will include all of the interactions with the database server. The first line establishes a new connection to MySQL. It includes the variables we created for connecting to the server. These variables, or values for these parameters, must be in the order shown here.

Once you have successfully connected to the database server, you can execute SQL statements. I left out the lines for querying the database to keep this part simple. We'll look at that in a bit.

If the program is not successful in connecting to MySQL, the `rescue` block will handle the errors and display them to the user using `puts`. Regardless of whether the processing of the queries is successful, the `ensure` will make sure that the connection to MySQL is closed at the end of the program.

Querying MySQL

In the previous section, we examined the process for starting a simple Ruby program and connecting to a MySQL server, and looked at how to disconnect from it. Let's now see how to query a database while connected to MySQL or MariaDB with the Ruby API.

We'll do a very simple query to get a list of Avocet birds from the `birds` table. To do this, we'll first create a variable to store the `SELECT` statement we want to execute. Then we'll execute it with a `query( )` call. Here's how that part of the program would look:

```
sql = "SELECT common_name, scientific_name
       FROM birds
       WHERE common_name LIKE '%Avocet%'"

rows = con.query(sql)

rows.each do |row|
  common_name = row[0]
  scientific_name = row[1]
  puts common_name + ' - ' + scientific_name
end
```

After the `query( )`, you can see that we're using an `each` statement to go through each of the rows of the results, storing each row in an array called `row`. Then we're temporarily storing each element of the `row` array in the `common_name` and `scientific_name` variables. We're using `puts` to display each variable with a hyphen between them and a newline at the end.

Sample MySQL/Ruby Program

Although it's easier to discuss the components of a program in separate pieces, it can be confusing to see how they come together. A complete Ruby program follows that uses the MySQL/Ruby module. This program has a very different purpose from the snippets we showed earlier. It will check the backup directory for backup files in accordance with our backup policy (this task was discussed in "Developing a Backup Policy" on page 307). The program will display to the administrator a list of backup files for the past several days. It will also store a report of its findings in the backup_reports table in the server_admin database in MySQL:

```ruby
#!/usr/bin/ruby

require 'mysql'

# create date variables
time = Time.new
yr = time.strftime("%Y")
mn = time.strftime("%m")
mon = time.strftime("%b")
dy = time.strftime("%d")

# variables for connecting to mysql
user = 'admin_backup'
password = 'its_password_123'
host =  'localhost'
database = 'server_admin'

# create other initial variables
bu_dir = "/data/backup/rookery/"
admin_name = "Lena Stankoska"

bu_report =  "Back-Up File Report\n"
bu_report += "----------------------------------------------------\n"
puts bu_report

it = 0
num = 7


begin
    # connect to mysql and query database for back-up policies
    con = Mysql.new host, user, password, database
    sql = "SELECT policy_id, backup_name, frequency,
           tables_include, file_format_prefix
           FROM backup_policies"
    policies = con.query(sql)

    policies.each_hash do |policy|      # loop through each row, each policy
```

```ruby
      # capture fields in variables
      bu_name = policy['backup_name']
      bu_pre = policy['file_format_prefix']
      bu_freq = policy['frequency']

      # assemble header for policy
      bu_header = "\n" + bu_name + " (performed " + bu_freq + ")\n"
      bu_header += "(" + bu_pre + "yyyy-mmm-dd.sql) \n"
      bu_header += "-------------------------------------------------------\n"
      bu_report += bu_header
      puts bu_header

    until it > num do          # iterate through 7 back-up files (i.e., days)
       bk_day = dy.to_i - it

       # assemble backup filename
       bu_file_suffix = yr + "-" + mon.downcase + "-" + bk_day.to_s + ".sql"
       bu_file = bu_pre + bu_file_suffix
       bu_path_file = bu_dir + bu_file

       # get info. on back-up file if it exists
       if File::exists?(bu_path_file)
          bu_size = File.size?(bu_path_file)
          bu_size_human = bu_size / 1024

          bu_file_entry = bu_file + " (" + bu_size_human.to_s + "k)"
          bu_report += bu_file_entry + "\n"
          puts bu_file_entry
       end
       it +=1
    end
    it = 0
  end
end

begin
    # insert report text accumulated in backup_reports table
    con = Mysql.new host, user, password, database
    sql = "INSERT INTO backup_reports
           (report_date, admin_name, report)
           VALUES (NOW(), ?, ?)"
    prep_sql = con.prepare sql
    prep_sql.execute(admin_name,bu_report)

rescue Mysql::Error => e
    puts e.errno
    puts e.error

ensure
```

```
        con.close if con
    end
```

This Ruby program has comments throughout it to explain the various sections of the code. However, I'd like to summarize it and highlight a few parts.

First, we get the current date to create variables that we'll use to determine the name of back-up files. These are based on the backup policies shown in Table 14-2.

Skipping ahead, you can see that we create a variable, bu_report, for storing text for a report. This report is displayed on the screen for the user as it goes along and will in the end be inserted into the backup_reports table.

Going back to the first begin block, we execute a SELECT to get a list of backup policies from the backup_policies table. This table includes the file format prefix (e.g., *rookery-class-*) used to make each backup file. This is followed by the date format that each filename uses (*yyyy-mm-dd.sql*). We store these policies in a hash named policies. Using an each statement, we go through each policy to form a header for each and then execute an until statement to check for the backup files on the server for the past week. For each backup file found, the bu_report is appended with the name of the file and its size.

The next begin block executes an INSERT statement to save the contents of bu_report, along with the date and the administrator's name in the backup_reports table. The results for one sample row in that table follow:

```
*************************** 62. row ***************************
   report_id: 62
 report_date: 2014-10-20 14:32:37
  admin_name: Lena Stankoska
      report: Back-Up File Report
-------------------------------------------------------

rookery - full back-up (performed weekly)
(rookery-yyyy-mmm-dd.sql)
-------------------------------------------------------
rookery-2014-oct-20.sql (7476k)
rookery-2014-oct-13.sql (7474k)

rookery - bird classification (performed daily)
(rookery-class-yyyy-mmm-dd.sql)
-------------------------------------------------------
rookery-class-2014-oct-20.sql (2156k)
rookery-class-2014-oct-19.sql (2156k)
rookery-class-2014-oct-18.sql (2156k)
rookery-class-2014-oct-17.sql (2154k)
rookery-class-2014-oct-16.sql (2154k)
rookery-class-2014-oct-15.sql (2154k)
rookery-class-2014-oct-14.sql (2154k)
rookery-class-2014-oct-13.sql (2154k)
```

```
birdwatchers - full back-up (performed weekly)
(birdwatchers-yyyy-mmm-dd.sql)
- - - - - - - - - - - - - - - - - - - - - - - - - - - - - - - - - - - - - - - - - - - - - - - - - - - -
birdwatchers-2014-oct-20.sql (28k)
birdwatchers-2014-oct-13.sql (24k)

birdwatchers - people (performed daily)
(birdwatchers-people-yyyy-mmm-dd.sql)
- - - - - - - - - - - - - - - - - - - - - - - - - - - - - - - - - - - - - - - - - - - - - - - - - - - -
birdwatchers-people-2014-oct-20.sql (6k)
birdwatchers-people-2014-oct-19.sql (6k)
birdwatchers-people-2014-oct-18.sql (6k)
birdwatchers-people-2014-oct-17.sql (4k)
birdwatchers-people-2014-oct-16.sql (4k)
birdwatchers-people-2014-oct-15.sql (4k)
birdwatchers-people-2014-oct-14.sql (4k)
birdwatchers-people-2014-oct-13.sql (4k)

birdwatchers - activities (performed daily)
(birdwatchers-activities-yyyy-mmm-dd.sql)
- - - - - - - - - - - - - - - - - - - - - - - - - - - - - - - - - - - - - - - - - - - - - - - - - - - -
birdwatchers-activities-2014-oct-20.sql (15k)
birdwatchers-activities-2014-oct-19.sql (15k)
birdwatchers-activities-2014-oct-18.sql (15k)
birdwatchers-activities-2014-oct-17.sql (15k)
birdwatchers-activities-2014-oct-16.sql (15k)
birdwatchers-activities-2014-oct-15.sql (13k)
birdwatchers-activities-2014-oct-14.sql (13k)
birdwatchers-activities-2014-oct-13.sql (13k)
```

More Information

If you would like to learn more about using Ruby with MySQL, there's a manual (*http://www.tmtm.org/en/mysql/ruby/*) provided by Tomita Masahiro, the creator of the MySQL Ruby module. You might also find *Learning Ruby* (O'Reilly) by Michael Fitzgerald useful.

SQL Injection

An API program that accesses MySQL or MariaDB and is available to the public, on the Web or from some other public access point, could be used to attack the database server. Someone could maliciously manipulate the data given to the web page containing a script, or the application that sends data to the server through an API. Specifically, a hacker could embed an SQL statement in the data to be injected into the database. This is known as *SQL injection*. The purpose could be to destroy data, retrieve sensitive or valuable information, or create a user with all privileges and then access the server to steal information.

The vulnerability is related to the fact that string values are contained in quotes. To inject SQL into a string value, a hacker just needs to close the open quote, add a semicolon, and then start a new SQL statement. With numeric values, one can add an extra clause without a quote and get at data.

For an example of an SQL injection, let's look the SQL statement used in the PHP API section, but without a placeholder. Suppose we embedded the $search_parameter variable inside the SQL statement like this:

```
$sql_stmnt = "SELECT common_name, scientific_name
              FROM birds
              WHERE common_name LIKE '%$search_parameter%'"
```

Instead of entering a common name of a bird, suppose that a hacker entered the following when using the API program, including the single quotes:

```
'; GRANT ALL PRIVILEGES ON *.* TO 'bad_guy'@'%'; '
```

That will change our SQL statement to read like this:

```
SELECT common_name, scientific_name FROM birds
WHERE common_name LIKE '%';

GRANT ALL PRIVILEGES ON *.* TO 'bad_guy'@'%';

'%';
```

This results in three SQL statements instead of just the one intended. The hacker would receive a blank list of birds for the first. More important, based on the second SQL statement, the system might create for him a user account with all privileges, accessible from anywhere and without a password. If the user account within the API program has GRANT TO and ALL privileges for all of the databases, the bad_guy user account would be created and have unrestricted access and privileges. The last bit of the malicious SQL statement would just return an error because it's incomplete and doesn't contain an SQL statement.

One method of preventing SQL injection with a MySQL API is to use placeholders instead of literal values. We used these in previous examples in this chapter. This method will isolate the data that will be added to the SQL statement. It does this by escaping single and double quotes. It may not seem like much, but it's fairly effective.

The previous SQL statements intended by the hacker will look instead as follows if placeholders are used:

```
SELECT common_name, scientific_name FROM birds
WHERE common_name LIKE '%\';

GRANT ALL PRIVILEGES ON *.* TO \'bad_guy\'@\'%\';

%';
```

Because the quote marks the hacker entered are escaped, MySQL will treat them as literal values and won't see them as the end of string values. Therefore, it won't start a new SQL statement when it encounters the semicolons he entered. It won't return the names of any birds, because the value won't equal any rows in the table. More important, a bad_guy user won't be created.

Summary

An API is very useful to create programs for users who don't know how to use MySQL, or users for whom you don't want to access MySQL directly. It provides you a much higher level of security and control over users, especially unknown users accessing your databases through the Web. Additionally, when MySQL doesn't have a function to get information you want from a database, you can write an API program to accomplish what you want and to supplement MySQL. As a result, the APIs are very powerful tools for customizing MySQL and MariaDB.

The API programs we reviewed in this chapter select data from a database, and some insert or update data in a database. Some were very simple and some were much more involved. We did very little error checking and performed only simple tasks. Despite how basic and minimal some of the examples were, they should be sufficient to give you an idea of how to write an API program to connect with MySQL and MariaDB and to query a database. The rest is a matter of knowing the related programming language and MySQL well, and using the many API functions available to make better applications. To that end, at the end of each section, you were given suggestions on learning more about each API.

Exercises

For the exercises in this chapter, use the API for whichever language you prefer. If you have no preference, use PHP for the exercises. It's the most popular and probably the easiest to learn.

1. Write an API program that connects to MySQL and queries the rookery database. Have the program execute a SELECT statement to get a list of birds. Use a JOIN to access the birds, bird_families, and bird_orders tables to select the bird_id, common_name, and scientific_name from the birds table, as well as the scientific_name from both the bird_families and bird_orders tables. Joins were covered in "Joining Tables" on page 156. Use the LIMIT clause to limit the results to 100 birds. When you're finished, execute the program from the command line, or a web browser if using the PHP API.

2. Write an API program that accepts data from the user of the program. It may be from the command line or from a web browser, if using the PHP API. Design the program to connect to MySQL and the birdwatchers database. Have it execute an INSERT statement to add data given by the user to the humans table, just data for the formal_title, name_first, and name_last columns. Set the value for join_date by using the CURDATE( ) function, and set the membership_type column to *basic*.

After you write this program, use it to enter the names of a few fictitious people. Then log into MySQL with the mysql client to verify that it worked.

3. Log into MySQL and use the CREATE TABLE statement to create a table named backup_logs in the server_admin database (the CREATE TABLE statement was covered in "Creating Tables" on page 47). We created the server_admin database at the beginning of this chapter. Design the backup_logs table however you want, but be sure to include columns to record the date and time, and the name of a backup file.

Use the GRANTS statement to give the admin_backup user account the INSERT and SELECT privileges (at a minimum) for this new table (this was covered extensively in "SQL Privileges" on page 258).

An example of a backup shell script was included in "Creating Backup Scripts" on page 289. Try writing an API program that can be executed from the command line, not from a web browser, to perform the same tasks as the shell script shown in that section. Have it call the mysqldump utility—don't try to develop your own backup utility. When you're finished, test the program to see whether it makes a backup file and gives it the correct name based on the data. This exercise may be beyond your abilities, though. If it is, skip this exercise and try again in the future when you're much more experienced in using the API.

After you've verified that this API program makes backups correctly, have it connect to MySQL to record that it has run successfully. Use the INSERT statement to insert a row with the date the program ran and the name of the backup file it created. When finished, run the program again and check the table in MySQL to make sure it logged the information.

Once you're sure the API program works properly, add a line to cron or another scheduling program to automatically execute the backup program you wrote. Set it to run some time soon so you can verify it works with cron. You can remove it from cron when you're finished.

4. Write an API program that will select a list of bird families to display to the user. Devise a way for the user to select a bird family from the results to get a list of birds in the family. If you're using an API program like PHP that may be used in a web browser, create links for the bird families to take them to the same API program to list the birds in the family selected.

If you're writing an API program that will be executed from the command line, provide the user with the family_id next to the name of each bird family. Instruct the user to run the program again, but with the family_id entered after the command to get a list of the birds for a family chosen. Create the program in such a way that if no family_id is entered, the user gets a list of families, but if a family_id is entered, the user gets a list of birds in the family. Try running the program to make sure it works properly.

Index

Symbols

!= construct, 124, 127
% (percent sign), 78, 101, 254
& (ampersand), 327
() (parentheses), 36
* (asterisk), 37
, (comma), 36, 120
; (semicolon), 31
<> construct, 124
[ ] (square brackets), 91, 327
^ (caret), 129
_ (underscore), 75
| (vertical bar), 129

A

ABS() function, 193, 245
absolute values, 193, 245
ADD COLUMN clause, ALTER TABLE statement, 61, 63
ADD INDEX clause, ALTER TABLE statement, 82
adding dates and time, 217–222
AddType directive, 349
administrative user accounts
    about, 265
    for bulk importing, 267
    for granting privileges, 268–269
    for making backups, 265

for restoring backups, 266
AFTER keyword, 64
aggregate functions
    about, 229
    calculating group of values, 235–240
    concatenating values for groups, 240–241
    counting values, 230–235
ALL privileges, 259, 298, 365
ALTER clause, ALTER TABLE statement, 71–73
ALTER EVENT statement, 260
ALTER FUNCTION statement, 259
ALTER privilege, 259, 266, 270
ALTER PROCEDURE statement, 259
ALTER ROUTINE privilege, 259
ALTER TABLE statement
    about, 50
    ADD COLUMN clause, 61, 63
    ADD INDEX clause, 82
    ALTER clause, 71–73
    AUTO_INCREMENT option, 74, 76, 94
    basic syntax, 61
    CHANGE COLUMN clause, 64, 71–73, 140
    DROP COLUMN clause, 63
    DROP PRIMARY KEY clause, 84
    dump files and, 287
    indexes and, 80–85
    MODIFY COLUMN clause, 66
    ORDER BY clause, 79
    SQL privileges and, 259

We'd like to hear your suggestions for improving our indexes. Send email to index@oreilly.com.

ALTER USER statement, 272
altering tables
about, 59
additional method for, 74–77
dynamic columns, 68–71
essential changes, 61–68
indexes and, 80–85
prudence when, 59–61
renaming tables, 77–78
reordering tables, 79–80
setting column default value, 71–73
setting value of AUTO_INCREMENT, 73
_AMP packages
about, 11
Linux binary distributions, 12–13
Mac OS X distributions, 11, 13–16
Windows distributions, 16–19
ampersand (&), 327
ANALYZE TABLE statement, 260
AND operator, 103, 123
anonymous users, removing, 25
APIs (application programming interfaces)
about, 337
C language, 338–342
creating user accounts, 338
Perl DBI module, 342–348
PHP language, 348–353
Python language, 353–357
Ruby language, 357–364
SQL injection, 364–366
apt-get utility, 12
arguments, functions and, 179
AS clause, SELECT statement, 103, 125
ASC option, 122
asterisk (*), 37
AUTO_INCREMENT option
about, 48, 92
ALTER TABLE statement, 74, 76, 94
setting value of, 73
AVG() function, 237, 239
Axmark, David, xix

B

backups
about, 279
creating scripts for, 289–290
database, 60, 280–282, 288
developing policies, 307–311
dump files and, 282–288

restoring, 292–306
table, 60, 290–292
user accounts for making, 265
user accounts for restoring, 266
BEGIN statement, 305
BENCHMARK() function, 173
BINARY data type, 198
binary logs, recovering from, 300–306
BINARY option, 130
bind_param() function, 351
bind_result() function, 351
BIT data type, 64
BLOB data type, 55, 69, 199
built-in functions (see functions)
bulk exporting data, 333–335
bulk importing data
checking accuracy of, 320–323
field and line definitions, 327–330
loading data basics, 318–324
mapping fields, 324–326
from outside MySQL, 330–333
preparing to import, 315–318
selecting imported data, 323–324
setting columns, 326
user account for, 267
watching for warnings, 319–320

C

C API
about, 338
compiling with C includes, 342
complete minimal program, 341
connecting to MySQL, 339
querying MySQL, 340
caret (^), 129
case sensitivity, 33, 130
case, setting for strings, 182
CAST() function, 196–199
CEILING() function, 244
CHANGE COLUMN clause, ALTER TABLE
statement, 64, 71–73, 140
CHANGE MASTER TO statement, 260
changing tables (see altering tables)
CHAR data type
CONVERT() function and, 198
space allocation, 48
storing dates, 205
character classes, 131
character names, 131

SET statement
creating variables, 242
dump files and, 283, 291
formatting column elements, 186
GLOBAL flag, 217, 260
subqueries and, 166
SHOW BINARY LOGS statement, 260, 300
SHOW COLUMNS statement
LIKE clause, 67
NOT NULL clause, 67
usage example, 73, 100
SHOW CREATE TABLE statement, 52–54, 75, 286
SHOW CREATE VIEW statement, 260
SHOW DATABASES privilege, 260
SHOW DATABASES statement
about, 47, 293, 296
restoring backups and, 299
SQL privileges and, 260, 262
SHOW ENGINE statement, 260
SHOW GRANTS statement
about, 254
SQL privileges and, 261, 268
usage examples, 257, 269
SHOW INDEX statement, 81–83
SHOW MASTER STATUS statement, 260, 301, 303
SHOW PROCESSLIST statement, 260, 272
SHOW SLAVE STATUS statement, 260
SHOW TABLES statement
about, 34
LIKE clause, 78
restoring backups and, 293
SQL privileges and, 261
SHOW VARIABLES statement, 217, 303
SHOW VIEW privilege, 260, 265
SHOW WARNINGS statement
bulk importing and, 319
inserting data and, 97, 106
updating data and, 140
SHUTDOWN privilege, 260
SIGN() function, 246
SIGNED data type, 198
slash-g (\g), 31
SLEEP() function, 206
source distributions, 21–23
SPACE() function, 185
spaces
padding strings with, 185

trimming in strings, 183
SQL injection, 364–366
SQL statements
canceling, 32
clause execution order, 65
conditional, 284
inserting and manipulating data, 36–40
overview, 34–36
selecting multiple items, 120
structure of, 36
subqueries and, 166
unifying results, 153–156
square brackets [ ], 91, 327
ssh tool, 261
startup items, 15
statements (see SQL statements)
STDDEV() function, 239
storage engines, 53
STRCMP() function, 192–193
string functions
about, 179
compressing strings, 199
converting string types, 196–199
extracting text from strings, 185–188
formatting strings, 180–185
searching strings and using lengths, 188–196
STR_TO_ADD() function, 222
STR_TO_DATE() function, 222
subqueries
about, 166–167
column, 169–170
FIND_IN_SET() function and, 190
performance considerations, 173
row, 170–172
scalar, 167–169
table, 172
SUBSTRING() function
about, 186–189
usage examples, 141, 240, 323, 327
SUBSTRING_INDEX() function, 187
subtracting dates and time, 217–222
SUM() function, 235
Sun Solaris platform, 19–21
SUPER privilege, 260, 272
symbolic links, creating, 15
SYSDATE() function, 206

T

table subqueries, 172

setting passwords, 272
user roles and, 274–276
user roles, 274–276
USING clause
  DELETE statement, 150, 165
  USING operator comparison, 164
USING operator, 157, 164
UTF-8 character set, 55

V

VALUES() function, 91–93, 98–100, 102
VARCHAR data type, 48, 69
variables, creating, 242
VARIANCE() function, 239
vertical bar (|), 129
vsdbutil utility, 16

W

web forms, 351
WHERE clause
  DELETE statement, 97, 149, 150, 165
  IN operator and, 122, 173
  LIKE operator and, 127–128
  MATCH() AGAINST() function and, 193
  QUARTER() function and, 221
  SELECT statement, 37, 40, 66, 103, 107, 120,
    122–124, 138, 156, 159
  SIGN() function and, 247
  STRCMP() function and, 193
  subqueries and, 167, 169, 170, 173
  UPDATE statement, 65, 109, 138–141, 144,
    145
Widenius, Michael "Monty", xix, 3
Windows distributions, 16–19
WinZip utility, 17

Y

YEAR data type, 204
YEAR() function, 209
yum utility, 12, 343, 353, 358

Z

zeros, padding with, 210

About the Author

Russell J.T. Dyer is a writer and editor living in Milan, Italy. He is currently working for MariaDB Ab as its Curriculum Manager. He worked previously for six years at MySQL, Inc., as its Knowledge Base Editor. He wrote *MySQL in a Nutshell* (O'Reilly), and has also written hundreds of articles on software (his specialty being MySQL), travel, photography, and economics.

You can find his first novel, *In Search of Kafka*, for sale on Amazon (*http://bit.ly/in_search_of_kafka*)—it was also edited by Andy Oram. It's a fun read about a computer programmer who has inadvertently gotten himself into trouble with the law. See Russell's website (*http://russelljtdyer.com*) for more information about him and his works.

Colophon

The animals on the cover of *Learning MySQL and MariaDB* are banded angelfish (*Apolemichthys arcuatus*), so named for the black band that runs on either side of each fish's body from the eye to its tail. The banded angelfish's laterally svelte body and soft dorsal fin are typical of the other marine angelfish in its Pomacanthidae family. Known also as bandit angelfish, members of this species inhabit the caves and ledges of rocky reefs found at moderate depths in the waters around Hawaii and the Johnson Atoll.

The behavior of marine angelfish differs widely between species, and members of the Pomacanthidae family are as likely to form monogamous pairs as gather in groups of one male marine angelfish to several females. As protogynous hermaphrodites, marine angelfish are capable of changing sex from female to male when the single male member of such a group dies or is otherwise removed.

Sponges constitute the bulk of the banded angelfish's diet, though it also eats algae and certain invertebrates. Difficulty replicating the banded angelfish's diet is a major impediment to the efforts of collectors who would keep banded angelfish in aquaria. Nevertheless, commercial aquarium fishermen appear to have thinned the population at normal diving depths on certain reefs.

Many of the animals on O'Reilly covers are endangered; all of them are important to the world. To learn more about how you can help, go to *animals.oreilly.com*.

The cover image is from *Cuvier's Animals*. The cover fonts are URW Typewriter and Guardian Sans. The text font is Adobe Minion Pro; the heading font is Adobe Myriad Condensed; and the code font is Dalton Maag's Ubuntu Mono.

O'REILLY®

There's much more where this came from.

Experience books, videos, live online training courses, and more from O'Reilly and our 200+ partners—all in one place.

Learn more at oreilly.com/online-learning

CPSIA information can be obtained
at www.ICGtesting.com
Printed in the USA
LVHW101536050821
694591LV00022B/528

9 781449 362904